WRITING WITH SKILL, LEVEL TWO

LEVEL 6 OF THE COMPLETE WRITER

by

Susan Wise Bauer

STUDENT TEXT

This book is to be used in conjunction with *Writing With Skill, Level Two: Level 6 of The Complete Writer, Instructor Text* (ISBN 978-1-933339-60-3)

Available at www.welltrainedmind.com or wherever books are sold

© 2013 Well-Trained Mind Press
Reprinted May 2021 by Bradford & Bigelow
Cover design by Sarah Park and Justin Moore
Cover illustration by Jeff West

Publisher's Cataloging-In-Publication Data
(Prepared by The Donohue Group, Inc.)

Bauer, S. Wise.
   Writing with skill. Level two, Student text / by Susan Wise Bauer.

      p. : ill. ; cm. — (The complete writer ; level 6)

   "This book is to be used in conjunction with Writing With Skill, Level Two: level 6 of The Complete Writer, Instructor Text."—T.p. verso.
   Interest grade level: 6–8.
   ISBN: 978-1-933339-61-0

   1. English language—Composition and exercises—Study and teaching (Middle school) 2. English language—Rhetoric—Study and teaching (Middle school) I. Title. II. Title: Writing with skill. Level two, Instructor text.

LB1631 .B385 2012
808/.0712   2012921120

TABLE OF CONTENTS

Introduction

OVERVIEW OF THE YEAR'S SEQUENCE

This is Level Two of the *Writing With Skill* series.

Level One was divided into seven sections: Basic Skills, Building Blocks for Composition, Sentence Skills, Beginning Literary Criticism in Prose and Poetry, Research, and Final Project. These sections gave you step-by-step instructions in the foundational skills needed for writing brief compositions in history, science, and literary criticism.

When you're first learning an unfamiliar skill, you need to focus on one thing at a time. But now that you've mastered the basics, your assignments don't need to be separated out into units. Instead, you'll go back and forth between compositions in history, science and literary criticism. At the same time, you'll learn how to make your sentences more interesting, your research more effective, and your note-taking more productive.

In the first level of this course, you reviewed narrative summaries, learned how to construct one-level outlines, and were introduced to two-level outlines. This year, you'll use narrative summaries in your writing, practice two-level outlines, and be introduced to three-level outlines.

In Level One, you learned the basics of documentation: footnotes, endnotes, note-taking, and avoiding plagiarism. This year, you'll put those basics to use in almost everything you write.

In Level One, you learned how to write seven kinds of forms: chronological narratives of past events and of scientific discoveries, descriptions of places and persons, scientific descriptions, biographical sketches, and sequences of natural processes. In Level Two, you'll practice combining these forms together, and also learn to write sequences in history, as well as explanations by comparison and explanations by definition in both science and history. You'll also find out how to round your compositions into fully-formed essays by adding introductions, conclusions, and well-written titles.

In Level One, you were introduced to thesaurus use and learned how to transform sentences by exchanging nouns and adjectives, active and passive verbs, indirect objects and prepositional phrases, infinitives and participles, and main verbs and infinitives. In Level Two, you'll also learn about added and intensified adjectives, using metaphors in place of adverbs, phrase-for-word substitution, and exchanging negatives for positives (and vice versa),

In Level One, you learned about protagonists, antagonists, and supporting characters in stories; about inversion, surprise stories and idea stories, metaphor, simile, and synecdoche. This year, you'll cover stories-within-stories, different points of view, foreshadowing, comparing stories to each other, and writing about longer works of fiction.

In the first level of this course, you learned about the basics of poetry: rhyme and meter, onomatopoeia and alliteration, sonnet and ballad form, and the relationship between form and meaning. This year, you'll learn how to compare poems to each other and how to combine poetry analysis with biographical sketches.

You wrapped up the last weeks of Level One with an independent final project that used several of the forms you learned over the course of the year. This year, you'll complete several different independent projects by combining forms together, and you'll also learn how to find your own original topics by brainstorming.

Finally, you'll practice a whole new kind of writing by modelling your own work on classic essays.

GENERAL INSTRUCTIONS

Each day's work is divided into several steps. Complete each step before moving on to the next. It is your responsibility to read the instructions and follow them carefully. Go slowly, and make sure that you don't skip lines or sections.

Whenever you see this symbol, ✦, you're about to see the answer to a question asked in the text. Stop reading until you've answered the question yourself. It's usually best to answer the question out loud—this forces you to put the answer into specific words (rather than coming up with a vague idea of what the answer might be). Only after you've answered the question out loud should you read the answer below the line.

Whenever you have trouble, ask your instructor for help. Many of the assignments tell you to "Check your work with your instructor." Before you show any work to your instructor, read through it a final time, checking for basic grammar and punctuation mistakes.

If you are writing by hand, make sure that your handwriting is legible! If you are working on a word processor, print out your work and read it through on paper before handing it in. (Sometimes it is difficult to see mistakes when you are reading on a screen.)

Plan to work on your writing four days per week.

Last year, you put together a Composition Notebook with six different sections in it:

> **Narrations**
> **Outlines**
> *Topoi*
> **Copia**
> **Literary Criticism**
> **Reference**

You can use this same notebook for this year's work. You'll be using all of the sections except for the first, but you may find it useful to look back at your narrations occasionally.

If you want to start a new notebook (or if you've *lost* last year's notebook!), you can make a new notebook and divide it into five sections, leaving out **Narrations**. However, this workbook assumes that you will be able to look back at the pages you added to the **Reference** section in Level One. These were:

> *Topoi* **Chart**
> > Chronological Narrative of a Past Event
> > Chronological Narrative of a Scientific Discovery

Description of a Place
Scientific Description
Description of a Person
Biographical Sketch
Sequence: Natural Process
Literary Terms
Sentence Variety Chart
Time and Sequence Words
Points of View

If you no longer have these reference pages, you'll need to recreate them for your new notebook. Ask your instructor for help!

WEEK 1: SUMMARIES AND OUTLINES

Day One: How (and Why) to Write Summaries

 Focus: Writing brief narrative summaries

Remember: you are responsible for reading and following the instructions! Your instructor is available to check your work, and to help if you have difficulty, but you should be able to do most of your work independently.

STEP ONE: Understand the purpose of writing summaries

One of the most important skills in writing is the ability to sum up a series of events or thoughts in just a few sentences.

Think about it. When you write, you can't just put down *everything* that crosses your mind. Instead, you have to select *which* thoughts fit together and make sense. If you can't do this, your writing simply won't hold a reader's interest.

To see what I mean, read the following two paragraphs from the classic biography *Mary, Queen of Scots*, by Emily Hahn. They describe the murder of Mary's husband, Lord Darnley, and his servant, William Taylor, in 1567.

> At about two o'clock Edinburgh was awakened by a terrific explosion. The noise had come from the direction of Kirk o' Fields. Most of the citizens rushed there to find out what had happened. It was an amazing sight. The King's house and the long hall leading to the new house next door were gone. Only heaps of stone rubble were left of the whole solid edifice. Thick stone walls and arched cellars were all in ruins.
>
> At first they could not find the King's body. That was because they were looking where it should have been, among the stones. Finally someone stumbled across two bodies in the garden, a long way from the ruined house. One corpse was Darnley's; the other was Taylor's.[1]

---

1. Emily Hahn, *Mary, Queen of Scots* (New York: Random House, 1953), pp. 102–104.

1

Emily Hahn was a skilled, well-loved writer, and she knew the importance of summary. Imagine if she had written her two paragraphs without summarizing . . .

It was a cold night. Winters in Edinburgh are cold, and that year, February had been dry (not too much snow) but down below freezing every single night, and cloudy during the days. At about two o'clock AM on February 10, most of Edinburgh—although not the southern parts of the city, which were too far away—was awakened by a terrific explosion. The explosion sounded as if it had been caused by gunpowder. They could hear fire roaring and bricks crashing down. The noise had come from the direction of Kirk o' Fields. It was so loud that many people thought 25 or 30 cannon had been fired off. Most of the citizens rushed there to find out what had happened. The road itself was blocked, so many of them had to climb over rubble or go around through the fields. It was an amazing sight. The King's house and the long hall leading to the new house next door were gone. Only heaps of stone rubble were left of the whole solid edifice. Thick stone walls and arched cellars were all in ruins. The trees and shrubs nearby had been beaten into shreds by the falling stones.

At first they could not find the King's body. That was because they were looking where it should have been, among the stones. Darnley had been ill—he had been suffering from smallpox, and Mary had been visiting him every day. But he was far too ill to have left the house on his own. Finally someone stumbled across two bodies in the garden, a long way from the ruined house. One corpse was Darnley's; the other was Taylor's. They were lying under a tree. Darnley's fur-lined, velvet cloak lay nearby. The people who found the bodies carried them to the chapel nearby.

All of the details in the second version are taken from contemporary accounts of Darnley's death (accounts written by people who lived at the time). But Emily Hahn chose not to use them. Here are all of the bits of information she intentionally left out:

~~It was a cold night. Winters in Edinburgh are cold, and that year, February had been dry (not too much snow) but down below freezing every single night, and cloudy during the days.~~ At about two o'clock ~~AM on February 10, most of~~ Edinburgh—~~although not the southern parts of the city, which were too far away~~—was awakened by a terrific explosion. ~~The explosion sounded as if it had been caused by gunpowder. They could hear fire roaring and bricks crashing down.~~ The noise had come from the direction of Kirk o' Fields. ~~It was so loud that many people thought 25 or 30 cannon had been fired off.~~ Most of the citizens rushed there to find out what had happened. ~~The road itself was blocked, so many of them had to climb over rubble or go around through the fields.~~ It was an amazing sight. The King's house and the long hall leading to the new house next door were gone. Only heaps of stone rubble were left of the whole solid edifice. Thick stone walls and arched cellars were all in ruins. ~~The trees and shrubs nearby had been beaten into shreds by the falling stones.~~

At first they could not find the King's body. That was because they were looking where it should have been, among the stones. ~~Darnley had been ill—he had been suffering from smallpox, and Mary had been visiting him every day. But he was far too ill to have left the house on his own.~~ Finally someone stumbled across two bodies in the garden, a long way from the ruined house. One corpse was Darnley's; the other was Taylor's. ~~They were lying under a tree. Darnley's fur-lined, velvet cloak lay nearby. The people who found the bodies carried them to the chapel nearby.~~

Can you hear how much more effective and dramatic Emily Hahn's version is? If you can't, read both versions out loud.

Summarizing teaches you to pick out the most important, most fitting, most sense-filled pieces of information. When you write briefly and powerfully, readers believe what you write. They are gripped by it. They are *convinced* by it. Writing summaries gives you the opportunity to practice brief and powerful writing, without putting you under the pressure of coming up with ideas (and information) to write about.

Summaries can also be useful parts of longer papers. When you write about a novel, you'll often need to provide a short summary of part of the plot. And in a science or history paper, you may need to briefly sum up someone else's research or conclusions.

STEP TWO: Understand how to write a narrative summary

There are two primary ways to sum up a series of events or thoughts. The first is to write a "narrative summary"—several brief sentences that highlight the most important events or ideas in a passage. The second is to outline the passage (you'll review that skill tomorrow).

Here is a long paragraph describing the arrival of the Armada, the enormous naval force sent by King Philip II of Spain to attack the English. This excerpt from a classic book of stories from history, *The Book of Brave Adventures*, tells how the Armada first came into view of the English shore in late July, 1588.

Through the night great signal fires burned on the shore, and men on horseback hurried from town to town carrying torches and shouting out the news that at last the Spanish fleet had come. From cottage and castle men answered the call, forming into companies and marching towards London to protect the queen. The clouds that had covered the sky at the beginning of the evening cleared away and a bright moon filled the world with soft light. By its glow the Spanish general saw a sight that made him uneasy. Under the shelter of the darkness the English fleet had crept around his own vessels and was now behind instead of in front of him. Before he could decide what to do, a line of small, swift English ships was passing rapidly up and down the circle of heavy Spanish galleys and warships, firing over and over again into their heavy timbers. The sailors and soldiers of the Armada hurried to their guns and tried to sink their enemy's vessels; but the lighter English boats, with their sharp prows and low decks, passed by so swiftly that they could not be hit. Showers of bullets rained down on the poor Spaniards, who could not get out of the way because of the great bulk and slowness of their ships. One of the largest ships of the Armada was captured, and many of the small supply boats. All the next day from dawn to sunset the one-sided fight went on; at last [the Spanish admiral] Medina Sidonia gave his fleet the signal to retreat. With torn sails and blood-stained decks the Armada turned her prows toward the French coast, where they anchored safely in a sheltered harbor.[2]

How would you write a brief narrative summary of this paragraph? You would ask yourself: What happens at the beginning of this paragraph? What happens next? What happens at the end?

Here's how you might answer these questions:

What happens at the beginning of this paragraph? The Spanish Armada arrives and the English come out to fight for their country.

What happens next? The English ships were faster than the Spanish ships and rained showers of bullets on them.

What happens at the end? The Spanish Armada retreated towards France.

Your finished summary might sound like this:

When the Spanish Armada arrived, the English came out to fight. Their small, fast ships were quicker than the Spanish ships, and rained so many bullets on them that the Spanish ships retreated towards France.

If you're writing a summary of a science passage with less of a "story" in it, you might need to ask slightly different questions. Read the following paragraph, which describes a scientific process:

Jellyfish . . . have no blood vessels or heart as we know them, but they do have a circulation. The "bell" of a jellyfish is composed of muscles and nerves. In order to swim, jellyfish contract the muscles of the bell and propel themselves along, instead of relying on ocean currents to drift aimlessly (although they do that too, part of the time). When the bell relaxes, it expands and draws water up into a network of canals. When the bell

---

2. D. D. Calhoun, *The Book of Brave Adventures* (New York: The Macmillan Co., 1915), pp. 75–77.

contracts, seawater is squeezed back out of the canals. The canals percolate through the entire muscular bell, so that each cell in the jellyfish comes into contact with seawater. Seawater can be considered the "blood" of the jellyfish, because it contains oxygen and some nutrients, and the canals can be thought of as their blood vessels. The rhythmic beating of the bell—so obvious when you see a jellyfish swimming in the water—is analogous to the beating of our hearts. So, when a jellyfish needs to swim faster, the bell contracts more frequently, which automatically ensures that oxygen will be circulated through the bell at a faster rate.[3]

In this case, you'd need to ask yourself: What exactly does this passage describe? What are the two or three most important parts of that description? What do they do?

What exactly does this passage describe? The circulatory system of a jellyfish.

What are the two or three most important parts of that description? The bell and the canals.

What do they do? The canals of the bell suck up seawater, and the seawater gives the jellyfish oxygen and nutrients.

Your finished summary might sound like this:

> The circulatory system of a jellyfish is made up of a network of canals in the "bell." When the bell expands and contracts, the canals suck up seawater. The seawater brings oxygen and nutrients up into the bell.

STEP THREE: **Practice**

Finish today's work by writing brief narrative summaries of the following three paragraphs. Each summary should be two to three sentences long. Try using the two sets of questions suggested below:

> *What happens at the beginning of this paragraph?*
> *What happens next?*
> *What happens at the end?*

or

> *What exactly does this passage describe?*
> *What are the two or three most important parts of that description?*
> *What do they do?*

(These questions are only tools, so if you don't find them helpful, don't feel obliged to use them.)

If you need help, ask your instructor. When you're finished, show your work to your instructor.

---

3. Eric P. Widmaier, *Why Geese Don't Get Obese (And We Do)* (W. H. Freeman, 1999), pp. 69–71.

Paragraph #1

Louis XV did not care how his people suffered. He danced and drank and enjoyed himself. It did not hurt his appetite to think that there were millions of people in France who could not get enough dry bread for their children. There were twenty-five million of these poor people, farmers, blacksmiths, carpenters, and bakers, so there were twenty-five million people who were glad when the cruel old king died. They hoped that his heir, Louis XVI, would be kinder. But when a great crowd of them went to the royal palace at Versailles with a list of their grievances, the king would not read it, and ordered the two peasants who carried it to be hanged. From this act, they knew that in spite of his gentle face, in spite of his sweet and kind young wife, Marie Antoinette, and his little son and daughter, the new king would be no more merciful than the old one. The lords went on demanding oats and hens as fees; the tax men still came for their money, and the cruel ministers who advised the king how to rule France went on making harsher laws than ever. The only man among these advisers who was a true friend to the wretched people, Necker by name, was removed from his office. The others would not listen to the pleas of the starving peasants.[4]

Paragraph #2

From its headwaters in the Rocky Mountains to the Gulf of California, the Colorado River drops over 13,000 vertical feet. This steep drop, occurring over a relatively short distance, churns up a river that is fast and furious, dropping an average of 7.7 feet per mile—25 times steeper than the mighty Mississippi. Because a river's erosive power increases exponentially with its speed, the Colorado would be a highly destructive river in any part of the world. But in the desert Southwest—a crumbling landscape filled with soft rocks and sparse vegetation—its erosive power is monumental. As the Colorado enters the Southwest, it grinds away at the region's barren rocks, picking up tiny particles of sediment along the way. The more sediment the river picks up, the more abrasive it becomes. The more abrasive it becomes, the more sediment it picks up. This vicious cycle feeds on itself until the Colorado is (quite literally) a river of liquid sandpaper. Before massive dams plugged the Colorado, the river's sediment loads were phenomenal. Back then, the Colorado carried an average of 235,000 tons of sediment through the Grand Canyon *each day.* "Too thick to drink, too thin to plow," was how one early explorer described it. The river's composition was often

---

4. Calhoun, pp. 110–111.

two parts sediment to one part water, and because the sediment had a high concentration of iron-oxide, the virgin Colorado had a distinct reddish hue.[5]

Paragraph #3

The rights of treasure-trove were those which gave full power to dukes and counts over all minerals found on their properties. It was in asserting this right that the famous Richard Coeur de Lion, King of England, met his death. Aedmar, Viscount of Limoges, had discovered in a field a treasure of which, no doubt, public report exaggerated the value, for it was said to be large enough to model in pure gold, and life-size, a Roman emperor and the members of his family, at table. Aedmar set aside what was considered the sovereign's share in his discovery; but Richard, refusing to concede any part of his privilege, claimed the whole treasure. On the refusal of the viscount to give it up he appeared under arms before the gates of the Castle of Chalus, where he supposed that the treasure was hidden. On seeing the royal standard, the garrison offered to open the gates. "No," answered Richard, "since you have forced me to unfurl my banner, I shall only enter by the breach, and you shall all be hung on the battlements." The siege commenced, and at first did not seem to favor the English, for the besieged made a noble stand. One evening, as his troops were assaulting the place, in order to witness the scene, Richard was sitting at a short distance on a piece of rock, protected with a target—that is, a large shield covered with leather and blades of iron—which two archers held over him. Impatient to see the result of the assault, Richard pushed down the shield, and that moment decided his fate. An archer of Chalus, who had recognised him and was watching from the top of the rampart, sent a bolt from a crossbow, which hit him full in the chest. He died of his wound twelve days later; first having, however, graciously pardoned the bowman who caused his death.[6]

5. James Kaiser, *Grand Canyon: The Complete Guide,* 4th ed. (Destination Press, 2011), p. 203.

6. Paul Lacroix and Robert Naunton, *Manners, Custom and Dress during the Middle Ages and During the Reniassance Period* (Kessinger Publishing, 2010), p. 22.

Day Two: How (and Why) to Construct an Outline

 Focus: Constructing two-level outlines

In the last day's work, you learned that there are two primary ways to sum up a series of events or thoughts: narrative summary and outlining. Today, you'll review how to construct a two-level outline.

When you see the symbol ✦, be sure to stop until you have completed all directions!

STEP ONE: Understand the difference between a two-level outline and a narrative summary

When you write a narrative summary, you are trying to condense a passage of writing into fewer words so that the reader gets the most important facts without having to plow through unnecessary details. When you write an outline, you're doing something different. Instead of summarizing the passage's most interesting information, you're looking for the passage's most central thought—the event or idea that every other sentence in the passage relates to.

Look back again at yesterday's passage about the Spanish Armada.

Through the night great signal fires burned on the shore, and men on horseback hurried from town to town carrying torches and shouting out the news that at last the Spanish fleet had come. From cottage and castle men answered the call, forming into companies and marching towards London to protect the queen. The clouds that had covered the sky at the beginning of the evening cleared away and a bright moon filled the world with soft light. By its glow the Spanish general saw a sight that made him uneasy. Under the shelter of the darkness the English fleet had crept around his own vessels and was now behind instead of in front of him. Before he could decide what to do, a line of small, swift English ships was passing rapidly up and down the circle of heavy Spanish galleys and warships, firing over and over again into their heavy timbers. The sailors and soldiers of the Armada hurried to their guns and tried to sink their enemy's vessels; but the lighter English boats, with their sharp prows and low decks, passed by so swiftly that they could not be hit. Showers of bullets rained down on the poor Spaniards, who could not get out of the way because of the great bulk and slowness of their ships. One of the largest ships of the Armada was captured, and many of the small supply boats. All the next day from dawn to sunset the one-sided fight went on; at last [the Spanish admiral] Medina

Sidonia gave his fleet the signal to retreat. With torn sails and blood-stained decks the Armada turned her prows toward the French coast, where they anchored safely in a sheltered harbor.[7]

I gave you the following narrative summary of this paragraph:

> When the Spanish Armada arrived, the English came out to fight. Their small, fast ships were quicker than the Spanish ships, and rained so many bullets on them that the Spanish ships retreated towards France.

If I were outlining the paragraph instead of summarizing it, I'd begin by finding the single central event or idea. Instead of writing answers to the questions I suggested in the last lesson ("What happens at the beginning of this paragraph? What happens next? What happens at the end?"), I would ask myself two questions: What is the main thing or person that this passage is about? (The Spanish Armada.) Why is that thing or person important? (It arrived at England, which started the fight between the English and Spanish navies.)

So my outline would begin like this:

I.   The Spanish Armada arrives in England

(You should remember from last year that the main points of an outline are given Roman numerals: I, II, III, IV, V, etc.)

Now that I've found the main point of the passage, I need to look for subpoints. Last year, you learned that subpoints give important information about the people, things, or ideas in the main point. In this passage, the subpoints should give only the *most important information* about the Spanish Armada and its arrival in England.

Here's how I would outline the passage:

I.   The Spanish Armada arrives in England
      A. The English attack
      B. The Armada retreats to France

You might be tempted to write an outline that looks like this:

I.   The Spanish Armada arrives in England
      A. The English all came out to fight
      B. The English fleet surrounded the Armada
      C. The Spanish ships were too slow to get out of the way
      D. The fight went on all the next day

---

7. Calhoun, pp. 75–77.

E.   Finally the Armada retreated

But remember that *subpoints are not details*. These are all details of *how* the English attacked. The fact that the English attacked, and the fact that the Armada then retreated, are the most important facts in the passage—and all you need to know to understand what happened when the Spanish Armada arrived in England.

If you were doing a three-level outline (you'll begin practicing these this year), those details would go underneath your subpoints, like this:

I.   The Spanish Armada
      A.   The English attack
           1.   Men come from all over England to join the defense
           2.   The English navy surrounds the Spanish fleet
           3.   The light English ships outmaneuver the Spanish
      B.   The Armada retreats to France
           1.   Spanish ships are captured
           2.   The Spanish admiral orders a retreat

Remember: Narrative summaries can have details in them. Three-level outlines can have details in them. But two-level outlines should simply contain the most important facts.

Let's look at one more example. Here's the narrative summary of the jellyfish passage from the last lesson:

> The circulatory system of a jellyfish is made up of a network of canals in the "bell." When the bell expands and contracts, the canals suck up seawater. The seawater brings oxygen and nutrients up into the bell.

Now, read through the passage one more time. Jot down in the box an idea of what the main point might look like. After you've done this (and only after!), look at my answer below.

> Jellyfish . . . have no blood vessels or heart as we know them, but they do have a circulation. The "bell" of a jellyfish is composed of muscles and nerves. In order to swim, jellyfish contract the muscles of the bell and propel themselves along, instead of relying on ocean currents to drift aimlessly (although they do that too, part of the time). When the bell relaxes, it expands and draws water up into a network of canals. When the bell contracts, seawater is squeezed back out of the canals. The canals percolate through the entire muscular bell, so that each cell in the jellyfish comes into contact with seawater.│ Seawater can be considered the "blood" of the jellyfish, because it contains oxygen and some nutrients, and the canals can be thought of as their blood vessels. The rhythmic beating of the bell—so obvious when you see a jellyfish swimming in the water—is analogous to

the beating of our hearts. So, when a jellyfish needs to swim faster, the bell contracts more frequently, which automatically ensures that oxygen will be circulated through the bell at a faster rate.[8]

I.

    A.

    B.

◆

Were you able to come up with a main point?

Since every single sentence in the passage describes some part of a jellyfish's circulation, my main point was:

I.   Jellyfish circulation

Now go back through the passage and look for two subpoints. Passages of scientific description, like this one, will often be divided into sections that describe different parts or elements of the main point. You'll see a small vertical line where this division happens. Try to come up with a phrase describing what part of a jellyfish's circulation each section of the passage describes.

Write each subpoint in the box above. Then, look at my answer below.

◆

Here is the outline I came up with:

I.   Jellyfish circulation
    A. The "bell" of the jellyfish
    B. The jellyfish's "blood"

The first part of the description tells how the bell works; the second explains how seawater carries oxygen into the bell as it expands and contracts.

---

8. Widmaier, pp. 69–71.

STEP TWO: **Understand the purpose of an outline**

Narrative summaries teach you to write succinctly and powerfully; they can also be used as shorter parts of longer papers. Outlines have different purposes.

An outline helps you understand exactly how a piece of writing is structured—and you can use that knowledge to write your own compositions. Both of the passages in this lesson are forms, or *topoi,* that you studied in the first level of this course; the Spanish Armada passage is a chronological narration of a historical event, and the jellyfish paragraph is a scientific description. You'll continue to use outlining this year to help you understand and master new *topoi.*

Outlining is also an excellent way to remember what you've read. The best way to study a piece of writing is to take notes on it, and outlining is an organized note-taking method. If you needed to study for a history test, the two-level outline:

> I.   The Spanish Armada arrives in England
>   A. The English attack
>   B. The Armada retreats to France

would help you remember that the English beat the Spanish Armada back—exactly the information you'd want to memorize for your test.

A three-level outline will probably be more useful as you study for science exams. If you were taking notes on the jellyfish passage, your outline might look like this:

> I.   Jellyfish circulation
>   A. The "bell" of the jellyfish
>   1. Made up of muscles and nerves
>   2. Expands and draws water up into canals
>   3. Contracts and squeezes water back up
>   B. The jellyfish's "blood"
>   1. Seawater carries oxygen and nutrients
>   2. Flows through the canals, or "blood vessels"

As you master three-level outlines later this year, you can begin to use them in your science studies as well.

STEP THREE: **Practice**

Finish today's work by writing two-level outlines of the paragraphs from the last lesson. Use your own paper.

Keep three things in mind as you write:

1. To find the main point, ask: What is the main thing, idea, or person that this passage is about? Why is that thing or person important? To find subpoints, ask: What is the most important information about the main point?

2. Be consistent in tense. Look back at the correct and incorrect versions of the Spanish Armada outline on pp. 9–10. Circle each verb in the incorrect version (the one where all the details have been turned into subpoints). Then, return to this page.

◆

You should have circled the following verbs:

arrives, came, surrounded, were, went, retreated

The first verb is the present tense, but the rest are past tense. You should try to use the same verb tense throughout your outline. (In the correct outlines, I've used all present tense, but you could choose past instead.)

3. Some guides to outlining will tell you that you should use all complete sentences or all complete phrases in your outline. When you're outlining someone else's writing, this doesn't always work. Sometimes a phrase will seem more natural than a sentence, and vice versa. Don't worry about mixing the two.*

If you need help, ask your instructor. When you're finished, show your work to your instructor.

Paragraph #1

> Louis XV did not care how his people suffered. He danced and drank and enjoyed himself. It did not hurt his appetite to think that there were millions of people in France who could not get enough dry bread for their children. There were twenty-five million of these poor people, farmers, blacksmiths, carpenters, and bakers, so there were twenty-five million people who were glad when the cruel old king died. They hoped that his heir, Louis XVI, would be kinder. But when a great crowd of them went to the royal palace at Versailles with a list of their grievances, the king would not read it, and ordered the two peasants who carried it to be hanged. From this act, they knew that in spite of his gentle face, in spite of his sweet and kind young wife, Marie Antoinette, and his little son and daughter, the new king would be no more merciful than the old one. The lords went on demanding oats and hens as fees; the tax men still came for their money, and the cruel ministers who advised the king how to rule France went on making harsher laws than ever. The only man among these advisers who was a true friend

---

*NOTE: #2 and #3 are both intended to get you into habits that will make outlines more useful for you in the future. Eventually, you'll want to outline compositions of your own before you write them. It won't matter if your outline is part phrases and part sentences, but if your outline mixes past and present tense, your composition will tend to do the same.

to the wretched people, Necker by name, was removed from his office. The others would not listen to the pleas of the starving peasants.[9]

Paragraph #2

From its headwaters in the Rocky Mountains to the Gulf of California, the Colorado River drops over 13,000 vertical feet. This steep drop, occurring over a relatively short distance, churns up a river that is fast and furious, dropping an average of 7.7 feet per mile—25 times steeper than the mighty Mississippi. Because a river's erosive power increases exponentially with its speed, the Colorado would be a highly destructive river in any part of the world. But in the desert Southwest—a crumbling landscape filled with soft rocks and sparse vegetation—its erosive power is monumental. As the Colorado enters the Southwest, it grinds away at the region's barren rocks, picking up tiny particles of sediment along the way. The more sediment the river picks up, the more abrasive it becomes. The more abrasive it becomes, the more sediment it picks up. This vicious cycle feeds on itself until the Colorado is (quite literally) a river of liquid sandpaper. Before massive dams plugged the Colorado, the river's sediment loads were phenomenal. Back then, the Colorado carried an average of 235,000 tons of sediment through the Grand Canyon *each day*. "Too thick to drink, too thin to plow," was how one early explorer described it. The river's composition was often two parts sediment to one part water, and because the sediment had a high concentration of iron-oxide, the virgin Colorado had a distinct reddish hue.[10]

Paragraph #3

The rights of treasure-trove were those which gave full power to dukes and counts over all minerals found on their properties. It was in asserting this right that the famous Richard Coeur de Lion, King of England, met his death. Aedmar, Viscount of Limoges, had discovered in a field a treasure of which, no doubt, public report exaggerated the value, for it was said to be large enough to model in pure gold, and life-size, a Roman emperor and the members of his family, at table. Aedmar set aside what was considered the sovereign's share in his discovery; but Richard, refusing to concede any part of his privilege, claimed the whole treasure. On the refusal of the viscount to give it up he appeared under arms before the gates of the Castle of Chalus, where he supposed that the treasure was hidden. On seeing the

---

9. Calhoun, pp. 110–111.
10. Kaiser, p. 203.

royal standard, the garrison offered to open the gates. "No," answered Richard, "since you have forced me to unfurl my banner, I shall only enter by the breach, and you shall all be hung on the battlements." The siege commenced, and at first did not seem to favor the English, for the besieged made a noble stand. One evening, as his troops were assaulting the place, in order to witness the scene, Richard was sitting at a short distance on a piece of rock, protected with a target—that is, a large shield covered with leather and blades of iron—which two archers held over him. Impatient to see the result of the assault, Richard pushed down the shield, and that moment decided his fate. An archer of Chalus, who had recognised him and was watching from the top of the rampart, sent a bolt from a crossbow, which hit him full in the chest. He died of his wound twelve days later; first having, however, graciously pardoned the bowman who caused his death.[11]

Day Three: Practicing Summaries and Outlines

 Focus: Writing brief narrative summaries and two-level outlines

STEP ONE: Prepare

Now that you've reviewed both summaries and outlines, you'll practice writing both.

Remember, to write a narrative summary, try using one of the following sets of questions:

What happens at the beginning of this paragraph?
What happens next?
What happens at the end?

What exactly does this passage describe?
What are the two or three most important parts of that description?
What do they do?

A narrative summary should give the most important information from the passage along with a couple of interesting details.

---

11. Lacroix and Naunton, p. 22.

A two-level outline should give the central, organizing idea in each paragraph, along with the most essential information about that idea. To write a two-level outline, find the main point by asking:

What is the main thing, idea, or person that this passage is about? Why is that thing or person important?

To find subpoints, ask:

What is the most important information about the main point?

Both your narrative summaries and your outlines should use consistent tense throughout. Make sure that you use complete sentences in the narrative summary, but you can use sentences, phrases, or a mix in the outline.

STEP TWO: **Narrative summary and outline**

The passage below, from *The Emperors of Chocolate,* is about Milton Hershey's attempts, beginning in 1900, to find a new formula for blending milk and chocolate into milk chocolate. Milton Hershey, a native of Pennsylvania, believed that he could discover a way to make milk chocolate that would be better than the methods used for centuries in Europe. But despite trial after trial, he couldn't get the milk and chocolate to combine, consistently, without burning, lumping, or spoiling.

First, write a narrative summary of three to four sentences. Notice that the tense of the selection changes from past tense (when the writer is describing what Milton Hershey did a century ago) to present tense (when he describes current attitudes in Europe). The tense of your narrative summary should remain consistent with the passage—so it's appropriate to shift from past to present when you are summarizing this final section.

After you've finished your narrative summary, put it aside and construct a two-level outline of the passage. You'll notice that the text below is separated into three sections by spaces. Treat each section as if it were a single paragraph. In the last section, the author has begun a new paragraph with each direct quote; this is correct form, but all four of the short paragraphs created by the quotes are related to the same main point. Each section should have one main point and at least one subpoint.

When you've finished both your narrative summary and your outline, show them to your instructor. If you have difficulty, ask your instructor for help.

— — —

. . . [I]t took many more trials before Hershey hit on a workable solution: Using a heavy concentration of sugar, Hershey boiled the milk mixture slowly under low heat in a vacuum. When the batch came out, it was smooth as satin, like a batch of still-warm taffy. The concoction blended effortlessly with other ingredients, resulting in a chocolate that was light brown in color and mild to the taste. But something else had happened in the process that no one understood. In making the milk solution, Hershey had hit upon a method (as chemists would later explain) that allowed the lipase enzymes in the milk to break down the remaining milk fat and produce flavorful free fatty acids. In other words, it was slightly soured.

Whether Hershey noticed the off-note flavor in the final product is not clear. All we know is that the process was hailed as a triumph and was replicated in the plant, where Hershey began churning out milk chocolate with this unusual flavor, distinct from any of its European counterparts. And from the moment the public tasted it, Hershey's new chocolate was a success. No one in America had eaten anything like it, and by 1907, the year Hershey's Kisses were introduced, sales had reached nearly $2 million, far outstripping Hershey's own expectations.

. . . The American public's love for Hershey's chocolate baffles European connoisseurs, who say Hershey's chocolate is offensive, if not downright inedible. Known in the industry as "barnyard" or "cheesy" chocolate, Hershey's unique, fermented flavor has never sold in Europe, despite attempts by the company to market it there.

"Milton Hershey completely ruined the American palate with his sour, gritty chocolate," said Hans Scheu, a Swiss national who is president of the Cocoa Merchants' Association. "He had no idea what he was doing."

Like most Europeans, Scheu despises the Hershey flavor and believes Milton Hershey could not possibly have intended to invent it.

"Who in their right mind would set out to produce such a sour chocolate?" he asked. "There is no way Mr. Hershey did this on purpose; it had to be a mistake."[12]

– – –

STEP THREE: **Outline and narrative summary**

Now reverse the order: write your outline first, and your narrative summary second.

Your outline of the following excerpt should have five main points, one for each paragraph. You'll notice that the fourth and fifth paragraphs cover more than one process. It is acceptable for your main points to contain both, like this:

12. Joël Glenn Brenner, *The Emperors of Chocolate* (Crown Business, 2000), pp. 109–111.

IV.   Tempering and molding
    A.   Heating, cooling, reheating
    B.   Molds in a variety of shapes and sizes

Alternatively, you could use a more general statement such as

IV.   After the conching

in which case your main points would need to be

    A.   Tempering
    B.   Molding

Either is acceptable (and you may copy one of the above when you get to Paragraph 4).

Your narrative summary should be no more than five sentences in length and should list the steps involved in making chocolate.

> One example of eating chocolate is sweet chocolate, a combination of unsweetened chocolate, sugar, cocoa butter, and perhaps a little vanilla. Making it involves melting and combining these ingredients in a large mixing machine until the mass has the consistency of dough. Milk chocolate, the most common form of eating chocolate, goes through essentially the same mixing process, except that it involves using less unsweetened chocolate and adding milk.
>
> Whatever ingredients are used, the mixture then travels through a series of heavy rollers set one atop the other. During the grinding that takes place here, the mixture is refined to a smooth paste ready for conching.
>
> Conching is a flavor development process that puts the chocolate through a "kneading" action and takes its name from the shell-like shape of the containers originally employed. The conches, as the machines are called, are equipped with heavy rollers that plow back and forth through the chocolate mass anywhere from a few hours to several days. Under regulated speeds, these rollers can produce different degrees of agitation and aeration in developing and modifying the chocolate flavors . . .
>
> After the . . . conching machines, the mixture goes through a tempering interval—heating, cooling, and reheating—and then at last into molds to be formed into the shape of the complete product. Molds take a variety of shapes and sizes, from the popular individual-size bars available to consumers to a ten-pound block used by confectionery manufacturers.
>
> When the molded chocolate reaches the cooling chamber, cooling proceeds at a fixed rate that keeps hard-earned flavor intact. Bars are then removed from the molds and passed along to wrapping machines to be packed for shipment.[13]

---

13. R. O. Parker, *Introduction to Food Science* (Albany, N.Y.: Delmar, 2003), p. 408.

Day Four: Copia

 Focus: Reviewing skills in sentence writing

Today, you will begin your first exercises in *copia*—rephrasing, rewriting, and rewording sentences.

STEP ONE: **Review basic thesaurus use**

If you're comfortable with thesaurus use, continue on to the exercise. If not, you may need to go back and review Week 3 of Level One: Using the Thesaurus.

The simplest way to rewrite a sentence is to choose *synonyms* for the most important words. You've probably learned the basic definition of a synonym: it is a word that means the same, or almost the same, as another word. *Fear* and *terror* are synonyms; they mean almost the same thing. *Run* and *jog* are synonyms. So are *loud* and *noisy,* and *joy* and *happiness.*

But although "word that means the same" is a good definition for an elementary-level writer, you should remember that "almost the same" is a more accurate definition. No word ever means *exactly* the same thing as another word; if that were the case, you wouldn't need two words. English words may overlap in their basic meaning, but they have different *shades* of meaning. *Joy* is more complete, more overwhelming than *happiness.* *Terror* is more intense than *fear.*

You should always remember shades of meaning when you choose synonyms. Consider the following sentence, from the Sherlock Holmes adventure called *The Speckled Band*:

> Imagine, then, my thrill of terror when last night, as I lay awake, thinking over her terrible fate, I suddenly heard in the silence of the night the low whistle which had been the herald of her own death.

In this sentence, "thrill" stands for the basic meaning of: startling, strong sensation. Look up "thrill" in your thesaurus, and you'll find the following synonyms for startling, strong sensations:

inspiration, satisfaction, frenzy, tumult, tingle

But in *The Speckled Band,* the thrill is a bad thing: terrifying, negative, horrible. A synonym for *thrill* in this sentence has to convey this shade of meaning. So you would not choose one of the following synonyms:

> *Imagine, then, my inspiration of terror when last night, as I lay awake . . .*
> *Imagine, then, my satisfaction of terror when last night, as I lay awake . . .*
> *Imagine, then, my tingle of terror when last night, as I lay awake . . .*

The first two sentences suggest that the strong sensation is pleasant. The third suggests that it isn't all that strong. So if you were to choose a synonym for *thrill,* you'd want to make sure that the essential meaning ("strong, sudden") is combined with an implication of dreadfulness.

> *Imagine, then, my frenzy of terror when last night, as I lay awake . . .*
> *Imagine, then, my tumult of terror when last night, as I lay awake . . .*

The synonyms *frenzy* and *tumult* both work, because both of them have strong negative suggestions to go along with the essential "sudden, strong" meaning of "thrill."

As you complete the following exercise, try to think about shades of meaning.

For each underlined noun, adjective, and verb, find four synonyms in your thesaurus. List those synonyms on the lines provided. Remember that you must provide noun synonyms for nouns, adjective synonyms for adjectives, and verb synonyms for verbs.

After you've found the synonyms, rewrite each sentence twice on your own paper, choosing from among the listed synonyms. Do not repeat any of the synonyms. When you've finished, read your sentences out loud and listen to how the sound and rhythm change with each new set of adjectives, nouns, and verbs.

When you're finished, show your work to your instructor.

Only <u>heaps</u> of stone <u>rubble</u> were left of the whole <u>solid</u> <u>edifice.</u>

heaps: ___bundle___ ___stack___ ___jumble___ ___ton___

rubble: ___debris___ ___ruins___ ___wreck___ ___residue___

solid: ___tight___ ___sturdy___ ___stable___ ___concrete___

edifice: ___pile___ ___house___ ___building___ ___skyscraper___

The others would not <u>listen</u> to the <u>pleas</u> of the <u>starving</u> peasants.

listen: ___hear___ ___attend___ ___mind___ ___hark___

pleas: ___cry___ ___appeal___ ___desire___ ___pleading___

starving: ___hungry___ ___famished___ ___starved___ ___thin___

STEP TWO: **Transforming nouns to adjectives and vice versa**

In the first level of this course, you learned that descriptive adjectives can be turned into nouns and placed into prepositional phrases that modify the original noun.

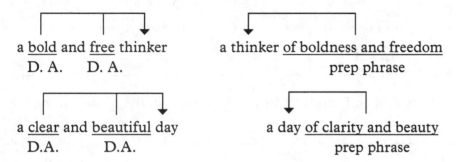

This works in reverse as well. When a prepositional phrase modifies a noun, you can usually turn the noun of the phrase into a descriptive adjective.

In the following sentences, transform as many adjectives into nouns/descriptive prepositional phrases as possible. Don't worry if your new sentences sound strange and awkward. Sometimes, transforming a sentence improves it; sometimes it doesn't. But you won't know until you try!

Hershey's unique, fermented flavor has never sold in Europe.

Hershey's hard, murky flavor has never sold in Europe.

In spite of his gentle face and his sweet and kind young wife, the king was unmerciful.

In spite of his floorboard face and his doorknob blanket wife, the king was unmerciful.

A bright moon filled the world with soft light.

A tree moon filled the world with green light.

In the following sentences, find any descriptive prepositional phrases and transform them into adjectives.

The sailors and soldiers of the Armada hurried to the guns.

The bloody sailors and soldiers of the Armada hurried to the guns.

Imagine, then, my thrill of terror when I suddenly heard the whistle in the silence of the night.

Imagine, then, my jumpy thrill of terror when I suddenly heard the whistle in the silence of the night.

The Colorado River picks up tiny particles of sediment along the way.

The Colorado River picks up green tiny particles of sediment along the way.

When you are finished, show your work to your instructor.

STEP THREE: **Rewriting original sentences**

You'll finish up today's assignment by rewriting two of your own sentences.

Look back over the work you completed in Days 1–3. Choose two sentences from any of the assignments (they don't have to be from the same project). Make sure that each sentence has at least one noun, one action verb, and one adjective. In one of the sentences, the adjective should be in what's called the "attributive" position—it should come before the noun, not after a linking verb (the "predicate" position).

           attributive position   predicate position
           The <u>fragrant</u> flower was <u>lovely</u> and <u>rare</u>.

In the sentence with the attribute adjective, turn the adjective into a noun that's part of a descriptive prepositional phrase, as in the exercise above. Using your thesaurus, replace the noun and verb in the sentence with synonyms.

In the other sentence, replace the adjective (it can be in the predicate position), noun, and verb all with synonyms.

When you're finished, show your work to your instructor.

Week 2: Narrations and Sequences in History, Part I

Day One: Chronological Narration

 Focus: Reviewing chronological narrations
of past events

Today, you'll review a *topos* (form of writing) you learned in the first level of this course: the chronological narration in history. For this lesson, you'll find it useful to have the "*Topoi*" section of your Composition Notebook on hand.

STEP ONE: **Read**

Your first assignment is to read the following selection about the siege of Stirling Castle in 1304.

Here's what you should know before you read: Between 1296 and 1328, Scotland and England fought the First War of Scottish Independence. The English king, Edward I, invaded Scotland and claimed to rule it, but the Scots resisted.

The siege of the Scottish Stirling Castle was part of this war. Stirling Castle lay on the River Forth, and protected the north of Scotland. Edward I needed to conquer it before he could control the north.

In the first paragraph, Berwick and Newcastle are both cities in the north of England. Aberdeen, Brechin, and Glasgow are Scottish cities that had already been seized by the English. In the second paragraph, London, Lincolnshire, and Northumberland are all in England; Perth and Dunblane are Scottish cities which had already surrendered. Burgundy is a region in France (Edward I had friends and allies in France).

Sir William Oliphant was the "Constable" of Stirling Castle, meaning that he was the officer responsible for keeping the castle safe.

> It was in late April that the siege began in earnest. At the beginning of
> the month the castle had been cut off from supplies, and the boats retained
> by the garrison below the castle on the Forth had been seized by English

forces. Initial orders for the assembly of the siege train had been issued a month earlier, in March, when the English constable of Edinburgh Castle had been ordered to repair his siege engines and send them to Stirling. English ships from Berwick and Newcastle sailed north with the components of engines stowed within their holds and laid upon their decks. In the fortress town of Berwick the core of the siege train began to take shape, Master Reginald the Engineer receiving two siege engines from Brechin, sixteen beams of another engine called *Forster* and eighteen beams from Aberdeen.

On 21 April 1304, with the siege about to begin, Edward I was still not satisfied. The king ordered that all the iron and great stones stored in Glasgow should immediately be seized and sent to Stirling Castle for the use of his siege engines. He also instructed his son and heir, the future Edward II, to strip as much lead as he could for the siege engines from the roofs of the churches in Perth and Dunblane, the only exception being where the roofs covered the altars. Large numbers of workmen were drafted in to undertake work on the engines and prepare for the assault on the castle. Batches of tools were sent north, including "pickes" and "stonaxes." Crossbows were delivered in large quantities, over twenty-four thousand crossbow bolts arriving in one instance alone, while the sheriffs of London, Lincolnshire and Northumberland, and the mayor of Newcastle, were required to provide substantial numbers of bows and enormous quantities of arrows. Cotton thread, sulphur and saltpetre were also delivered, the ingredients necessary for the making of Greek fire. To prepare this volatile, highly flammable liquid fire (the precise mixture of which still eludes historians and chemists to this day), Edward I employed the services of the Burgundian expert Jean de Lamouilly. Launched at the castle by means of siege engines, this Greek fire, most probably contained in earthenware pots, would have exploded with startling ferocity. Its use against Stirling Castle was one of the first instances in which the English deployed what was essentially a gunpowder weapon.

Yet this remained a period in which the science of fortification held sway over that of assault, in which methods of defense were superior to those of attack. Despite the unprecedented array of siege engines, the walls of Stirling Castle remained impervious to the hail of missile fire to which they were subjected. The English built a battering ram, but when brought into action it was found ineffective due to a fault in its construction. Impatient at the lack of success, Edward I rode dangerously close to the walls, his advanced age failing to temper his characteristic boldness. The king became increasingly troubled by the prolonged nature of the siege as it dragged on into summer. But Edward still had one card to play, and in terms of the most sophisticated technology, he had saved the very best until last.

For several weeks a team of fifty men headed by five master carpenters had been working intensively on the construction of the greatest of all English siege engines, a trebuchet of such size and proportion that it dwarfed all others. It was a weapon that was appropriately christened the *Warwolf*. In fact, it was so substantial that it was still not ready when [Sir William] Oliphant finally offered the unconditional surrender of the castle on 20 July. However, Edward was so determined to witness the *Warwolf* in action that he refused to accept the offer of surrender until his gargantuan trebuchet had flexed its timber limbs and pounded Stirling Castle with a further heavy barrage. When the garrison were finally allowed to exit the battered castle, they came before the English king in symbolic humility, barefoot and with ashes on their heads as they pleaded for mercy. According to some accounts, Edward was only prevented from having them disembowelled and hanged by the intervention of his queen; however, it is possible this may have been no more than an act of conventional posturing on the part of the king. Having won widespread admiration for their courageous resistance, the garrison were led off into England and captivity. With the conclusion of the three-month siege of Stirling, the last remnant of Scottish resistance had finally been eliminated.[14]

STEP TWO: **Review the form of a chronological narrative**

This passage is a chronological narrative about a past event—the first form you learned in the last level of this course.

A chronological narrative answers the questions: Who did what to whom? (Or: What was done to what?) In what sequence? Before going on, review the definition and format of a chronological narrative. The chart in your notebook should look like this:

Chronological Narrative of a Past Event

Definition: A narrative telling what happened in the past and in what sequence

Procedure	Remember
1. Ask *Who did what to whom?* (Or, *What was done to what?*)	1. Select your main events to go with your theme.
2. Create main points by placing the answers in chronological order.	2. Make use of time words.
	3. Consider using dialogue to hold the reader's interest.

14. David Cornell, *Bannockburn: The Triumph of Robert the Bruce* (Yale University Press, 2009), pp. 14–15.

This particular excerpt doesn't use dialogue, but it does follow the rest of the definition. Take a minute now and circle five time words in the passage. You may want to use the Time and Sequence Words appendix from Level One. If you can't find it your instructor has a copy.

STEP THREE: **Two-level outline**

Now go back through the excerpt and try to come up with a two-level outline, with one main point for each paragraph. Each paragraph contains a series of events, but all of those events center on a particular happening, or a specific phase of the siege. The main points should be numbered I, II, III, and IV. They can be either phrases or sentences.

Let's walk through the first paragraph together.

The first sentence of the first paragraph ("It was in late April that the siege began in earnest") is a summary sentence which does *not* state the theme of the first paragraph. In fact, the siege itself is not described until the third paragraph.

So how can you find the theme? Start by listing the main events in the paragraph.

Supplies to castle cut off
Boats seized by the English
Orders for siege issued (a month before)
English ships bring parts of siege engines
Siege engines arrive from Brechin and Aberdeen

All of these events have to do with the first preparations for the siege—the very beginning stages. So you could phrase your main point as

I.   Early English preparations for the siege

or

I.   The beginning stages of the siege

or

I.   The siege of Stirling Castle begins

Now, look back at the list of main events. Your subpoints (the most important pieces of information *about* the preparation for the siege) will be drawn from this list.

Can any of the events be combined under a single heading? If so, the events are actually details that both describe aspects of the same overall thing. "Supplies to castle cut off" and "boats seized by the English" both have to do with the castle being isolated from the outside world at the beginning of the siege, so you could make your first subpoint "Castle cut off." If you were completing a three-level outline, those details would appear like this:

I.   Early English preparations for the siege
   A. Castle cut off
     1. Supplies cut off
     2. Boats of garrison seized

For this outline, though, you only need to come up with major subpoints, not details.

The last two events both have to do with the parts of siege engines arriving, so they could be combined as well. The completed outline of your first paragraph might look like this:

I.   Early English preparations for the siege
   A. Castle cut off
   B. Orders for siege issued (a month before)
   C. Siege engines arrive

Follow the same procedure and try to come up with main points and subpoints for the next three paragraphs.

If you need help, ask your instructor. Show your completed outline to your instructor.

Day Two: Historical Sequence

 Focus: Understanding the form of a sequence in history

STEP ONE: **Read**

Begin by reading the following passage carefully.

In the second paragraph, you will see several unfamiliar terms: *Balearic fundae, balearic slings,* and *fonevals.* All of these are medieval names for siege engines; historians are still not sure exactly what these siege engines looked like. The *mangonel* mentioned in the third paragraph is a type of catapult.

— — —

The massively strong castles that developed in the central medieval period made life difficult for besiegers. The old siege methods were still used and could be successful, but there was an increased demand for more powerful weapons to assist the attackers.

The first major original siege weapon of the Middle Ages was the trebuchet. The main point of difference with this weapon from others was that it worked by means of a counterweight. It remains uncertain at what date the trebuchet first appeared. The first clear evidence is from the thirteenth century, but it is probable that experiments with counterweights occurred at least in the previous century. Possible early appearances include at Lisbon in 1147, where we hear of Balearic *fundae*, William the Lion of Scotland's engine at Wark in 1174 (which had a sling), Richard the Lionheart's "balearic slings" in the late twelfth century, and Jaime I of Aragon's fonevols. Any or all of these might have been trebuchets, but in no case does the literary evidence allow us to be certain.

The trebuchet depended on the use of a long and fairly flexible wooden arm, like that on the man-gonel but supported by a pivot on a frame. The shorter and thicker end of the arm carried a crate, or something similar, that could be loaded with very heavy weights—perhaps stones or lead—to act as a counterweight. To the longer and thinner end of the arm was attached a sling. This end had to be winched down, thus lifting the counterweight into the air. The sling was then loaded with the missile, perhaps a large rock. A lever released the arm, which pivoted up into the air, carried by the counterweight dropping at the other end. The thin arm rose and the sling was thrown over and forwards, thus releasing the rock.

It is probable that there were experiments with the trebuchet in the twelfth century. By the thirteenth century the weapon had certainly arrived, and was soon recognized as the most powerful of all siege engines. The effect of the counterweight, and the extra power engendered by using a sling, meant that larger rocks could be hurled than had hitherto been possible, and they could be thrown with considerable force. Besiegers now had better hopes of battering down strong walls.[15]

— — —

15. Matthew Bennett et al., *Fighting Techniques of the Medieval World, AD 500–AD 1500: Equipment, Combat Skills, and Tactics* (Amber Books/St. Martin's Press, 2005/2006), p. 201.

STEP TWO: **Construct a one-level outline**

Now go back through the excerpt and construct a one-level outline ONLY.
   It may be useful to ask yourself the following questions:

I.   *What need does this paragraph introduce?*
II.   *What background information does this paragraph supply?*
III. *What process does this paragraph describe?*
IV.   *What result does this paragraph describe?*

   If you have difficulty, ask your instructor for help. When you are finished, show your work to your instructor.
   Be sure not to look ahead to the next steps until you are done.

STEP THREE: **Construct a two-level outline of the third paragraph**

For the purpose of today's lesson, you will now do a two-level outline of the third paragraph *only*.
   Hint: This outline should have two subpoints. The first subpoint covers the first three sentences of the paragraph; the second, the last four.
   If you have difficulty, ask your instructor for help. When you are finished, show your work to your instructor.
   Do not look ahead at Step Four until your instructor prompts you.

STEP FOUR: **Write down the pattern of the *topos***

A three-level outline of the third paragraph would resemble the following:

III. Trebuchets
    A. Description
        1. Short and thick end loaded with weights
        2. Long and thin end had a sling
    B. How they work
        1. Thin end winched down
        2. Sling loaded with missile
        3. Arm released
        4. Counterweight dropped
        5. Missile launched

This paragraph is an example of your new *topos:* a sequence in history.
   Last year, you learned to write a sequence in science. For your reference, here's what that sequence included:

Sequence: Natural Process

Definition: A step by step description of a cycle that occurs in nature

Procedure	Remember

1. Describe the natural process chronologically, step by step.
2. Decide which other elements to include.
    a. Introduction/summary
    b. Scientific background
    c. Repetition of the process

(You should have this in the Reference section of your Composition Notebook.)

When you were introduced to this *topos*, you learned that a sequence is similar to a chronological narrative. Both list a series of events in the order that they happen. But while a chronological narrative tells you about events that happened *once*, a sequence lists events that happen over and over and over again.

Richard the Lionheart was killed only once. The siege of Stirling Castle in 1304 only happened once. But a trebuchet was used over, and over, and over again.

In science, a sequence describes an often-repeated natural process. In history, a sequence describes an often-repeated process as well. A sequence in history might describe the functioning of a historical machine—a trebuchet, a wind-driven grain mill, a Roman aqueduct. Or it might describe a process that was often repeated in the past: the malting of barley into beer, the progress of a typical siege, the steps in the harvesting of an ancient crop.

Looking back at your outline, you will see that the third point contains two distinct parts: a description of the trebuchet, and then a step-by-by step explanation of how it works. These are the most central elements of the historical sequence. If you look at the outline as a whole, you'll see other optional elements in the other paragraphs.

I.	Strong castles made sieges difficult	*Introduction*
II.	Experiments with new siege engines	*Historical background*
III.	Trebuchets	*Sequence itself*
	A. Description	*Description*
	1. Short and thick end loaded with weights	
	2. Long and thin end had a sling	
	B. How they work	*Step-by-step explanation*
	1. Thin end winched down	
	2. Sling loaded with missile	
	3. Arm released	
	4. Counterweight dropped	
	5. Missile launched	
IV.	Stronger siege engines	*Result/consequence*

You'll examine this pattern again in the next day's work.

Finish up today's lesson by copying the following onto a blank sheet of paper in the Reference section of your Composition Notebook.

Sequence: History

Definition: A step-by-step description of a process, machine, or cycle in history

Procedure	Remember

1. Provide an introductory description.
2. Describe the functioning of the process, step by step.
3. Decide which other elements to include.
   a. Introduction
   b. Historical background
   c. Results/consequences

Day Three: Practicing the *Topos*

 Focus: Learning how to write
a descriptive sequence

Today, you'll make a practice run at the descriptive sequence.

To write a good descriptive sequence in history, you need to do research, take notes, and document your information. Before you go through the multiple steps involved in writing a true historical sequence, you'll practice the *form* of the historical sequence—by giving a step-by-step description of a not-so-historical machine in your own house.

STEP ONE: **Review the pattern of the *topos***

Keep in mind the two central elements of the *topos:* a clear description of the parts of the machine, followed by a step-by-step description of how it works. One or more additional elements might be included: introduction, historical background (a discussion of how the machine developed over time), and results or consequences.

Read the following historical sequence, describing the first metal "submarine." Invented by Robert Fulton, the *Nautilus* was funded by the French government during Napoleon's wars with England. Even though Fulton was English, he built the ship for France because the English were, at first, uninterested in paying for it.

You will need to know the following terms: A "knot" is a measure of speed at sea; a ship going at 20 knots is moving at about 23 miles per hour. A "conning tower" is a raised tower;

an officer in the conning tower can see where the ship is going. The "scuttles" are thick glass panes that serve as windows. "Ballast" is heavy material used to weigh the ship down.

description

gear

Launched in May 1800, *Nautilus* was 21 feet 4 inches long and 7 feet in diameter. She was built of copper on iron frames and . . . had an estimated collapse depth of about 30 feet; Fulton wisely restricted dives to 25 feet. A folding mast with a collapsible curiously-shaped sail was hoisted on the surface and a two-bladed propeller, rotated by a handwheel, was capable of driving her at one or two knots submerged so long as the muscles of the crew held out. A bell-shaped conning tower with thick glass scuttles enabled the navigator to see where he was going when the craft was awash and a magnetic compass proved reasonably reliable under water. There were three ballast tanks. . . .

[I]t was arranged that *Nautilus* should be taken to Brest where the craft made a fully submerged run lasting between seven and eight minutes . . . Fulton took her only just below the surface. . . . A few days later, increasing his intrepid ship's company from one to three, Fulton took the boat down by means of ballast and diving rudders to the bottom at maximum diving depth. The crew remained in total darkness (candles would have burned too much oxygen) for one hour. Later, a compressed air cylinder was installed to increase the endurance to one hour and forty minutes.

step by step
(how it works)

result

But it was the extremely low speed and very limited range of *Nautilus* that finally dissuaded the French from following the venture any further. Napoleon did not believe the craft was any use and called Fulton a senseless fool. However, on the other side of the Channel, the British government appreciated the dangers of an effective submarine, if one should ever be developed. It might well put the mighty Royal Navy out of business. Fulton, disgusted with the French, came to England, unabashed at changing sides . . .[16]

16. Richard Compton-Hall, *The First Submarines: The Beginnings of Underwater Warfare* (Penzance: Periscope Publishing, 2003), pp. 83–84.

In the blanks to the left of the excerpt, identify the paragraphs. One paragraph is a description of parts; identify this as "Description." One explains how the submarine works; identify this as "Step-by-step process." One paragraph contains one of the additional elements of the *topos*. Try to identify it as introduction, historical background, or results/consequences.

When you are finished, show your work to your instructor.

STEP TWO: **Choose the topic for the composition**

Now that you've reviewed another example of a historical sequence, you'll get ready to practice the form yourself.

Your first task: choose a household appliance or machine.

Then: Describe the appliance or machine. Then explain, step-by-step, how it works.

Your finished composition will be three paragraphs long and at least 290 words long. In this particular part of the assignment, you will be writing two paragraphs (you'll add to them in the next step). The total word count for these two paragraphs should be at least 250 but not longer than 500 words.

Try to finish this assignment independently. You don't need to show your work until the end of Step Four.

STEP THREE: **Add one or more of the optional elements**

Your composition should also include one of the optional elements: an introductory paragraph, a paragraph of historical development, or a paragraph describing the results/consequences of the machine's use.

If you choose development or results, you'll have to make something up. If you decided to write about a blender, for example, you might write,

> *At first, cooks who wanted to blend ingredients together had to use their hands. Eventually, one cook learned how to use a spoon, and many others followed his lead. The invention of the electric motor made it possible to bring power into the blending process.*

(For this exercise, inventing facts is perfectly fine!)

If you don't want to invent a history or a set of consequences, write an introductory paragraph like the one found in the trebuchet excerpt instead.

You must write at least 40 additional words. You may also choose to add more than one of the optional elements.

STEP FOUR: **Proofread**

Today, you'll add one more step to your compositions: proofreading them before showing them to your instructor.

You'll be developing your proofreading skills over the course of this year. Here are the basic steps in proofreading that you'll always start with:

1) Go somewhere private and read your composition out loud. Listen for any parts that sound awkward or unclear. Try to rewrite them so that they flow more naturally when you're reading out loud. READ OUT LOUD. DO NOT SKIP THIS STEP!

2) Check for spelling by looking, individually, at each word that might be a problem. When you read a word in context, as part of a sentence, your eye often sees what it expects to see: a properly spelled word. Looking at words one at a time, without reading the rest of the sentence, makes it easier to see misspellings. If you're unsure about a word, look it up in a dictionary.

3) Check your commas. Commas are the most frequently misused punctuation mark. Wherever there is a comma, ask yourself: Do I need this?

Commas should primarily be used to:

    a) separate words in a list,

    b) indicate a natural pause or break in a sentence, or

    c) prevent misunderstanding.

(They are also used in dialogue, but that shouldn't be an issue in this composition.)

If you're using a comma for some other purpose, ask yourself if it is really necessary.

When your composition has been proofread, show it to your instructor.

Day Four: Copia

 Focus: Reviewing skills in sentence writing

Today, you'll review a few more of the sentence-transformation skills you learned in the first level of this course: transforming infinitives to participles and main verbs to infinitives.

STEP ONE: Review transforming infinitives to participles

Read the following two sentences out loud.

> In the fortress town of Berwick, the core of the siege train began **to take** shape.

> In the fortress town of Berwick, the core of the siege train began **taking** shape.

In the first sentence, the main verb *began* is followed by an infinitive. An infinitive is a verb form that starts with *to*. Write *inf.* over the bolded **to take** in the first sentence.

In the second sentence, the main verb is followed by a participle. A participle is a verb form that ends with *-ing*. Write *part.* over the bolded **taking** in the second sentence.

When a main verb is followed by an infinitive, you can often change that infinitive to a participle. In the next two sentences, underline the main verb twice. Write *inf.* over the infinitive and *part.* over the participle.

> Milton Hershey could not possibly have intended to invent sour chocolate.

> Milton Hershey could not possibly have intended inventing sour chocolate.

◆

In both sentences, you should have underlined the main verb *have intended*. *To invent* is the infinitive; *inventing* is the participle. (Notice that the transformed sentence is not quite as easy to read as the first. One reason to practice copia is to see which version sounds better.)

You may need to reword slightly or insert additional punctuation.

> A compressed air cylinder was installed **to increase** the endurance to one hour and forty minutes.

> A compressed air cylinder was installed, **increasing** the endurance to one hour and forty minutes.

Not every infinitive can be changed into a participle. Read the next two sentences out loud.

> The English constable of Edinburgh Castle had been ordered to repair his siege engines.

> The English constable of Edinburgh Castle had been ordered repairing his siege engine.

The first sentence makes sense; the second doesn't. Always read your transformed sentences out loud to make sure that they still make sense!

STEP TWO: **Review transforming main verbs to infinitives**

As you saw in the last step, a main verb can be followed by an infinitive that completes its meaning. But you can also transform a main verb into an infinitive. Read the following two sentences out loud, listening to the differences in sound.

New siege engines changed the way wars were fought.

New siege engines began to change the way wars were fought.

With your pencil, underline the word *changed* in the first sentence twice. Write "main verb" above it. In the second sentence, underline *began* twice. Write "main verb" above it. Then underline *to change* once and write "inf." above it.

In the second sentence, the main verb has been changed to an infinitive. But since that leaves the sentence without a main verb, a new main verb has to be provided. This changes the meaning of the sentence a little bit. If I had decided to use other main verbs, the meaning of the sentence would change yet again.

New siege engines continued to change the way wars were fought.

New siege engines needed to change the way wars were fought.

New siege engines attempted to change the way wars were fought.

When you change the main verb to an infinitive, you have the opportunity to add another level or shade of meaning to your sentence.

Here's one more consideration. When you change the main verb to an infinitive, you'll need to choose a new main verb—and there are certain verbs that go along with infinitives better than others. Here's a short list:

VERBS THAT ARE OFTEN FOLLOWED BY INFINITIVES

agree	aim	appear	arrange	ask	attempt
beg	begin	care	choose	consent	continue
dare	decide	deserve	dislike	expect	fail
forget	get	hesitate	hope	hurry	intend
leap	like	love	ought	plan	prefer
prepare	proceed	promise	refuse	remember	start
strive	try	use	wait	want	wish

STEP THREE: **Practice transformations**

In the following sentences, decide whether to transform an infinitive into a participle or a main verb into an infinitive. (Remember that you'll need to choose a new main verb if you turn a main verb into an infinitive.) Rewrite each sentence, transformed, on the line that follows.

The white kitten was purring.

The white kitten was starting to pur

Alice turned the pages to look for some part she could read.

Alice turned the pages looking for some part she could read.

She didn't like to confess that she couldn't make it out at all.

She didn't like to confess that she couldn't make it out at all.

Alice did not notice the Rose's last remark.

Alice didn't notice the Rose's last remark.

However fast they went, they never passed anything.

However fast they went, they never passed anything.

STEP FOUR: **Rewriting original sentences**

You'll finish up today's assignment by rewriting two of your own sentences.

Look back over the work from this week. Choose two sentences from your own work. In both sentences, try to transform the main verb into an infinitive, adding a new main verb from the list above.

Then change one other major adjective or noun in each sentence with a synonym. Use your thesaurus to choose new and interesting synonyms.

When you're finished, show your work to your instructor.

WEEK 3: NOTE-TAKING AND DOCUMENTATION

Day One: Footnotes, Endnotes, In-text Citations, and Works Cited

 Focus: Reviewing proper format for documentation

This week, you'll review last year's lessons on correct documentation and practice taking notes of your own—which you'll use in Week 4's assignment.

Today's lesson will briefly cover the type of citations you learned in Level One of this course, and will also introduce you to a couple of alternative ways of documenting your work.

STEP ONE: **Review footnotes and endnotes**

Footnotes and endnotes both give essentially the same information; the only difference is where the notes appear in the final draft of the paper.

When you quote from another writer's work, the quote should be followed by a superscript number that comes *after* the closing quotation marks.

> In *Beowulf,* the monster Grendel is described as "greedy and grim" and "malignant by nature."[2]

The superscript number refers to the following information:

> Seamus Heaney, *Beowulf: A New Verse Translation* (W. W. Norton, 2001), p. 11.

If the information is placed at the bottom of the page where the quote appears, it is called a footnote. If it appears at the very end of the paper, it is called an endnote.

If you use a word processor to write, you can use the program's tools to insert either footnotes or endnotes (both are correct). If you are handwriting a paper, it is much simpler to use endnotes.

Remember the following rules:

1) Footnotes and endnotes should follow this format:

Author name, *Title of Book* (Publisher, date of publication), p. #.

If there are two authors, list them like this:

Author name and author name, *Title of Book* (Publisher, date of publication), p. #.

If your quote comes from more than one page of the book you're quoting, use "pp." to mean "pages" and put a hyphen between the page numbers.

Author name, *Title of Book* (Publisher, date of publication), pp. #-#.

If a book is a second (or third, or fourth, etc.) edition, put that information right after the title.

Author name, *Title of Book,* 2nd ed. (Publisher, date of publication), p. #.

If no author is listed, simply use the title of the book.

Title of book (Publisher, date of publication), p. #.

All of this information can be found on the copyright page of the book.

2) Footnotes should be placed beneath a dividing line at the bottom of the page.[17] If you are using a word processor, the font size of the footnotes should be about 2 points smaller than the font size of the main text.

3) Endnotes should be placed at the end of the paper, under a centered heading, like this:

ENDNOTES

[2] Seamus Heaney, *Beowulf: A New Verse Translation* (W. W. Norton, 2001), p. 11.

For a short paper (three pages or less), the endnotes can be placed on the last page of the paper itself. A paper that is four or more pages in length should have an entirely separate page for endnotes.

---

17. Like this.

4) The second time you cite a book, your footnote or endnote only needs to contain the following information:

² Heaney, p. 12.

STEP TWO: **Review in-text citations**

In-text citations are often used in scientific writing. Instead of inserting an endnote or footnote, you would write the last name of the author, the date of the book, and the page number in parentheses, after the closing quotation mark but before the closing punctuation mark.

> In *Beowulf,* the monster Grendel is described as "greedy and grim" and "malignant by nature" (Heaney, 2001, p. 11).

All of the other publication information about the book goes on the Works Cited page.

STEP THREE: **Review the Works Cited page**

The Works Cited page should be a separate page at the end of your paper. On it, you should list, in alphabetical order by the last name of the author, all of the books you've quoted from.

WORKS CITED

Heaney, Seamus. *Beowulf: A New Verse Translation*. New York: W. W. Norton, 2001.

Remember the following rules:

1) The Works Cited entries should be formatted like this:

Last name, first name. *Title of Book*. City of publication: Publisher, date.

If the work has no author, list it by the first word of the title (but ignore the articles a, an, and the).

2) If the city of publication is not a major city (New York, Los Angeles, London, New Delhi, Tokyo), include the state (for a U.S. publisher) or country (for an international publisher).

Housley, Norman. *Contesting the Crusades*. Malden, Mass.: Blackwell, 2006.

Jackson, Peter. *The Seventh Crusade, 1244–1254: Sources and Documents*. Aldershot, England: Ashgate, 2007.

Generally, you should use standard state abbreviations rather than postal code abbreviations for U. S. states.

If you have difficulty finding the city of publication, visit the website worldcat.org. Type the title and author into the search box. The city of publication will be included in the search results.

STEP FOUR: **Practice correct form in documentation**

In the spaces provided, write the footnotes, endnotes, or in-text citations for each quote. Use the copyright pages, covers and other details provided to find the information for your notes. Pay attention to where your commas, periods, and parentheses go.

Here's something to keep in mind: When a book has a subtitle (a separate second phrase explaining more about the main title), it is always set off from the main title (the first phrase) with a colon, even if the colon is not on the book cover itself.

Remember that, when handwriting, you indicate italics by underlining the words to be italicized.

#1. Winnie-the-Pooh

Winnie-the-Pooh once made a very profound statement: "It's a funny thing about accidents. You never have them until you're having them."[1]

Winnie-the-Pooh

1

The quote comes from page 235 of the following book:

It was published in 2001 by Dutton Children's Books.

#2 ʒ *Rabindranath Tagore*

The Sepoy Mutiny of 1857 "had shaken the British rule in India at its very foundation."[2]

2

The quote comes from page 66 of the following book:

© 1993 A.K. Basu Majumdar

First published in 1993
by Indus Publishing Company
FS-5, Tagore Garden, New Delhi

ISBN 81-85182-92-2

All rights reserved. No part of this book may be reproduced
in any manner without written permission of the publisher

Published by M.L. Gidwani, Indus Publishing Company
FS-5, Tagore Garden, New Delhi 110027, and printed at
Efficient Offset Printers, Shahzada Bagh, New Delhi

#3 *Max Planck*

The quantum physicist Max Planck studied the movement of heat in three ways: conduction, convection, and radiation.[3]

3

The quote comes from page 14 of the following book:

It was written by Jane Weir and published by Capstone Press in 2009. The subtitle is "Revolutionary Physicist."

#4 *EGYPTIAN Mythology*

Although the word *hippopotamus* comes from the Greek for "water horse," the Egyptians thought of hippopotami as "water pigs" instead of "water horses."[4]

---

[4]

The quote comes from page 142 of the following book. The subtitle is "A Guide to the Gods, Goddesses, and Traditions of Ancient Egypt."

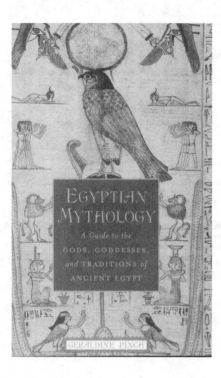

OXFORD
UNIVERSITY PRESS

Oxford   New York
Auckland   Bangkok   Buenos Aires
Cape Town   Chennai   Dar es Salaam   Delhi   Hong Kong   Istanbul
Karachi   Kolkata   Kuala Lumpur   Madrid   Melbourne   Mexico City   Mumbai
Nairobi   São Paulo   Shanghai   Taipei   Tokyo   Toronto

Copyright © 2002 by Geraldine Pinch

STEP FIVE: **Understand variants in documentation**

The style described in this lesson is the most common one for student papers. It is known as "Turabian," after Kate Turabian, the head secretary for the graduate department at the University of Chicago from 1930 until 1958. Kate Turabian had to approve the format of every doctoral dissertation and master's thesis submitted to the University of Chicago. These papers were supposed to follow the format of the University of Chicago *Manual of Style,* but the *Manual of Style* is huge and complicated and many students couldn't figure out exactly how to use it. So Kate Turabian wrote a simplified version of the *Manual of Style,* intended just for the use of students writing papers. Known as *A Manual for Writers of Research Papers, Theses, and Dissertations,* her book has sold over eight million copies. Turabian is a streamlined variation of full Chicago Manual style.

Notice that in Turabian, the format in footnotes and on the Works Cited page is slightly different. A footnote uses this format:

First name, last name, *Title* (Publisher, date), page #.

while a Works Cited entry uses this format:

Last name, first name. *Title.* City of publication: publisher, date.

Turabian style is almost always acceptable, but once you begin writing for other teachers and professors, you might find that one of them prefers another style. Just for your information, here is a brief summary of how each of the major styles formats a Works Cited entry. Notice differences in capitalization, punctuation, author's name, and placement of the different elements.

Turabian (most common for students)

Cooper, Susan. *Silver on the Tree.* New York: Atheneum, 1977.

Chicago Manual of Style

Cooper, Susan. 1977. *Silver on the Tree.* New York: Atheneum.

APA (American Psychological Association, the standard for science writing)

Cooper, S. (1977). *Silver on the tree.* Atheneum. *[Note: Until 2019 the APA format also included the city of publication.]*

Harvard

COOPER, S. (1977). *Silver on the tree.* New York, Atheneum.

MLA (Modern Language Association, more often used in the arts and humanities)

Cooper, Susan. *Silver on the Tree.* New York: Atheneum, 1977. Print.

Using the above as your model, compose three different Works Cited pages for the following two books. Use your own paper, centering the title WORKS CITED at the top of the page. First, create a Works Cited page in Turabian format. Second, create a Works Cited page in APA format. Third, create a Works Cited page using any of the other three formats (the same format for the whole page, please!). When you are finished, you will have three Works Cited pages in three different formats (Turabian, APA, and your choice), each with 2 citations.

When you are finished, show your work to your instructor.

#1: Notice that this book has a subtitle (the two lines at the very bottom of the cover). The subtitle should follow the main title and be separated from it with a colon. The publisher should simply be Random House.

2009 Random House Trade Paperback Edition

Copyright © 2008 by Richard Preston

All rights reserved.

Published in the United States by Random House Trade Paperbacks, an imprint of The Random House Publishing Group, a division of Random House, Inc., New York.

RANDOM HOUSE TRADE PAPERBACKS and colophon are trademarks of Random House, Inc.

Originally published in hardcover in the United States by Random House, an imprint of The Random House Publishing Group, a division of Random House, Inc., in 2008.

Portions of this book appeared in different form in *The New Yorker*.

Grateful acknowledgment is made to Jean-François Ruppol, M.D., for permission to reprint an excerpt from his unpublished narrative "Ebola 2," translated into English from French by Richard Preston and William T. Close. Used by permission of Jean-François Ruppol, M.D.

LIBRARY OF CONGRESS CATALOGING-IN-PUBLICATION DATA

Preston, Richard
Panic in level 4/Richard Preston.
   p.   cm.
"Portions of this book appeared in different form in *The New Yorker*."
ISBN 978-0-8129-7560-4
1. Medicine, Popular. 2. Science. 3. Science writers. I. Title.
RC81.P856   2008   616.02'4—dc22   2007041770

Printed in the United States of America

www.atrandom.com

987654321

Handwritten:

<u>Works cited</u>

Preston, Richard. Panic in level 4: Cannibals, Killer Viruses and other Journeys to the Edge of Sience. New York: Random House, 2008.

#2. This edition is the *latest* one published, although the dates of other editions are noted on the copyright page. The publisher is simply "Harcourt" ("Young Classics" and "Odyssey Classics" are series names that don't need to appear on the Works Cited page).

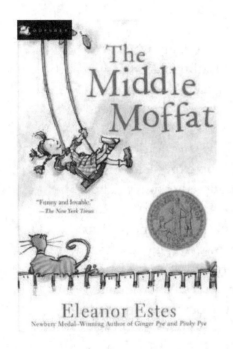

First Harcourt Young Classics edition 2001
First Odyssey Classics edition 2001
First published 1942

www.harcourt.com

Library of Congress Cataloging-in-Publication Data
Estes, Eleanor, 1906–   .
The middle Moffat/Eleanor Estes; illustrated by Louis Slobodkin.
      p.   cm.
Sequel to: *The Moffats.*
Sequel: *Rufus M.*
"An Odyssey/Harcourt Young Classic."
Summary: Follows the adventures and misadventures of ten-year-old
Jane Moffat living with her widowed mother and three siblings in their new
home in Cranbury, Connecticut, in the early twentieth century.
[1. Family life—Connecticut—Fiction.   2. Moving, Household—Fiction.
3. Connecticut—Fiction.]   1. Slobodkin, Louis, 1903–   , ill.   II. Title.
PZ7.E749Mi   2001
[Fic]—dc21   00-37030
ISBN 0-15-202523-5   ISBN 0-15-202529-4 (pb)

Printed in the United States of America
C E G H F D B
C E G H F D B (pb)

Day Two: Common Knowledge and Plagiarism

Focus: Reviewing the definition of plagiarism

STEP ONE: Understand common knowledge

By this point, you should know that every direct quote in your writing must be documented with a footnote, endnote, or in-text citation.

In the last level of this course, you also learned that you should add a note or citation anytime you use someone else's words and ideas—even if you change the words around or use your own phrasing. Borrowing words and ideas without giving proper credit is *plagiarism*—literally, "kidnapping" someone else's work and taking it for yourself.

Read the following passage carefully. It comes from my book *The History of the Renaissance World*, published by W. W. Norton, and it describes the invasion of the Chinese empire, ruled by the Song dynasty, by the northern tribes known as Jurchen. The Jurchen had been nomads not long before—they had barely begun to think of themselves as a people—so the Song government despised them as barbarians. But they were strong fighters, and by AD 1130, the Jurchen army had pushed its way into China all the way to Kaifeng, which was the Song capital city.

The emperor Song Gaozong, who had just turned twenty when Kaifeng fell, was forced to move from hiding to place to hiding place. He grew so desperate that he sent an embassy to the Jurchen generals, offering to become their vassal if the raids would only stop: "I have no one to defend me," he wrote, "and no place to run."[1]

But the Jurchen did not want vassals. The Song scorn was not entirely undeserved; the Jurchen were mounted soldiers with no experience of running a state, no mechanism for administering a conquered country. They wanted to conquer China, not run it as an occupied land.

So Song Gaozong's plea was rejected, and the battles continued. But this turned out to be the saving of the Song. As fighting dragged on, the northern warriors struggled with unfamiliar southern heat. The terrain, crosshatched with streams and canals, slowed their horses. They had no experience with water warfare, but they now faced the barrier of the Yangtze. The Jurchen troops, growing fatter with plunder and loot, were less inclined to ride hard and far. And the Song themselves, adjusting to their exile, were mounting an increasingly powerful resistance by ship.[2]

---

[1] Yuan-Kang Wang, *Harmony and War: Confucian Culture and Chinese Power Politics* (New York: Columbia University Press, 2001), p. 80.

[2] Peter Allan Lorge, *War, Politics and Society in Early Modern China, 900–1795* (New York: Routledge, 2005), p. 55.

The first footnote is there because of the direct quote in the first paragraph. I took those words from Yuan-Kang Wang's book, so I needed to give him credit.

There are no direct quotes in the third paragraph. So why is there a footnote to Peter Allan Lorge's book *War, Politics, and Society in Early Modern China?*

As I was researching the Jurchen invasion of the Song, I found that many historians describe the Jurchen invasion of the southern Song land—an invasion that ultimately failed. But I took the explanation for the failure directly from Peter Allan Lorge's book. He suggested that the Jurchen failed because 1) they had no experience with fighting over water, and 2) they were growing more comfortable, so less willing to fight hard.

Those were Peter Allan Lorge's ideas, so, even though I put them into my own words, I needed to give him credit.

What about the second paragraph?

The statement that the Jurchen were mounted soldiers with no experience of running a country is simply a statement of fact. Anyone could conclude this by looking at the history of the Jurchen. I saw a mention of this fact in every history of the Jurchen I consulted.

This is "common knowledge"—a piece of information widely known by a large group of people. You don't have to footnote common knowledge.

Generally, the following are considered to be common knowledge:

Historical dates	"The Jurchen conquered Kaifeng in 1127."
Historical facts	"The Jurchen were nomads."
Widely accepted scientific facts	"The Yangtze River floods during the rainy season."
Geographical facts	"The source of the Yangtze is in the Tanggula Mountains."
Definitions	"Nomads move from place to place instead of settling down in one area."
Proverbs and sayings	"A watched pot never boils."
Well-known theories and facts	"Flooding makes farmland more fertile because the floods leave silt behind."
Anything that can be learned through the senses	"Silt is black, thick soil." "A boiling pot emits large clouds of steam."

How about the conclusions that the Jurchen "did not want vassals" and "wanted to conquer China, not run it as an occupied land"? I came up with that on my own after reading multiple books about the Jurchen. If another historian uses that idea after reading *The History of the Renaissance World,* I hope she gives me credit.

When I write, I don't use footnotes for broad statements of fact that can be found in many books, like "Walter Tyrrel shot King William II with an arrow in 1100." That piece of information can be found in dozens of books about English history. But if I then write, "After shooting the king, Walter Tyrrel jumped on his horse, struck it with his spurs, and galloped away without anyone in pursuit," I would insert a footnote. Those details come from one specific source: William of Malmesbury's twelfth-century history, *The Deeds of the Bishops of England.*

It isn't always easy to distinguish common knowledge from information that should be footnoted. If you're in doubt, footnote.

STEP TWO: **Practice**

Mark each sentence CK (for "common knowledge") or NF (for "needs footnote"). When you're finished, check your answers with your instructor. Don't worry if you have trouble deciding. Your instructor will provide explanations for each answer, if necessary.

_CK_   Motion sickness is caused by a conflict between what the eye sees and what the inner ear feels.

NE "Conditioned motion sickness" can strike a student pilot at the mere sight of an airplane, if the student has suffered from motion sickness during every previous flight.

CK Tibet has been a Buddhist country since the fifth century.

NE Buddhism came to Tibet during the rule of the 28th king of the Yarlung Dynasty, King Thori Nyatsen.

CK The peak of Mount Everest is 29,029 feet above sea level.

CK The Indian mathematician Radhanath Sikdar was the first surveyor to discover that Mount Everest is the highest mountain on earth.

NE Studies suggest that it takes 45.6 days for the human body to adapt to life at an altitude of 13,000 feet above sea level.

NE Only one percent of the names of the feudal lords in the *Domesday Book* are Anglo-Saxon; the rest of the names are Norman.

NE William II's heir was his brother Robert, Duke of Normandy.

CK California bedrock was often very rich in gold.

CK Neil Armstrong walked on the moon on July 21, 1969.

NE Right before he walked on the moon, Neil Armstrong said, "I'm going to step off the LEM now."

STEP THREE: **Research**

Using an Internet search engine, find and read at least two articles about three of the people on the list (that's a total of *six* articles). Search for each name, with quotes around it, plus the word *plagiarism*.

> Fareed Zakaria
> Jonah Lehrer
> Stephen Ambrose
> Doris Kearns Goodwin
> Chris Anderson

When you are finished, report back to your instructor. Explain orally (and briefly—a couple of sentences is fine) why each public figure was accused of plagiarism.

Day Three: Taking Notes

Focus: Practicing note-taking

There's one more skill to review before you get back to writing: taking notes.

The first step in writing is selecting a topic—something we'll work on a little later this year. The second step is to find out more about your topic through reading and taking notes.

While taking notes, remember to write down all the information you'll need to construct footnotes later on. Never trust your memory! The notes that you take today won't be used for writing until next week. By then, you'll have forgotten the authors, publishers, and dates of your sources. You may even have forgotten the titles. And unless you use quotation marks to set off direct quotes, you won't remember which sentences are direct quotations and which ones are your own paraphrases.

STEP ONE: Review the rules for taking notes

Last year, you learned four rules for note-taking.

1. Always write down the full bibliographical information of your source (author, full title, city of publisher, publisher, date) as if you were entering it on a Works Cited page.

2. Always quote directly and use quotation marks around the exact words of your source. You can combine this with brief paraphrases that sum up information you're not going to quote directly.

3. Always write the page number of quotes right next to the words themselves.

4. If you are reading a book or resource online, never copy and paste words into your notes. Type them out yourself (this will force you to pick only the most important information).

You can take your notes onto 3x5 (index) cards and then arrange the cards in order when you start to write. Use a different card for each quote, write the full bibliographical information about the source on the first card, and then just write the author's last name at the top of each remaining card.

Or, create a document in your word processor for your notes. Type the full information for each book before you start to take notes on it. Then, make a list of important quotes (with page numbers!) under each book's title.

STEP TWO: **Take notes about the California Gold Rush**

Next week, you'll write an essay that combines a chronological narrative about a past event with the new form you've just learned, the descriptive sequence in history. Today's assignment is to take notes on the information you'll need to write that composition.

The chronological narrative will be about the California Gold Rush, and the descriptive sequence will explain exactly how panning for gold works.

Rather than telling you how many notes to take on each source (as I did last year), I'll tell you that the chronological narrative should be at least 200 words long, but not longer than 400 words. It should cover at least four major events of the Gold Rush. The descriptive sequence should be 75–150 words in length. It *must* contain both a physical description of the tools used in panning gold, and a step-by-step explanation of the process itself.

Before you begin to take notes, read through all of the sources from beginning to end.

The photos are provided for your reference. You'll want to look at them as you write your descriptive sequence, but you don't need to make notes about them. The following excerpts have been slightly condensed; ignore the gaps in the text, which contained irrelevant information.

When you're finished taking your notes, show them to your instructor.

The first resource has no author; the editors of *Life* decided to publish it anonymously. When there is no author, list the resource alphabetically in your works cited by the first main word in the title ("Gold") and simply omit the mention of an author completely.

"The Gold Country." In *Life,* Feb. 2, 1948, p. 44

JAMES WILSON MARSHALL arose at sunup on Jan. 24, 1848. Around him on the wild banks of California's American River, on a site near the present town of Coloma, were the green timbers of a sawmill which he was building for a man named John Sutter, a wealthy Swiss trader and landowner. While Sutter still dozed in his fort and trading post at Sacramento, a day's journey on horseback to the west, Marshall went down to the riverbank to inspect the unfinished tailrace of his mill. It was a dry cut, 50 rods in length, filled with rocks still only partially blasted out. During the night Marshall had diverted water into it to carry away the earth and powdered stone. Now the water had been turned out again, leaving only shallow pools in the cut. Marshall looked into one of these pools and saw a yellow speck which caught the early morning sun. He bent over to pick it up, and as he did so he saw another yellow flake and then another. In a little while he had a half ounce of dust which he put in the crown of his white woolen hat. Then he went about his business, seeming to his nine workmen to be no moodier or more temperamental than he ordinarily was. But at nightfall Marshall suddenly turned to the others and said, "Boys, I think I've found a gold mine." They laughed at him.

Next day, when the tailrace was emptied once more, Marshall looked anxiously among the pools. This time there was no doubt. The torrent of water had swept away the light earth and rock powder, leaving a litter of heavy yellow grains on the bottom. Marshall scooped up a full three ounces of it, hefted it in his hands, ground it between his teeth, hammered it flat between two stones. Soon he was on his horse with a heavy pouch in his pocket, riding alone down the Sierra foothills in a driving rain toward Sutter's fort. When he got there, wild-eyed and spattered with red mud, he shoved Sutter into his bedroom, called for bowls of water and apothecaries' scales, and locked the door. Together the men feverishly tried the metal, using every test Sutter could remember. It was 23-carat gold.

For a time Sutter tried to keep the discovery secret. It was no use. Word leaked out slowly at first, then in a wild stream. All over California men dropped their tools, left their farms and trading posts,

44

(also on page 44)

deserted ships in the harbors and stampeded toward Sutter's mill. A few skeptics, chiefly Spanish and Mexican landowners who bitterly resented the American conquest of California, tried to hold them back by saying that the gold talk was only a Yankee trick. That, too, was no use. The word spread back east, overland or by the long route around Cape Horn, and by spring of the next year thousands of emigrants who called themselves forty-niners were headed west. The Gold Rush was on. In the next 10 years more than 365,000 people reached California or died trying to get there, singing to the tune of *Oh, Susanna!* new words which went, "I'm bound for Sacramento with my washbowl on my knee." Some of the forty-niners actually used washbowls to pan the gold dust out of the river beds. Others tore at the gravel with their bare hands or with knives or shovels, sold to them by Trader Sutter, who was always glad to oblige. Some struck it rich and others failed, but only a handful ever went home again. They stayed in California and made a thriving territory and then a state out of a remote area which might otherwise have remained empty for many years.

In the century since Marshall's discovery, more than $2¼ billion in gold has been taken out of California. Most of the old claims have long since been worked out although dredges and deep mines are still in operation. A few wistful oldtimers still comb the hills, searching for a new rich lode to rouse the sleepy Sierra again, and the whole length of the gold country, as shown on the following 11 pages of color photographs, is filled with the scars and landmarks left by the forty-niners. A stone monument on the bank of the American River marks the site of Sutter's mill, and a hundred cities and towns—some of them deserted and quietly decaying in the woods—mark the locations of the miners' camps. But James Marshall himself, the man who bent over to pick up something bright that caught his eye in the tailrace, left nothing behind him. He was elbowed aside in the rush of gold-seekers and never made a fortune from his discovery. He wandered aimlessly around the gold fields for many years and finally died, penniless and all alone in a shack not far from Sutter's mill.

Historical photographs:

THE FORTY-NINERS

A CHRONICLE OF THE
CALIFORNIA TRAIL AND EL DORADO
BY STEWART EDWARD WHITE

NEW HAVEN: YALE UNIVERSITY PRESS
TORONTO: GLASGOW, BROOK & CO.
LONDON: HUMPHREY MILFORD
OXFORD UNIVERSITY PRESS
1920

CHAPTER IV

GOLD

THE discovery of gold—made, as everyone knows, by James Marshall, a foreman of Sutter's, engaged in building a sawmill for the Captain—came at a psychological time.[1] The Mexican War was just over and the adventurous spirits, unwilling to settle down, were looking for new excitement. Furthermore, the hard times of the Forties had blanketed the East with mortgages. Many sober communities were ready, deliberately and without excitement, to send their young men westward in the hope of finding a way out of their financial difficulties. The Oregon question, as has been already indicated, had aroused patriotism to such an extent that westward migration had become a sort of mental contagion.

It took some time for the first discoveries to leak out, and to be believed after they had gained

[1] January 24, 1848, is the date usually given.

55

---

56   THE FORTY-NINERS

currency. Even in California itself interest was rather tepid at first. Gold had been found in small quantities many years before, and only the actual sight of the metal in considerable weight could rouse men's imaginations to the blazing point.

Among the most enthusiastic protagonists was one Sam Brannan, who often appeared afterwards in the pages of Californian history. Bran-

The following begins on page 57 (text about Brannan's character and personal history has been cut)

light, he went far. Though there were a great many admirable traits in his character, people were forced to like him in spite of rather than because of them. His enthusiasm for any public agitation was always on tap.

In the present instance he rode down from Sutter's Fort, where he then had a store, bringing with him gold-dust and nuggets from the new placers. "Gold! Gold! Gold from the American River!" shouted Brannan, as he strode down the street, swinging his hat in one hand and holding aloft the bottle of gold-dust in the other. This he displayed to the crowd that immediately gathered. With such a start, this new interest brought about a stampede that nearly depopulated the city.

---

58 **THE FORTY-NINERS**

The fever spread. People scrambled to the mines from all parts of the State. Practically every able-bodied man in the community, except the Spanish Californians, who as usual did not join this new enterprise with any unanimity, took at least a try at the diggings. Not only did they desert almost every sort of industry, but soldiers left the ranks and sailors the ships, so that often a ship was left in sole charge of its captain. All of American and foreign California moved to the foothills.

The following is from page 60:

The first gold was often found actually at the roots of bushes, or could be picked out from the veins in the rocks by the aid of an ordinary

GOLD 61

hunting-knife. Such pockets were, to be sure, by no means numerous; but the miners did not know that. To them it seemed extremely possible that gold in such quantities was to be found almost anywhere for the mere seeking. Authenticated instances are known of men getting ten, fifteen, twenty, and thirty thousand dollars within a week or ten days, without particularly hard work. Gold was so abundant it was much easier to dig it than to steal it, considering the risks attendant on the latter course. A story is told of a miner, while paying for something, dropping a small lump of gold worth perhaps two or three dollars. A bystander picked it up and offered it to him. The miner, without taking it, looked at the man with amazement, exclaiming: "Well, stranger, you are a curiosity. I guess you haven't been in the diggings long. You had better keep that lump for a sample."

The following is from page 62:

The first news of the gold discovery filtered to the east in a roundabout fashion through vessels from the Sandwich Islands. A Baltimore paper published a short item. Everybody laughed at the rumor, for people were already beginning to discount California stories. But they remembered it. Romance, as ever, increases with the square of the distance; and this was a remote land. But soon there came an official letter written by Governor Mason to the War Department wherein he said that in his opinion, "There is more gold in the country drained by the Sacramento and San Joaquin rivers than would pay the cost of the late war with Mexico a hundred times over." The public immediately was alert. And then, strangely enough, to give direction to the restless spirit seething beneath the surface of society, came a silly popular song. As has happened many times before and since, a great movement was set to the lilt of a commonplace melody. Minstrels started it; the public caught it up. Soon in every quarter of the world were heard the strains of

GOLD   63

Oh, Susannah! or rather the modification of it made to fit this case:

"I'll scrape the mountains clean, old girl,
  I'll drain the rivers dry.
I'm off for California, Susannah, don't you cry.
Oh, Susannah, don't you cry for me,
I'm off to California with my wash bowl on my
    knee!"

The public mind already prepared for excitement by the stirring events of the past few years, but now falling into the doldrums of both monotonous and hard times, responded eagerly. Every man with a drop of red blood in his veins wanted to go to California. But the journey was a long one, and it cost a great deal of money, and there were such things as ties of family or business impossible to shake off. However, those who saw no immediate prospect of going often joined the curious clubs formed for the purpose of getting at least one or more of their members to the El Dorado. These clubs met once in so often, talked over details, worked upon each other's excitement, even occasionally and officially sent some one of their members to the point of running amuck. Then he usually broke off all responsibilities and rushed headlong to the gold coast.

"Pan for gold this summer—here's how and where," by Bob Behme. In *Popular Mechanics*, July 1974 (Vol. 142, No. 1), pp. 82–85.

Finding gold. A noble metal, gold is dense with a unique color. Nothing exactly duplicates its look or feel. It bears the chemical symbol Au, has an atomic number of 79 and weight of 197.2. A cube 14 inches square would weigh one ton. Since it is heavy it is found wherever it settles to the bottom of a stream. The most likely places include roots and grasses along a bank, in bedrock crevices, behind boulders, in sandbars, and in places where the current slows or changes direction . . . (p. 83)

How to pan. The object is to concentrate heavier materials in the bottom of the pan as you float off the lighter "fines" as clay, sand and dirt. Fill a pan half full of sand and clay. Submerge it so it fills with water. Then remove larger rocks and break up clay, dirt balls and sod with your hand. Incline the pan away from your body and move it with a quick circular motion so that it swirls, churning the contents. Let the water flow gently over the lip of the pan, flushing away the silt, and repeat until only the heavier materials, generally black in color, remain. If you are lucky, the black sand will hold gold flakes and possibly nuggets. (p. 84)

Days of Gold: The California Gold Rush and the American Nation, by Malcolm J. Rohrbough. Berkeley, Calif.: University of California Press, 1997.

From the beginning . . . gold was readily accessible to the most inexperienced mining novice with the simplest and most inexpensive kinds of equipment. The first gold-mining techniques were simple. Gold was found in the nooks and crannies of old, dry streambeds and in the bottoms of existing watercourses, where it had been left by thousands of years of movement of water, which had carried the mineral downstream until the velocity of the water was insufficient to support the gold's weight. In turn, water was a crucial agent in early gold mining, as a force for separating the gold once again from the deposits around it. The first miners quickly mastered the primitive techniques by which moving water flowing through a tin pan would separate the lighter sand and gravel, which would be carried off by the force of the water, from the heavier gold particles, which would sink to the bottom of the pan, where they could be easily retrieved and stored in a small sack. All that was necessary to join the race for wealth was a shovel and a pan. (p. 12)

Day Four: Copia

 Focus: Reviewing skills in sentence writing

STEP ONE: **Review transforming active into passive verbs**

Look carefully at these sentences, drawn from this week's readings:

> Song Gaozong's plea was rejected.

> Gold was discovered at Sutter's Mill by James Marshall.

Underline the subject of each sentence once and the complete verb (main verb plus helping verbs) twice.

✦

You should have underlined:

> plea   was rejected
> gold   was discovered

Both of these verbs are in the passive voice, which means that the subject receives the action of the verb. The plea didn't do anything. Neither did the gold. In both sentences, someone or something else *did* the action of rejecting and discovering.

In a sentence with a verb in the active voice, the subject does the action of the verb. Most sentences can be rewritten so that the voice changes from passive to active. Read the next two sentences out loud:

> subject active verb   direct object
> The Jurchen rejected Song Gaozong's plea.
> subject   active verb   direct object
> James Marshall discovered   gold   at Sutter's Mill in 1848.

In the original version of the first sentence, you are not given any information about *who* or *what* performed the action of the verb. Sometimes, sentences are written in the passive voice because the author doesn't have this information. In the case of Song Gaozong and the Jurchen, we don't actually know which official, general, or ruler decided to ignore Song Gaozong's request. To rewrite my original sentence in the active voice, I have to choose a new subject, someone who's actually *doing* the rejecting. My only choice is the broad, vague subject "the Jurchen."

Other times, the actor in the sentence is found in a prepositional phrase following the passive verb. In the second sentence, James Marshall does the actual discovering. If you wanted the focus of the sentence to be on the gold, you would write, "Gold was discovered by James Marshall." If you wanted the focus to be on James Marshall, you would write, "James Marshall discovered gold."

To sum up: Passive verbs can be transformed into active verbs by supplying a new subject. Sometimes you'll need to invent this subject; sometimes, you can locate it in the prepositional phrase after the passive verb.

STEP TWO: Review transforming indirect objects into prepositional phrases

In the first level of this course, you also learned how to transform an indirect object into an object of a preposition.

Remember: an indirect object is a word that is indirectly affected by an action verb. In the sentence:

>   S   V   IO   DO
> The discovery of gold brought California a host of new settlers.

"host" is the direct object; it receives the action of the verb "brought" (meaning that the host of settlers was the thing brought). "California" is the indirect object. California didn't get "brought" somewhere. But the action of bringing did affect California; it ended up with a whole lot of new residents.

Indirect objects can be taken out of their place (between the verb and the direct object), and paired up with a preposition to express the same meaning:

>   S   V   DO   PREP   OP
> The discovery of gold brought a host of new settlers to California.

In this transformed sentence, the indirect object has become the object of the preposition "to."

STEP THREE: Practice transformations

Read each of the following sentences and decide whether it contains a passive verb that could be active, or an indirect object that could become the object of a preposition. In the blank next to each sentence, write "p" for "passive verb" or "io" for "indirect object."

Then rewrite each sentence on your own paper.

For the sentences with passive verbs, decide whether you can find a new subject in a prepositional phrase. If not, make a new subject up from your imagination.

For the sentences with indirect objects, simply transform each indirect object into the object of a preposition.

When you're finished, read both the original sentences and your sentences out loud. Sometimes, the revised sentence will sound better—and sometimes the original will be much clearer than the rewritten sentence! Place a checkmark by any of your sentences that sound like improvements on the original.

Show your completed work to your instructor.

1. More people in Africa are killed by hippos than by lions. _____
2. The hippopotamus's sudden grunt gave the young boy quite a scare. _____
3. Hippos were hunted by Egyptians because the large animals damaged their crops. _____
4. Only one small animal is allowed near the hippo. _____
5. The white sandpiper bird offers the hippo relief from parasites. _____
6. The formidable hippo guarantees the bird safety. _____
7. This relationship between two animals is called symbiosis. _____
8. You will be taught about symbiosis when you study biology. _____

Week 4: Narrations and Sequences in History, Part II

Day One: Analyzing Models

 Focus: Understanding how *topoi* fit together

STEP ONE: **Read**

Read the following description of kangaroo-hunting, written in the nineteenth century by a man who was visiting the British colonies in Australia.

As you may already know, in the late eighteenth century, the British government decided to send convicted prisoners to the continent of Australia in order to make British prisons less crowded. These prisoners were given the task of establishing a British colony in Australia. The colony was known as New South Wales. In 1803, the colony spread to the southern island of Tasmania, which the British called Van Diemen's Land.

Sir William Denison was the governor of New South Wales from 1855 until 1861. A *lurcher* is a type of hound.

"Kangaroo-Hunting in the New Australian Colonies"

I have not yet, in this veritable record, described any of our kangaroo-hunts, and what is Van Diemen's Land without a kangaroo-hunt?

Sometimes, when Sir William Denison comes to the country for "high hunting," with his aides-de-camp and secretaries, I am told he hunts with a pack of beagles, and a great field of horsemen; but this is not our style, nor indeed the usual style. The proper dog for this sport is a kind of powerful greyhound bred for the purpose; and two of them are enough.

One day, not long ago John Knox and I rode out with Mr. Reid and his two dogs, one a small thorough-bred greyhound, the other a large strong kangaroo dog, very like what is called in England a lurcher, but of finer make and taller stature.

We took the direction of the Blue Hill, westward, and soon found our-selves in a hilly, rocky, desolate and thickly-wooded region, littered by dead, prostrate trees, and cut up by hundreds of precipitous gullies running in all directions. The little hills are all so like one another, that to fix a landmark is impossible. Save by the position of the sun, you cannot tell towards what point of the compass you are going. The trees are so dense on the sides of all the hills, and the ground is so rough with broken and burned stumps, rocks, and holes, that fast riding is out of the question.

The dogs keep close to our horses' feet, as we slowly penetrate this wilderness, until at last, from behind a huge decaying log, with a shrill chir-rup of terror, bounds a kangaroo. In three huge leaps, springing on hind legs and nervous tail, he is out of our sight, and away behind the bushes and down the rocky gorge.

But from the moment his mouselike ears appear, as he rises to his first bound, the dogs are on his trail. The hounds also are out of sight in an instant; and we hold in our horses, and stand motionless, awaiting the result.

In five or ten minutes they will have either worried him, or lost him altogether. In either case they will come straight back to where they left us; and, the moment they appear, we shall know by their expression whether they have done their business. If the kangaroo has got away, they will slink back with drooping ears and penitent eyes, and lie down to pant at our feet. If they have slain the enemy, they will come bounding through the trees, with their heads high and their jaws bloody, and before coming quite up to us, they will turn and trot off, and so bring us to the spot where he lies dead.

We listen, and for a while can hear the crash of the dead branches as the dogs rush on—and then, occasionally, a short angry bark—and then dead silence. Presently, shame-faced, they come panting along. They do not dare look us in the face, but approach in a zig-zag manner and lie down on their sides, heaving as if their ribs would burst. We do not reproach them; their own failure is punishment enough.

We proceed still farther amongst the hills, and presently another kan-garoo breaks cover. Again, the dogs disappear in a twinkling. We hear a sharp, angry, almost constant barking. Then there is silence. And then, from the distance of a mile, rings the loud yell of one of the dogs. They are worrying the enemy. We dare not move in that direction, lest we should miss the dogs among the winding gullies, but wait impatiently. Finally they appear, with slow steps and trailing tails, but with triumph in their eyes.

—John Mitchel, *Jail Journal: or, Five Years in British Prisons*
(New York: Office of the "Citizen," 1854), pp. 291–292.

STEP TWO: **Analyze**

Using the text below, try to identify the three different *topoi* that make up this composition. Consult the *topoi* section of your Composition Notebook as you work.

The first two paragraphs serve as an introduction and are already labeled for you.

The first *topos* is made up of the five paragraphs in bold print. Write the name of the *topos* in blank 1.

The second *topos* is found in the italicized paragraph. Write its name in blank 2. (Ignore blank 3 for right now.)

The third *topos* is found in the paragraph written in regular type. Write its name in blank 4.

When you are finished, show your work to your instructor. Your instructor has further directions for you.

"Kangaroo-Hunting in the New Australian Colonies"

INTRODUCTION

I have not yet, in this veritable record, described any of our kangaroo-hunts, and what is Van Diemen's Land without a kangaroo-hunt?

Sometimes, when Sir William Denison comes to the country for "high hunting," with his aides-de-camp and secretaries, I am told he hunts with a pack of beagles, and a great field of horsemen; but this is not our style, nor indeed the usual style. The proper dog for this sport is a kind of powerful greyhound bred for the purpose; and two of them are enough.

1. *Chronhar Pastevent*

One day, not long ago John Knox and I rode out with Mr. Reid and his two dogs, one a small thorough-bred greyhound, the other a large strong kangaroo dog, very like what is called in England a lurcher, but of finer make and taller stature.

2. *Desc of a Place*

3. *Sequence History*

We take the direction of the Blue Hill, westward, and soon find ourselves in a hilly, rocky, desolate and thickly-wooded region, littered by dead, prostrate trees, and cut up by hundreds of precipitous gullies running in all directions. The little hills are all so like one another, that to fix a landmark is impossible. Save by the position of the sun, you cannot tell towards what point of the compass you are going. The trees are so dense on the sides of all the hills, and the ground is so rough with broken and burned stumps, rocks, and holes, that fast riding is out of the question.

The dogs keep close to our horses' feet, as we slowly penetrate this wilderness, until at last, from behind a huge decaying log, with a shrill chirrup of terror, bounds a kangaroo. In three huge leaps, springing on hind legs and nervous tail, he is out of our sight, and away behind the bushes and down the rocky gorge.

But from the moment his mouselike ears appear, as he rises to his first bound, the dogs are on his trail. The hounds also are out of sight in an instant; and we hold in our horses, and stand motionless, awaiting the result.

4. ___Sequence/___ ___History/___ In five or ten minutes they will have either worried him, or lost him altogether. In either case they will come straight back to where they left us; and, the moment they appear, we shall know by their expression whether they have done their business. If the kangaroo has got away, they will slink back with drooping ears and penitent eyes, and lie down to pant at our feet. If they have slain the enemy, they will come bounding through the trees, with their heads high and their jaws bloody, and before coming quite up to us, they will turn and trot off, and so bring us to the spot where he lies dead.

We listen, and for a while can hear the crash of the dead branches as the dogs rush on—and then, occasionally, a short angry bark—and then dead silence. Presently, shamefaced, they come panting along. They do not dare look us in the face, but approach in a zig-zag manner and lie down on their sides, heaving as if their ribs would burst. We do not reproach them; their own failure is punishment enough.

We proceed still farther amongst the hills, and presently another kangaroo breaks cover. Again, the dogs disappear in a twinkling. We hear a sharp, angry, almost constant barking. Then there is silence. And then, from the distance of a mile, rings the loud yell of one of the dogs. They are worrying the enemy. We dare not move in that direction, lest we should miss the dogs among the winding gullies, but wait impatiently. Finally they appear, with slow steps and trailing tails, but with triumph in their eyes.

STEP THREE: Review the *topos* Sequence: History

The sequence you identified in the last assignment only had one element from your *topoi* chart: the step-by-step process of a kangaroo hunt. Because the sequence was part of a longer composition, the chronological narrative served as both introduction and historical background.

Here is a sequence in history that contains both the step-by-step process and two other elements from your chart. Identify each element and label it in the margin of your paper.

"Aborigines" are the native peoples of Australia, who lived on the continent before the British colonists arrived.

Intro-
ductory
Desc.

The stone axe of the aborigines resembles the stone axes found in Europe. This useful and indispensable implement is of various sizes. It is made chiefly of green stone, shaped like a wedge, and ground at one end to a sharp edge. At the other end it is grasped in the bend of a doubled piece of split sapling, bound with kangaroo sinews, to form a handle, which is cemented to it with a composition of gum and shell lime.

Step by
step

This cement is made by gathering fresh wattle gum, pulling it into small pieces, masticating it with the teeth, and then placing it between two sheets of green bark, which are put into a shallow hole in the ground, and covered up with hot ashes till the gum is dissolved. It is then taken out, and worked and pulled with the hands till it has become quite stringy, when it is mixed with lime made of burnt mussel shells, pounded in a hollow stone— which is always kept for the purpose—and kneaded into a tough paste.

results

This cement is indispensable to the natives in making their tools, spears, and water buckets.

—James Dawson, *Australian Aborigines* (Melbourne: Walker May & Co., 1881), p. 24.

When you are finished, show your work to your instructor.

Day Two: Review Notes and Write the Narration

Focus: Writing a chronological
narration from notes

Over the next two days, you will write a composition of at least 250 but not more than 500 words. This composition will contain a chronological narrative and a descriptive sequence in history.

Today, you'll write a draft of the chronological narrative. Tomorrow, you'll write the descriptive sequence, combine the two parts of the composition into one whole essay, and proofread your work.

STEP ONE: **Read back through notes**

Open the document containing last week's notes on the Gold Rush. (Or pull out your notecards.) Read carefully through your notes.

STEP TWO: **Arrange your notes in chronological order**

First, separate out your notes about how gold panning works. You'll use these tomorrow when you write your sequence.

Now, arrange your notes in chronological order.

You learned how to do this in Week 29 of last year, when you wrote a chronological narrative about Julius Caesar. Here's a very quick review of what you were told to do:

> *You took notes about Caesar's actions from two books,* **The Delphian Course** *and* **Caesar's Commentaries on the Gallic War.** *In this step, you'll put the notes from both books together into one chronological list, cutting out unnecessary repetition.*
>
> *From* **Caesar's Commentaries,** *you might have written down the following three events:*
>
> *Caesar found out about the senate's decree "at Ravenna, on the 10th of January, 49 BC." (xiii)*
>
> *Caesar "crossed the Rubicon . . . and advanced into Italy." (xiii)*
>
> *As he marched through Italy, "town after town threw open its gates" to him. (xiii)*
>
> *From* **The Delphian Course,** *you might have written down:*
>
> *Caesar "completed his Gallic campaign" in 49 BC. (480)*
>
> *The senate was afraid of Caesar and "asked him to disband his soldiers." (480)*
>
> *Caesar refused and "crossed the Rubicon, the stream north of Rome." (480)*
>
> *Put those two lists together so that all of the events are in order, and then cross out notes that repeat the same information:*
>
> *Caesar "completed his Gallic campaign" in 49 BC. (480)*
>
> *The senate was afraid of Caesar and "asked him to disband his soldiers." (480)*
>
> *Caesar found out about the senate's decree "at Ravenna, on the 10th of January, 49 BC." (xiii)*
>
> *Caesar refused and "crossed the Rubicon, the stream north of Rome." (480)*
>
> ~~*Caesar "crossed the Rubicon . . . and advanced into Italy." (xiii)*~~
>
> *As he marched through Italy, "town after town threw open its gates" to him. (xiii)*
>
> *If you're using a word processor, create a new document and cut and paste information from both lists of events into it. If you're using note cards, simply arrange the cards in order and set aside the ones that have repeated information.*

Repeat these same steps for your information about the Gold Rush.

If you need help, show your work to your instructor. If not, go on to the next step.

STEP THREE: **Divide notes into main points**

Here's one more review from Week 29 of Level One:

> *Before you can write your chronological narrative about Caesar, you need to make yourself an outline. You're going to do this by dividing your list of events up into groups and giving each group a phrase or sentence that explains what it's about.*
>
> *Imagine that these are the first eight notes that you have on your list.*
>
> Caesar "completed his Gallic campaign" in 49 BC. (480)
>
> The senate was afraid of Caesar and "asked him to disband his soldiers." (480)
>
> The senate told Caesar "to resign the governorship of both Gauls and disband his army." (xiii)
>
> Caesar found out about the senate's decree "at Ravenna, on the 10th of January, 49 BC." (xiii)
>
> Caesar refused and "crossed the Rubicon, the stream north of Rome." (480)
>
> As he marched through Italy, "town after town threw open its gates" to him. (xiii)
>
> Caesar reached the capital "sixty days after the edict of the senate." (xiii)
>
> Caesar entered Rome and "brought order instead of turmoil to the city." (480)
>
> *The first four events are all leading up to the senate's decree, so you can group them all together and describe them like this:*
>
> I.   The senate's decree to Caesar
>
> Caesar "completed his Gallic campaign" in 49 BC. (480)
>
> The senate was afraid of Caesar and "asked him to disband his soldiers." (480)
>
> The senate told Caesar "to resign the governorship of both Gauls and disband his army." (xiii)
>
> Caesar found out about the senate's decree "at Ravenna, on the 10th of January, 49 BC." (xiii)
>
> *Give each group a title or description. If you're using a word processor, give the titles Roman numerals and type them into your document, using the same format as above:*
>
> II. Title for second group of notes
>
> event
>
> event
>
> event

and so on. If you're using note cards, write each title on a separate
note card and place it in front of the group of cards that it describes.

When you've finished this step, you'll have a two-level outline that you can use to write your narrative.

Aim for four or five main groups of events.

If you need help, show your work to your instructor. If you feel comfortable with your outline, go on to the next step.

STEP FOUR: **Write the narration**

Take a minute to review the Chronological Narrative of a Past Event chart in the Reference section of your notebook.

Using the outline you have created, write one paragraph about each group of events. Your narrative should be at least 200 words but not longer than 400. If you use an idea that is not common knowledge, be sure to use a footnote even if you put the idea into your own words.

The *Life* article has no listed author and is also a magazine article. Here is how you should format it for a footnote:

"The Gold Country" (*Life*, Feb. 2, 1948), p. 44.

The second time, just call it "The Gold Country."

On your Works Cited page, the article should be alphabetized as if "Gold" were the author's name, like this:

"The Gold Country." In *Life*, Feb. 2, 1948, p. 44.

In your composition, include at least one line of dialogue (something one of the characters actually said). If you didn't include dialogue in your notes, go back to the sources and choose a line. (Often, when you write, you will find yourself returning to the sources to find something that you didn't know you needed.)

When you are finished, show your composition to your instructor.

Day Three: Write the Sequence and Complete the Composition

 Focus: Writing a sequence describing a historical process

STEP ONE: Read back through notes

Go back through the notes you took about panning for gold. Look carefully at the photographs in last week's lesson.

STEP TWO: Write the sequence

Write a sequence that includes
> 1) a description of the pan used for panning gold and
> 2) a step-by-step description of the gold panning process

This sequence should be at least 50 words long, but no longer than 100 words. (It's a pretty simple process, so 100 words would have to be a flowery and elaborate sequence!)

STEP THREE: Combine the narration and sequence into a full composition

Now, decide where to insert the sequence into your chronological narrative. Look for a place where you mention gold miners, discuss their daily routines, or talk about gold found in a stream.

You may need to write a transitional sentence to go at the beginning of your sequence; something like "Panning for gold was difficult work" or "Many gold miners used gold pans to search for gold." (If you can't come up with your own sentence, you can use one of mine.)

Place a title at the top of your first page. You'll work on writing good titles a little later this year, when we talk more about selecting topics. This composition can just be titled "The Gold Rush."

Insert a Works Cited page at the end of your document.

STEP FOUR: **Proofread**

Repeat the basic steps of proofreading from Week 2 (Day 3):

1) Read your composition out loud. Listen for awkward or unclear sections. Rewrite them so that they flow more naturally.
2) Check spelling by looking, individually, at each word that might be a problem.
3) Check your commas.

Add the following step:

4) Check the punctuation and capitalization on your footnotes, your Works Cited page, and any direct quotes (including your required line of dialogue).

When you are confident that your composition is finished, show it to your instructor.

Day Four: Copia

Focus: Added and intensified adjectives

STEP ONE: **Understand the purpose of added and intensified adjectives**

So far, you've reviewed five kinds of sentence transformation learned in Level One of this course:

descriptive adjectives ⟷ nouns
passive verb ⟷ active verb
indirect object ⟶ object of the preposition
infinitives ⟷ participles
main verb ⟷ infinitive

Today, you'll learn a new skill: transforming a sentence by adding and intensifying adjectives.
Read the following two sentences.

My heart stood still, stopped dead short by a terrible cry, by the cry of great triumph and of severe pain.

My heart stood still, stopped dead short by an exulting and terrible cry,
by the cry of inconceivable triumph and of unspeakable pain.

The second sentence is from the novel *Heart of Darkness,* by Joseph Conrad. Compare the first version of the sentence (which just says that the narrator heard a cry of triumph and pain) with Conrad's version of the sentence. In Conrad's sentence, underline each adjective.

by a   cry, by the cry of   great triumph and of   severe pain.
by an exulting and terrible cry, by the cry of inconceivable triumph and of unspeakable pain.

Joseph Conrad uses two methods to make his sentence gripping and colorful.

First, he *intensifies* his adjectives. "Great" and "severe" are both useful adjectives, but Conrad chose to think: What is the most intense kind of greatness there is? A greatness that is *so* great that it is . . . *inconceivable.* What is the most intense pain possible? A pain so severe that it is . . . *unspeakable.*

Second, he *adds* adjectives. The cry isn't just terrible. It is both terrible *and* exulting.

Conrad often uses intense and added adjectives. Here is another sentence from *Heart of Darkness:*

I had blundered into a place of cruel and absurd mysteries.

Underline the adjectives that Conrad uses to describe the mysteries.

Once again, notice that he uses not just one adjective, but two. And both are *intense* adjectives. *Cruel* is a stronger description than *unkind* or *bad. Absurd* is a stronger word than *silly.*

How do you know if one adjective is more intense than another? That's a judgment call, so often there's not a clear right or wrong answer. Intense adjectives are more specific and less common than milder adjectives.

You shouldn't add adjectives that are exact synonyms. If Conrad had written "cruel and harsh mysteries" or "horrible and terrible cry," his sentences would be less powerful (and less interesting). But "exulting" and "absurd" add different shades of meaning.

STEP TWO: **Practice intensifying adjectives**

Using your thesaurus, write two intensified adjectives for each of the following words.

frightening   _____   _____

large   _____   _____

enjoyable   _____   _____

embarrassed   _____   _____

STEP THREE: **Add to the Sentence Variety chart**
Add the following principle and illustration to the Sentence Variety chart.

adjective ⟶ intensified adjective

The sun was bright.
The sun was incandescent.

adjective ⟶ added adjective

He leaped into the cold water.
He leaped into the cold and murky water OR
He leaped into the cold, murky water.

STEP FOUR: **Practice sentence variety**

Using your own paper or a word processing document, rewrite the following sentences by intensifying each adjective and adding a second adjective. Each sentence is adapted from Charles Dickens' classic novel *Oliver Twist*.

Use your thesaurus to find intense adjectives. You can also use your thesaurus to find second adjectives, but try to introduce adjectives that have different shades of meaning. For example, given the sentence:

The boy was poor.

you would look up "poor" in your thesaurus. "Penniless" is a more intense synonym for poor:

The boy was penniless.

But you don't want to choose another synonym of "poor" for your second adjective. Instead, pick one of the synonyms and look up the entry for *that* word. Another synonym for "poor" is "destitute." Under the entry for "destitute," you would find the synonym *exhausted*. So your sentence could now read:

The boy was penniless and exhausted.

The two adjectives go together, but don't mean exactly the same thing.

When you are finished, show your work to your instructor, who has the original versions of the sentences for you to compare to your own.

The girl fixed him with a sharp look.
At that time of day, the streets were quiet.
He was a nice gentleman.
The alley was dirty.
Oliver was in high spirits.

Week 5: Explanation by Comparison, Part I

Day One: Two-Level Outline

 Focus: Constructing a two-level outline of a comparison in nature

STEP ONE: **Read**

Read the following brief essay about tigers and cats (written by novelist Boris Fishman).

— — —

A cat snoozing on a couch may not remind you of a tiger, but in many ways the two animals are almost identical. In the scientific system that classifies all living things, cats and tigers belong to the same family, *Felidae*, which also includes lions and leopards, who are technically known as "big cats."

It's common knowledge that tigers are fierce hunters, but it's less well known that those cuddly cats are as well. Like tigers, cats have strong, flexible, and fast bodies; quick reflexes; and sharp claws and teeth suited to killing animals. Tigers and cats even kill their prey similarly, by sinking the long canine teeth on the sides of their mouths into their victims' necks and crushing their spinal cords.

Tigers and cats share sharp senses of smell, sight, and hearing. They need six times less light than human beings in order to see things. Both cats and tigers can hear higher-pitched sound than humans, which is useful for

hunting because the animals cats and tigers like to eat, like rodents, make noise
in these high frequencies.

And while it may seem that people keep only one of the two animals as pets,
that isn't the case. In the United States alone, there are 12,000 pet tigers, more
than 4,000 of them in Texas. Of course, there are 86 million pet cats—so cats
definitely have the edge in numbers!

There are obvious differences between tigers and cats. For one, tigers are
much bigger. (The heaviest cat to have ever lived weighed 46 pounds, which is
only half the amount of meat that a tiger can consume in a single meal!) And
only tigers can roar, whereas cats have to satisfy themselves with purring. (Inter-
estingly, scientists still don't know how or why cats purr.) As any cat owner
knows, cats don't like water, but tigers love it. They are powerful swimmers who
can cross four miles of water in a single trip. Tigers and cats belong to different
genera in the *Felidae* family—*Felis* (cats) and *Panthera* (tigers).

There's a much more serious difference between the two animals. Because of
their close association with human beings, cats can be found almost anywhere in
the world. In the United States alone, there are 60 million feral (non-domestic) cats.
But tigers are scarce. At the beginning of the 20th century, there were more than
100,000 wild tigers living in a territory stretching from the Caspian Sea in southern Europe to Siberia in northern Asia and Indonesia in southern Asia. Today, that
number is closer to 2,000, in an area that is less than one-tenth as large.

Human mythology celebrates both tigers and cats, though it's a little more
admiring of tigers. In ancient Egypt, cats were considered sacred animals. Statues of goddesses often depicted them as felines. And Muhammad, the prophet
of Islam, loved cats so much that "he would do without his cloak rather than
disturb one that was sleeping on it." But many people have negative superstitions
about cats, seeing them as bringers of bad luck who keep company with witches.
During the Black Plague, cats were exterminated because people thought that
they had caused the epidemic. (In fact, cats could have helped because they ate
the rats that actually carried the disease that caused the Black Plague.)

Tigers, on the other hand, have enjoyed only the best associations. Especially in eastern Asia, where many tigers have existed in the wild, the animal
represents royalty, fearlessness, and wrath. Tigers are the national animals of
Bangladesh, Nepal, India, Malaysia, North Korea, and South Korea (not to
mention the mascots of a countless number of sports teams).

The two animals have a little sibling rivalry going on when it comes to
popularity. Though one recent poll found cats to be the most popular domestic
pet, another poll found tigers to be the most beloved animal overall. One animal
specialist explained why this way: "We can relate to the tiger, as it is fierce and
commanding on the outside, but noble and discerning on the inside."[1]

--- --- ---

[1]David Ward, "Humankind's favourite animal is a tiger" (*The Guardian*, Dec. 5, 2004, www.guardian.co.uk)

STEP TWO: **Begin the two-level outline**

Your assignment is to make a two-level outline of this passage, but today, you'll approach the outline a little differently.

Up until now, you've been told to outline by finding the main point of each paragraph and then looking for subpoints within the paragraph. But in this passage, the paragraphs *are* the subpoints.

Look at the first four paragraphs and complete the following statement: "Each paragraph tells you how cats and tigers are _____."

Your answer to this question should help you find the first main point of the passage—the point that the first four paragraphs *all* relate to. Each of the first four paragraphs is a *subpoint*, giving more information about the main point. So your outline should look like this:

I.   (Main point that all four paragraphs relate to)
  A. (Main point of Paragraph 1)
  B. (Main point of Paragraph 2)
  C. (Main point of Paragraph 3)
  D. (Main point of Paragraph 4)

On your own paper, try to complete this outline. Check your work with your instructor when you are finished.

STEP THREE: **Finish the two-level outline**

Now that you've gotten the idea, finish the outline of the passage.

Here's a hint for you: It should follow this pattern.

II.
  A. (Main point of Paragraph 5)
  B. (Main point of Paragraph 6)
III.
  A. (Main point of Paragraphs 7 AND 8 combined)
  B. (Main point of Paragraph 9)

You might find II.A. (the main point of Paragraph 5) and III (the overall main point that Paragraphs 7–9 all relate to) particularly challenging. Give it a good try first, but then don't be reluctant to ask your instructor for help.

You've done something difficult and important today—you've outlined a piece of writing as a *whole*, rather than just approaching it paragraph by paragraph. That's a huge step. You probably deserve some chocolate. (Hershey's, if you like barnyard flavors—Godiva, if you don't!)

Day Two: Analyzing the *Topos*: Explanation by Comparison in Science

Focus: Learning the form of comparison/contrast

STEP ONE: Examine model passage

Read the following passage:

1. *Similarity feed*

2. *Similarity Cold blood*

4. *Differences Skin, claws, and young*

Time was when the only good snake was a dead one. Fortunately, as we have come to understand that every species has a place in the global environment, that attitude is almost a thing of the past. We now know that the fear of reptiles and amphibians is not instinctive, but is learned by children, usually from people who are simply uninformed. The fact is that many of these animals make excellent neighbors because they eat rodents or insects.

Both reptiles and amphibians are cold-blooded, meaning they depend on the sun or other heat source to stay warm. Beyond that, there are several differences between the two groups. 3. *Transition 1st*

Reptiles—the snakes, turtles, lizards, and crocodilians—have scales or plates, and their toes have claws. (The clawless Leatherback sea turtle is an exception.) Young reptiles are miniature versions of their parents.

Amphibians—the salamanders, toads, and frogs—have moist skins, and most have no claws. Their young have a larval stage, usually passed in the water (such as the tadpole of a frog) before they change into their adult form. In fact, the word *amphibian* is based on Greek words meaning "living a double life."

5. *Differences Most Skin, no claws,*

—Roger Conant, Robert C. Stebbins, & Joseph T. Collins,
Peterson First Guide: Reptiles and Amphibians
(New York: Houghton Mifflin Company, 1992), pp. 4–5.

Like the passage you read in the last day's work, this excerpt discusses the similarities and differences between two natural phenomena (in both cases, living things).

The comparison begins in the first paragraph: People fear both reptiles and amphibians. This is a similarity—maybe not between the animals themselves, but in the reactions people have to them. On the first line, write "Similarity: People fear them."

The first sentence of the second paragraph contains a second similarity. On line 2, write, "Similarity: They are _____" and fill in the blank.

The authors then use the last sentence of the second paragraph to transition from similarities to differences. On line 3, write "Transition."

The third paragraph begins to highlight the differences between reptiles and amphibians by describing the skin, feet, and young of reptiles (scales, claws, and miniature versions). On the fourth line, write "Differences: Scales, claws, young."

The final paragraph finishes the contrast by describing the skin, feet, and young of amphibians (moist skin, no claws, larvae). On line 5, write "Differences: Moist skin, no claws, larvae."

STEP TWO: **Write down the pattern of the *topos***

Like the passage that you outlined in the last lesson, this passage explains what two living creatures are by comparing them to each other.

This form of writing is called *explanation by comparison and contrast*. It is one of the most useful *topoi* you will learn. Comparison and contrast gives the reader a clear, straightforward picture of what two things are like by explaining how they are the same and how they are different.

When you set out to write an explanation, you'll have to decide how to organize your comparisons (similarities) and contrasts (differences). In the comparison of cats and tigers, Boris Fishman used the *point-by-point* method. He listed one quality after another and, for each, compared cats and tigers.

Scientific family?	Cats, yes.	Tigers, yes.
Fierce hunters?	Cats, yes.	Tigers, yes.
Sharp senses?	Cats, yes.	Tigers, yes.
Kept as pets?	Cats, yes.	Tigers, yes.
Size?	Cats, small.	Tigers, bigger.
Sound?	Cats, purr.	Tigers, roar.
Water?	Cats, hate.	Tigers, love.
Numbers?	Cats, millions.	Tigers, 2,000

The authors of *Peterson First Guide* started out by using the same method for comparisons.

People fear them?	Amphibians, yes.	Reptiles, yes.
Coldblooded?	Amphibians, yes.	Reptiles, yes.

But when they began to give contrasts, they changed to the *subject by subject method*. They described three things about reptiles, and then the same three things, in the same order, about amphibians.

Reptiles	Skin
	Feet
	Young
Amphibians	Skin
	Feet
	Young

The point-by-point method is very clear and easy to write, but it can get monotonous (like a very long tennis match, where the ball goes back . . . and forth . . . and back . . . and forth . . . and back . . .). The subject-by-subject method gives your writing a better forward flow, but requires the reader to keep all of the points of the first subject in mind while reading the second—so you wouldn't want to list more than three or four points of comparison for one subject before going on to the next.

Alternating methods, as in *Peterson First Guide,* can give your composition variety and hold the reader's interest.

Copy the following onto a blank sheet of paper in the Reference section of your Composition Notebook.

Explanation by Comparison/Contrast

Definition: A comparison of similarities and differences

Procedure

1. Decide which aspects of the subjects are the same, and which are different.
2. Choose a method for comparing and contrasting.
   a. Point-by-point
   b. Subject-by-subject

Remember

1. Use both methods to give variety.

STEP THREE: **Read**

You'll finish today's assignment by taking notes on the following information. In the next day's work, you'll use it to write a comparison of your own.

This is less complicated than the Gold Rush assignment. Tomorrow's comparison can be brief, and because all of the information in the sources below comes under the heading of common knowledge (widely accepted scientific facts, well-known theories, and things learned through the senses), you don't have to worry about documentation.

Instead, divide a sheet of paper into two columns. Label one "platypus" and the other "beaver." In each column, jot down facts about these two animals, using the source material below. Aim for 12–15 notes per animal.

The first few notes are done for you, just to give you a sense of what kinds of facts you're looking for. Read the excerpt from *The International Wildlife Encyclopedia* carefully before looking at the notes. Then, take your own notes using the pattern I've provided, or else copy my notes into your column.

Maurice Burton, ed., *The International Wildlife Encyclopedia,* **Vol. 1 (New York: Marshall Cavendish Corp., 1989), p. 1987.**

That the platypus, a mammal, lays eggs and suckles its young was not known when the first specimen was discovered . . . The term *monotremes* refers to the spiny anteaters and the platypus, both of which are egg-laying mammals and the only members of the order Monotremata.

. . . Usually two soft-shelled white eggs are laid [by the female platypus], each 1/2 inch (1.3 cm) in diameter. The eggs often stick together, which prevents them from rolling away . . . Before retiring to lay her eggs, the female blocks the tunnel at intervals with earth up to 8 inches (20 cm) thick, which she tamps into position with her tail . . . The young platypus is naked and blind, and its eyes do not open for 11 weeks. It is weaned at nearly 4 months old, when it takes to the water.

SAMPLE NOTES

PLATYPUS

Mammal
Monotremes—egg-laying mammals
Lays two soft-shelled white eggs
Eggs stick together
Female lays eggs in a tunnel
Young is naked and blind
Eyes open in 11 weeks
Weaned at nearly 4 months

Notice that you don't need to note down the authors, books, and page numbers as long as you are jotting down scientific facts.

Now, continue to take notes on the following sources on your own.

Jack Myers and John Rice, *The Puzzle of the Platypus: And Other Explorations of Science in Action* **(Honesdale, Penn.: Boyds Mills Press, 2008), pp. 20, 22, 23.**

(p. 20)   People who had seen the platypus said that it made a living by diving to scoop up worms and crayfish between the long upper and lower lips of its bill. Onshore, it used its claws to dig burrows in the riverbank. It was amphibious, living both in water and on land.

(p. 22)   Study of the platypus's insides showed that it has a cloaca, a structure found in birds and reptiles. This is an opening—a single opening for all body wastes, both feces and urine. In birds and reptiles, the cloaca also serves as a passageway for laying eggs.

Further study found glands that were much like the milk-producing mammary glands of mammals. Then, observations on living animals found actual production of milk.

(p. 23)   Scientists . . . placed the platypus in a special group of mammals, the monotremes ("one-opening" animals). This just says that of all the classes of animals, the platypus is most like the mammals. Then it says that they are different from other mammals in having only one opening in the body cavity.

Note to student: Although "monotreme" means "one-opening," it refers only to mammals that have one body opening ("cloaca") and also lay eggs.

Tom Grant, *The Platypus: A Unique Mammal* (Sydney, Australia: University of New South Wales Press, 1995), pp. 2, 5.

(p. 2)   The platypus is streamlined like other mammals which live in water, such as the otters and beavers, but it is much smaller than these animals. It propels itself through the water using alternate kicks of its webbed front limbs, while most other aquatic animals . . . kick with their back feet . . . The platypus has a covering of dense waterproof fur over all of its body except for its feet and bill (beak). The bill looks a bit like that of a duck, with nostrils on top just back from the tip, but, unlike the duck's bill, it is soft and rubbery.

(p. 5)   The possession of hair and mammary glands certainly places the platypus into the class Mammalia and scientists now recognise that it is certainly a "different" mammal.

Karen McGhee and George McKay, *The Encyclopedia of Animals: A Complete Visual Guide* (Washington, D.C.: National Geographic, 2007), p. 66.

Like other mammals, monotremes are covered in fur, lactate to feed their young, and have a four-chambered heart, a single bone in the lower jaw, and three bones in the middle ear. They are unusual, however, because they lay eggs rather than give birth to live young, and also have some anatomical similarities to reptiles, such as extra bones in their shoulders . . . With its duck-like bill, webbed feet, furred body, and beaver-like tail, the platypus has fascinated scientists since the first specimen was sent to Britain in 1799.

Leonard Lee Rue III, *Beavers* (Stillwater, Minn.: Voyageur Press, 2002), pp. 18, 21.

(p. 18)   The beaver's favorite foods are the twigs and bark from aspen, willow, and alder saplings. In the spring and summer, beavers will also eat skunk cabbage, grasses, and berries. Beavers have to eat a lot of these fibrous foods to get the nutrition they need. An adult beaver will need 1 1/2 to 2 pounds (0.7–0.9kg) of food per day for body maintenance . . . The  beaver gains nutrition from the tree's outer and inner barks; it cannot break down the lignin in the wood itself.

(p. 21)   When a beaver, or a pair of beavers, move into a new area, its first priority is shelter. If there is a streamside bank higher than 24 inches (67 cm), the beaver can dig a bank burrow. The beaver dives beneath the water's surface and, using the strong claws on its forefeet, digs an underwater tunnel into the bank. The beaver will dig the tunnel to slope upwards, above the water level, where it will excavate a small chamber.

Marshall Cavendish Corporation, *Encyclopedia of the Aquatic World* (New York: Marshall Cavendish, 2004), pp. 183, 194.

(p. 183)   Beavers are unusual among mammals in that they have a cloaca, a single chamber into which the intestinal, urinary, and reproductive ducts open. Amphibians, reptiles, and birds have a cloaca; mammals more typically have two openings.

(p. 194)   Beavers are not prolific breeders and invest a lot of time raising each litter of young. Young beavers are dependent on their parents for up to two years.

     Beavers are monogamous. Each beaver group consists of a breeding pair, their offspring from the previous year, and kits from the current year.

The yearlings help their parents raise the next litter by babysitting and providing food for the kits.

Beaver kits are born fully furred, with eyes open, and with their incisors already present. Newborn beavers are 12 inches (30 cm) long and weight just over 1 pound (0.5 kg). At first the kits have soft fur that insulates them against cold, but they do not have tough protective guard hairs. The fluffy fur makes beaver kits so buoyant that they cannot exit through the lodge's underwater entrances . . . Four is the usual number of kits in a litter, but up to eight or nine is possible.

John O. Whitaker and William John Hamilton, *Mammals of the Eastern United States* (Ithaca, N.Y.: Comstock, 1998), pp. 262–263.

(p. 262)   The beaver is the largest North American rodent, and between its size and its large, scaly paddle-like tail, it can be confused with no other North American mammal. The color is uniformly reddish brown to blackish brown . . . The ears, short and rounded, are dark blackish brown. The hind legs are longer than the front legs, the hips thus higher than the shoulders when the animal is walking. The skull and teeth are massive, a necessity for cutting tough wood such as oak and maple . . .

(p. 263)   The reproductive organs are internal and open into a common . . . cloaca . . .

Day Three: Practicing the *Topos*

 Focus: Writing an explanation by comparison/contrast

STEP ONE: **Organize platypus notes**

Take the notes from the last day's work and organize them into groups, by topic. Give each group a title.

Start with the platypus notes. For example, if I were organizing the notes I took on the very first source, I would divide them up like this:

CLASSIFICATION
Mammal
Monotremes—egg-laying mammals

BABIES
Lays two soft-shelled white eggs
Eggs stick together
Female lays eggs in a tunnel
Young is naked and blind
Eyes open in 11 weeks
Weaned at nearly 4 months

If necessary, you may borrow my two topics to get you started.

Cut and paste (or rearrange) your notes so that all the notes that belong to a single topic are grouped together. You should be able to find at least four different topics.

When you are finished, show your work to your instructor.

STEP TWO: **Organize beaver notes**

Now take your beaver notes and organize them into the same categories. If you have additional beaver notes that don't fall into those groupings, put them under the heading "Other."

When you are finished, show your work to your instructor.

STEP THREE: **Choose topics for your comparison/contrast**

Now that you've organized your notes, you should be able to figure out the similarities and differences between the two animals.

Remember that you're writing an explanation by comparison and contrast—that means that your composition needs to be structured around 1) what is similar and then 2) what is different.

In your notes, underline, highlight, or circle the things that are *the same*—that both animals have in common.

Then, choose *two* topics or groupings that contain *differences* between the two animals.

You won't use the rest of the material. Any time you write a comparison and contrast, you will need to pick and choose among the material, deciding to use only the facts that make your composition flow easily forward. So pick the topics that you think will be the easiest to write about.

STEP FOUR: **Write the comparison**

Now you'll write the actual comparison and contrast, using the directions below.

If you are confused at any point, ask your instructor for help.

DIRECTIONS

First, write a paragraph explaining how the two animals are the same. Do this before you move on.

Second, using one of the topics/groups you selected, write a paragraph explaining how the two animals are *different*. Make use of the point-by-point method.

This paragraph will have three parts—read a), b), and c) below before you write!

a) Begin the paragraph with a sentence that says, in your own words, "Beavers and platypuses[18] are different in _____ [fill in the blank with the topic]."

b) Continue by addressing the facts in the group that apply to both platypuses and beavers. For example, if you are writing about appearances, you might write:

The platypus has a bill like a duck, but the beaver has massive front teeth. The platypus is smaller than the beaver.

c) Conclude by describing the facts that apply only to platypuses, and then the facts that apply only to beavers. You will never find *exact* parallels between two living things, so you will need to give yourself room to finish out the paragraph without finding perfect, point-by-point contrasts for every fact.

Finish the paragraph before you move on.

Third, using the second topic/group selected, write a paragraph explaining how the two animals are *different,* using the subject-by-subject method.

a) First, write several sentences describing the platypus, fact by fact.

b) Then, write several sentences describing the beaver, fact by fact.

---

18. Scientists differ on what the plural of "platypus" should be. "Platypuses" is used by many; others just use "platypus" (in the same way that "one deer" and "many deer" have the same form). Some even use "platypi," because the Latin plural ends in -i (even though the word "platypus" is derived from the Greek). You may choose any of these options when you write.

STEP FIVE: **Proofread**

Repeat the basic steps of proofreading:

1) Read your composition out loud. Listen for awkward or unclear sections. Rewrite them so that they flow more naturally.
2) Check spelling by looking, individually, at each word that might be a problem.
3) Check your commas.

When you're finished, show your work to your instructor.

Day Four: Copia

Focus: Introduction to simile

Today, you'll begin to build the skills needed for a more complex set of sentence transformations.

STEP ONE: **Understanding simile**

Read the following sets of sentences out loud.

He was very large and very fat.
He looked, in fact, very much like a colossal bowl of jelly, without the bowl.

There was an ominous stillness.
For an instant there was an ominous stillness, as if even the air was holding its breath.

The higher they went, the darker it became.
The higher they went, the darker it became, though it wasn't the darkness of night, but rather more like a mixture of lurking shadows and evil intentions which oozed from the slimy moss-covered cliffs and blotted out the light.

The second sentence in each pair is from Norman Juster's classic adventure *The Phantom Tollbooth*. Each one of Norman Juster's sentences contains a *simile*.
In the second sentence of each pair, find and underline the word *like* or *as*.
Then, circle the set of words that follow each underlined word.
Here's what you should have circled . . .

✦

a colossal bowl of jelly, without the bowl
if even the air was holding its breath
a mixture of lurking shadows and evil intentions

Each one of these phrases is a *simile*.

You studied similes very briefly in the first level of this course. Let's review: **A simile is a comparison between two things, introduced by the words *like* or *as* (or *as if*).** In the first sentence, a fat man is compared to a bowl of jelly. In the second, stillness is compared to a living creature holding its breath. In the third, darkness is compared to shadows and evil intentions.

In a good simile, the comparison reminds the reader of the most important, or most striking, or most interesting thing about the subject. Norman Juster wants you to focus in on how formless, quivering, and bulgy the fat man is . . . so he chooses *jelly* (which is formless, quivering and bulgy). He wants you to *feel* the stillness, so he reminds you of how it feels to hold your breath and be completely motionless. And he wants you to *sense* just how threatening and scary the darkness is, so he compares it to "lurking" shadows and "evil intentions."

STEP TWO: **Identifying simile**

In the following sentences, underline the simile. Draw an arrow from the simile back to the subject—the word the simile describes by comparison.

Oh, my Luve's like a red, red rose,
That's newly sprung in June
     (Robert Burns)

[The door] was opened by another footman in livery, with a round face, and large eyes like a frog.
     (Lewis Carroll, *Alice in Wonderland*)

[Meg] tried to get rid of the kitten, which had scrambled up her back and stuck like a burr just out of reach.
     (Louisa May Alcott, *Little Women*)

As Anne sits at the window, she can look down on the sea, which this morning is calm as glass.
     (Charlotte Bronte, *Letters*)

The wrath of the monarch's eye dazzled like the lightning in the sky.
     (Jean Racine)

The sun to me is dark, and silent as the moon.
   (John Milton, *Samson Agonistes*)

He squeaks like a hurt chicken.
   (Alexander Wilson)

The vast clouds fled, countless and swift as leaves on autumn's tempest.
   (Percy Bysshe Shelley)

Yellow butterflies flickered along the shade like flecks of sun.
   (William Faulkner, *The Sound and the Fury*)

STEP THREE: **Invent new similes**

Now it's your turn to find similes.

On your own paper, rewrite the sentences from Step Two by finding your own simile. Try to choose a simile that expresses the meaning in the brackets below. So, for example, a good answer to

Oh, my Luve's like [something fresh, beautiful, and new]

would not be

Oh, my Luve's like rain after a long drought.

It's very nice to say that your love is like rain after a long drought, but that simile doesn't convey *fresh, beautiful,* and *new*. It might convey

Oh, my Luve's like [something that saves me when I'm desperate]

but that's a whole different set of ideas.

Oh, my Luve's like the first grass of spring

would be a better simile (although perhaps not quite as good as Robert Burns's!).

As you're working on your similes, use the following meanings:

Oh, my Luve's like [something fresh, beautiful, and new].

The door was opened by another footman in livery, with a round face, and large eyes like [something rather stupid].

Meg tried to get rid of the kitten, which had scrambled up her back and stuck like [something uncomfortable and annoying].

As Anne sits at the window, she can look down on the sea, which this morning is calm as [something smooth].

The wrath of the monarch's eye dazzled like [something frightening and destructive].

The sun to me is dark, and silent as [something very distant].

He squeaks like [something powerless and silly].

The vast clouds fled, countless and swift as [something passing, temporary, soon gone].

Yellow butterflies flickered along the shade like [something incredibly bright].

When you are finished, show your sentences to your instructor.

WEEK 6: INTRODUCTIONS AND CONCLUSIONS

Day One: How to Write an Introduction

 Focus: Learning the structure of introductions

STEP ONE: Understand three types of introduction

When you wrote last week's composition about the beaver and the platypus (the comparison/contrast), you were told to begin with a paragraph explaining how the two animals are the same. Your composition probably started something like this . . .

> The beaver and the platypus both belong to the mammal family. They have fur and nurse their young. Both beavers and platypuses dig out burrows for their homes, using their claws. And, unlike other mammals, both have a single opening in their body, called the *cloaca*.

That's a perfectly good paragraph about similarities. But it's missing something: an *introduction.*

Today, you'll return to your comparison and give it an introduction.

In order to understand what a good introduction does, let's look at three different introductions to three different essays about animals. We'll start with the first paragraph of Boris Fishman's comparison of cats and tigers.

> A cat snoozing on a couch may not remind you of a tiger, but in many ways the two animals are almost identical. In the scientific system that classifies all living things, cats and tigers belong to the same family, *Felidae*, which also includes lions and leopards, who are technically known as "big cats."

The first sentence of this paragraph *introduces* Fishman's first set of comparisons by telling you, ahead of time, what the conclusion of his entire essay will be: Although there are important contrasts between cats and tigers, their *similarities* are much more important than their differences. The *introduction by summary* provides one or two sentences at the beginning of a composition that tell the reader exactly what the composition is about and what its most central conclusion will be.

Introduction by summary is one of the simplest forms of introduction. Here's a second kind, from the comparison of reptiles and amphibians you looked at last week:

> Time was when the only good snake was a dead one. Fortunately, as we have come to understand that every species has a place in the global environment, that attitude is almost a thing of the past.[19]

This kind of introduction, the *introduction by history,* looks back in time, telling you something about the subject's history: In the past, snakes were usually just killed, but now that attitude has changed.

An introduction by history gives you a snippet of information about past attitudes, an idea of how the subject has developed over time, or a brief scene from history. Here's another *introduction by history,* this one about beavers [*extirpate* means "to remove" or "to destroy completely"]:

> Two beaver species inhabit our world: the North American and the Eurasian beaver. Both had been extirpated over large areas by the beginning of the 20th century. But during the past 50 years . . . each of the species has traveled along a different trajectory. In the United States, reintroduction of the North American beaver in its former range has been so successful that burgeoning populations have no choice but to move into developed land . . . In Europe, meanwhile, reintroductions have given some countries their first beavers in decades. Still small in numbers, these new populations are being carefully nurtured.[20]

This introduction by history tells how the beaver population has developed over time: Fifty years ago, beavers were uncommon. Then they were reintroduced. Now there are almost too many beavers in North America, and the population in Europe is starting to grow. The introduction tells you how beaver populations have developed over time.

Here's one more introduction from history, this one using a brief scene from history to introduce an essay about scientific controversy over the platypus:

---

19. Conant, Stebbins, and Collins, p. 4.
20. Dietland Müller-Schwarze, *The Beaver: Natural History of a Wetlands Engineer* (Comstock, 2003), p. ix.

It all began harmlessly enough. Nearly 10 years after settlement, in November 1797, at Yarramundi Lagoon just north of Sydney, Governor John Hunter watched an Aboriginal guide wait patiently to spear a platypus as it surfaced. Hunter sent the skin and a sketch to the Literary and Philosophical Society in Newcastle-upon-Tyne . . .[21]

The third type of introduction, *introduction by anecdote,* starts by telling a story. This story might be drawn from personal experience, as in the introduction to *Reptiles & Amphibians for Dummies:*

Most reptile and amphibian owners can point with unerring accuracy to the moment they got hooked on these animals. For me, it was when I walked across the street at age 6 to the open lots west of my home in Albuquerque, New Mexico. The lots were filled with tumbleweeds, tufts of scrub grass, and a few (very few, thank goodness) scraggy, low cholla cactus. Dashing from clump to clump were blue-tailed skinks. Less active but lying quietly amidst concealing gravel patches were the sand lizards. I never knew what occupied the fist-sized tunnels, but imagined they might be rattlesnakes. I spent most of my summers exploring those lots. . .[22]

An *introduction by anecdote* can also take the form of an invented scene—a story that you make up, based on what you know about the subject. Here are two examples, both taken from books that compare and contrast animals.

You wake up one morning and are walking sleepily toward the kitchen when all of a sudden, your pet cat rubs against your leg. She seems cute and friendly, but what your pet is really doing is acting like a wild cat![23]

It is feeding time. In the dense Indian jungle, an enormous Bengal tiger drags his fresh kill to a hiding place. Thousands of miles away on a dusty African plain, a male lion takes the first bite of a zebra that his lionesses have just killed. No animal dares to get in his way.[24]

There are many other ways to introduce a composition, but these three are the most common (and the most useful).

---

21. Penny Olsen, *Upside Down World: Early European Impressions of Australia's Curious Animals* (National Library of Australia, 2010), p. 14.

22. Patricia Bartlett, *Reptiles & Amphibians for Dummies* (Wiley, 2003), p. 1.

23. Jenni Bidner, *Is My Cat a Tiger? How Your Pet Compares to its Wild Cousins* (Lark Books, 2006), p. 7.

24. Isabel Thomas, *Lion vs. Tiger* (Heinemann Library, 2007), p. 4.

STEP TWO: **Create an Introduction reference page**

Keep this information on hand as you write by adding it to the Reference section of your Composition Notebook.

At the top of a sheet of paper, center the word INTRODUCTIONS. Beneath it, write the following information:

1. Introduction by Summary
   One or more sentences that tell the reader what the composition is about and what its most central conclusion will be

2. Introduction by History
   a. Information about past attitudes towards the subject
   b. Description of how some aspect of the subject has changed or developed over time
   c. Brief scene from history

3. Introduction by Anecdote
   a. A story drawn from personal experience
   b. An invented scene, based on your knowledge of the subject

STEP THREE: **Practice**

Finish today's work by writing three brief introductions to your platypus and beaver comparison: one introduction by summary, one introduction by history, and one introduction by anecdote. Each introduction can be as short as one sentence or as long as three or four.

If you have difficulty with any of these introductions, ask your instructor for help.

1. Introduction by Summary

In one or more sentences, tell the reader whether the beaver and the platypus are more alike than they are different—or vice versa.

2. Introduction by History

Using the following information, write one or more sentences (you'll probably need at least two) describing past attitudes towards the platypus.

Ever since the first specimen (a dried skin) of the platypus arrived in Britain from Australia in about 1798, the species has been surrounded by controversy. This first specimen was thought to be a fake animal which a taxidermist had made by stitching together the beak of a duck and the body parts of a mammal! Even when it was found to be real, the species was not accepted as actually being a mammal.[25]

When the first platypus specimens from Australia were sent back to England in 1798, people thought they were two unrelated animals sewn together. A faked-up mermaid (which was commonly fabricated from monkey remains and fishtails) was more understandable. At least mermaids were well-known mythical creatures. But who would believe an otter-and-duck combination?

In the end, scientists discovered that the platypus was not only real, but even weirder than was immediately apparent.[26]

3. Introduction by Anecdote

Write a description, one sentence or more, set in the present tense, of both a platypus and a beaver carrying out some daily activity. Your end result should resemble the lion-and-tiger introduction in Step Two.

Alternately, if you've ever seen a platypus, write one or more sentences about your reactions. (If you feel creative, you could *pretend* that you've seen a platypus and write about your *possible* reaction.)

When you've finished your three introductions, show them to your instructor. Together, decide which one is the most effective introduction to your composition.

Day Two: How to Write a Conclusion

> Focus: Learning the purpose and structure of conclusions

STEP ONE: **Understand three types of conclusion**

When you first meet someone, you say "hello." When you leave, you say "goodbye." An introduction is a composition's "hello" to the reader. Today, you'll learn how to say "goodbye" by writing a strong conclusion.

There are many ways to conclude an essay, but let's look at three of the most common.

---

25. Grant, p. 5.

26. Margaret Mittelbach and Michael Crewdson, *Carnivorous Nights: On the Trail of the Tasmanian Tiger* (Random House, 2005), p. 225.

First, you can summarize your conclusions. *Conclusion by summary* is similar to *introduction by summary*; the difference is that, by the end of the essay, you've given the reader plenty of specific details. So when you write a conclusion by summary, you should use a couple of those details.

How would *conclusion by summary* work for Boris Fishman's essay on cats and tigers? You could simply write,

> Despite their many differences, cats and tigers are very much alike.

But using a few of the details from the essay would make this a much more effective conclusion.

> Cats and tigers may be very different in size, in the way they sound, and in their love of water. But as their hunting habits and their sharp senses show us, they have just as many similarities as differences.

Notice how I went back and mentioned specifics: size, sound, love of water, etc.

Here's another example of *conclusion by summary*. Reread this excerpt from *Peterson First Guide: Reptiles and Amphibians* (you saw this in Day Two of last week's lesson). Notice the bolded sentences I have added to the end.

> Time was when the only good snake was a dead one. Fortunately, as we have come to understand that every species has a place in the global environment, that attitude is almost a thing of the past. We now know that the fear of reptiles and amphibians is not instinctive, but is learned by children, usually from people who are simply uninformed. The fact is that many of these animals make excellent neighbors because they eat rodents or insects.
>
> Both reptiles and amphibians are cold-blooded, meaning they depend on the sun or other heat source to stay warm. Beyond that, there are several differences between the two groups.
>
> Reptiles—the snakes, turtles, lizards, and crocodilians—have scales or plates, and their toes have claws. (The clawless Leatherback sea turtle is an exception.) Young reptiles are miniature versions of their parents.
>
> Amphibians—the salamanders, toads, and frogs—have moist skins, and most have no claws. Their young have a larval stage, usually passed in the water (such as the tadpole of a frog) before they change into their adult form. In fact, the word *amphibian* is based on Greek words meaning "living a double life."
>
> **Despite their cold-blooded nature, amphibians and reptiles are actually quite different. Scales and claws set reptiles apart, and young amphibians look nothing like young reptiles!**

(One consideration: At the end of a short composition, conclusion by summary can sound repetitive. After all, the reader *just* learned those details two minutes ago! You'll probably find it useful for slightly longer compositions.)

Second, you can end with a personal statement or opinion—your own reaction to what you've just written. The *conclusion by personal reaction* tells the reader what *you* think. So Mr. Fishman's composition might have ended:

> I can understand why so many people like tigers—but give me a cat
> any day. I'd far rather have a cat sleeping on the end of my bed than a pet
> tiger caged in my backyard!

Telling the reader which animal is *your* favorite brings the composition to a nice, neat end.

A *conclusion by personal reaction* to the reptile and amphibian comparison might sound like this:

> Even though amphibians and reptiles are different in many ways, they
> seem very much alike to me. I'd be happy to have either a frog or a turtle for
> a pet, and snakes and salamanders both give me the shivers.

Here again, the reader finds out what *you* think: In your opinion, the similarities are a lot more important than the differences.

Another way to write a personal reaction would be to mention your own experience with the subject (very much like the *introduction by anecdote*, except at the end of the composition instead of the beginning). The reptile-amphibian comparison could end like this:

> I have kept both turtles and frogs as pets. Both of them needed to be
> kept warm during the winter. But I have to say that I find baby turtles much
> more appealing than frog larvae!

Third, you can end by posing a question to the reader. The *conclusion by question* asks the *reader* to react—so in a way, it's similar to the *conclusion by personal reaction*.

The cat-tiger comparison might end like this:

> Tigers may be noble, but remember: they can eat over ninety pounds
> of meat in a single meal! If you had a choice between a tiger or cat for a pet,
> could you afford to feed it?

or

> Even though tigers are magnificent animals, the number of pet cats in
> the world tells me that most people actually prefer the tiger's smaller rela-
> tive. What would your preference be—tiger or cat?

Both conclusions take the last part of the comparison and contrast (how people react personally to cats and tigers) and ask the reader to have an opinion about it.

Keep this in mind as you write: All of these sample conclusions have more than one sentence. A conclusion written as a separate paragraph should have a minimum of two sentences. Sometimes, you may find it more natural to write a single-sentence conclusion. In that case, attach that sentence to the last paragraph of the essay, like this:

> The two animals have a little sibling rivalry going on when it comes to popularity. Though one recent poll found cats to be the most popular domestic pet, another poll found tigers to be the most beloved animal overall. One animal specialist explained why this way: "We can relate to the tiger, as it is fierce and commanding on the outside, but noble and discerning on the inside."[1] **Tigers may be noble and discerning—but I'd rather have a pet cat snoozing on *my* sofa!**

[1]David Ward, "Humankind's favourite animal is a tiger" (*The Guardian*, Dec. 5, 2004, www.guardian.co.uk)

STEP TWO: Create a Conclusion reference page

Keep this information on hand as you write by adding it to the Reference section of your Composition Notebook.

At the top of a sheet of paper, center the word CONCLUSIONS. Beneath it, write the following information:

GENERAL: A paragraph of conclusion should contain at least two sentences. Single-sentence conclusions should be written as the last sentence of the final paragraph.

1. Conclusion by Summary
   Write a brief summary of the most important information in the passage, including specific details

2. Conclusion by Personal Reaction
   a. Personal statement
   b. Your opinion about the material
   c. Your own experience with the subject

3. Conclusion by Question
   Ask the reader to react to the information

STEP THREE: **Practice**

Finish today's work by writing three brief conclusions to your platypus and beaver comparison: one conclusion by summary, one conclusion by personal reaction, and one conclusion by question.

One of these conclusions (you can choose which one!) may be a one-sentence conclusion attached to your last paragraph. However, the other two *must* be separate paragraphs (so should have at least two sentences each).

If you have difficulty with any of these introductions, ask your instructor for help.

1. Conclusion by Summary

Come to a decision: Are they more alike or more different? Which details will make this clear to the reader? (This may sound very much like the introduction by summary you wrote in the last day's work—that's perfectly fine.)

2. Conclusion by Personal Reaction

Which would you rather have for a pet? Or, which animal is more interesting? Or, have you ever seen a beaver or platypus? If so, what did you think about it?

3. Conclusion by Question

Ask the reader a question. Which animal does the *reader* like better? Can you think of another question to ask?

Day Three: Introductions and Conclusions: Further Practice

 Focus: Practicing introductions and conclusions

STEP ONE: **Analyze**

Read the following essay, taken from *Mark Twain's Autobiography*. Mark Twain's real name was Samuel Clemens. He lived 1835–1910 and is best known as the author of *The Adventures of Tom Sawyer* and *The Adventures of Huckleberry Finn*.

This essay uses comparison and contrast to describe the Mississippi River.

"Two Ways of Seeing a River"

Now when I had mastered the language of this water and had come to know every trifling feature that bordered the great river as familiarly as I knew the letters of the alphabet, I had made a valuable acquisition. But I had lost something, too. I had lost something which could never be restored to me while I lived. All the grace, the beauty, the poetry had gone out of the majestic river!

I still keep in mind a certain wonderful sunset which I witnessed when steamboating was new to me. A broad expanse of the river was turned to blood; in the middle distance the red hue brightened into gold, through which a solitary log came floating, black and conspicuous; in one place a long, slanting mark lay sparkling upon the water; in another the surface was broken by boiling, tumbling rings, that were as many-tinted as an opal; where the ruddy flush was faintest, was a smooth spot that was covered with graceful circles and radiating lines, ever so delicately traced; the shore on our left was densely wooded, and the sombre shadow that fell from this forest was broken in one place by a long, ruffled trail that shone like silver; and high above the forest wall a clean-stemmed dead tree waved a single leafy bough that glowed like a flame in the unobstructed splendor that was flowing from the sun. There were graceful curves, reflected images, woody heights, soft distances; and over the whole scene, far and near, the dissolving lights drifted steadily, enriching it, every passing moment, with new marvels of coloring.

I stood like one bewitched. I drank it in, in a speechless rapture. The world was new to me, and I had never seen anything like this at home. But as I have said, a day came when I began to cease from noting the glories and the charms which the moon and the sun and the twilight wrought upon the river's face; another day came when I ceased altogether to note them. Then, if that sunset scene had been repeated, I should have looked upon it without rapture, and should have commented upon it, inwardly, in this fashion: "This sun means that we are going to have wind to-morrow; that floating log means that the river is rising, small thanks to it; that slanting mark on the water refers to a bluff reef which is going to kill somebody's steamboat one of these nights, if it keeps on stretching out like that; those tumbling 'boils' show a dissolving bar and a changing channel there; the lines and circles in the slick water over yonder are a warning that that troublesome place is shoaling up dangerously; that silver streak in the shadow of the forest is the 'break' from a new snag, and he has located himself in the very best place he could have found to fish for steamboats; that tall dead tree, with a single living branch, is not going to last long, and then how is a body ever going to get through this blind place at night without the friendly old landmark?"

No, the romance and the beauty were all gone from the river. All the value any feature of it had for me now was the amount of usefulness it could furnish toward compassing the safe piloting of a steamboat. Since those days, I have pitied doctors from my heart. What does the lovely flush in a beauty's cheek mean to a doctor but a "break" that ripples above some deadly disease? Are not all her visible charms sown thick with what are to him the signs and symbols of hidden decay? Does he ever see her beauty at all, or doesn't he simply view her professionally, and comment upon her unwholesome condition all to himself? And doesn't he sometimes wonder whether he has gained most or lost most by learning his trade?

When you have finished reading the essay, ask your instructor for directions.

STEP TWO: Review the Introduction and Conclusion charts in your Reference Notebook

In the last step of this lesson, you'll write an introduction and conclusion to a brief essay. Prepare for this assignment by going back to your Reference Notebook and reviewing the three types of introduction and the three types of conclusion.

STEP THREE: Write an introduction and conclusion

Read the following comparison/contrast essay carefully.

When you're finished, write an introduction and a conclusion. Choose the type you prefer from your charts. Both should be separate paragraphs, at least two sentences in length.

Introduction by summary and conclusion by summary are very similar. DO NOT CHOOSE TO WRITE BOTH! If you write an introduction by summary, pick another kind of conclusion (and vice versa).

Introduction by anecdote and conclusion by personal reaction are also similar. Don't write both!

If you have difficulty coming up with an introduction and conclusion, ask your instructor for ideas.

If you were to look at Venus and Earth side by side, they might appear to be twins. Earth's diameter (measured at the equator) is 12,756 kilometers (7,926 miles) compared to Venus's 12,100 kilometers (7,518 miles). The difference in their diameters is less than the width of Texas, which for a planet is barely noticeable. Earth and Venus have very similar masses as well, meaning that the surface gravity on each planet is nearly the same. If you stood on Venus, you would weigh about 90% of what you weigh on Earth, and you probably wouldn't notice much of a difference.

However, Venus is much hotter than Earth. The average surface temperature on Earth is 14 degrees Celsius (57 degrees Fahrenheit), or the temperature of a cool autumn day. But on Venus the average surface temperature is 462 degrees Celsius (864 degrees Fahrenheit), making it the hottest planet in our solar system. Even Mercury, which is closer to the sun than Venus, has an average temperature of only 167 degrees Celsius (332 degrees Fahrenheit).

How did Venus get so hot? The thick atmosphere of Venus is composed mostly of carbon dioxide. Once sunlight passes through the atmosphere, it is trapped by the atmosphere and continues to heat the planet. This is called the greenhouse effect. Just like the glass roof of a greenhouse, which allows sunlight to come in but not go out, the atmosphere of Venus traps the sun's heat. Earth doesn't suffer from this horrendous heat because the planet's atmosphere is less than 1% carbon dioxide, allowing it to "breathe" better than Venus.

Here is additional information that you might find useful:

Neil F. Comins and William J. Kaufmann, *Discovering the Universe* (New York: W. H. Freeman, 1996), pp. 206–207.

Unlike Mercury, Venus is intrinsically bright because it is completely surrounded by light-colored, highly reflective clouds. Because visible light telescopes cannot penetrate this thick, unbroken layer of clouds, we did not even know how fast Venus rotates until 1962. In the 1960s, however, both the United States and the Soviet Union began sending probes there. The Americans sent fragile, lightweight spacecraft into orbit near the planet. The Soviets, who had more powerful rockets, sent more durable spacecraft directly into the Venusian atmosphere.

. . . Finally, in 1970, the Soviet probe *Venera* (Russian for "Venus") *7* managed to transmit data for 23 minutes directly from the Venusian surface. Soviet missions continued until 1985, measuring a surface temperature of 750 [degrees] K[elvin] (900 F) and a surface air pressure of 90 atm, among other things. This value is the same pressure you would feel if you were swimming 0.82 km (2700 ft) underwater on Earth.

In contrast to Earth's present nitrogen- and oxygen-rich atmosphere, Venus's thick atmosphere is 96% carbon dioxide, with the remaining 4% mostly nitrogen . . . Soviet spacecraft also discovered that Venus's clouds are confined to a 20-km-thick layer located 48 to 68 km above the planet's surface.

Kenneth R. Lang and Charles A. Whitney, *Wanderers in Space: Exploration and Discovery in the Solar System* (Cambridge: Cambridge University Press, 1991), p. 72.

> Venus has boiled dry, like a kettle left too long on a stove. And there are no seasons such as we know on Earth. Her terrain is gloomy; 98 per cent of the sunlight is captured at higher levels in the dense, cloudy atmosphere. As a result of the atmosphere's peculiar filtering action, the rocky surface of Venus is bathed in the dim light of an orange sky.

Vicki Cameron, *Don't Tell Anyone, But—: UFO Experiences in Canada* (Burnstown, Ont., Canada: General Store Pub. House, 1995), p. 147

> Venus holds the prize for Most Frequently Seen as a UFO.
> Venus normally appears brighter than any other star, low in the western sky after sunset or just above the eastern horizon in the early morning. Like all planets, Venus seems to wander about the sky during the year, although it's really travelling a known path.
> About every two years, Venus appears extremely bright, in the evening and in the morning. It's so bright it remains visible after the sun rises. Various effects in the atmosphere make it ripple in rainbow colours, dance, or appear to head right for you on a collision course.

Day Four: Copia

 Focus: Introduction to Metaphor

STEP ONE: **Understanding metaphor**

Last week, you worked on similes. This week, you'll advance to metaphors.

Similes and metaphors are two related types of figurative language. Like a simile, a metaphor is a comparison between two things, but a metaphor does not use the words "like" or "as."

In *King Lear,* William Shakespeare wrote,

> Methought his eyes were two full moons.

This sentence contains a metaphor, because it directly compares eyes to full moons. If the sentence read, "Methought his eyes were <u>like</u> two full moons," it would be a simile, because it uses the word "like." The metaphor says, instead, that the eyes *were* moons.

You studied metaphors briefly in the first level of this course. Let's review: **A metaphor is a comparison that does not use "like" or "as." It simply describes one thing in terms of another.**

Of course, when you read this metaphor, you realize that eyes are not moons. Your brain inserts a "like" or "as" somewhere in there. But the metaphor itself is more powerful than a simile, because it is so much more direct.

Sometimes metaphors are found with linking verbs, as in this sentence. Other times metaphors can follow action verbs. Those metaphors are sometimes more difficult to identify.

Each of the following sentences describes rain by comparing it to another object. Practice identifying metaphors by circling each comparison that you see. (If you have trouble, ask your instructor.)

> The rain was a curtain of silver needles.
> (Shirley Rousseau Murphy, *Unsettled*)

> The patter of rain was a gentle lullaby to Amy.
> (Edward Payson Roe, *Nature's Serial Story*)

> The rain came down in white sheets, making a mighty roar.
> (Victor Villaseñor, *Rain of Gold*)

> The rain came down in long knitting needles.
> (Enid Bagnold, *National Velvet*)

> Where in the world was the rain? Those blinding cataracts she had
> endured day after day?
> (Ann Patchett, *State of Wonder*)

After circling the comparisons, underline each main verb twice. Write "l.v." above the linking verbs and "a.v." above the action verbs. Check your answers with your instructor before going on.

As you can see from the above sentences, metaphors don't always have to follow linking verbs.

Good metaphors give the reader a picture of the subject. Roe wanted to describe rain as soft and pleasant, so he compared it to a "gentle lullaby," whereas Bagnold wanted to describe rain as sharp and piercing so she compared it to "long knitting needles." Metaphors describe an unfamiliar subject by comparing it to a different familiar thing.

STEP TWO: Identifying metaphor

In the following sentences, underline the metaphor. Draw an arrow from the metaphor back to the subject—the word the metaphor describes by comparison. There may be more than one metaphor. If you're unsure, ask your instructor for help.

Hope is the thing with feathers/That perches in the soul.
(Emily Dickinson, "Hope")

His face is all . . . knobs, and flames of fire.
(Shakespeare, *King Henry V*)

His eyes were bars, and behind them was a fierce, unfed animal.
(Jeanette Winterson, *Lighthousekeeping*)

All the world's a stage, and all the men and women merely players.
(Shakespeare, *As You Like It*)

Death is a Dialogue between the Spirit and the Dust.
(Emily Dickinson, "Death is a Dialogue between")

CHALLENGE ASSIGNMENT (Optional)

Now you know the basics about metaphor. If you'd like to go further, complete the next assignment too.

Read the passage below from *Lighthousekeeping* by Jeanette Winterson. The author and Pew are caretakers for the lighthouse. A sou'wester is a waterproof hat with a floppy brim.

Above me was the kitchen where Pew cooked sausages on an open cast-iron stove. Above the kitchen was the light itself, a great glass eye with a Cyclops stare.

Our business was light, but we lived in darkness. The light had to be kept going, but there was no need to illuminate the rest. Darkness came with everything. It was standard. My clothes were trimmed with dark. When I put on a sou'wester, the brim left a dark shadow over my face. When I stood to bathe in the little galvanised cubicle Pew had rigged for me, I soaped my body in darkness. Put your hand in a drawer, and it was darkness you felt first, as you fumbled for a spoon. Go to the cupboards to find the tea caddy of Full Strength Samson, and the hole was as black as the tea itself.

The darkness had to be brushed away or parted before we could sit down. Darkness squatted on the chairs and hung like a curtain across the stairway. Sometimes it took on the shapes of the things we wanted: a pan, a bed, a book. Sometimes I saw my mother, dark and silent, falling towards me.

Darkness was a presence. I learned to see in it, I learned to see through it, and I learned to see the darkness of my own.

Pew did not speak. I didn't know if he was kind or unkind, or what he intended to do with me. He had lived alone all his life.

The first night, Pew cooked the sausages in darkness. No, Pew cooked the sausages *with* darkness. It was the kind of dark you can taste. That's what we ate: sausages and darkness.[27]

There are many descriptions of the darkness in this passage. Some use figurative language, and some do not. For example, look in the last paragraph. *The first night, Pew cooked the sausages in darkness. No, Pew cooked the sausages* with *darkness.* One of these sentences is a metaphor, and one is not. Can you tell which one is the metaphor?

The second sentence is a metaphor, because it compares darkness to a food that you could eat with sausages. The first sentence is not a metaphor, because it simply tells you that it was dark when Pew was cooking the sausages.

Read through the passage again, and underline each metaphor and simile. If it is a simile, circle the word *like* or *as*. If an entire sentence is a metaphor, you can underline the whole sentence.

STEP THREE: **Invent new metaphors**

Now it's your turn to write metaphors.

Look back at the metaphors you identified in Step One.

On your own paper, rewrite these two metaphors about rain.

The rain came down in [something sharp and stabbing].

The patter of rain was [something quiet and soothing].

Now, read (or reread) the following lines from the optional exercise. In this, the author describes the darkness as something you can feel, something that is a part of everyday life, such as soap or clothing.

It was the kind of dark you can taste.

Darkness squatted on the chairs and hung like a curtain across the stairway.

---

27. Jeanette Winterson, *Lighthousekeeping* (Boston: Houghton Mifflin Harcourt, 2006), pp. 19–21.

Our business was light, but we lived in darkness. The light had to be kept going, but there was no need to illuminate the rest. Darkness came with everything. It was standard. My clothes were trimmed with dark. When I put on a sou'wester, the brim left a dark shadow over my face. When I stood to bathe in the little galvanised cubicle Pew had rigged for me, I soaped my body in darkness. Put your hand in a drawer, and it was darkness you felt first, as you fumbled for a spoon. Go to the cupboards to find the tea caddy of Full Strength Samson, and the hole was as black as the tea itself.

On your own paper, rewrite the following metaphors for darkness.

It was the kind of dark you can [sense or experience].

Darkness [did something a house pet might do].

I [did some everyday task] with darkness.

Darkness was [something alive].

When you are finished, show your metaphors to your instructor.

WEEK 7: EXPLANATION BY COMPARISON, PART II

Day One: Three-Level Outline

 Focus: Constructing a three-level outline of a comparison in history

STEP ONE: **Read**

Read the following excerpt from *Collapse: How Societies Choose to Fail or Succeed*, by Jared Diamond. Here, he is comparing the nations of Haiti and the Dominican Republic, both of which occupy the island of Hispaniola in the Caribbean.

— — —

Why did the political, economic and ecological histories of these two countries—the Dominican Republic and Haiti—sharing the same island unfold so differently?

Part of the answer involves environmental differences. The island of Hispaniola's rains come mainly from the east. Hence the Dominican (eastern) part of the island receives more rain and thus supports higher rates of plant growth. Hispaniola's highest mountains (over 10,000 feet high) are on the Dominican side, and the rivers from those high mountains mainly flow eastwards into the Dominican side. The Dominican side has broad valleys, plains and plateaus and much thicker soils . . .

In contrast, the Haitian side is drier because of that barrier of high mountains blocking rains from the east. Compared to the Dominican Republic, the area of flat land good for intensive agriculture in Haiti is much smaller, as a higher percentage of Haiti's area is mountainous. There is more limestone terrain, and the soils are thinner and less fertile and have a lower capacity for recovery . . .

. . . Haiti was a colony of rich France and became the most valuable colony in France's overseas empire. The Dominican Republic was a colony of Spain, which by the late 1500s was neglecting Hispaniola and was in economic and political decline itself. Hence, France was able to invest in developing intensive slave-based plantation agriculture in Haiti, which the Spanish could not or chose not to develop in their side of the island. France imported far more slaves into its colony than did Spain.

As a result, Haiti had a population seven times higher than its neighbor during colonial times—and it still has a somewhat larger population today, about ten million versus 8.8 million. But Haiti's area is only slightly more than half of that of the Dominican Republic. So Haiti, with a larger population and smaller area, has double the Republic's population density . . .

. . . [A]s a legacy of their country's slave history and slave revolt, most Haitians owned their own land, used it to feed themselves and received no help from their government in developing cash crops for trade with overseas European countries. The Dominican Republic, however, eventually did develop an export economy and overseas trade.[28]

— — —

STEP TWO: **Find four areas of comparison**

Jared Diamond starts his comparison of Haiti and the Dominican Republic with an introductory question. As you can see, *introduction by question* is another method of beginning an essay. Unlike *conclusion by question,* which asks the reader to react, this kind of introduction asks a question that you will then answer in the essay.

After this introduction, Diamond compares and contrasts the two countries in *four different ways.* On your own paper, list the four areas of comparison.

Here's a hint: The first comparison is found in paragraphs 2 and 3 combined. The second comparison is in the fourth paragraph, the third comparison in the fifth, and the fourth comparison is contained in the last paragraph.

If you have difficulty, ask your instructor for help. When you are finished, show your work to your instructor.

STEP THREE: **Complete a three-level outline**

In this essay, Jared Diamond does a point-by-point comparison of Haiti and the Dominican Republic. Here's the overall structure:

---

28. Jared Diamond, *Collapse: How Societies Choose to Fail or Succeed* (Penguin, 2005), pp. 339–340.

I.   Introduction
II.   Environment
       A. Dominican
       B. Haitian
III.   Colonial history
       A. Haiti
       B. Dominican Republic
IV.   Population
       A. Haiti
V.   Trade
       A. Haitians
       B. Dominicans

Notice that Diamond avoids monotony by changing the order in which he gives the comparisons: first the Dominican environment and then the Haitian; the reverse order when he discussions colonial history. When he talks about population, he only addresses Haitian population directly, just referring to the Dominican Republic in passing.

The actual comparisons are found in the details of the paragraphs, which belong in the third level of an outline.

Study the following outline carefully. Compare the details listed in the second main point (II. Environment) to the second and third paragraphs. Then, try to complete the outline by filling in the details for main points III, IV, and V. (It's OK to have one more or less details than the numbers suggest you should have!)

When you are finished, show your work to your instructor. Ask for help if you need it.

I.   Introduction
II.   Environment
       A. Dominican
           1. More rain
           2. Higher rates of plant growth
           3. Higher mountains
           4. Rivers flow eastward
           5. Broad valleys, plains, plateaus
           6. Much thicker soil
       B. Haitian
           1. Drier
           2. Barrier of high mountains
           3. Less flat land
           4. More limestone
           5. Thinner, less fertile soil

III.   Colonial history
    A. Haiti
        1.
        2.
        3.
        4.
    B. Dominican Republic
        1.
        2.
        3.
        4.
IV.   Population
    A. Haiti
        1.
        2.
        3.
        4.
V.   Trade
    A. Haitians
        1.
        2.
        3.
    B. Dominicans
        1.

Day Two: Note-Taking

Focus: Taking notes for a comparison
of two people

As you can see from yesterday's excerpt, comparisons and contrasts can be used for many different subjects—in history as well as in science. You can compare and contrast countries (as Jared Diamond did in *Collapse*), people, rivers, castles, fortresses, villages, or mountains. You can compare and contrast events in history—battles, discoveries, or crises of various kinds. You can even write a comparison/contrast between something in its present form, and how it was at an earlier point in time ("In the sixteenth century, Cairo had 150,000 people living in it and covered only two square miles. Today, Cairo has 1.3 million residents and occupies over 62 square miles").

Now that you've practiced writing a comparison in science and seen an example of a history comparison, you'll work on a historical comparison of your own.

STEP ONE: **Add to the Introduction chart**

Before you start work on your comparison, make an addition to your Introduction chart. On it, write:

> 4. Introduction by Question
>   Ask a question that you will answer in your essay.
>   *Example:* "Since X and Y are so similar in _____, why are they so
>   different in _____?"

Jared Diamond used this method to introduce his comparison of Haiti and the Dominican Republic.

STEP TWO: **Take notes**

You'll spend the rest of today taking notes for a comparison of two historical figures—the brothers Wilbur and Orville Wright.

Take your notes in a way that will help you organize your composition when you return to it tomorrow. Divide a sheet of paper into two columns. Write "Similarities" and "Differences" over the columns.

If a piece of information applies to both brothers, put it in the "Similarities" column. If it only applies to one, list the brother's name and then put the information after it.

Use the last name(s) of the author and the page numbers to identify your source. You can refer back to the full publication information in this book when you construct your footnotes and Works Cited page.

The first notes have been done for you. Read the following excerpt carefully *before* you examine the chart that follows. (In the excerpts, the numbers in parentheses are page numbers.)

Tara Dixon-Engel & Mike Jackson, *The Wright Brothers: First in Flight* (New York: Sterling Publishing, 2007), pp. 2–7.

> (2) They weren't always two serious-looking men in starched collars
> and dark hats. In fact, as boys, Orville and Wilbur Wright were typical
> brothers, teasing each other, disagreeing on any and all topics, and dream-
> ing of new experiences and distant horizons. They both enjoyed tinker-
> ing with mechanical devices and it was this early interest in "how things
> worked" that would lead them into the bicycle business and, later, fuel their
> dream of flight . . .
>
> (6) As Wilbur and Orville aged, their personalities began to gel. In fact,
> they complemented each other in strengths and weaknesses. Orville was
> an outgoing student, and somewhat of a mischief-maker, while Wilbur had

inherited his mother's shyness. Will's tendency toward daydreaming did not win him any points in school, but it was the sign of a sharp mind that was always in motion, always exploring questions and seeking answers. Wilbur found a home as an athlete and gymnast, while Orville was a (7) budding businessman from the age of six onward. In addition to collecting scrap metal to sell to a junkyard, the young man built and sold kites to his neighborhood friends. Neither brother especially enjoyed schoolwork or, perhaps, being tied to a disciplined classroom setting. Both were curious and loved to learn, but they preferred to choose the subject themselves.

Now, compare the following notes to the excerpt:

Similarities	Differences
"typical brothers, teasing each other, disagreeing . . . dreaming of new experiences and distant horizons." (Dixon-Engel & Jackson, p. 2) "both enjoyed tinkering with mechanical devices" (D-E & J, p. 2) "Neither brother especially enjoyed schoolwork" but "Both were curious and loved to learn" (D-E & J, p. 7)	Orville: outgoing, mischief-maker (D-E & J, p. 6) Wilbur: shy, daydreaming, "sharp mind that was always in motion" (D-E & J, p. 6) Wilbur: "athlete and gymnast" (D-E & J, p. 6) Orville: "budding businessman from the age of six," collected scrap metal and sold kites (D-E & J, p. 7)

(Notice that I abbreviated the authors' names after the first note—as long as you can identify where the material came from, you don't need to write the same names over and over again.)

Now take your own notes on the first excerpt (or copy mine, if you want!). Continue on by taking notes on the following excerpts. When you are finished, show your work to your instructor.

Orville Wright & Fred C. Kelly, *How We Invented the Airplane: An Illustrated History* (New York, David McKay, 1953), p. 3. (The following is from the introduction by Fred C. Kelly.)

Wilbur Wright was four years older than Orville . . . Neither Wilbur nor Orville ever attended college; and, for unusual reasons, neither was formally graduated from high school, though each attended high school the full time required for a diploma. Wilbur had about finished school in Richmond at the time of [his family's] move to Dayton; and to be graduated he would have had to return to Richmond to be present with his class on commencement day. But he did not consider the mere diploma important enough to justify the bother of the trip. He took an extra year in high school at Dayton, studying Greek and trigonometry. When Orville came to his final year in high school, he thought he might wish to go to college and took special studies that included Latin. Though he learned more than if he had followed the prescribed course, he, too, had to do without a diploma.

Their first interest in bicycles was racing; but as their interest grew, they arranged in December, 1892, to start the Wright Cycle Co., to sell, repair, and manufacture bicycles. They opened for business in the spring of 1893.

When they were youngsters, Wilbur naturally treated Orville as a "kid brother," and Orville thought he sometimes did so after they were grown; but there was great devotion and understanding between them. From the time they got into the bicycle business, they always had a joint bank account, and neither paid the slightest attention to what the other drew out for his own use.

Stephanie Sammartino McPherson & Joseph Sammartino Gardner, *Wilbur & Orville Wright: Taking Flight* (Minneapolis: Lerner Publishing Group, 2004), pp. 26–28.

(26) By this time, their older brothers and many of their friends had married. Orville developed a close friendship with a young woman named Agnes Osborn, a friend of Katharine's. Dressed in his best suit, Orville played chess with Agnes, took her on boat rides, and played pranks on her. As much as he enjoyed her company, however, the relationship didn't become a lasting romance. Both Wilbur and Orville were happy as bachelors. They relished their roles as uncles and . . . (27) felt very close to all their nieces and nephews.

If the brothers felt any discontent at all, it came from their longing for broader opportunities. "Intellectual effort is a pleasure to me," Wilbur told his father, "and I think I would be better fitted for reasonable success in some of the professions than in business." Wilbur wanted to grapple with issues and ideas. The bicycle shop provided an income, but it did not satisfy Wilbur's growing impatience for more creative challenges.

In 1896, the year the Wrights began making their bicycles, a horseless carriage appeared on the streets of Dayton. (28) Wilbur and Orville spent hours discussing the newfangled vehicle with its owner, their friend Cordy Ruse. Certainly the mechanical car had many problems. Sometimes it even lost parts on the road! Still, Orville feared the new means of transportation would eventually take business away from the bicycle. Maybe they should consider building horseless carriages, he told his brother.

But that wasn't the challenge Wilbur sought. Like many others, he laughed at horseless carriages. "To try to build one that would be any account, you'd be tackling the impossible," he declared. "Why, it would be easier to build a flying-machine."

Tom D. Crouch, *The Bishop's Boys: A Life of Wilbur and Orville Wright* (New York: W.W. Norton, 1989), pp. 49–50.

(49) In later years Wilbur and Orville would point to a very strong relationship stretching far back into their childhood. In the will prepared in May 1912 shortly before his death, Wilbur stressed that the two had been "associated . . . in all hopes and labors, both of childhood and manhood." And on another occasion he wrote: "From the time we were little children, my brother Orville and myself lived together, played together, worked together, and, in fact, thought together. We usually owned all of our toys in common, talked over our thoughts and aspirations so that nearly everything that was done in our lives has (50) been the result of conversations, suggestions, and discussions between us."

Those words have been cited time and again to illustrate the lifelong bond between the two brothers. In fact, Wilbur was overstating their relationships as children in order to underscore the importance of the full partnership that they enjoyed as adults. As boys they were close, and as far apart, as any brothers separated by a four-year difference in age. They would scarcely begin to bridge that gulf in a serious way until 1889, the year in which Orville left high school and Wilbur emerged from a period of extended illness and depression . . .

When the brothers were away from home in later years, Wilbur tended to write to his father. Orville, far more often, directed his letters to [their sister] Katharine. They are charming letters, flecked with warmth and humor. Within the family circle, Orville was generally regarded as being much less articulate than his brothers, yet his letters to Katharine are among the clearest and most human documents among the thousands of pieces of Wright family correspondence.

Stephen Kirk, *First in Flight: The Wright Brothers in North Carolina* (Chicago: R.R. Donnelley & Sons, 2003), pp. 18–19.

(18) The Wrights often squabbled during their early business dealings, with one or the other brother feeling he was saddled with an unfair share of the work . . . It was mainly to avoid ill feelings resulting from their work with gliders that they resolved to blur the distinctions between them and present all their ideas as joint conceptions. This attitude grew on them

to the point that they even signed their checks "Wright Brothers," with a simple "W.W." or "O.W." the only indication of the signer.

Differences between the two are not difficult to find.

(19) Wilbur was older, balder, and a more avid correspondent. He was the more visionary of the two. . . . But Wilbur was also prone to depression. One of the defining incidents of his life came in his late teens, when he was inadvertently clubbed in the face while playing a hockey-type game with neighborhood boys. His injuries drove him into a three-year-long withdrawal from friends and family. Aside from the risks he later took in his flight experiments, he seems to have considered himself a kind of invalid-in-waiting from that point. Worn down by lawsuits and stricken with typhoid at age forty-five, he died rather easily.

Orville was probably closer to his younger sister, Katharine, than he was to Wilbur. He was more shy than Wilbur, but also more of a prankster. A dapper dresser, he wore a mustache and had a touch of vanity. Disliking the suntanned look he acquired on the Outer Banks, he would adjourn to the bathroom with a lemon every morning upon getting back to Dayton and set to rubbing his face with its juice, with the result that his skin returned to its normal paleness weeks before Wilbur's.

Day Three: Practicing the *Topos*, Part I

> Focus: Organizing a comparison/contrast of two historical figures

STEP ONE: **Organize the similarities and differences**

Today, you'll use the notes you took on Wilbur and Orville Wright, inventors of the first working airplane, to write a comparison and contrast between the two men.

Look back at the reference notes in your Composition Notebook. Reread the description of "Explanation by Comparison/Contrast." The first step is to decide which aspects of the subjects are the same, and which are different. You've already begun to organize your notes in similarities and differences. Now, you need to group those similarities and differences into larger categories (those are the "aspects"). For example, the excerpts talk about Wilbur and Orville being bachelors, enjoying being uncles, and writing to their father and to their sister Katharine. You probably noted that Orville was closer to his sister, Wilbur to his father. All of those have to do with *family relationships*.

Go through the rest of your similarities and differences and try to organize them into three or four additional categories.

If you have trouble, ask your instructor for help.

When you're finished, show the categories to your instructor. Don't go on to the next step until then!

STEP TWO: **Plan the composition**

Now that you've taken notes and organized them into larger categories, you've essentially already come up with an outline for your composition. For each category, discuss first the similarities between the two brothers, and then the differences. Here's an example of how you might organize the aspect/category "family relationships":

II. Family relationships
    A. Similarities between the two brothers
       "typical brothers, teasing each other, disagreeing" (Dixon-Engel &
          Jackson, p. 2)
       Remained bachelors (McPherson & Gardner, p. 26)
       Enjoyed being uncles (M & G, p. 26)
    B. Differences between them
       1. Orville
          Orville wrote to his sister Katharine (Crouch, p. 50)
          Orville closer to Katharine (Kirk, p. 19)
       2. Wilbur
          Wilbur wrote letters to his father (Crouch, p. 50)

Now choose four categories that you'll write about in your composition. Give each category a Roman numeral. Organize the appropriate notes under each category, following the pattern above. (You can use my outline above if you choose to write about family relationships!)

If one category contains *only* similarities or *only* differences, that's fine.

STEP THREE: **Write the body of the composition**

Using your outline as a guide, write one or two paragraphs to describe each aspect. Depending on how much information you have, you can either write a paragraph about similarities and then a second about differences, or write a paragraph combining the two.

The facts about Orville and Wilbur Wright are found in many biographies. If you use your own words, you don't need to footnote. But be sure to use quotation marks and to insert a footnote if you use the exact words from *any* of the sources!

The paragraph does not need to say specifically, "They were the same in . . ." or "They were different because . . ." Instead, you can simply write about the similarities and then the differences. For example a paragraph based on the outline above might sound like this:

> As children, Wilbur and Orville Wright teased each other and argued with each other. Neither man ever got married, and both of them enjoyed being uncles. But Orville was closest to his sister Katharine and wrote her many letters. Wilbur was closer to his father than to his sister.

(If you need to use this paragraph to get you started, go ahead. But try to change at least a few of the words to make it more your own.)

Instead of working towards a minimum number of words, try to produce a minimum of six paragraphs.

When you're finished, show your work to your instructor.

Day Four: Practicing the *Topos*, Part II

 Focus: Completing a comparison/contrast of two historical figures

Today, you'll finish off your comparison and contrast of Wilbur and Orville Wright by writing an introduction and a conclusion to your essay.

STEP ONE: **Write an introduction**

Look back at the Introductions page in the Reference section of your Composition Notebook. Decide which kind of introduction you will use.

You may write a one-sentence introduction rather than writing a separate paragraph—but if you do, remember that your conclusion (see Step Two) *must* be a separate paragraph of two sentences or more.

You may need to look back over the sources listed on Day Two. Some of the information there will be helpful if you decide to write an introduction by history or an introduction by anecdote—and might not have made it onto your chart of similarities and differences.

If you need help, ask your instructor.

STEP TWO: **Write a conclusion**

Look back at the Conclusions page in the Reference section of your Composition Notebook. Decide which kind of conclusion you will write. If you wrote a one-sentence introduction, your conclusion should be a separate paragraph.

Look back at the sources if necessary.
If you need help, ask your instructor.

STEP THREE: **Assemble the Works Cited page**

If your composition contains any footnotes, put the sources used on a Works Cited page, using the correct format.

STEP THREE: **Proofread**

Add the introduction, conclusion, and Works Cited page to the body of your essay.
Repeat the basic steps of proofreading:

1) Read your composition out loud. Listen for awkward or unclear sections. Rewrite them so that they flow more naturally.
2) Check spelling by looking, individually, at each word that might be a problem.
3) Check your commas.

Today, add one additional step:

4) As you read, listen for repeated nouns, verbs, and modifiers. If you find yourself using the same noun or verb more than twice, use your thesaurus to find an alternative. If you use a modifier (adverb, adjective, or prepositional phrase acting as an adjective or adverb) more than once, find another word. (Phrases like "In the same way" or "In contrast" tend to be overused in comparisons!)

When you're finished, show your work to your instructor.

I. Intro

II.

III.

IV.

V.

education
Personality
bicycles
goals

Pick 3 out
of 4

Conc

WEEK 8: FINDING A TOPIC

This week, you will research your own project on a topic that you choose yourself.

Let's do a quick review: The first level of this course ended with an independent project. You were given a list of the seven *topoi* you studied last year, and were assigned the job of combining at least two of them into a composition.

Over the next two weeks, you will complete a similar (but shorter) assignment with a slightly different focus. Next week, you'll work on note-taking and writing. But this week, you'll focus in on one particular skill: *how to choose a topic.*

This week, work independently as much as possible (but ask for help if you need it). Show your work to your instructor at the end of each day.

Day One: Brainstorming in History

 Focus: Finding a topic in history

Instead of beginning with particular *topoi*, you'll start by brainstorming topics that might interest you in history and in science.

You'll need five blank sheets of paper for today's work.

STEP ONE: Use the four Ws to find broad subjects

Turn your first piece of paper sideways. Along the top, write the words WHEN, WHERE, WHAT, and WHO, like this:

WHEN	WHERE	WHAT	WHO

Now you're ready to begin brainstorming.

Under the heading WHEN, write at least three words or phrases describing a period in time: a century, a decade, a year, or a period (like "The Roaring Twenties").

Under the heading WHERE, write at least three geographical designations: countries, cities, rivers, mountains, etc. (such as "Mount Everest").

Under the heading WHAT, write down at least four events or things from history: inventions, discoveries, explorations, wars, languages, customs, etc. ("The Civil War" or "smallpox")

Under the heading WHO, write down at least three names of famous people from history—anyone from Julius Caesar to Margaret Thatcher.

If necessary, flip through the index of a history encyclopedia or atlas for ideas.

STEP TWO: **Use the other 3 Ws to narrow a subject**

Look back over your paper. Circle one name or phrase in each column that seems potentially the most interesting to you.

What did you circle in the "When" column? Write it in the center of your second blank sheet of paper. Now ask yourself: Where? What? Who? And try to come up with at least two answers for each question. Three or four answers are much better.

Here's an example.

Imagine that you chose "The Roaring Twenties." Now ask yourself: Where did the Roaring Twenties happen?

You probably won't know the answer to that. So to help yourself brainstorm, use the Internet. Enter the terms "Roaring Twenties" and "where" into a search engine such as Google, Bing, or Yahoo.

When I do this, the first link that comes up is the "Roaring Twenties" entry on Wikipedia. You might remember this paragraph from the first level of *Writing With Skill*:

> You may *not* use Wikipedia. Wikipedia is not professionally edited or fact-checked. Anyone can post anything on Wikipedia. Usually, other users will identify and remove mistakes—but if you happen to use Wikipedia five minutes after someone has posted bad information (which people sometimes do just for fun), you won't realize that you're writing down false facts.[29]

That's still true! But you're not doing research right now—you're just trying to come up with as many connected ideas and bits of information as possible. If there's a mistake in the information, you'll discover it as soon as you start taking notes. So go ahead and use Wikipedia if your search engine turns it up.

---

29. Susan Wise Bauer, *Writing With Skill, Level One Student Workbook* (Peace Hill Press, 2012), p. 478.

When I click on the Wikipedia link, I discover that the Roaring Twenties was centered at large cities: Chicago, New Orleans, Los Angeles, New York, Philadelphia, Paris, and London. That certainly gives me plenty of answers to the question "where."

Write your newly-discovered words or phrases around the word at the center of your brainstorming paper, like this:

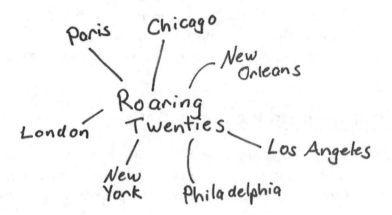

Now do the same for "what" and "who." Remember to put quotes around words or phrases that belong together. Your answers to "what" will probably be phrases or even short sentences; when I search for "Roaring Twenties" and "what," I come up with "decade following World War I", "time of unprecedented prosperity," "jazz," and "speakeasies." For "who," I find "flappers," "Sinclair Lewis," "Edith Wharton," and "suffragettes." (Notice that "who" can be answered with either proper names or categories of people.)

If possible, use a different color of pencil or pen for the "what" answers, and a third color for the "who" answers.

Here's how my brainstorming map looks now. You can't see the colors, but I used a regular pencil for "where," a purple pencil for "what," and a green pencil for "who."

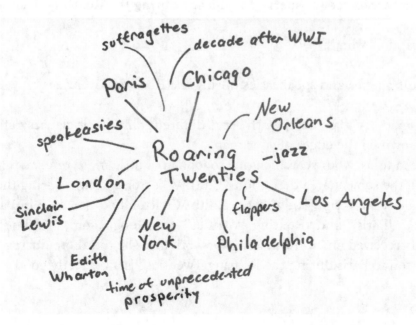

You should now have a completed brainstorming map for your chosen entry in the "When" column.

STEP THREE: **Complete the brainstorming maps**

Now finish your remaining three maps. For your chosen entry in the "where" column, ask, "When? What? Who?" For the "what" entry, ask "When? Where? Who?" And you can figure out on your own what to ask for the "who" entry!

Remember to use different colored pens or pencils for the answers to each of the "W" questions.

STEP FOUR: **Finish defining the subject area**

Now you'll take the final step in defining your subject.

Choose your favorite brainstorming map. Pick one answer each from *two* of the categories (this will be easier if you've used different colors) and put them together with your central subject.

For example: I asked "Who? What? Where" about the Roaring Twenties. So I need to pick a "who" answer and a "where" answer and put them together with "Roaring Twenties":

> Suffragettes in Paris during the Roaring Twenties

or

> Flappers in Philadelphia during the Roaring Twenties

I could also pick one of the "what" answers to go with a "where" answer:

> Jazz in New Orleans during the Roaring Twenties
> Unprecedented prosperity in Chicago during the Roaring Twenties

or a "who" and a "what":

> Suffragettes and speakeasies during the Roaring Twenties

Using your own map, try to come up with three different phrases or clauses defining subject areas. Jot them down on the edges of your map.

You may need to use your search engine to look up a little more information. For example, if I came up with the subject area definition "Edith Wharton in Paris during the Roaring Twenties," I would want to find out whether Edith Wharton had ever *been* in Paris. If I enter "Edith Wharton," "Paris," and "Roaring Twenties" into Google.com, I find out that Edith Wharton actually received an award in Paris for work that she did there during World War I. So "Edith Wharton in Paris during the Roaring Twenties" is a perfectly good subject. (I don't know what her work was or what the award was called, but that's OK; I'm not doing research yet.)

When you are finished, show your work to your instructor.

Day Two: Brainstorming in Science

 Focus: Finding a topic in science

You'll need five more sheets of paper for today's work.

STEP ONE: Use the four Ws to find broad subjects

Turn your first piece of paper sideways. Along the top, write the words WHAT, WHERE, WHO, and WHY. "When" is a good question for history, but since science is about *explanation,* "why" is a more useful question for you to ask.

Under the heading WHAT, write down at least six names or phrases describing scientific phenomena, natural objects, or occurrences. As you do so, think about the major fields of scientific research: biology, chemistry, physics, astronomy, geology. If you have trouble, browse through the index of a science encyclopedia or glance through the table of contents of a science survey textbook. Examples might include: frogs, the atom, the speed of light, supernovas, and continental drift.

Under the heading WHERE, write at least three physical places, such as outer space, the ocean (deep or shallow?), the Sahara desert, or just "deserts." (You can use one of mine, but you have to come up with the other two on your own.)

Under the heading WHO, write down at least four names of famous scientists.

Under the heading WHY, write down the names of at least two scientific theories. (Here's an example: Johannes Kepler's "Laws of Planetary Motion.") If you can't think of any scientific theories, enter "scientific theory" and "example" into your Internet search engine and skim through the results.

STEP TWO: Use the other 3 Ws to narrow a subject

Look back over your paper. As you did yesterday, circle one name or phrase in each column that seems potentially the most interesting to you.

What did you circle in the "What" column? Write it in the center of your second blank sheet of paper. Now ask yourself: Where? Who? Why? Try to come up with at least two answers for each question; three or four answers are much better. Use different colored pens or pencils to write the answers in a brainstorming map around your central term.

Here's how I would do this.

In my "What" column, I circled "space dust." (I've always thought "space dust" was a fascinating phrase.) I entered "space dust" and "where" into my Internet search engine, and after that entered "space dust" and "who" and "space dust" and "why." Here's what my completed map looks like. The single-underlined words are in answer to "where" (places space dust is found), the double-underlined words are in answer to "who" (scientists who have made discoveries about space dust), and the plain words are in answer to "why" (observations and theories about space dust).

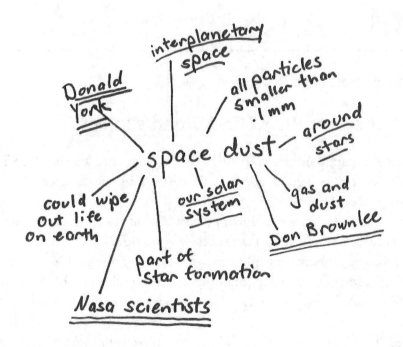

STEP THREE: **Complete the brainstorming maps**

Now create brainstorming maps for your favorite entries under the Where, Who, and Why headings. When you're finished, you should have four finished maps.

STEP FOUR: **Finish defining the subject area**

Choose your favorite brainstorming map. Using the same method as yesterday, come up with three different phrases, sentence fragments, or sentences, defining subject areas that you might do further research in. Jot them on the edge of your map.

Using the map above, I chose the "why" answer "could wipe out life on earth" and the "where" answer "interplanetary space" to come up with:

Space dust is in interplanetary space and could wipe out life on earth.

Using a "who" and "where" answer, I googled "Donald York," "space dust," and "around stars" to make sure that Donald York's experiments had something to do with dust around stars. They do, so I came up with

> Donald York and space dust around stars

Other subject area definitions might be:

> NASA scientists and space dust in our solar system
> Space dust, star formation, and our solar system

When you are finished, show your work to your instructor.

Days Three and Four: Pre-Reading

Focus: Initial research

You'll spend the next couple of days doing general reading about one of your subject areas.

Each step has a suggested amount of time for you to spend on it. This is only a very general guideline; you and your instructor may decide together to change it.

You should have two completed brainstorming maps with tentative subject areas written on them, one in history and one in science. Choose one.

You haven't yet picked a *topos*, so you don't know whether you'll be writing a chronological narration, a biographical sketch, a comparison and contrast, or some other form. You'll make this decision *after* you finish your general reading. The reading will give you an idea of what sorts of information are available about your subject; that will help you choose the appropriate *topoi*.

STEP ONE: **Prepare for the library visit**   **30–60 minutes**

Your goal is to end up with five sources that tell you something helpful about your general subject area.

With your instructor, plan a library visit. Before the visit, prepare by making an initial list of titles to look for by using your local library's online catalog. (Most local libraries have online catalogs now, but if yours doesn't, you'll have to perform this step at the library.)

Visit the library's website and look for the link "Catalog" or "Library Catalog." Once you're on the catalog page, you should see a dropdown menu that gives you an option of searching title keywords, subject area keywords, author names, etc. Generally, start off by searching for "title keyword." If that doesn't bring you any results, search for "subject key-word" instead.

Start by typing in the word or phrase at the center of your brainstorming map. For me, that would be "Roaring Twenties" (from the map I did for Day One). When I search by "title keyword," I instantly see at least six nonfiction books, shelved in the young adult section, about different aspects of the Roaring Twenties. That's a good sign—it means there are plenty of resources available.

Make a quick list of the titles and call numbers that you might want to investigate. Then, choose one of the subject area definitions that you jotted down on your map. Do a similar search for the keywords in the definition.

For example, I jotted down "Suffragettes and speakeasies during the Roaring Twenties." A title keyword search for "Suffragettes" only brings up one book, *33 Things Every Girl Should Know About Women's History: From Suffragettes to Skirt Lengths to the ERA*. But the catalog page for that book also contains a link to the subject area "Women's rights—History—Juvenile literature." When I click on the link, I find nine more books. So I've learned that books about suffragettes are more likely to be under the heading "Women's rights—History."

When I search for "speakeasies," the same thing happens. I only find one title. But there is a link on the page to the subject heading "Prohibition—United States—History," which leads me to more books.

Searching for these titles before going to the library will save you frustration. If you're unable to find more than one or two books, you should choose another subject area definition and try using its keywords for your search. And if *none* of your subject area definitions are giving you good keywords for searching, you might consider choosing another brainstorming map.

STEP TWO: **Collect resources**   **1–3 hours**

Now it's time for your library visit. Be sure to take your brainstorming map with you!

You should already have a preliminary list of titles to locate. Ask the reference librarian for help finding the books, if necessary. Glance on either side of the titles to see whether nearby books might also have something interesting to say about your subject area.

Pull at least 10–12 books off the shelf and take them to a place where you can examine them more closely. Using the index, make sure that at least one of the keywords in your subject area appears in the book!

For example, if I am researching "Suffragettes and speakeasies during the Roaring Twenties" and I pull a book called *The Roaring Twenties* off the shelf, I want to make sure that the word "suffrage" or the word "speakeasies" appears in the index. If I can't find anything about speakeasies *or* suffrage in any of the books about the Roaring Twenties, I might need to pick another subject area from my brainstorming map.

Try to bring home at least six books that relate to your subject. (You'll only need five sources, but one will probably turn out to be unhelpful.)

STEP THREE: **Do initial reading**   **At least 3 hours**

Your last task this week is simply to read.

Read the chapters or sections of each book that relate to your topic. Don't take notes yet—you don't know what information you'll need. But be sure to use bookmarks (torn slips of notebook paper are fine) or Post-It Notes to mark pages where you find interesting information.

You'll return to these pages next week as you settle on a final form for your composition.

WEEK 9: COMPLETING THE COMPOSITION

Last week, you worked on the new skill of finding, defining, and reading about a subject area for your composition. This week, you'll decide which *topoi* best fit your subject, take notes, and complete your composition.

You should work as independently as possible this week, but be sure to ask for help whenever you feel the need.

At the end of each day, show your instructor your completed work. However, your instructor should not evaluate your composition until you have finished the final proofreading step in Day Four.

Day One: Choosing the Right *Topos*

Focus: Matching form to content

STEP ONE: **Review the *topoi***

Before you can begin taking notes, you'll need to make a tentative decision about the form of your composition. Your composition will need to be at least 500 words in length (that includes your introduction and conclusion, but not your Works Cited page). It can be just one *topos,* or it can combine two or three.

Last year, you learned the following forms:

> *Chronological narrative of a past event*
> *Chronological narrative of a scientific discovery*
> *Description of a place*
> *Scientific description*
> *Description of a person*
> *Biographical sketch*
> *Sequence: Natural process*

So far this year, you've added:

Sequence: History
Explanation by comparison/contrast

Turn to the Reference section of your Composition Notebook and review the details of each form by reading *carefully*. Then, think back through your preliminary reading. Which *topoi* seem to fit the information best?

Here are some questions to ask yourself:

Does the reading tell you about a series of events? If so, you may want to write a chronological narrative.

Does the reading contain lots of visual details? If so, you may want to write a description—of a place, person, or scientific phenomenon.

Does the reading give you information about the character and life of a particular person? If so, you may want to write a biographical sketch—either alone, or combined with a chronological narrative of some important part of the person's life.

Does the reading explain a series of events that happened, or happens, more than once? If so, you may need to write a sequence.

Does the reading draw comparisons? If so, you may be looking at a comparison/contrast. But remember that comparison/contrast is a very flexible form. By doing a little additional research, you can turn almost any set of details into a comparison and contrast. You can compare a chronological narrative (say, the events leading up to and during the Battle of Hastings) to another chronological narrative (by researching another historic battle, you could describe how the two battles are the same and how they are different). You can compare one person to another, one series of events to another, or one description to another.

STEP TWO: **Make a preliminary plan**

Now that you've made a tentative decision about the form of your composition, make a preliminary plan. Decide what sorts of details you'll need to fill out your composition, so that you don't take lots of unnecessary notes.

For your chosen *topoi*, jot down the answers to the questions below on a piece of a paper. (Don't just answer the questions in your head!) If necessary, go back to the lessons listed to review the forms of each *topos*.

Chronological narrative of a past event
WWS1, Week 4, Days 3–4; Week 6, Days 3–4
     What is the theme of the narrative—its focus?
     What are its beginning and ending points?
     Will you use dialogue? Who will speak?

Chronological narrative of a scientific discovery
WWS1, Week 5, Days 3–4; Week 7, Days 3–4
>Will you need a background paragraph explaining the circumstances before the discovery?
>Can you quote from the scientist's own words?

Description of a place
WWS1, Week 8, Days 3–4; Week 9, Days 3–4; Week 10, Days 3–4
>What purpose will this description fulfill?
>What is your point of view?
>What metaphors or similes will make the description more vivid?

Scientific description
WWS1, Week 12, Days 3–4; Week 13, Days 3–4; Week 14, Days 3–4
>What are the parts of the object or phenomenon?
>What is your point of view? Will you use more than one?
>What figurative language can make the description more visual?

Description of a person
WWS1, Week 16, Days 2–3; Week 17, Days 2–3; Week 18, Days 2–3
>What aspects will be included?
>Will you slant the description in a positive or negative direction?
>Will you use an overall metaphor to give clues about the person's character?

Biographical sketch
WWS1, Week 19, Days 2–3; Week 20, Days 2–3
>What will the focus be—life events, or the subject's accomplishments/work?
>>If life events, which ones will be included?
>>If accomplishments/work, will they be listed chronologically or by topic?
>What aspects from the Description of a Person chart should be included?

Sequence: Natural process
WWS1, Week 21, Days 2–3; Week 22, Days 2–3
>What other elements will you include?
>>Introduction/summary?
>>Scientific background?
>>Repetition of the process?

Sequence: History
WWS2, Week 2, Days 2–3; Week 4, Days 1–3
>What other elements will you include?
>>Introductory paragraph?

Historical development?
Results/consequences?

Explanation by comparison/contrast
WWS2, Week 5, Days 2–3; Week 7, Days 1, 3–4

Will point-by-point or subject-by-subject comparison work better?
Can you use both?
Will you need to do additional research to complete your comparison?

STEP THREE: **Begin taking notes**

Finish today's work by taking notes on one of your sources. If you need to review the proper format, review Week 3, Day Three.

Choose the source that you think will be the most helpful. The number of notes that you will take will vary. However, for a short composition you should try never to take more than 20 notes from any individual source.

After you've finished taking your notes, you should have some idea of how well the details in your source will fit into your chosen *topos*. If necessary, go back to the list of *topoi* and adjust your plan. (You may realize, for example, that what you thought were events in a sequence actually fit better into a chronological narrative—or that the details you intended to use in a place description are actually better suited to a comparison or contrast.)

When you're finished, tell your instructor which *topos* you've chosen, and show your notes.

Day Two: Finish Taking Notes

Focus: Gathering information

Today's assignment is simple: Take notes from your remaining sources.

You should have done preliminary reading from about six books. When you did this reading, you probably found at least one or two books that weren't particularly helpful. Choose three of the remaining books and take notes from them.

Try not to create duplicate notes—if you've learned a fact from one book, there's no need to note it again when you find it in another. You may end up only taking two or three notes from the last book that you use.

Day Three: Draft the Composition

 Focus: Writing an initial draft from notes

STEP ONE: **Place your notes in order and divide them into main points**

Take your notes from yesterday and arrange them in order.

This order will depend on the form you've chosen for your composition. Here's a quick review. You don't have to read all of the following, just the section that deals with the *topos* you've chosen:

This year, you've already reviewed arranging notes in chronological order for a **chronological narration** (Week 4, Day 2) and writing a **sequence in history** from notes (Week 4, Day 3). You have also practiced arranging notes in the correct order to write a **comparison/contrast** (Week 5, Day 3 and Week 7, Day 2).

You used notes to write a **personal description** and a **description of a place** in Week 29 of Level 1. You organized the personal description by reading through your notes and using scratch paper to jot down aspects from the Description of the Person chart that the notes described; you then organized your notes so that they were grouped together by aspect. For the place description, you followed the same procedure, using the Description of a Place chart. (If you need a more detailed review, go back to Level 1, Week 29 and reread the instructions for Day 3 and Day 4.)

You used notes to write a **sequence of a natural process** and a **scientific description** in Week 30 of Level 1. You organized them by placing them so that all of the events in the sequence were listed in order, eliminating the notes that simply repeated information. You divided them so that each group covered a different stage of the sequence. (If you need more review, go back to Level 1, Week 30, Days 2–3.)

You used notes to write a **biographical sketch** in Week 31 of Level 1. You had the choice of organizing them chronologically (for a listing of major life events), or else organizing them into a brief summary of life events followed by a survey of the subject's accomplishments and achievements.

STEP TWO: **Write the *topos* (or *topoi*)**

Using your ordered notes, write your composition. In most cases, you'll probably want to write one paragraph for each group of notes, but if it seems more natural to combine groups or to use more than one paragraph, that's fine.

Be sure to quote directly from at least two of your sources. Make sure that all direct quotes and anything which is not common knowledge is footnoted.

Check your *topoi* chart one more time to make sure that you have included the required elements.

Since your complete composition, including introduction and conclusion, should be at least 500 words long, aim to have at least 450 words in this initial draft.

STEP THREE: **Write an introduction and conclusion**

Review the Introductions and Conclusions chart in the Reference section of your Composition Notebook.

Choose one kind of introduction and another kind of conclusion. (That means you can't do an introduction by summary *and* a conclusion by summary, and you should be careful that your introduction by anecdote and conclusion by personal reaction don't sound too similar.)

Write a draft of your introduction and a draft of your conclusion. Assemble the entire composition. Make sure that you have 500 words or more.

Now put your composition away until tomorrow at the earliest. You should show your instructor that the composition is finished, but your instructor shouldn't offer suggestions or criticisms until you've had a chance to complete Day Four's work.

Day Four: Finalize the Composition

 Focus: Revision and proofreading

STEP ONE: **Title**

Begin today's work by reading carefully through your composition from beginning to end (silently is fine; see Step Two).

Now it's time to give the essay a title.

When you finished your composition at the end of Level 1, you were asked to give it a very simple title—just the name of an event, person, place, or process. But you should now begin to work towards more complex titling.

What is the event, person, place, or process that your composition discusses? Jot it down on a scratch piece of paper. Now, think about the *topos* (or *topoi*) that you used to write your paper. Can you come up with a phrase that includes both the event/person/place/process *and* a description of the *topos*?

Here are a few examples to help you out.

If you wrote about Abraham Lincoln and decided to do a chronological narrative of a past event, you'd want to combine Abraham Lincoln and the event:

The Assassination of Abraham Lincoln

or perhaps

Abraham Lincoln Declares War.

A biographical sketch might be titled:

Who Was Abraham Lincoln?

or even

A Character Sketch of Abraham Lincoln.

But if you planned to compare and contrast Abraham Lincoln with another historical figure, you could title your paper:

The Similarities between Abraham Lincoln and George Washington

or

The Differences between Abraham Lincoln and Chairman Mao.

The chronological narrative of a scientific discovery could be titled, very simply:

The Discovery of the Polio Vaccine

or

How a Vaccine for Polio was Discovered.

A scientific description could be titled:

How Polio Vaccines Work

or

The Polio Vaccine and How It Functions.

You can title the description of a place by using your final evaluation of it:

The Beauties of the Grand Canyon

or

The Dangers of the Grand Canyon.

And finally, sequences can be titled with the name of the sequence itself:

How Galaxies Are Formed

or

The Formation of Galaxies.

If you have chosen to use two or more *topoi* in your composition, choose the *topos* that seems most important or central for your title.

When you have come up with your title, center it at the top of your first page. Use initial capitals, but do not put your title in all caps.

STEP TWO: **Revise**

Using your *topoi* chart, check to make sure that all of the required elements of your chosen *topos* are included in your paper. If you are missing one, return to your notes (or sources if necessary) and add it in.

Now read your composition out loud. Listen for awkward or unclear sections. Rewrite them so that they flow more naturally.

Finally, read your composition out loud a second time. Listen for repeated nouns, verbs, and modifiers. If you find yourself using the same noun or verb more than twice, use your thesaurus to find an alternative. (This doesn't include the name of your actual subject, of course!) If you use a modifier (adverb, adjective, or prepositional phrase acting as an adjective or adverb) more than once, find another word.

STEP THREE: Assemble the Works Cited page

Put the sources used in your footnotes on a Works Cited page, using the correct format.

STEP FOUR: Proofread

1. Read through the paper one more time, looking for sentence fragments or run-on sentences.
2. Check the format of your footnotes and Works Cited page. (If necessary, look back at Week 3, Day 1).
3. Check your spelling by looking, individually, at each word that might be a problem.

When you have finished proofreading and corrected any errors, give your paper to your instructor for evaluation.

WEEK 10: THE EMBEDDED STORY

Introduction to Weeks 10-11

In the first level of *Writing With Skill,* you spent eight weeks working on skills in beginning literary criticism: identifying protagonists, antagonists, and conflicts; learning basic vocabulary for literary techniques; and writing brief literary analysis essays about fiction and poetry.

In this second level, you'll build on those basic skills and develop a few new ones. Instead of spending an entire month writing about fiction and another month on poetry, you'll work on these intermediate skills for a couple of weeks at a time, interspersed with your other writing assignments.

You should glance back through the list of literary terms you completed in the first level of this course before beginning Week 10's work.

Day One: Read

Focus: Reading

STEP ONE: **Learn about the author**

"The Open Window" was written by a British author named Hector Hugh Munro. He was actually born in Burma in 1870, because his father was an English official in British-controlled India. But he grew up in England, because his mother died and his father sent him to live with two aunts back at home.

He began to write short stories, essays, and newspaper articles when he was in his twenties. He published his short stories under the pen name Saki, which he borrowed from a very popular book of Persian poems called *The Rubaiyat of Omar Khayyam.*

When World War I began in 1914, Munro lied about his age in order to join the British army (he was 44, too old for regular enlistment). He fought for two years before he was killed by a German sniper in November of 1916.

"The Open Window" was first published early in 1914, in a collection of short stories called *Beasts and Superbeasts*.

Before you read, you should know that the word "romance" in the last line is not used in the modern sense of "boy meets girl." It has the older sense of "tales of daring, excitement, and brave deeds."

STEP TWO: **Read**

Get in a comfortable place and read the story from beginning to end. Enjoy yourself. Eat a cookie.

STEP THREE: **Reread**

Now read through the story a second time.

Why do you think you were told to do a second reading? Tell your instructor why you think this second reading was assigned. If you don't know, your instructor will explain. (Hint: it has to do with the genre of the story, which you should be able to recognize.)

Day Two: Think

 Focus: Finding the story within the story

As you learned last year, it's always easier to write about a story if you've talked about it first. In the steps below, you'll see lines and definitions. In each of the steps, your instructor will carry on a dialogue with you. At the end of each dialogue, write a brief observation on the lines. These observations will help you construct your brief essay tomorrow.

STEP ONE: **Identify the protagonist and antagonist**

Protag.- Mr. Nuttle, worried easily

Antag- Vera, makes up stories,
wants to play/scare Mr Nuttle,

She got What She wanted,

STEP TWO: **Find the story within the story**

Story #1: _____

_____

_____

_____

_____

_____

Story #2: _____

_____

_____

_____

_____

_____

"Not only does the unfortunate Mr. Nuttel fall victim to the story's joke, but so does the reader. The reader is at first inclined to laugh at Nuttel for being so gullible. However, the reader, too, has been taken in by the story and must come to the realization that he or she is also inclined to believe a well-told and interesting tale."

—Nozar Niazi and Rama Gautam, *How to Study Literature: Stylistic and Pragmatic Approaches* (New Delhi: PHI, Ltd., 2010), p. 164

STEP THREE: Examine the author's language

#1 _____ = _____

#2 _____ = _____

#3 _____ = _____

ironic language: _____

_____

EXAMPLE   OPPOSITE TO REALITY BECAUSE . . .

_____

_____

_____

_____

Day Three: Write

 Focus: Writing about the story

Today, you'll write a brief essay following the pattern you learned in Level One of this course: a brief summary of the story, followed by two or three paragraphs explaining the most central issues with the story's structure and function.

STEP ONE: **Write the summary**

Begin by writing a brief narrative summary of the story. This summary should be five to ten sentences in length, and may be either one or two paragraphs.

You should be comfortable writing summaries by now, but if you need help, ask your instructor.

STEP TWO: **Write the analysis**

Now you'll write an analysis of how the story works. This analysis should have four parts:

1. A description of the story-within-a-story structure (two to three sentences),
2. The way that the central story fools both the reader and Mr. Nuttel (two to three sentences),
3. The way Saki uses word choice to make the ghost story more effective, and
4. The way Saki uses irony to hint at the trick he is playing on us.

You can combine these into two or three paragraphs or else write a separate short paragraph for each.

Remember that you should use either present tense ("Saki structures this story by telling *two* stories") or past tense ("Saki structured this story by telling *two* stories") throughout.

Be sure to quote directly from the story at least twice. You do not need to footnote these quotes, since it is very clear that you are using "The Open Window" as your source.

If you have trouble getting started, you can use my opening sentence above ("Saki structures this story by telling *two* stories") as your first sentence. If you're still stuck, ask your instructor for help.

STEP THREE: **Proofread**

Before you give your essay to your instructor, proofread it using the following steps:

1. Read your composition out loud. Listen for awkward or unclear sections. Rewrite them so that they flow more naturally.
2. Read your composition out loud a second time. Listen for repeated nouns, verbs, and modifiers. If you find yourself using the same noun or verb more than twice, use your thesaurus to find an alternative. If you use a modifier (adverb, adjective, or prepositional phrase acting as an adjective or adverb) more than once, find another word.
3. Look for sentence fragments or run-on sentences. Correct them if you find them.
4. Check to make sure that you have quoted directly from the story at least twice.
5. Make sure that all five required elements are present—narrative summary plus the four parts listed above.
6. Check your spelling by looking, individually, at each word that might be a problem.

Day Four: Literary Language

 Focus: Understanding point of view

Today, you'll use "The Open Window" and excerpts from a few other works to learn more about *point of view*.

STEP ONE: **Review point of view**

In the first level of this course, you were introduced to *point of view*. Take a minute now to review what you've already learned.

1. First-person point of view uses the pronouns *I, we, my,* and *mine*. You learned about this when you read from Helen Keller's autobiography in Level 1, Week 3:

> **We** walked down the path to the well-house, attracted by the fragrance of the honeysuckle with which it was covered. Someone was drawing water and **my** teacher placed **my** hand under the spout. As the cool stream gushed over one hand, she spelled into the other the word *water*, first slowly, then rapidly. **I** stood still, **my** whole attention fixed upon the motions of her fingers.
>
> —Helen Keller, *The Story of My Life*
> (Doubleday, Page & Company, 1903), p. 24.

2. In the same lesson, you learned that third-person point of view uses third-person pronouns and names. You were given the following third-person version of the same paragraph:

> **Helen and Miss Sullivan** walked down the path to the well-house, attracted by the fragrance of the honeysuckle with which it was covered. Someone was drawing water and **Helen's** teacher placed **her** hand under the spout. As the cool stream gushed over one hand she spelled into the other the word *water*, first slowly, then rapidly. **Helen** stood still, **her** whole attention fixed upon the motions of her fingers.

3. In Weeks 9 and 13, you learned that when writing a description, you need to think of your *point of view* as a narrator—where are you in relation to the thing being described? You were given four options:

1. From above, as though you were hovering over the place. This is sometimes called the "impersonal" point of view, because you're not directly involved in the place itself; you're looking over it as a detached observer.

2. From inside it, as though you were part of the place, standing still in the middle of it at a particular point and looking around.

3. From one side, as though you were standing beside the place looking at it from one particular angle.

4. Moving, as though you were walking through the place, or around it.

STEP TWO: Understand first, second, and third-person point of view in fiction

In short stories and novels, "point of view" has a very particular meaning. "Point of view" has to do with who the narrator of the story is and how much that narrator knows.

Read the following descriptions and examples carefully.

1) First-person point of view ("I") gives a very immediate, but limited, perspective. First-person allows you to hear a character's most private thoughts–but in exchange, you can only see what happens within the character's line of sight, and you can only know those facts that the character is herself aware of.

> I could only look upwards; the sun began to grow hot, and the light offended my eyes. I heard a confused noise about me; but in the posture I lay could see nothing except the sky. In a little time I felt something alive moving on my left leg, which advancing gently forward over my breast,

came almost up to my chin; when bending my eyes downward as much as I
could, I perceived it to be a human creature not six inches high, with a bow
and arrow in his hands, and a quiver at his back.
  —Jonathan Swift, *Gulliver's Travels*

2) Second-person ("You walk down the street and open the door . . .") is unusual. It is
generally found only in experimental literary works and in adventure games. Like first-person
point of view, second-person keeps the reader intimately involved with the story. But second-
person also tends to limit the writer to the present tense, cutting off any reflection on the past.

You are about to begin reading Italo Calvino's new novel, *If on a winter's night a traveler.* Relax. Concentrate. Dispel every other thought. Let the
world around you fade. Best to close the door; the TV is always on in the
next room.
  —Italo Calvino, *If on a winter's night a traveler*

3) Third-person tells the story using third-person pronouns—he, she, it, they—and proper
names. There are four kinds of third-person stories, but these three are the most common:

a) Third-person limited. This tells the story from the viewpoint of one
particular character, delving into that character's mind, but using the third-
person pronouns (he or she) rather than the first-person pronouns. This
allows the writer to gain a little bit of distance from the story, but still limits
the writer to those events that the viewpoint character can actually see and
hear.

With this excellent resolve for the future, Goodman Brown felt
himself justified in making more haste on his present evil purpose. He
had taken a dreary road, darkened by all the gloomiest trees of the forest, which barely stood aside to let the narrow path creep through, and
closed immediately behind. It was all as lonely as could be . . . [H]e
passed a crook of the road, and, looking forward again, beheld the
figure of a man, in grave and decent attire, seated at the foot of an old
tree.
  —Nathaniel Hawthorne, *Young Goodman Brown*

b) Third-person multiple. This point of view allows the writer to use
the third-person viewpoints of several different characters, jumping from
the "inside" of one character to the "inside" of another in order to give multiple perspectives.

Clutching his broken glasses to his face, Harry stared around. He had emerged into a dingy alleyway . . . Feeling jumpy, Harry set off, trying to hold his glasses on straight and hoping against hope he'd be able to find a way out of here.

Peeves was bobbing overhead, now grinning wickedly, surveying the scene; Peeves always loved chaos.

"Don't be silly, Ron, I've got to keep up," said Hermione briskly. Her spirits were greatly improved by the fact that all the hair had gone from her face and her eyes were turning slowly back to brown.

—J. K. Rowling, *Harry Potter and the Chamber of Secrets*

c) The omniscient point of view–the most popular until the nineteenth century–puts the writer in the place of God. He can see and explain everything—events, thoughts in anyone's head, secrets. The narrator can even give opinions and ideas and talk directly to the reader ("Gentle reader, what depths of guilt such a man must feel!" is an example of the omniscient point of view.)

Here is an example of the omniscient point of view in which the narrator knows what's going on in both character's heads better than they do:

Aunt March put on her glasses and took a look at the girl, for she did not know her in this new mood. Meg hardly knew herself, she felt so brave and independent, so glad to defend John and assert her right to love him, if she liked. Aunt March saw that she had begun wrong, and after a little pause, made a fresh start . . .

—Louisa May Alcott, *Little Women*

STEP THREE: **Understand the point of view of "The Open Window"**

Now look back at "The Open Window" and try to decide which point of view the narrator of the story uses.

As you do, think particularly about the following lines:

Privately he doubted more than ever whether these formal visits on a succession of total strangers would do much towards helping the nerve cure which he was supposed to be undergoing.

"Do you know many of the people round here?" asked the niece, when she judged that they had had sufficient silent communion.

Romance at short notice was her specialty.

When you've decided, tell your instructor your conclusions.

WEEK 11: COMPARING STORIES

Day One: Read

Focus: Reading

STEP ONE: **Learn about the author**

"The Monkey's Paw" was written by William Wymark Jacobs. Born in 1863, Jacobs grew up in London. He worked for the British postal service and wrote stories in his spare time. His first book of short stories was published in 1896; by the time he died in 1943, he had written over 150 stories and published 12 different story collections. Many of Jacobs's stories feature British colonials (residents in British colonies in India and other countries) who have just returned home.

You may find some unfamiliar vocabulary in the story. "Rubicund" means "ruddy, flushed, red." "Fakir" was the name that British officers in India often used for local Muslim and Hindu monks, particularly those who claimed to be able to do miracles. An "antimacassar" is a decorative drape that goes on the back of a sofa or chair to help keep it clean. "Simian" means "monkey-like."

Something that is "prosaic" is everyday, ordinary, comfortable. Someone who is "credulous" believes tall tales easily. "Bibulous" means "having to do with drink."

A "fusillade," often used to describe a whole collection of gunshots let off at once, means a "general discharge" or all-at-once outpouring.

STEP TWO: **Read**

Get in a comfortable place and read the story from beginning to end. Enjoy yourself. Eat a cookie.

Day Two: Think

> Focus: Understanding story structure,
> story climax, and foreshadowing

In each of the steps below, your instructor will carry on a dialogue with you. At the end of each dialogue, write a brief observation on the lines provided. These observations will help you construct your brief essay at the end of the week.

STEP ONE: **Identify the protagonist**

Mr. White

STEP TWO: **Examine the structure of the story**

#1: 3 phases of mystery

#2: 3 times of something happens.

#3: 3 examples

STEP THREE: **Understand the pivot point**

pivot point: the moment at which the main character changes goals, wants, or direction

_____

_____

_____

_____

_____

_____

_____

_____

_____

STEP FOUR: **Identify the climax of the story**

story climax: the point of greatest tension or conflict

TENSION BETWEEN

_____ Mr. White _____ and _____ Mrs. White _____

_____ Mr. White _____ and _____ What's on the Porch _____

_____ and _____

STEP FIVE: **Learn about foreshadowing**

foreshadowing: giving the reader clues about what will happen later in the story

Day Three: Compare

 Focus: Comparing similarities and differences

Beginning in Week 5 of this year's work, you practiced writing comparisons—using similarities and differences to organize compositions in history and in science. Today, you'll do the same in literature by comparing "The Monkey's Paw" to "The Open Window." The sentences and paragraphs you write today will become part of this week's composition, which you'll finish tomorrow.

STEP ONE: Add to the Literary Terms chart

Review what you learned in Day Two by adding the following definitions to your Literary Terms chart:

> pivot point: the moment at which the main character changes goals, wants, or direction
> story climax: the point of greatest tension or conflict
> foreshadowing: giving the reader clues about what will happen later in the story

STEP TWO: Compare structure

Using your own scratch paper (or word processing program) write two to four sentences describing the structure of "The Open Window." If necessary, glance back at Week 10, Day Three and the work you did in Step Two.

Then, write three to six sentences describing the structure of "The Monkey's Paw." Be sure to discuss the pivot and the parts into which the story is divided.

When you are finished, show your work to your instructor.

STEP THREE: Compare story climaxes

Write two to three sentences describing what happens at the climax of "The Open Window."

Then, write three to four sentences describing what happens at the climax of "The Monkey's Paw."

When you are finished, show your work to your instructor.

STEP FOUR: **Compare language**

Write three to four sentences describing how Saki uses word choice in "The Open Window" to create suspense and to fool the reader. You can choose to use sentences from the essay you wrote last week, or write new sentences.

Then, write four to six sentences describing how W. W. Jacobs uses word choice to make his story more effective. Discuss his use of repeated threes, but also look for vocabulary that heightens the sense of horror, especially towards the end of the story. If you have difficulty, ask your instructor for help.

When you are finished, show your work to your instructor.

Day Four: Write

> Focus: Writing a comparison and contrast
> of two stories

Today, you'll write a brief essay comparing the structure, story climaxes, and language of "The Monkey's Paw" and "The Open Window."

For this comparison, you won't need to write a narrative summary; you can assume that your readers are already familiar with the stories. Instead, you'll write a point-by-point comparison and then provide an introduction and conclusion.

STEP ONE: **Write the first point-by-point comparison**

Look at the two sets of sentences you wrote about the structure of the two stories. Ask yourself: What is similar about the structure of the stories? Try to sum up this similarity in one sentence. Then, combine the sentences into a paragraph describing what is different about how each story is put together.

If you have difficulty, ask your instructor for help.

When you're finished, show your work to your instructor (just to make sure that you're on the right track).

STEP TWO: **Write the second and third comparisons**

Use the same strategy to write about the story climaxes. Write a sentence telling what is the same about the climaxes. Then, describe the differences by telling what happens in each one.

Now finish your comparison by describing what is the same about the way both authors use language. Then, describe precisely what each one does—and how they are different. You may use either one or two paragraphs for each comparison.

Remember that you should use either present tense or past tense throughout.

You should quote each story at least once in your section comparing the language that the two authors use. You do not need to footnote the quotes as long as you clearly indicate which story you are quoting.

If you need help, ask your instructor. If you are comfortable with your work, you do not need to show it until the composition is finished and proofread.

STEP THREE: **Write an introduction and conclusion**

Finish your composition by writing an introduction by summary and a conclusion by personal reaction. If you need to review these forms, go back to Week Six, Days One and Two.

Your introduction by summary should say whether you think the stories are more alike or more different, and what the greatest similarity or difference is. It should also include the titles and authors of both stories.

Your conclusion by personal reaction should say which story you prefer and why.

The introduction and conclusion should each be an independent paragraph.

STEP FOUR: **Proofread**

Before you give your essay to your instructor, proofread it using the following steps:

1. Read your composition out loud. Listen for awkward or unclear sections. Rewrite them so that they flow more naturally.

2. Read your composition out loud a second time. Listen for repeated nouns, verbs, and modifiers. If you find yourself using the same noun or verb more than twice, use your thesaurus to find an alternative. If you use a modifier (adverb, adjective, or prepositional phrase acting as an adjective or adverb) more than once, find another word.

3. Pay special attention to your transitions. When you are writing a comparison/contrast paper, it is very easy to overuse the words "but," "however, "on the one hand," and "on the other hand." If necessary, look up "however" and "but" in your thesaurus to find substitutes.

4. Look for sentence fragments or run-on sentences. Correct them if you find them.

5. Check to make sure that you have quoted directly from each story.

6. Make sure that your composition includes introduction, three sets of comparisons/contrasts, and conclusion.

7. Check your spelling by looking, individually, at each word that might be a problem.

Week 12: Explanation by Definition: Essential and accidental properties

This week you'll begin to investigate a new *topos: explanation by way of definition.*

You can organize a whole composition around defining something. You've probably never looked up the definition of "definition," but Webster's Dictionary says that a definition is "a statement expressing the nature of something."

Over the next few weeks, you will learn how to explain *the nature of something.* In other words, you will describe the characteristics of something—what makes it different, unique, *itself.*

First, you'll practice this in science. Then, you'll exercise those same skills on a topic in history.

Day One: Essential Properties and Accidental Properties

Focus: Answering the question "What is it"?

You won't be writing an original composition today—just reading and thinking. Complete the following steps *slowly and carefully!*

STEP ONE: Review scientific description

You've already practiced the first part of *explanation by way of definition.* Last year, you learned to write a *scientific description*—a visual and structural description of an object or phenomenon. A description is one of the building blocks you'll use when you write full definitions.

Take a minute now to review the form of the scientific description. Read the following chart out loud.

Scientific Description

Definition: A visual and structural description of an object or
phenomenon

Procedure	Remember
1. Describe each part of the object or phenomenon and tell what it is made from.	1. Consider using figurative language to make the description more visual.
2. Choose a point of view.	2. Consider combining points of view.

When you first learned about scientific descriptions, back in Week 12 of Level One of this
course, you learned how to describe the parts of an object and tell what each part is made of,
while also giving the reader a clear picture of what the object looks like. Among the examples
given was this excerpt from Bill Bryson's *A Short History of Nearly Everything:*

> Whatever their size or shape, nearly all your cells are built to funda-
> mentally the same plan: they have an outer casing or membrane, a nucleus
> wherein resides the necessary genetic information to keep you going, and a
> busy space between the two called the cytoplasm. The membrane is not, as
> most of us imagine it, a durable, rubbery casing, something that you would
> need a sharp pin to prick. Rather, it is made up of a type of fatty material
> known as a lipid, which has the approximate consistency "of a light grade of
> machine oil," to quote Sherwin B. Nuland . . .
> If you could visit a cell, you wouldn't like it. Blown up to a scale at
> which atoms were about the size of peas, a cell itself would be a sphere
> roughly half a mile across, and supported by a complex framework of gird-
> ers called the cytoskeleton. Within it, millions upon millions of objects—
> some the size of basketballs, others the size of cars—would whiz about like
> bullets. There wouldn't be a place you could stand without being pummeled
> and ripped thousands of times every second from every direction.[30]

This description gives you the parts of the cell (membrane, nucleus, cytoplasm, skeleton)
and tells you what they are made of (genetic information, lipids). It also uses figurative language (peas, basketballs, and bullets) to give you a sense of what the cell *looks* like.

---

30. Bill Bryson, *A Short History of Nearly Everything* (Random House, 2004), p. 377.

Your assignment in Week 12 was to describe the parts of a volcano and explain what each part was made from, using at least one metaphor (figurative language). (If you can find that description, you should read back through it now. But if it's lost forever, I understand.)

The following week, you added one more element to your description. You learned that, when writing a scientific description, you can use either a *removed* or *present* point of view.

You were given two examples. Let's review them now.

The first is written from a *removed* point of view. The narrator of this paragraph knows a lot about volcanoes, but he isn't actually *there* as the volcano erupts.

> Sometimes an explosive eruption produces a cloud of volcanic debris so full of fragments that it is too heavy to rise very high into the atmosphere. Such an emulsion of gas and fragments forms a pyroclastic flow, the most dangerous kind of volcanic hazard. Pyroclastic flows can travel at speeds of more than 100 kilometers per hour, flattening and burning almost every-thing in their paths. Small pyroclastic flows often race down the valleys on a volcano's flanks, but larger masses that are expelled at high speeds . . . can sweep over small hills or across large flat areas.[31]

The second is an eyewitness description written by the Roman lawyer Pliny the Younger after he lived through the eruption of Mount Vesuvius in the year 79.

> Ashes were already falling, not as yet very thickly. I looked round: a dense black cloud was coming up behind us, spreading over the earth like a flood. . . . We had scarcely sat down to rest when darkness fell, not the dark of a moonless or cloudy night, but as if the lamp had been put out in a closed room. You could hear the shrieks of women, the wailing of infants, and the shouting of men; some were calling their parents, others their chil-dren or their wives, trying to recognize them by their voices. . . . A gleam of light returned, but we took this to be a warning of the approaching flames rather than daylight. However, the flames remained some distance off; then darkness came on once more and ashes began to fall again, this time in heavy showers. We rose from time to time and shook them off, otherwise we should have been buried and crushed beneath their weight.[32]

A description written from the present point of view tells the reader what the narrator is seeing, hearing, feeling, smelling, and/or tasting.

---

31. Robert Decker and Barbara Decker, *Volcanoes*, 4th ed. (W. H. Freeman & Co., 2006), p. 125.
32. Pliny the Younger, *The Letters of the Younger Pliny*, trans. and ed. Betty Radice (Penguin Books, 1963), Book VI.

STEP TWO: Understand essential properties and accidental properties

When you write a scientific description, you give the reader basic answers to two important questions:

> *What is it?*
> *How does it work?*

Those questions, asked even more carefully, can also help you to write a definition—an explanation of the nature of a scientific object. To them, you'll add a third question: "Where does it belong?"

For this week, you'll just concentrate on "What is it?"

When you answer this question for the reader, you are describing the *properties* of an object. You can write perfectly serviceable descriptions without understanding exactly what a property is, but it's time to stretch your mind (and to prepare yourself for the upper-level writing you'll be doing later in your student years). So take a few minutes now to think about properties.

A property is something that belongs to the object. The philosopher Aristotle said that there are two different kinds of properties: essential and accidental. What's the difference? Here's how one philosopher puts it:

> *Essential properties are those that define a thing as the sort or kind that it is; accidental properties are all other properties of a thing.*[33]

Think about cows for a minute. All cows chew a cud, have a four-part stomach, and contain cow DNA. These are "essential properties" of cows. If an animal doesn't chew its cud, have a four-part stomach, and contain cow DNA, it isn't a cow. These essential properties *make* a cow a cow.

Many cows are brown. But being brown is not necessary to being a cow. It is an "accidental property." Some cows may be black or white.

Sometimes, cows are outfitted with sunglasses. The sunglasses are not an essential part of being a cow. In Aristotle's language, they are also "accidental properties."

When you answer the question "What is it?" you're describing the essential and accidental properties of a scientific object or phenomenon.

In the following list of properties, underline *only* those that are **essential properties.** When you're finished, show your work to your instructor. (The first one should be easy. The second might be a little harder—consult an encyclopedia or online resource if necessary. For an exercise like this, Wikipedia is perfectly acceptable.)

---

33. Richard Cross, "Duns Scotus: *Ordinatio.*" In *Central Works of Philosophy, Volume 1: Ancient and Medieval,* ed. John Shand (McGill-Queens, 2005), p. 230.

father
    thirty-seven
    blond
    male
    protective
    accountant
    parent
    tall

tornado
    visible
    wedge-shaped
    black
    rotating
    touching ground
    noisy
    form in afternoon
    destructive

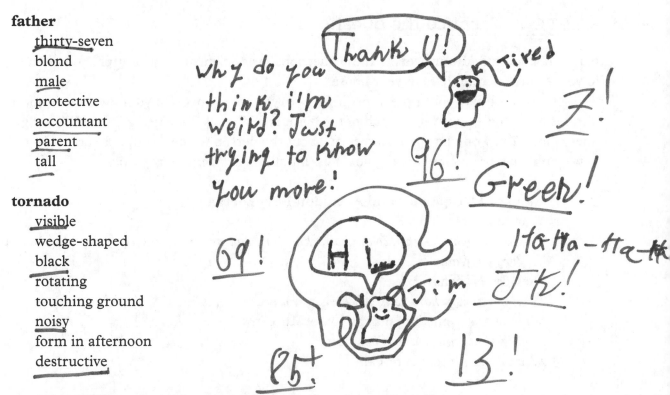

STEP THREE: Examine the questions about properties

When you define an object, you start out by describing its essential properties and its accidental properties. Asking the following questions will help you identify these.

Read these questions out loud to your instructor. If any of them are unclear, ask for explanations.

1. **Essential Properties and Accidental Properties**
    What does it look like?
    How does it behave?
    What senses come into play as you observe it?
    What do those senses reveal?
    Is your observation passive (watching/listening) or active (experimenting/collecting/probing)?
    What sorts of measurements (temperature, quantity, time, etc.) are necessary to your observation?
    What does it resemble?
    What is it made of?
    What sort of structure does it have?
    What is its extent in space?
    What is its extent in time?
    Which properties are essential?
    Which are accidental?

STEP FOUR: **Practice the questions**

Now you'll identify the answers to these questions for a scientific object or phenomenon close to you—someone who lives in your house.

Choose a sibling, your parent, or (if necessary) a family pet. On your own paper, jot down phrases or sentences answering each of the "properties" questions, using the additional guidelines below. You won't be writing an essay about the person (or pet) you're describing—right now, you're just practicing *thinking* about essential and accidental properties.

1. **Essential Properties and Accidental Properties**
   What does it look like?
   > *Size (height, weight), color (hair, skin, fur), outline (arms and legs? how many?), clothes (or fur), features . . .*
   How does it behave?
   > *Expressions, characteristic behaviors, habits,* bad *habits . . .*
   What senses come into play as you observe it?
   > *Sight, hearing, smell, touch, taste . . .*
   What do those senses reveal?
   > *. . . ?*
   Is your observation passive (watching/listening) or active (experimenting/collecting/probing)?
   > *Which of your observations so far happen when you're not actually talking to the person/pet? Which come from the person/pet doing his/her/its own thing while you just watch?*
   What sorts of measurements (temperature, quantity, time, etc.) are necessary to your observation?
   > *You're probably using measurements for height and weight . . . are there any others?*
   What does it resemble?
   > *Do you know another person/pet that your subject looks like?*
   What is it made of?
   > *You don't have to go into too much detail here . . . but describe basic blood/bone/hair or fur . . .*
   What sort of structure does it have?
   > *How many arms, legs, toes/fingers/claws? How about the face—eyes, nose, mouth, or muzzle?*
   What is its extent in space?
   > *How much physical space does it take up?*
   What is its extent in time?
   > *How long has it been alive?*
   Which properties are essential?
   > *What makes the person or pet* it??
   Which are accidental?
   > *What could be different about other siblings/parents/pets, and yet make them still siblings/ parents/pets?*

Day Two: Analyze

> Focus: Studying a model answering the question
> "What is it?"

STEP ONE: **Read**

Carefully read the following paragraphs from *A Naturalist's Guide to the Arctic*, by E. C. Pielou.

When the arctic sky is totally dark—which it never is, of course, in high summer—the chances are favorable for seeing a display of the *aurora borealis*, or northern lights. In good displays, the glowing, shimmering, flickering lights sometimes take the form of arcs or bands, sometimes of rippling draperies, and sometimes of rapidly pulsating patches of light streaming upward toward the sky. The color is usually pale green, very occasionally red or violet.

Contrary to legend, the aurora makes no sound: it is silent. Reports of shushing sounds probably mean that the observer was hearing the swish of dry snow blown over hard snow crust, and of crackling sounds that the observer was hearing the static crackle of dry woolen or synthetic clothes. (It is noteworthy that reports of audible auroras seem always to refer to displays on intensely cold nights, and never to those on warm nights, in populous, mid-latitude regions.)

The aurora is caused by electrically charged particles streaming earthward from the sun and striking atoms and molecules (chiefly of oxygen and nitrogen) in the rarefied upper atmosphere. Subatomic particles are dislodged from the atoms and molecules hit, and energy is liberated in the form of light. The same thing happens in a glowing neon sign, in which molecules of the rare gas neon are the targets. The colors of the aurora depend on the varying energy of the incoming particles (the missiles) and on the chemical nature of the atmospheric atoms and molecules struck (the targets). The common pale green aurora is emitted by oxygen; the rarer reds and violets come from both oxygen and nitrogen, struck by particles with different energies. This electrical activity commonly takes place at between 100 and 300 km above the ground.[34]

---

34. E. C. Pielou, *A Naturalist's Guide to the Arctic* (Chicago: The University of Chicago Press, 1994), pp. 13–14.

STEP TWO: **Answer the questions**

This is the first part of an explanation by definition. It answers many of the questions you practiced in the last lesson.

Your task now: to identify which questions the paragraph answers.

Using the list of questions from Step Three of Day One, go back through the paragraphs about the *aurora borealis*. On the worksheet below, answer each question. If the paragraphs do not provide you with an answer, draw a line through the question and continue on. The first one is done for you.

When you are finished, show your work to your instructor.

What does it look like?   pale green, occasionally red or violet, glowing, shimmering, flickering,

pulsating patches of light ~~Bright~~ Bright

How does it behave? It Shimmers, it flickers, Pulsates

What senses come into play as you observe it? Sight, happiness

What do those senses reveal? Sight and Sound, (lacks of
no hearing in the eyes).

Is your observation passive (watching/listening) or active (experimenting/collecting/probing)?
Passive

What sorts of measurements (temperature, quantity, time, etc.) are necessary to your observation?
movement of particles

What does it resemble? A rainbow, color of lights,
neon sign.

What is it made of? nitrogen, oxygen, Particles

What sort of structure does it have? atoms and molecules is
what it interacts with.

What is its extent in space? ___*100- 300 Km above*___

What is its extent in time? ___*Artic, cold places, At night*___
___*time*___

Which properties are essential? ___*~~At night time~~ atoms,*___
___*molecus struck by electricly ta Partides.*___

Which are accidental? ___*the color, shape, height*___

STEP THREE: **Two-level outline**

Now that you've seen how the author E. C. Pielou describes the essential and accidental properties in an essay, look a little more closely at the way in which he organizes his thoughts.

Complete the following two-level outline of the passage. If you have trouble, ask your instructor for help.

I. *Appearance*

   A. *Shape*

   B. *Color*

II.   Sound

   A. *Silent*

   B. *noises around*

III. *Causes*

   A. *light*

   B. Colors

Day Three: Write About Essential and Accidental Properties

Focus: Writing answers to the question
"What is it?"

Today you'll prepare to write an explanation by definition that answers the questions about essential and accidental properties. Your finished composition will be at least 150 words in length (but can be longer if you want).

You'll write about volcanoes and volcanic eruptions—the same topic you covered in Level One when you wrote scientific descriptions. But this week's composition will be much more closely focused on the *properties* of the volcano.

STEP ONE: **Read**

Read back through the questions you'll be asking one more time. Then, read through the following passages without stopping to take notes.

Jacqueline Dineen, *Natural Disasters: Volcanoes* (Mankato, Minn.: The Creative Company, 2005), pp. 6–10.

(6) Volcanoes are openings in the surface of the earth, from which molten rock, called magma, and gases can escape.

The earth is made up of three layers—the crust, the mantle, and the core. The crust is the outermost layer of rock and can be quite thin. The continental crust is between 18 and 30 miles thick, but the oceanic crust is only about 3 miles thick.

The crust feels solid, but it consists of giant plates . . . that float on the upper mantle. The upper mantle is made of hot, molten rock called magma, which is always moving. Pressure in the mantle forces magma to the surface.

Volcanic eruptions occur where the rising magma finds a way through a crack or weakness in the earth's crust, usually at the edges of plates. These are called plate margins . . .

(10) Volcanoes are, in a sense, the safety valves in the earth's crust, releasing the build-up of pressure caused by gases beneath the earth's surface.

The strength of a volcanic eruption depends on the type of magma and the amount of gases trapped in it. The magma formed when plates pull apart is very fluid. The gases in it have time to escape and there is no volcanic eruption. When the plates collide, however, the magma formed is much thicker and stickier. Gases become trapped in it and escape explosively in a huge cloud of steam and dust thousands of feet high. Surges of red-hot lava flood out of the volcano's crater at speeds of up to 600 feet per second. Lava will flow from the volcano as long as there is enough pressure to force it to the surface. After such violent eruptions, the entire volcano often collapses into its empty magma chamber, forming a steep-sided depression called a caldera.

Peter Clarkson, *Volcanoes* (Stillwater, Minn.: Voyageur Press, Inc., 2000), pp. 7–8.

(7) In July 1963 a trip to Iceland opened my eyes to all manner of volcanic phenomena. I marveled at real volcanic craters; bubbling springs of boiling mud; hot pools that suddenly drained for a few seconds before exploding vertically in a geyser; streams flowing from beneath glaciers with sulfur-coated rocks in their beds, indicating thermal activity under the ice . . . A small cone of ash had been breached by the sea on one side and, as each new wave flowed into the crater, the volcano responded with an explosive ejection of ash and rock mixed with a cloud of steam. I remember feeling warm inside the aircraft but I suspect this was excitement rather than temperature . . .

(8) Anyone who has seen a volcano in eruption will be overawed by the display of immense power that the Earth exhibits. The column of smoke may rise several miles into the atmosphere; streams of lava may flow down the mountainside burning everything in their paths; explosive activity may remove a large part of the original structure of the mountain by reducing it to a dust that is shot into the air. Rocks as large as houses may be thrown hundreds of feet into the air and a blanket of ash may settle over the land, burning and suffocating all life beneath its pall.

Pliny the Younger, "Pliny to Tacitus," trans. Cynthia Damon. In Ronald Mellor, ed., *The Historians of Ancient Rome: An Anthology of the Major Writings,* second ed. (New York: Routledge, 2004), pp. 534–536.

The following passage is from a letter written in 79 AD by Pliny the Younger to the historian Tacitus. Pliny the Younger survived the eruption of Mount Vesuvius, which destroyed the Italian city of Pompeii.

(534) The carts that we had ordered brought were moving in opposite directions, though the ground was perfectly flat, and they wouldn't stay in place even with their wheels blocked by stones. In addition, it seemed as though the sea was being sucked backwards, as if it were being pushed back

by the shaking of the land. Certainly the shoreline moved outwards, and many sea creatures were left on dry sand. Behind us were frightening dark clouds, rent by lightning twisted and hurled, opening to reveal huge figures of flame. These were like lightning, but bigger. At that point the Spanish friend urged us strongly: "If your brother and uncle is alive, he wants you to be safe. If he has perished, he wanted you to survive him. So why are you reluctant to (535) escape?" We responded that we would not look to our own safety as long as we were uncertain about his. Waiting no longer, he took himself off from the danger at a mad pace. It wasn't long thereafter that the cloud stretched down to the ground and covered the sea. It girdled Capri and made it vanish, it hid Misenum's promontory. Then my mother began to beg and urge and order me to flee however I might, saying that a young man could make it, that she, weighed down in years and body, would die happy if she escaped being the cause of my death. I replied that I wouldn't save myself without her, and then I took her hand and made her walk a little faster. She obeyed with difficulty, and blamed herself for delaying me.

Now came the dust, though still thinly. I look back: a dense cloud looms behind us, following us like a flood poured across the land. "Let us turn aside while we can still see, lest we be knocked over in the street and crushed by the crowd of our companions." We had scarcely sat down when a darkness came that was not like a moonless or cloudy night, but more like the black of closed and unlighted rooms. . . . It grew lighter, though that seemed not a return of day, but a sign that the fire was approaching. The fire itself actually stopped some distance away, but darkness and ashes came again, a great weight of them. We stood up and shook the ash off again and again, otherwise we would have been covered with it and crushed by the weight. I might boast that no groan escaped me in such perils, no cowardly word, but that I believed that I was perishing with the world, and the world with me, which was a great consolation for death.

STEP TWO: **Take notes**

Now you'll take notes for your own description. The description should cover both the volcano and the volcanic eruption, since the eruption answers the question "How does it behave?"

Today, try a slightly different method of taking notes.

On your own paper, write each question and then look for the answers to that question in the passages provided. Jot down the answers. Be sure to record the author and page number of the passage where you found specific pieces of information.

Here's an example of how some of your answers might look:

Question: What does it resemble?
Answer: A "safety valve in the earth's crust" (Dineen, p. 10)
    Rocks might be "as large as houses" (Clarkson, p. 8)
    Eruption has flames "like lightning, but bigger" (Pliny, p. 534)
    Cloud of ash "like a flood poured across the land" (Pliny, p. 535)
    Dark "like the black of closed and unlighted rooms" (Pliny, p. 535)

Question: What sorts of measurements (temperature, quantity, time, etc.) are necessary to
    your observation?
    Answer: Size, quantity, time, temperature

You would not need to have all of these answers, but you should aim to have at least two answers for each question. Some of the questions may not be addressed at all. If you find no answers, draw a line through the question and continue on.

Writers work in different ways. Some writers find it easier to take many notes and then go back through them, looking for a theme to emerge. Others find it easier to settle on a tentative theme first and then take very specific notes supporting it. As you continue to write, you'll find out which method suits you best.

Before you move on to the next step, show your work to your instructor.

STEP THREE: **Organize**

Finish up today's work by organizing your answers into groups.

You should be able to divide your answers into two main groups—because there are actually two separate (but related) objects/phenomena described. Volcanoes are described, but so are volcanic eruptions.

Organize your answers into the following two groups:

    I. Volcano
    II. Eruption

When you're finished organizing your answers, show your work to your instructor.

Day Four: Write About Essential and Accidental Properties

 Focus: Writing answers to the question "What is it?"

STEP ONE: **Write**

Now that your answers have been organized into the proper order, write the description. Keep the following rules in mind:

1) The description should have at least two paragraphs and be at least 150 words in length. Longer is just fine.

2) Cite each source at least one time. When you cite Pliny's letter in your footnote, use the following format:

> Pliny the Younger, "Pliny to Tacitus," trans. Cynthia Damon, in Ronald Mellor, ed., *The Historians of Ancient Rome: An Anthology of the Major Writings,* second ed. (Routledge, 2004), p. 534–535.

When you cite a work from a larger collection, you put the name of the work being cited in quotation marks and the name of the larger collection/book in italics.

3) Use at least one metaphor or simile—either from your sources, or from your own imagination.

Remember: you do *not* have to use all of the quotes and answers you've collected! Nor is it necessary for you to answer every question. For example, there's no reason in this particular description to explain to the reader that your observation of the volcano is passive, or that you are using the sense of sight. These questions will be much more useful to you when you do your own scientific observation instead of basing your work on what other people have written. Right now, you are just practicing the skill of sorting through details and putting them together into readable prose.

STEP TWO: **Assemble the Works Cited page**

Title a separate piece of paper "Works Cited." List your sources in alphabetical order. The letter by Pliny should be listed in the same format as in your lesson. Alphabetize Pliny under "P."

STEP THREE: **Title your description**

Now choose a title for your description.

In Week 9 you learned the following steps for choosing a title:

1. What is the event, person, place, or process that your composition discusses? Jot it down on a scratch piece of paper.

2. Now, think about the *topos:* explanation by definition, with a focus on the essential and accidental properties of a scientific object or phenomenon.

Can you come up with a phrase that includes both the event/person/place/process *and* a description of the *topos?*

Center your title at the top of the first page of your composition. Double-space between the title and the top line of your first paragraph.

If you need help, ask your instructor.

STEP FOUR: **Proofread**

Before handing your paper to your instructor, go through the following proofreading steps.

1) Read your paper out loud, listening for awkward or unclear sections and repeated words. Rewrite awkward or unclear sentences so that they flow more naturally.

2) Read through the paper one more time, looking for sentence fragments, run-on sentences, and repeated words. Correct fragments and run-on sentences. If you used the same noun or verb more than twice, pick an alternative from the thesaurus. If you used a modifier (adverb, adjective, or prepositional phrase acting as an adjective or adverb) more than once, find another word.

3) Check the format of your footnotes and Works Cited page.

4) Check your spelling by looking, individually, at each word that might be a problem.

When you are finished, give your paper to your instructor for evaluation.

Week 13: Explanation
By Definition: Function

This week, you'll work on the second part of an explanation by way of definition.

A fully-developed definition answers three questions:

What is it? [Essential and accidental properties]

How does it work?

Where does it belong?

Last week, you worked on describing the essential and accidental properties of an object or phenomenon. This week, you'll answer the second question: "How does it work?" (What is its *function*?)

Day One: Function

Focus: Answering the question
"How does it work?"

You won't be writing today—just reading and thinking. Complete the following steps *slowly and carefully!*

STEP ONE: Understand function

When you answered the question "What is it?", you painted a picture of what the object looks like—its essential and accidental properties. But you need more than this to really understand what an object or phenomenon *is*.

Read the following definition of a machine:

> There in the flickering light of the lamp was the machine sure enough, squat, ugly, and askew; a thing of brass, ebony, ivory, and translucent glimmering quartz. Solid to the touch—for I put out my hand and felt the rail of it—and with brown spots and smears upon the ivory, and bits of grass and moss upon the lower parts, and one rail bent awry.

171

This tells you what the machine looks like, what it resembles, what it is made of, its structure and extent in space—but your understanding of the machine is still incomplete, because you don't know what it *does*. Until the reader can understand the **function** of the machine, it remains mysterious.

Now read on:

> I gave it a last tap, tried all the screws again, put one more drop of oil on the quartz rod, and sat myself in the saddle . . . I took the starting lever in one hand and the stopping one in the other, pressed the first, and almost immediately the second. I seemed to reel; I felt a nightmare sensation of falling; and, looking round, I saw the laboratory exactly as before. Had anything happened ? For a moment I suspected that my intellect had tricked me. Then I noted the clock. A moment before, as it seemed, it had stood at a minute or so past ten; now it was nearly half-past three!
>
> I drew a breath, set my teeth, gripped the starting lever with both my hands, and went off with a thud. The laboratory got hazy and went dark . . . I pressed the lever over to its extreme position. The night came like the turning out of a lamp, and in another moment came tomorrow. The laboratory grew faint and hazy, then fainter and ever fainter. Tomorrow night came black, then day again, night again, day again, faster and faster still . . . I saw trees growing and changing like puffs of vapor, now brown, now green; they grew, spread, fluctuated, and passed away. I saw huge buildings rise up faint and fair, and pass like dreams. The whole surface of the earth seemed changing—melting and flowing under my eyes. The little hands upon the dials that registered my speed raced round faster and faster. Presently I noted that the sun belt swayed up and down, from solstice to solstice, in a minute or less, and that, consequently, my pace was over a year a minute; and minute by minute the white snow flashed across the world and vanished, and was followed by the bright, brief green of spring.

Now that you've read about how the machine works, do you have a better idea of what it is? The answer follows . . . so if you want to answer the question on your own, think of an explanation before you go on.

Both passages come from the *The Time Machine* by H. G. Wells.[35] The machine is a time machine that shoots into the future, stopping at AD 802,701—hundreds of thousands of years away.

The answer to "How does it work?" often overlaps with the answer to "How does it behave?" (one of the "essential and accidental properties" questions). But "How does it work?"

---

35. H.G. Wells, *The Time Machine: An Invention* (Kettering: Manor House, 1895), p. 210.

is a much more specific question. It also encompasses, "How does it interact with other things?" In the case of the time machine, you discover the effect that the time machine has on the person who uses it. When you define the function of a living thing, such as a wildcat or a cell or a cactus, you talk about how it grows and thrives in nature and how it is used or affected by other objects. When you define the function of a phenomenon, such as a volcanic eruption or the aurora, you explain not only what conditions cause it and what it does, but what is affected by it.

Read the following definition of *soil*. Notice that the first two paragraphs tell you about the properties of soil, while the third paragraph describes how soil behaves—and how it interacts with both the person examining it, with plant roots, and with water and air.

Soil is the layer of transition between the rock core of the Earth and the web of life on its surface. It is a very thin layer, measured in inches or feet, but it is the basis for all that stands between life and lifelessness.

essential accidental prop

Soil is a complex and dynamic mixture of several components: rock and mineral particles, water and dissolved substances, air, living organisms, and more or less decomposed organic matter. An "ideal" soil is said to contain a little less than 50 percent solid particles, 25 percent air, and less than 5 percent living organisms and organic matter. In actual soils, of course, the relative proportions of these components vary from region to region, and the makeup of any given soil changes with the weather and the seasons.

Sandy soil has a coarse, grainy, gritty texture. If you squeeze a handful and release it, sandy soil falls apart and runs between your fingers. Wet or dry, sandy soil is easy to dig and till and easy for plant roots to penetrate. Water and air pass freely through the large pores between sand particles, and sandy soil dries out quickly after a rain and doesn't hold a large reservoir of water.[36]

function

STEP TWO: **Examine the questions about function**

When you define the function of an object or phenomenon, you have to answer three major questions:

How does it work or behave?
Who/what needs it or uses it?
For what purposes?

36. Rita Buchanan and Roger Holmes, eds., *Taylor's Master Guide to Gardening* (New York: Houghton Mifflin Co., 1994), p. 525.

To give good, complete answers to these larger questions, you'll probably need to ask a series of more focused questions:

> *How does it work or behave?*
>> *Will a descriptive sequence help the reader understand how it works? What would the sequence describe?*
>> *Is its behavior predictable or unpredictable?*
>> *Does it work/behave differently under different circumstances?*
>>> *At different times?*
>> *Can its behavior be divided into phases?*
>>> *What separates the phases?*
>> *Is there a cause or trigger for its behavior?*
>> *What is the time frame for its behavior?*
>> *Where does the behavior take place?*
> *Who/what needs it or uses it?*
>> *Is anything dependent on it?*
>> *Is it dependent on anything else?*
>> *Who/what affects its working/behavior?*
> *For what purposes?*
>> *Is there more than one purpose?*
>> *Does the purpose change at different times?*
>> *Is the purpose dependent on any other conditions?*

Although you wouldn't need to ask *all* of these questions for any one object or phenomenon, a selection of them may help you decide what details belong in your definition.

Read these questions out loud to your instructor now. If any of them confuse you, ask your instructor for help.

STEP THREE: **Practice the questions**

Now, you'll identify the answers to these questions for a scientific object or phenomenon right outside your window: a tree.

Choose a tree that you can see outside (or, if you can't see any trees, a kind of tree that you already know something about). On your own paper, jot down phrases or sentences answering the "function" questions above. You can skip questions that don't seem to apply—but be sure to answer at least five of the work/behavior questions, and at least two out of the three questions under *"Who/what needs it or uses it?"* and *"For what purposes"*?

As you did last week, you'll just practice *thinking* about this category. You won't be writing an essay about the tree.

When you are finished, show your answers to your instructor.

Day Two: Take Notes About Function

 Focus: Taking notes in answer to the question "How does it work?"

Today you'll prepare to write an explanation by definition that answers the questions about function. Your finished composition will be at least 150 words in length (but can be longer if you want).

You'll write about Venus flytraps, how they work, and how they fit into the ecosystem.

STEP ONE: **Read**

Read back through the questions on function one more time. Then, read through the following passages without stopping to take notes.

Carl Zimmer, "Fatal Attraction," *National Geographic,* March 2010, Vol. 217, Issue 3, pp. 80–82.

(82) A hungry fly darts through the pines in North Carolina. Drawn by what seems like the scent of nectar from a flowerlike patch of scarlet on the ground, the fly lands on the fleshy pad of a ruddy leaf. It takes a sip of the sweet liquid oozing from the leaf, brushing a leg against one tiny hair on its surface, then another. Suddenly the fly's world has walls around it. The two sides of the leaf are closing against each other, spines along its edges interlocking like the teeth of a jaw trap. As the fly struggles to escape, the trap squeezes shut. Now, instead of offering sweet nectar, the leaf unleashes enzymes that eat away at the fly's innards, gradually turning them into goo. The fly has suffered the ultimate indignity for an animal: It has been killed by a plant.

The swampy pine savanna within a 90-mile radius of Wilmington, North Carolina, is the one place on the planet where Venus flytraps are native. It is also home to a number of other species of carnivorous plants, less famous and more widespread but no less bizarre. You can find pitcher plants with leaves like champagne flutes, into which insects (and sometimes larger animals) lose themselves and die. Sundews envelop their victims in an embrace

of sticky tentacles. In ponds and streams grow bladderworts, which slurp up their prey like underwater vacuum cleaners.

There is something wonderfully unsettling about a plant that feasts on animals. Perhaps it is the way it shatters all expectation.

Matilda Gollon, ed., *The Big Idea Science Book* (New York: DK Publishing, 2010), p. 78.

You might think all plants rely only on photosynthesis or absorb all their nutrients from the soil. Think again! Plants live in a wide variety of biomes and habitats such as forest, desert, and marsh. They have evolved adaptations, characteristics that help them survive in stressful environments. Some plant adaptations are especially unique. Places like rain forests and many swamps, for example, have very little fertile soil. Plants that inhabit these places cannot depend on the soil to fulfill all their nutritional needs. They must find other ways to survive. Some live on nutrients left in the dead matter of other plants. Others actually trap, kill, and digest insects. Because some plants like Indian pipe (white waxy plants) lack chlorophyll, they cannot make their own food to live. Instead, they have a parasitic relationship with fungi, where the plant's roots tap into the fungi and take the nutrients they need.

The Venus flytrap lives in certain boggy areas of North and South Carolina. Because the soil cannot provide all its nutrients, the Venus flytrap evolved as a carnivorous plant. Carnivorous plants are adapted to attract, capture, digest, and absorb insects and other tiny animals. The flytrap's jawlike leaves secrete sweet-smelling nectar. When an unsuspecting insect tickles the trigger hairs, the leaves snap shut. Digestive fluids break down the insect's soft parts, and the leaves absorb the nutrients. The plant releases the exoskeleton days later.

The inside surface of each leaf typically has 6 trigger hairs.

The prey must touch 2 trigger hairs or the same hair twice within about 20 seconds for the trap to close.

Audrey Anderson, "The Venus Flytrap's Circle of Life"

With deadly fangs that snap shut around its prey, the carnivorous Venus flytrap seems more at home in a science fiction film than in the backwoods of North or South Carolina. This unusual plant responds to a lack of nitrogen in the soil by capturing nutrient-laden flies and feasting upon them. Though quite intimidating in nature, the Venus flytrap is actually a small plant, about six inches in size, typically with seven leaves or fewer. At the end of each leaf is the flytrap, resembling an open clamshell with spiny, interlocking teeth. In good conditions, the perennial Venus flytrap produces lovely white flowers every spring.

How is a quiet swamp plant like the Venus flytrap capable of exhibiting such aggressive behavior? When the fly lands on the rosy leaves of the flytrap, his legs brush against tiny hairs on the trap. If only one hair is touched, nothing happens. This keeps the Venus flytrap from eagerly snapping shut every time a grain of sand or a raindrop falls on its leaf. But a lively little fly will most likely touch at least two hairs. At this point, enough charge has built up in the leaves that they snap shut, locking their spiky teeth together. Once the fly has been trapped, the hungry plant begins to secrete enzymes that turn its prey into an easily digested snack. The whole process takes about two weeks, after which the trap reopens, ready to lure its next victim.

The Venus flytrap's ingenious methods of carnivorousness do not protect it from typical plant predators such as raccoons, rodents, or caterpillars. Ironically, tiny aphids and grasshoppers will sometimes feast on the flytrap, if they manage to escape being eaten themselves. Without any poisons or systems of defense, the Venus flytrap may become a meal for a hungry mouse or caterpillar making its way through a swamp in North Carolina. Fortunately for the flytrap, its composition and texture make it an unpopular choice for most predators. However, if hungry enough, a swamp rat will make a meal out of the little plant. And for a brief moment, the flies all breathe a sigh of relief.

Michael Tierra, *Treating Cancer with Herbs: An Integrative Approach* (Twin Lakes, Minn.: Lotus Press, 2003), p. 157.

Dr. Helmut Keller, M.D., an oncologist and medical director of the Chronic Disease Control and Treatment Center in Bad Steben, Germany, first studied the Venus flytrap at Boston University in 1980. In order to find more support and freedom for his research he moved to Germany a year later. Carnivora® is a drug derived from the sterilized fresh juices of the Venus flytrap, which is native to the wet pinelands and sandy bays of North and South Carolina. Dr. Heller claims promising therapeutic results from its use for a variety of conditions including various types of cancer. Proponents of Carnivora® claim that it works to shrink solid tumors, but has no effect on non-solid cancers such as leukemia. It also stimulates the immune system to assist its anticancer properties. They also believe that it works best for those individuals who have not undergone chemo or radiation therapy.

STEP TWO: **Taking and organizing notes**

Now you'll take notes for your own description.

As you did last week, organize your notes as you take them. On your own paper, write each question, and then look for the answers to that question in the passages provided. Write down the answers. Be sure to record the author and the page number of where you found specific pieces of information. If there is no page number provided, record only the author's name.

You do not have to answer every question! For example, the passages don't really tell you whether the behavior of the Venus flytrap is predictable or unpredictable. You can deduce that it is predictable, but since the passages don't address this question directly, it's not an important or useful one for this particular topic.

When you're working through the descriptive sequence (under the main question "How does it work/behave?"), you may find it helpful to number the steps of the process by which the flytrap catches and eats its prey. Your notes would resemble the following:

Will a descriptive sequence help the reader understand how it works?
1. The flytrap produces "a sweet-smelling nectar" (Gollon, p. 78)
2. A fly is tempted by "the scent of nectar" (Zimmer, p. 82)
3.
4.
5. . . .
and so on.

As you answer the second and third questions (*Who/what needs it or uses it?* and *For what purposes?*) you might find it useful to put your notes into two columns, like this (one example of an answer is provided):

Who/what needs it?	**For what purpose(s)?**
Who/what uses it?	**For what purpose(s)?**
Aphids, grasshoppers, raccoons, rodents, caterpillars	Food (Anderson)
Is anything dependent on it?	**For what purpose(s)?**
Is it dependent on anything else?	**For what purpose(s)?**
Who/what affects its working/behavior?	**How?**

When you are finished, show your work to your instructor.

Day Three: Write About Function

Focus: Writing answers to the question
"How does it work?"

STEP ONE: Write

Now, use your notes to write a definition of the Venus flytrap that focuses on the *function* of the plant. Follow the basic order of your notes:

1) First, answer the question "How does it work/behave?"
2) Second, answer the questions "Who/what needs it or uses it? For what purpose?"

Follow these additional guidelines:

3) The description should have at least two paragraphs and be at least 150 words in length. Longer is just fine.

4) Be sure to cite each source at least one time. You will be citing two unusual sources this time, one from a magazine article (the Zimmer article), and one source written especially for this textbook (the Anderson passage). Use the following format for your footnotes:

Carl Zimmer, "Fatal Attraction," *National Geographic* (March 2010, Vol. 217:3), p. 82.

Audrey Anderson, "The Venus Flytrap's Circle of Life." In *Writing With Skill, Level Two* (Peace Hill Press, 2013), p. 176–177.

Remember, when you cite a work from a larger collection, which includes an article in a magazine, you put the name of the work being cited in quotation marks and the name of the larger collection/book in italics.

5) Use at least one metaphor or simile from your own imagination.

6) Use transitional words such as "first," "next," or "finally" when you describe the sequence of the Venus flytrap's function.

Remember: you do *not* have to use all of the quotes and answers you've collected! Although you should give a detailed description of function, you do not need to answer all questions—as long as your finished composition is the proper length.

Note that correct spellings of the plant include *Venus flytrap, Venus Flytrap, Venus' flytrap, Venus Fly Trap,* and *Venus's Fly-trap.* Choose one spelling and stick with it.

STEP TWO: **Assemble Works Cited Page**

Title a separate piece of paper "Works Cited." List your sources in alphabetical order.

   The Anderson piece should be listed as:

   Anderson, Audrey. "The Venus Flytrap's Circle of Life." In *Writing With Skill, Level Two*. Charles City: Peace Hill Press, 2013, pp. 176–177

   The Zimmer piece should be listed as:

   Zimmer, Carl. "Fatal Attraction." In *National Geographic,* March 2010, Vol. 217, Issue 3, pp. 80–82.

STEP THREE: **Title your composition**

Now choose a title for your essay. You may look back at Day Four, Step Three of last week if you need to review.

   Remember to center your title at the top of the first page of your composition. Double-space between the title and the top line of your first paragraph.

   As always, if you need help, ask your instructor.

STEP FOUR: **Proofread**

Before handing your paper to your instructor, go through the following proofreading steps.

   1) Read your paper out loud, listening for awkward or unclear sections and repeated words. Rewrite awkward or unclear sentences so that they flow more naturally.

   2) Read through the paper one more time, looking for sentence fragments, run-on sentences, and repeated words. Correct fragments and run-on sentences. If you used the same noun or verb more than twice, pick an alternative from the thesaurus. If you used a modifier (adverb, adjective, or prepositional phrase acting as an adjective or adverb) more than once, find another word.

   3) Check the format of your footnotes and Works Cited page.

   4) Check your spelling by looking, individually, at each word that might be a problem.

When you are finished, give your paper to your instructor for evaluation.

Day Four: Copia

Focus: Understanding and using
phrase-for-word substitution

STEP ONE: Understanding phrase-for-word substitution

When you were introduced to the first *copia* exercises, back in Week 16 of Level One, you were also introduced to the Renaissance scholar and theologian Desiderius Erasmus, who took the sentence "Your letter pleased me greatly" and rephrased it 195 different ways.

Among those sentences were:

> The words from your pen brought joy.
> The pages I received from you sent a new light of joy stealing over my heart.
> Your pearls of wisdom gave me pleasure.

All three of these sentences have the same basic structure as the original—there's a subject, an action verb, and a direct object. But in each of them, Erasmus has substituted a phrase (or clause)[37] for the noun "letter."

	S		V	DO
	<u>letter</u>		<u>pleased</u>	me

	S		V	DO
<u>words from your pen</u>			<u>brought</u>	joy

	S		V	DO
<u>pages I received from you</u>			<u>sent</u>	light

	S		V	IO	DO
<u>pearls of wisdom</u>			<u>gave</u>	me	pleasure

In each sentence, the phrase acts in exactly the same way as the original subject noun.

The first two sentences use very literal phrases in place of the noun "letter." What is a letter made up of? Words written on paper. "Words written on paper" could be substituted for "letter." Where did the words come from? Well, your brain ("Words from your brain" might

---

37. Just for your information: A *phrase* is a grouping of words that has a single grammatical function. A *clause* is different from a phrase in that it contains a verb. "Words from your pen" is a phrase (with no verb in it). "I <u>received</u> from you" is a clause that describes "pages" (verb is underlined).

work too), but in a very basic sense, the words came from the end of your pen. In the same way, the letter is, physically, pages that arrived because they were sent.

The third sentence uses a metaphor. You reviewed metaphors back in Week 6 (and if you don't remember the difference between a metaphor and a simile, go back and review Day Four of Week 5 *and* Day Four of Week 6 now). A metaphor describes something by comparing it to something else. Wise words from a loved one's letter are treasured. Pearls are treasured. So the letter can become "pearls of wisdom."

A third way to substitute a phrase for a word is to use a *kenning*—a method common in Norse and Old English poetry. A *kenning* substitutes a description of some quality that the noun possesses, or some function that it performs, for the noun itself. So, for example, an *arrow* might become a "slaughter shaft," or blood a "hot battle-sweat." Instead of *body,* a Norse poet might use the phrase "house for the bones." The *sea* becomes the "whale road," ships become "wave floaters."

Sometimes, using a phrase for a word can make a sentence too complicated and wordy, but phrase-for-word substitution can also make your writing more vivid, poetic, and engaging.

STEP TWO: **Changing whole phrases to words**

Each one of the following sentences contains an underlined phrase that has been substituted for a noun. Write a plain noun that could be used in place of each phrase on the blank line.

Be sure to get up before the lighting of the sky candle. ___Sunrise___

The groaning board was piled with cakes, cookies, and pies. ___table___

He peeled the elongated yellow fruit thoughtfully. ___banana___

The vitamin-laden liquid comes from cows. ___milk___

I was just admiring the fringed curtain of your eye. ___eyelashes___

He drove away in his shiny new status symbol. ___car___

Harry Potter's greatest enemy is He Who Must Not Be Named. ___Voldemort___

Just let me turn on the darkness destroyer. _____

I'm going to see a performance of the Scottish play. _____

STEP THREE: **Add to the Sentence Variety chart**

Add the following principle and illustration to the Sentence Variety chart.

word ⟶ phrase describing what the word is or does	letter ⟶ words from your pen
metaphor	letter ⟶ pearls of wisdom
kenning	sea ⟶ whale road

STEP FOUR: **Inventing and substituting new phrases for words**

The following sentences are taken from "The Lady Who Put Salt in Her Coffee," the first chapter of Lucretia P. Hale's classic novel *The Peterkin Papers*. For each underlined word, come up with two phrases that you can substitute for the original noun. One phrase should be based on the word's literal meaning; the other should involve a metaphor.

When you are finished, read the sentences aloud to your instructor, substituting the new phrases. Which versions of the sentences do you prefer?

It was a <u>mistake</u>.

_____ *wrong doing* _____

She had poured out a delicious cup of coffee, and, just as she was helping herself to cream, she found she had put in <u>salt</u> instead of <u>sugar</u>.

_____ *Spice instead of sweets* _____

_____

The <u>family</u> came in; they all tasted, and looked, and wondered what should be done, and all sat down to think.

_____ *group* _____

At last Agamemnon, who had been to <u>college</u>, said, "Why don't we go over and ask the advice of the chemist?"

_____ *School* _____

First he looked at the <u>coffee</u>, and then stirred it.

_____ *bean juice* _____

The herb-woman lived down at the very end of the street; so the boys put on their india-rubber boots again, and they set off.

Spice lady

As soon as the little old woman came, she had it set over the fire, and began to stir in the different herbs.

Flame

The children tasted after each mixture, but made up dreadful faces.

Kids

Week 14: Explanation By Definition: Genus

Remember, a fully-developed definition answers three questions:
> *What is it?* [Essential and accidental properties]
> *How does it work?* [Function]
> *Where does it belong?*

This week, you'll work on the third and final part of a definition: "Where does it belong?"

Day One: Introduction to Genus

Focus: Answering the question
"Where does it belong?"

STEP ONE: **Understand genus**

When you answer the question "Where does it belong?" you are describing the *genus* of the object or phenomenon you're defining.

You may have come across the word "genus" in your science studies. In modern biology, living things are divided up first into one of five *kingdoms* (protist, fungus, plant, bacteria, animal); then, each of the kingdoms is divided up into different *phyla* (so, for example, the plant kingdom is divided into five *phyla*—algae, mosses, ferns, trees with cones, and flowering trees and plants); then, each phylum is further divided into classes . . . and so on. You may have seen the following chart in your biology book:

Kingdom
Phylum
Class
Order
Family
Genus
Species

For the biologist, a *genus* is a class that contains several different species (so, for example, the Scots Pine tree is a species of pine tree that belongs to the genus *Pinus,* along with the species Red Pine, Japanese Black Pine, Arizona Pine, and others).

When Aristotle talked about *genus,* he meant something a little bit less scientific. For Aristotle, finding the *genus* of something was a way of grouping it together with things that were like it—and different from it. When he spoke of *genus,* he wanted to know: What larger group does it belong to?

So when you determine the genus of something, you look back at its essential and accidental properties, and you think about its function. And then you ask yourself: What other objects or phenomena have these properties, or function in this way?

There is often more than one way to answer this question. Think back to Week 12, when you studied essential and accidental properties. You listed the properties of a volcano. What other objects or phenomena have these properties, or function in this way?

Volcanoes and earthquakes both happen at plate margins, when tectonic plates shift—so you could identify volcanoes as belonging to the larger group "Phenomena caused by shifting tectonic plates." If you then investigated what other phenomena are caused by shifting tectonic plates, you'd discover that both mountains and oceanic trenches belong to the same group.

On the other hand, volcanoes also explode—a quality that earthquakes, mountains, and oceanic trenches don't share. What other objects in nature explode? Supernovas and solar flares are both explosions. Avalanches are a type of natural explosion. So are meteor impacts—and lightning strikes.

What's the purpose of identifying *genus*?

Grouping your object (or phenomenon) together with others forces you to think about *why* you're defining it—what the ultimate point of your essay will be. When you write about volcanoes, are you focusing in on a volcano as just one of the many things that happen at the edges of the earth's plates—simply another example of what shifts in the earth's crust bring about? Or will you present the volcano as one of the most destructive forces in nature—an explosive phenomenon that destroys everything it touches?

Like the questions you've asked about properties and function, questions about genus force you to think more deeply about what you're writing. (And that's why writing is such hard work—because you have to *think* in order to do it well.)

STEP TWO: **Examine the questions about genus**

Asking the following questions will help you think more deeply about genus.

You'll start by asking three basic questions:

> *What other objects or phenomena can it be grouped with?*
> *What are the qualities that lead you to group them together?*
> *What name can you give this group?*

In the case of the volcano, if you grouped it along with lightning, meteor strikes, and avalanches, you would be thinking about the volcano's explosion and its destructive power as the central qualities of the volcano—as opposed to its location at the edge of the earth's tectonic plates.

What name would you give this group? You don't have to get complicated: "Things That Explode in Nature" or "Destructive Natural Phenomena" would work.

You would then need to ask one more question:

> *In what significant ways is it different from the others in its group?*

Aristotle thought that finding genus also involved finding what he called "divisions"—differences between your object and other objects in the same group. If you were to group a volcano along with lightning, meteor strikes, and avalanches, you would also include in your description of genus the information that the volcano, unlike the other three, spews molten lava. Explosive, destructive power *groups* the volcano *together* with lightning, meteor strikes, and avalanches; lava *differentiates* it from the others.

Now read all four questions out loud to your instructor (this forces you to slow down and think).

STEP THREE: **Practice the questions**

Now you'll practice these questions.

Go back to Week 12, Day Two. Reread the description of the *aurora borealis* and look back through your answers to the question about its properties.

Now, jot down on your own paper answers to the following questions:

> *What other objects or phenomena can it be grouped with?*
> *What are the qualities that lead you to group them together?*
> *What name can you give this group?*
> *In what significant ways is it different from the others in its group?*

To answer these questions, you might need to do some investigation.

You can start with an encyclopedia or with Wikipedia. Although you should be suspicious of information found on Wikipedia (see Week 8, Day One, if you don't remember why), Wikipedia can be a good starting place when you're unfamiliar with a subject—particularly if you're reading up on subjects that don't arouse strong emotions in people. (For example, I'd be more inclined to trust Wikipedia's information about the chemical composition of fool's gold than its entry on the aims of the Republican Party or the responsibilities of the Pope.)

You can then follow up by doing an online book search for terms you find in the encyclopedia or Wikipedia.

Identifying genus often takes a little bit of additional research, since your original source materials may not include the information about *other* objects and phenomena that you need. Remember this—and make sure to allow time for it in future projects.

Ask your instructor for assistance if you need it. And when you're finished, show your work to your instructor.

Day Two: Take Notes on Properties or Function

 Focus: Preparing to answer the question "Where does it belong?"

Today you'll prepare to write an explanation by definition that answers last lesson's questions.

Before you can assign an object or phenomenon to a larger group, you have to know something about it—which means that you have to answer either the questions about properties, or the questions about function (or possibly even both!) before you can think about genus.

STEP ONE: Prepare

Start out by reviewing the questions about properties and function. Read these out loud to your instructor now.

Essential Properties and Accidental Properties
What does it look like?
How does it behave?
What senses come into play as you observe it?
What do those senses reveal?
Is your observation passive (watching/listening) or active (experimenting/collecting/probing)?
What sorts of measurements (temperature, quantity, time, etc.) are necessary to your observation?
What does it resemble?
What is it made of?

What sort of structure does it have?
What is its extent in space?
What is its extent in time?
Which properties are essential?
Which are accidental?

Function

How does it work or behave?
Will a descriptive sequence help the reader understand how it works?
   What would this sequence describe?
Is its behavior predictable or unpredictable?
Does it work/behave differently under different circumstances?
   At different times?
Can its behavior be divided into phases?
   What separates the phases?
Is there a cause or trigger for its behavior?
What is the time frame for its behavior?
Where does the behavior take place?
Who/what needs it or uses it?
   Is anything dependent on it?
   Is it dependent on anything else?
   Who/what affects its working/behavior?
For what purposes?
   Is there more than one purpose?
   Does the purpose change at different times?
   Is the purpose dependent on any other conditions?

STEP TWO: **Read**

Now that you've reviewed the questions, read through the following passages without stopping to take notes.

Craig Wallin, *Golden Harvest: How to Grow the Four Most Profitable Specialty Crops* (Anacortes, Wash.: HeadStart Publishing, 2012), p. 6.

> Bamboo has been called "the most useful plant in the world," and for more than half the human race that depend on it, life would be much different without it. This amazing plant, with over one thousand species, has qualities found in no other plant. For example:
>
> Some bamboo varieties can reach 120 feet in height, with hollow stems a foot in diameter.

Bamboo is the world's fastest growing plant. The record is 47.6 inches of growth in 24 hours.

Bamboo is tough. A grove of bamboo at ground zero in Hiroshima survived the atomic blast, and sprouted new shoots just days after the blast.

Bamboo is versatile, with over 1,500 products from medicines to scaffoldings.

Bamboo is native to every continent except Europe and Antarctica. It is found from the tropics to mountain tops. India has the largest reserves, with over 25 million acres.

Throughout Asia, bamboo is prized for its abundance and versatility. In China, it's called "friend of the people." The Chinese have long appreciated the beauty of bamboo. Chinese legend honored bamboo as one of the four "noble" plants, along with the orchid, plum and chrysanthemum.

Contrary to popular belief, bamboo is not a tree, but a primitive member of the grass family. Like grass, bamboo has a jointed hollow stem and rapid growth. The hollow stem, or cane, is called the "culm." Instead of roots, bamboo has rhizomes that spread out horizontally up to ten feet a year and form an interlocking web underground. This web of rhizomes prevents the earth from coming apart, which is why the Japanese have always considered a bamboo grove as one of the safest places during an earthquake.

Gale Beth Goldberg, *Bamboo Style* (Layton, Utah: Gibbs Smith, Publisher, 2002), p. 14.

The physiology of this remarkable plant is complex. Technically, it is a grass. Depending on growing conditions, some species stay low to the ground, reaching only six to twelve inches high. Other giant grasses tower above at heights of more than a hundred feet. Some plants are pencil-thin; others have diameters of nearly a foot. Some are hollow between the nodes; others are solid. Some gracefully grow tall and straight; others are irregularly shaped with crooks and bends and alternating humps, much like the protective shells turtles carry with them . . .

While trees contain cellulose fibers that are made only of lignin, bamboos contain cellulose fibers with lignin and silica—the same hard, glassy substance found in sand, and a big factor in bamboo's high density, strength, and hardness. Bamboo fibers are nearly ten times as long as those found in trees.

During bamboo's growth activity aboveground, the rhizomes, or underground stems, are also busy. The gnarly, dense network with smaller intertwining roots spreads to create a strong foundation in a growing zone found about two to three feet below the soil's surface.

Nancy Moore Bess, *Bamboo in Japan* (New York: Kodansha America, Inc., 2001), p. 65.

Bamboo serves many functions in the Japanese kitchen, but bamboo baskets make the most obvious contribution. Many home kitchens have five to ten *zaru,* simple woven bamboo basket-trays used to drain and rinse *soba* noodles, spinach, and blocks of tofu. In *soba* shops, cold *soba* noodles, the connoisseur's choice, are served on a square lacquered *zaru.* In displays and advertisements, the *zaru* is used to display seasonal fruit, freshly caught fish, or the first bamboo shoots of spring . . .

Another small basket—lidded, rectangular, and woven of fine *sasa* bamboo—is used as a lunch box (*o-bento*) throughout Japan. In competition with the brightly colored plastic version decorated with images of favorite cartoon characters, these baskets, lined with bamboo leaves (which are naturally anti-bacterial) and filled with rice, pickles, and a favorite treat, still appear at family outings and occasionally in the classroom . . .

Bamboo scoops for rice and round banded trays for steaming are still common in the Japanese kitchen . . . A variety of bamboo storage baskets are found in many Japanese homes, particularly in rural areas.

Daphne Lewis and Carol A. Miles, *Farming Bamboo* (Washington, D.C.: Smithsonian Institute/Daphne B. Lewis and Carol Miles, 2007), p. 2.

Bamboo can be grown to produce food and poles, to diversify farm operations, to spread labor needs over the year, and, of course, to increase farm income. Shoots are harvested in the spring and poles are harvested in summer and/or late winter. Leaves from harvested poles can be fed to livestock or made into silage. Bamboo can serve other purposes on the farm in addition to those of a cash crop. Bamboo groves can screen the farm from roads and neighbors, provide shade for pastures and farm buildings, and catch dust. It can thereby minimize the impact of farm operations on neighbors. Bamboo groves can protect riparian zones by capturing runoff that carries excess fertilizer and manure from pastures, fields and paddocks. The interwoven rhizome and root system can hold soil and organic debris, preventing them from entering streams and ponds. Farmlands subject to seasonal flooding can be planted with bamboo to prevent soil erosion and crop loss. Bamboo is an evergreen plant so its landscape and environmental functions continue throughout the year.

Bamboo . . . canes can be used for poles, charcoal, paper pulp, rayon, and laminated wood products including plyboo and composites. Many lumber, fiber, paper and rayon products are made from recycled fibers plus a small amount of virgin fibers. These virgin fibers could be produced from bamboo to replace the virgin fiber that is currently harvested from national and state forestlands in the United States.

William Cullina, *Native Ferns, Moss, and Grasses: From Emerald Carpet to Amber Wave* (Boston: Houghton Mifflin, 2008), p. 131.

Bamboos are giant grasses aspiring to be woody plants. They have evolved incredibly strong, resilient perennial stems composed primarily of lignin and cellulose (the molecules that make wood strong), and they have a tensile or bending strength and flexibility that surpasses that of most trees. Each aerial stem, or culm, grows from a creeping rhizome, popping up almost overnight like a spear point thrust up from the netherworld. The base of the culm is wrapped by sheaths that are attached at a knuckled collar, which gives the culm its characteristic jointed appearance once the sheaths drop off. The sheaths do take a few months to fall off, but they quickly dry and turn papery tan, wrapping the new canes and giving them a very attractive, hyphenated look. A few feet up, sheaths give way to 6- to 12-inch long, bright green, lance-shaped leaves that alternate up the rest of the cane as it expands.

Expansion is the key to bamboo's fast growth. The spear-pointed new culms are nearly fully formed, compressed canes that simply expand like a telescope as they fill with water. This is the same way the new twig growth on many trees such as oaks and pines commences. This inflation is much faster than the incremental cell-by-cell growth seen on most grasses and other herbaceous plants, and it means the tender new shoots . . . can grow tall and harden off faster than the herbivores can eat them.

STEP THREE: **Take notes**

Decide whether you'd rather take notes about properties or about function. Answering either set of questions will give you enough information to assign bamboo to a genus (that will be tomorrow's project).

Whichever category of questions you decide on, go back through the readings now and use them to jot down answers to the questions on your own paper. Use the same method as last week; write down each question, and then note the answers, recording the author and page number of specific pieces of information. Here's an example from last week:

> *Is there a cause or trigger for its behavior?*
> **Cause: The flytrap is carnivorous because the soil it grows in "cannot provide all its nutrients" (Gollon, p. 78)**

Trigger: Insects landing on the leaves brush at least two of the trigger hairs "or the same hair twice within about 20 seconds" (Gollon, p. 78)

What is the time frame for its behavior?
About two weeks for digestion (Anderson)

Where does the behavior take place?
Where the plant grows, in the "swampy pine savanna within a 90-mile radius of Wilmington, NC" (Zimmer, p. 82)

If you need help, ask your instructor.

Day Three: Write About Genus

 Focus: Writing answers to the question "Where does it belong?"

Today, you'll write two separate (brief) answers to the question "Where does it belong?"

When you write an explanation by definition, the descriptions of properties and functions will take up most of the paper. Identifying genus will be the briefest part of your composition. So today, you'll simply write a couple of paragraphs that could be added to a longer paper. You won't have to come up with a title (although you'll still have to proofread and format your footnotes properly).

STEP ONE: Examine examples

When you define the genus of an object or phenomenon, you try to answer the following questions:

> *What other objects or phenomena can it be grouped with?*
> *What are the qualities that lead you to group them together?*
> *What name can you give this group?*
> *In what significant ways is it different from the others in its group?*

Before you write, look at the brief examples below. The first is from *Protozoans, Algae & Other Protists*, by Steve Parker.

> Although protists are almost everywhere you look, you cannot see them. They are mostly microscopic life-forms, each made of one living unit called a cell. Some protists are like tiny animals because they take in or eat

food. They are often called protozoans. Other protists, the protophytans, are like tiny plants because they use the sun's light energy to grow. Some protists have traits of both plants and animals.

There are thousands of kinds of protists. The tiniest are so small that a thousand would fit into this "o." Others, such as algae, can grow bigger than a person.[38]

In just a few sentences, the author identifies the quality that groups protists together into a single genus: they are one-celled organisms. He then tells you some of the ways in which protists differ: protozoans eat food, protophytans use sunlight; some protists are smaller than a letter of the alphabet, others bigger than human beings.

Here's a second example of identifying genus, this one about (once more) volcanoes.

A volcano is a hole, usually a crack, connecting the exterior and the interior of the earth; from it are ejected, often with explosive violence, various materials, which are generally at a high temperature.

Volcanoes may be divided into classes depending upon the frequency of the eruptions which take place. **Active** volcanoes are those from which an eruption can be expected at any time. If there is no cessation of activity . . . we have a *constant* volcano, like Stromboli [a Sicilian volcano which has been erupting for the past 200 years]. If the eruption is followed more or less regularly by a period of rest, such a volcano is called *periodic,* like Vesuvius . . . If the period of rest extends into a great number of years, and is then followed by an eruption, the volcano is described as **dormant;** and in those cases where the activity seems to have ceased altogether, we have **extinct** volcanoes.[39]

The authors tell you briefly *two* qualities that group all volcanoes together. One is a property ("holes connecting the exterior and interior of the earth") and the other is a function ("eject materials at a high temperature"). Then, they tell you the differences between the different kinds of volcanoes.

Here's one final example, from the book *A Journey into a Wetland,* by Rebecca L. Johnson.

A swamp is a dark drippy place where land and water intertwine. It is full of creatures that slither and screech and splash. All life here is tied to the water that winds its way slowly around tree trunks and patches of squishy mud.

---

38. Steve Parker, *Protozoans, Algae & Other Protists* (Compass Point Books, 2009), p. 6.
39. Arthur Thomas Simmons and Ernest Stenhouse, *A Class Book of Physical Geography* (Macmillan & Co., 1912), p. 169.

A swamp is a type of wetland. A wetland is land that is covered with shallow water for all or part of the year. Some wetlands stretch for miles and miles. Other wetlands are no bigger than a playground or parking lot.[40]

This third excerpt shows how a discussion of genus might fit into a larger context. The author has spent most of the chapter talking about swamps—what they are, what's in them, how they function, what they look like, and so on. She then puts swamps into a genus—the larger group *wetlands,* which includes not just swamps but also bogs, marshes, sloughs, and other wet areas.

STEP TWO: Answer the question "Where does it belong?"

Now that you've seen examples of how to write about genus, it's your turn.

Rather than just answering this question one time, you'll do it twice—briefly.

Your first assignment: Write a single paragraph, at least three sentences long, explaining what larger group, scientifically speaking, bamboo belongs to. Also explain how bamboo is different from other members of that group. If you use exact words from your sources, or comparisons or ideas unique to those writers, be sure to footnote.

Optional: you can also include some information about how different types of bamboo differ from each other.

If you can't find the information you need in your notes, glance back at the passages about bamboo from the last lesson.

When you're finished, proofread your paragraph. By now, you should know what to look for—awkward sentences, misspelled words, incorrect punctuation, missing required elements. Don't forget to read your paragraph out loud.

Show your work to your instructor.

STEP THREE: Answer the question "Where does it belong?" in another way

Bamboo belongs to the grass family—but not every object or phenomenon you'll describe will fit easily into a scientific classification. Remember our illustration about volcanoes: they can be grouped together with other natural explosions, or with other events taking place at the edge of a tectonic plate.

Choosing a genus for your object can be a little more creative than just finding out how it is classified. Look back through your notes now. Decide which aspects of bamboo you would like to draw attention to. Then, choose a group of objects that have similar properties, or similar functions, to bamboo.

You may need to consult an encyclopedia or browse websites in order to do this. If you need help brainstorming, ask your instructor.

---

40. Rebecca L. Johnson, *A Journey Into a Wetland* (Carolrhoda Books, 2004), p. 7.

When you've done this, give your group a tentative name. This doesn't have to be a formal, recognized title. For example, "Things that grow by filling with water" is a perfectly good title. (However, don't choose this as your group—you'll have a very hard time finding other objects that go into it.)

Now write two paragraphs, each one at least two sentences long. The first paragraph should explain what qualities the group has, what the group is called, and why bamboo belongs in it. It should mention at least one other object or phenomenon that belongs in the group. The second paragraph should explain how bamboo *differs* from the other objects or phenomena in the group.

When you're finished with your two paragraphs, proofread them and then show them to your instructor.

Day Four: Copia

 Focus: Substituting similes for adverbs

STEP ONE: Understanding simile-for-adverb substitution

In your copia exercise last week, you studied how to substitute descriptive phrases for words. Today you will study a specific way of doing this: substituting similes for adverbs.

Recall the definition of a **simile** from Week 5, Day Four: **A simile is a comparison between two things, introduced by the words *like* or *as* (or *as if*).**

Today you will practice seamlessly working similes into your writing, by substituting them for adverbs. Erasmus did this in his own examples of copia. Examine his sentences below:

> S   V   DO ADV
> Your <u>letter</u> <u>pleased</u> me **greatly.**

> S   V   DO   SIMILE
> Your <u>letter</u> <u>pleased</u> me **as food does a glutton.**

In both sentences, the bolded words tell you more about the verb **pleased.** How much did the letter please Erasmus? Greatly; just like food pleases a glutton.

When you substitute a simile (a phrase or clause beginning with like or as) for an adverb, always think about what the adverb implies. For Erasmus, the sensation of getting a letter from his loved one was just as satisfying as a plateful of delicious food to a greedy man.

STEP TWO: **Changing whole phrases to adverbs**

Each one of the following sentences contains a simile. Write an adverb that could be used in place of each. Think carefully about the exact shade of meaning, sensation, and feel of the underlined simile. Try to choose an adverb that has that same shade of meaning. The first sentence has been done for you. You may want to use a thesaurus.

   When you are finished, show your work to your instructor.

He smiled, <u>like I do when Mom finds out about something I did that I shouldn't have done</u>.

   guiltily
—Jonathan Safran Foer, *Extremely Loud and Incredibly Close*

Past him, ten feet from his front wheels, flung the Seattle Express <u>like a flying volcano</u>.

   explosivly
—Sinclair Lewis, *Arrowsmith*

All day Tarzan followed Kulonga, hovering above him in the trees <u>like some malign spirit</u>.

   silently
—Edgar Rice Burroughs, *Tarzan of the Apes*

The silence overtook me <u>like a cancer</u>.

   dreadfully
—Jonathan Safran Foer, *Extremely Loud and Incredibly Close*

Then fear, disguised in the garb of mild-mannered doubt, slips into your mind <u>like a spy</u>.

   sneakily
—Yann Martel, *Life of Pi*

The calm sea opened up around me <u>like a great book</u>.

   fantascilly
—Yann Martel, *Life of Pi*

They nodded and smiled and kept on scrubbing me <u>as if I were the deck of a ship</u>.

   Homefully
—Yann Martel, *Life of Pi*

Doctors and nurses cared for me <u>as if I were a premature baby</u>.

gently
—Yann Martel, *Life of Pi*

He must face infection <u>as a soldier must face bullets</u>.

strongly ~~strength~~
—George Bernard Shaw, *Candida*

Rustling about the room, his softly-slippered feet making no noise on the floor, he moved <u>like a refined tiger</u>.

swiftly
—Charles Dickens, *A Tale of Two Cities*

There could not be fewer than five hundred people, and they were dancing <u>like five thousand demons</u>.

dancy
—Charles Dickens, *A Tale of Two Cities*

He was afraid of things, and skipped and dodged and scrambled around <u>like a woman who has lost her mind on account of the arrival of a bat</u>.

carefully
—Mark Twain, *Personal Recollections of Joan of Arc*

STEP THREE: **Inventing and substituting similes for adverbs**

Now, you will practice writing your own similes to substitute for adverbs. The following sentences were taken from *Tarzan of the Apes*, by Edgar Rice Burroughs.[41]

    When you are finished, read the sentences aloud to your instructor, substituting the similes for the adverbs. Which version sounds better to you?

In the meantime the lion had approached with quiet dignity to within ten paces of the two men, where he stood <u>curiously</u> watching them.

with bewilderment

---

41. Edgar Rice Burroughs, *Tarzan of the Apes* (New York: A.L. Burt Company Publishers, 1914).

He suffered <u>terribly</u> to see her so. _____ *greatly* _____

<u>Carefully</u> he lifted Tarzan to the cot. _____ *gently* _____

Tarzan of the Apes would have felt cold lead once again had not D'Arnot cried <u>loudly</u> to the man with the leveled gun.

_____ *noisly* _____

Arrows and bullets flew <u>thick and fast</u>. _____ *heavy and quickly* _____

He traveled <u>very slowly</u>, sleeping in the jungle at night. _____ *very hot   fast* _____

He beat <u>furiously</u> upon the heavy portal. _____

As Tarzan moved <u>steadily</u> onward, his mind was occupied with many strange and new thoughts.

_____ *carefully* _____

Jane Porter shuddered and looked <u>fearfully</u> up at the giant figure beside her.

_____ *scaredly* _____

<u>Gently</u> the door opened until a thin crack showed something standing just without.

_____ *carefully* _____

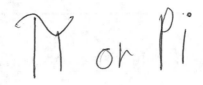

Week 15: Explanation by Definition Project

Now that you've spent so much time studying explanations by definition, you'll write your own—on a topic of your choice.

Your composition will need to be at least 500 words in length (usually, about two double-spaced typed pages of text). That includes your introduction and conclusion, but not your Works Cited page.

Instead of breaking your tasks down into four days, I'm going to give you a suggested amount of time to spend on each step, and let you (and your instructor) decide how many days to spread them out over. These are only *suggested* times! Everyone works at a different pace.

It's fine to take more than a week to work on this assignment; sometimes your pre-reading and note-taking will take more time than expected, and you may find after you start researching a topic that it isn't really suitable. When that happens, never be afraid to switch topics, even if you've already spent time researching your original idea. False starts are an important part of writing.[42]

Here's an overview of the steps:

Step One: Review the *topos*	20–30 minutes
Step Two: Brainstorm a topic	45–60 minutes
Step Three: Pre-reading	Time for library visit, plus 1–3 hours for reading
Step Four: Take notes	2–4 hours
Step Five: Draft the composition	2–4 hours
Step Six: Finalize the composition	1–3 hours

Before you start on Step One, read through the entire week's lesson.

Although you don't need to show your work to your instructor after each step, ask for help whenever you need it. Your instructor may ask to see your work at any time. Always be ready to show it!

---

42. When I wrote the first volume of my advanced world history series for adults, *The History of the Ancient World,* I wrote *thirty thousand words* about prehistory, archaeology, and civilizations that existed before writing was invented. I threw 25,000 of those words away! Turned out I had started in the wrong place—way too early! But if I hadn't written (and then cut out) all those pages, I would never have known *where* to start.

STEP ONE: **Review the *topos* (20–30 minutes)**

Before you start to look for a topic, review the questions you'll be trying to answer.

On a sheet of paper, copy down the following *topos* and place it into the Reference section of your Composition Notebook.

Explanation by Definition: Natural Object or Phenomenon
Definition: An explanation of properties, function, and genus

Procedure

1. Answer the following questions:
Essential Properties and Accidental
Properties
    What does it look like?
    How does it behave?
    What senses come into play as you observe it?
    What do those senses reveal?
    Is your observation passive (watching/listening)
        or active (experimenting/collecting/probing)?
    What sorts of measurements (temperature,
        quantity, time, etc.) are necessary to your
        observation?
    What does it resemble?
    What is it made of?
    What sort of structure does it have?
    What is its extent in space?
    What is its extent in time?
    Which properties are essential?
    Which are accidental?
Function
    How does it work or behave?
        Will a descriptive sequence help the reader
            understand how it works? What would the
                sequence describe?
        Is its behavior predictable or unpredictable?
        Does it work/behave differently under different
            circumstances?
            At different times?
        Can its behavior be divided into phases?
            What separates the phases?
        Is there a cause or trigger for its behavior?
        What is the time frame for its behavior?

Remember

1. Not all questions need to be answered.

2. Selection of genus can be based on either properties or function.

Where does the behavior take place?
Who/what needs it or uses it?
Is anything dependent on it?
Is it dependent on anything else?
Who/what affects its working/behavior?
For what purposes?
Is there more than one purpose?
Does the purpose change at different times?
Is the purpose dependent on any other
conditions?

Genus
What other objects or phenomena can it be grouped with?
What are the qualities that lead you to group them
together?
What name can you give this group?
In what significant ways is it different from the others in its
group?

STEP TWO: **Brainstorm a topic (20–30 minutes)**

To choose an object or phenomenon for study, you'll carry out a slightly simplified version of
the brainstorming you learned in Week 8.

Back then, you learned to ask four questions for topics in science: What? Where? Who?
Why? You'll follow the same procedure, but you won't ask *who*. "Who?" is a question that usually leads you in the direction of a biographical sketch (which you'll review later this year), or
possibly towards a narrative of scientific discovery.

Here's a reminder of the sequence you'll follow as you brainstorm. If you need more explanation, go back to Week 8 and read through the instructions for Day Two.

1. Write the words WHAT, WHERE, and WHY along the long side of a piece of paper.
Under WHAT, write six names or phrases describing scientific phenomena,
natural objects or occurrences. (Keep in mind: Biology, chemistry, physics,
astronomy, geology!)
Under WHERE, write at least three physical places.
Under WHY, write down the names of at least two scientific theories.

2. Circle one name or phrase in each column that seems potentially the most interesting to
you. Write the circled term from the WHAT column in the middle of a second blank sheet of
paper. Now ask yourself: Where? Why? Try to come up with at least two answers for each question. Use different colored pens or pencils to write the answers in a brainstorming map around
your central term.

3. Repeat #2 for the circled terms in the WHERE and WHY columns.

4. Because you are writing a definition, you do not need to complete the final brainstorming step of defining the subject area. It's already defined: you're writing a definition! But these

brainstorming maps should give some idea of which object or phenomenon is best suited to an explanation by definition. Pick the map that turned out the best—the one that you found the most information on, or that you found the most interesting. You will end up covering a number of the different topics on this brainstorming map. Remember that your paper will be easier to write if you pick something with a clear *function* as well as *properties*.

STEP THREE: **Pre-reading (Time for library visit, plus 1–3 hours for reading)**

Now you'll use your brainstorming map to help you locate titles for pre-reading.

The pre-reading you do for your definition by explanation won't need to be quite as extensive as the pre-reading you did for your independent project in Weeks 8–9. You should aim to end up with three sources that give you valuable information about your topic. You'll follow the same sequence as in Week 8; if you need reminders, go back to Day Three of Week 8 and read back through the lesson.

1. Make an initial list of titles to look for, using your local library's online catalog. Search for several different terms from your brainstorming map.

2. Take your brainstorming map with you and visit the library. Locate your chosen titles. Glance at the titles on either side on the shelf to see if they look useful. Pull six to eight books off the shelf and examine them. Use the indices to make sure that each book addresses your topic. Remember: you need information about properties *and* function. You can determine an appropriate genus yourself.

3. Try to bring home at least four books that relate to your subject.

4. Read the chapters or sections of each book that relate to your topic. Don't take notes yet; instead, use bookmarks or Post-It Notes to mark pages that you might want to use.

STEP FOUR: **Take notes (2–4 hours)**

Using proper form (see Week 3, Day Three, if you need a refresher), take notes from at least three of your books. The number you will take will vary; try not to take more than 20 notes from any one book.

Take notes in the way suggested in Day Three of Week 12 and Day Two of Week 13: As you take your notes, organize them by the question that they answer. If you don't remember how this works, read back through the instructions for both days now.

As you take your notes, you will constantly need to refer back to your Explanation by Definition chart. Look for answers to the questions on the chart, and note the answers underneath each question.

This is a different method of note-taking than the method used in Weeks 8–9, when you chose both your own subject and your own *topoi*. There are two different ways of preparing to write a paper: knowing ahead of time what kind of paper you'll write (as in this assignment), and deciding after you look at the available information what kind of paper you'll write (as in the Weeks 8–9 assignment). You'll be given both kinds of assignment in college, so you need to practice both.

Be sure that your notes answer at least four of the questions under Properties, and at least three to four of the questions under Function.

Whenever you find a piece of information that might help you place your subject into a group, list it under Genus. You'll probably want to put the *same* information into either Properties or Function; it's perfectly fine to duplicate your notes for Genus.

STEP FIVE: **Draft the composition (2–4 hours)**

Using your ordered notes, write your composition. Follow these guidelines:

First, describe the properties of your subject (in any order that you choose). Then, describe the function. Finally, identify the genus.

Aim for at least two to three paragraphs each for properties and function, one to two paragraphs for genus.

Quote directly from at least two of your sources. Make sure that all direct quotes and anything which is not common knowledge is footnoted.

Check your *topoi* chart one more time to make sure that you have included the required elements.

Since your complete composition, including introduction and conclusion, should be at least 500 words long, aim to have at least 450 words in this initial draft.

STEP SIX: **Finalize the composition (1–3 hours)**

1. Review the Introductions and Conclusions chart in the Reference section of your Composition Notebook. Choose one kind of introduction and another kind of conclusion. Write your introduction and conclusion. Make sure that you have at least 500 words total.

2. Choose a title. If necessary, look back at Week 9, Day Four, to review the process.

3. Assemble your Works Cited page, using the correct format.

4. Proofread, using the four-part process described in Week 13, Step Four.

When your composition is finished, show it to your instructor.

Week 16: Comparing Two Poems

Day One: Read

Focus: Reading

Overview of Weeks 16–18

You've spent the last four weeks writing about science. Now you'll change directions and do something completely different: write about poetry.

In the first level of this course, you wrote three different beginning literary analysis essays about three different poems: "The Bells," by Edgar Allan Poe; "Ozymandias," by Percy Bysshe Shelley; and "The Charge of the Light Brigade," by Alfred, Lord Tennyson. In this second level, you'll also spend three weeks writing about poetry, but you'll concentrate on bringing together some of the different skills you've learned.

First, you'll write a comparison/contrast of two poems. Then you'll work on combining the analysis of a poem with a biographic sketch of the poem's author.

As you did last year, you'll pay attention both to the meaning of the poems, and to the words and techniques the poets use.

Turn to Appendix II. The first two poems in the appendix, "The Road Not Taken" and "The Armful," are by the American poet Robert Frost.

Robert Frost (1874–1963) grew up in California and Massachusetts; he also lived in New Hampshire, England, Vermont, and Florida. He worked as a farmer, teacher, and writer. He won four Pulitzer Prizes for his poetry and published over thirty volumes of poetry, plays, and essays.

"The Road Not Taken" was originally published in 1916; "The Armful" was published in 1928.

Read each poem four times in a row, closely following these instructions.

STEP ONE: **Read silently**

Read the poem silently and slowly. Stop and look up the meanings and pronunciations of all words you don't know.

STEP TWO: **Read out loud**

Go to a private place and read the poem out loud, at a normal pace. Pronounce each word clearly. Pause at the end of each line so that you can hear the sound of each individual line.

STEP THREE: **Read for punctuation**

Read the poem out loud a second time. This time, ignore the line endings. Instead, pause at each comma; pause for a longer time at semicolons and colons; make the longest pause of all at periods. If there is no punctuation at the end of a line, read on without pausing. Use your voice to indicate exclamation points.

STEP FOUR: **Read for rhyme**

Read the poem out loud one last time, emphasizing the last syllable of every line. Listen for repeated rhymes.

Day Two: Examine Form

 Focus: Understanding meter and rhyme scheme

STEP ONE: **Review meter**

When you wrote about poetry in the first level of this course, you learned that *meter* is the rhythmical pattern of a poem. Poems written in regular meter have a repeating pattern of stressed and unstressed syllables. Each set of stressed and unstressed syllables is known as a *foot*.

In these lines from "Ozymandias," each *foot* is surrounded by parentheses. Within each foot, an accent mark is over each stressed syllable. A circumflex is over each unstressed syllable.

    ˇ   ´   ˇ   ´   ˇ   ´   ˇ   ´   ˇ   ´

(My name) (is O) (zyman) (dias, King) (of Kings):

    ˇ   ´   ˇ   ´   ˇ   ´   ˇ   ´   ˇ   ´

(Look on) (my works), (ye migh) (ty, and) (despair)!

Read those two lines out loud to your instructor. Use your voice to emphasize each stressed (marked with an accent) syllable.

Each line of this poem has five feet. Each foot has the same pattern: one unstressed syllable, followed by a stressed syllable. Last year, you learned that this meter is called **iambic pentameter.** An **iamb** is a foot with the pattern "unstressed-stressed." **Pentameter** means that there are five feet per line.

You also learned that in **trochaic** meter, each foot has the pattern "stressed-unstressed." **Anapestic** meter follows the pattern "unstressed-unstressed-stressed." And **dactylic** meter follows the pattern "stressed-unstressed-unstressed."

Label each line below as iambic, trochaic, anapestic, or dactylic. When you're finished, show your work to your instructor. Remember—reading poetry out loud is the very best way to hear the meter!

'Twas the night before Christmas, and all through the house   _____

Because I could not stop for Death,/ He kindly stopped for me   _____

Decked them with their brightest feathers   _____

Shall I compare thee to a summer's day?   _____

Bubble, bubble, toil and trouble.   _____

Black were her eyes as the berry that grows on the thorn by the wayside _____

STEP TWO: **Understand the meter of each poem**

Begin by marking the meter of "The Armful," which is very regular. On the copy of the poem below, mark stressed syllables with accents and unstressed with circumflexes. (Ignore the blanks to the right for the moment.)

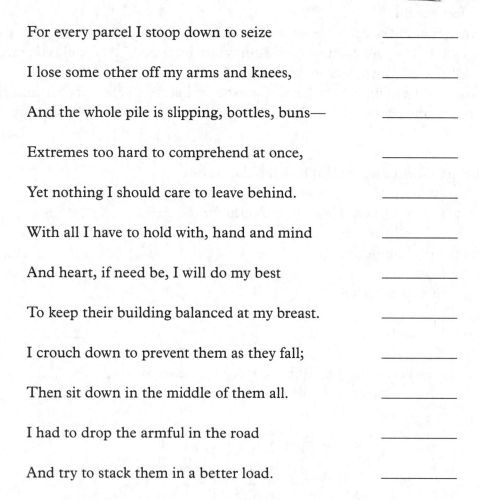

The Armful
by Robert Frost

For every parcel I stoop down to seize   _____

I lose some other off my arms and knees,   _____

And the whole pile is slipping, bottles, buns—   _____

Extremes too hard to comprehend at once,   _____

Yet nothing I should care to leave behind.   _____

With all I have to hold with, hand and mind   _____

And heart, if need be, I will do my best   _____

To keep their building balanced at my breast.   _____

I crouch down to prevent them as they fall;   _____

Then sit down in the middle of them all.   _____

I had to drop the armful in the road   _____

And try to stack them in a better load.   _____

When you are finished, circle each foot in the first two lines. What is the name of the poem's meter? Write the answer on the line below.

_____

When you are finished, show your work to your instructor. If you need help, ask for it!

◆

Now look carefully at the first stanza of "The Road Not Taken." See if you can mark the stressed and unstressed syllables in the first stanza. Here's a hint: there is one extra syllable in each line. Can you find it?

When you've done your best, show the stanza to your instructor. (You'll use the blanks to the right of the poem in the next step.)

The Road Not Taken
by Robert Frost

Two roads diverged in a yellow wood,   _____

And sorry I could not travel both   _____

And be one traveler, long I stood   _____

And looked down one as far as I could   _____

To where it bent in the undergrowth;   _____

After discussing the meter with your instructor, go on and mark the rest of the lines.

Then took the other, as just as fair,   _____

And having perhaps the better claim   _____

Because it was grassy and wanted wear,   _____

Though as for that the passing there   _____

Had worn them really about the same,   _____

And both that morning equally lay   _____

In leaves no step had trodden black.   _____

Oh, I marked the first for another day!   _____

Yet knowing how way leads on to way   _____

I doubted if I should ever come back.   _____

I shall be telling this with a sigh   _____

Somewhere ages and ages hence: _____

Two roads diverged in a wood, and I,   _____

I took the one less traveled by,   _____

And that has made all the difference.   _____

When you're finished, write the name of the meter on the line below.

_____

STEP THREE: **Understand the rhyme scheme of each poem**

Go back to "The Armful" and mark the rhyme scheme, using the blanks to the right of the poem.

Remember: a rhyme scheme is a pattern of repeating rhymes. You find a rhyme scheme by giving each line-ending sound a different letter of the alphabet, like this:

"Will you walk a little faster?" said a whiting to a snail,	A
"There's a porpoise close behind us, and he's treading on my tail.	A
See how eagerly the lobsters and the turtles all advance!	B
They are waiting on the shingle—will you come and join the dance?"	B
"You can really have no notion how delightful it will be	C
When they take us up and throw us, with the lobsters, out to sea!"	C
But the snail replied "Too far, too far!" and gave a look askance—	B
Said he thanked the whiting kindly, but he would not join the dance.	B

(Those are two stanzas from a poem by Lewis Carroll called "The Lobster Quadrille.")

The same ending sound always gets the same letter—that's why "advance," "dance," and "askance" are all given the letter B.

Show your work to your instructor. Answer the following question: Is the rhyme scheme regular or irregular?

Now do the same thing for "The Road Less Travelled." Show your work to your instructor. Answer the following question: Is the rhyme scheme regular or irregular?

STEP FOUR: **Complete the comparison chart**

Sum up your conclusions about meter and rhyme by completing the following chart.

	"The Armful"	"The Road Not Taken"
Name of meter?		
Which poem's meter is more regular? More irregular?		
Do any lines break the metrical pattern? If so, write them here.		
What is the rhyme scheme?		
Is the rhyme scheme regular or irregular?		
Which rhyme scheme is simpler? More complex?		

Day Three: Think

 Focus: Connecting form and meaning

In the first two steps of today's lesson, your instructor will carry on a dialogue with you. During these dialogues, you'll write brief answers in the spaces below. These answers will help you construct your short essay tomorrow.

STEP ONE: Discuss "The Armful"

What is the literal meaning of the poem? _____

_____

_____

_____

Where does the poem take place? _____

What do the things in the pile represent? _____

_____

What changes between the beginning and end of the poem? _____

_____

_____

How do the meter and rhyme relate to the meaning of the poem? _____

_____

_____

_____

STEP TWO: **Discuss "The Road Not Taken"**

What is the literal meaning of the poem?_____

_____

_____

_____

Where does the poem take place? _____

What do the roads represent? _____

_____

What changes between the beginning and end of the poem? _____

_____

_____

How do the meter and rhyme relate to the meaning of the poem? _____

STEP THREE: **List similarities and differences**

Finish up today's work by making a list of the similarities and differences between the two poems.

Using your own paper, begin by listing every similarity between the two poems, like this:

SIMILARITIES

Written in the first person

You can use phrases, not complete sentences. Try to come up with at least four similarities.

Next, list the differences. Be specific and use the following format:

DIFFERENCES

"The Armful"	"The Road Not Taken"
Narrator doesn't have to leave anything behind	**Narrator has to make a choice between two things**

If you have trouble, ask your instructor for help. Try to come up with at least three differences. You can use the examples above to start your lists.

Day Four: Write

> Focus: Writing about the poem

Today, you'll write about "The Armful" and "The Road Not Taken," using a *topos* that you covered a few weeks ago: explanation by comparison and contrast. Review the chart now:

Explanation by Comparison/Contrast

Definition: A comparison of similarities and differences

Procedure	Remember
1. Decide which aspects of the subjects are the same, and which are different.	1. Use both methods to give variety.
2. Choose a method for comparing and contrasting. a. Point-by-point b. Subject-by-subject	

You've already finished the first part of the procedure—deciding which aspects of the subjects are the same and which are different. Now, you'll use a point-by-point method to compare and contrast them.

Your final composition should be at least 250 words long.

Remember the following rules for quoting poetry:

Identify clearly which poem you're quoting.

Place the line number of the poem in parentheses after the closing quotation marks of the quote, like this: "In leaves no step had trodden black" (12)

If you quote two or three consecutive lines from a poem, use a forward slash mark followed by a space to show the division between the lines. Use exactly the same punctuation as in the original, except for the last line quoted; drop the punctuation of the last line completely, like this: "Two roads diverged in a wood, and I,/ I took the one less traveled by" (18–19).

If you quote four or more lines from a poem, double-space down, indent twice, and reproduce the lines exactly as they appear in the poem. This is called a "block quote." No quotation marks are needed.

STEP ONE: Write about similarities

Begin by writing a paragraph describing the similarities between the two poems. The paragraph should be 60–100 words long and should quote directly from at least one of the poems.

STEP TWO: Write about differences

Now write three short paragraphs, each one describing a difference between the two poems. Quote from each poem at least one time. All together, your three paragraphs should be at least 125 words long.

You can use the following phrases/words, but don't use any phrase/word more than once:

on the one hand . . . on the other hand

by contrast

however

but

Also, make sure that each one of your paragraphs has a different opening (in other words, don't begin each paragraph by saying, "In 'The Armful' . . . but in 'The Road Not Taken' . . . "). If you need help, ask your instructor.

You do not need to show your work to your instructor until it is proofread, but you may ask your instructor whether or not you're on the right track (or road!).

STEP THREE: Write an introduction and conclusion

Finish your composition by writing an introduction and conclusion.

Last year, you learned that an introduction should include the name of the poem, the name of the author, and the main topic, idea, or theme of the poem. For this comparison/contrast, you can begin by stating either a topic, idea, or theme that the poems have in common, or else by describing a difference between them.

Which should you pick? It depends on whether you think the poems are more alike, or more different. This type of introduction is very much like the Introduction by Summary you studied in Week 6:

1. Introduction by Summary

    One or more sentences that tell the reader what the composition is about and what its most central conclusion will be.

In the case of a literature paper, you also have to be sure to identify the works that you'll be writing about.

Your introduction should be a separate paragraph. It can be either a single sentence long, or more than one sentence.

Now, choose one of the following conclusions that you studied in Week 6:

2. Conclusion by Personal Reaction

    a. Personal statement
    b. Your opinion about the material
    c. Your own experience with the subject

3. Conclusion by Question

    Ask the reader to react to the information

Write a conclusion for your paper. Remember that a paragraph of conclusion should contain at least two sentences. Single-sentence conclusions should be written as the last sentence of the final paragraph.

STEP FOUR: Title and proofread your essay

Give your essay a title. It should include both poem titles and a phrase explaining that you are comparing and contrasting the two poems. (Ask your instructor if you need help.)

Now proofread your essay, using the following checklist:

1) Make sure that your paper is at least 250 words long.

2) Check for the required elements: introduction, one paragraph describing similarities, three paragraphs describing differences, and a conclusion.

3) Make sure that you quote directly from each poem at least once.

4) Read your paper out loud, listening for awkward or unclear sections and repeated words. Rewrite awkward or unclear sentences so that they flow more naturally.

5) Read through the paper one more time, looking for sentence fragments, run-on sentences, and repeated words. Correct fragments and run-on sentences. If you used the same noun or verb more than twice, pick an alternative from the thesaurus. If you used a modifier (adverb, adjective, or prepositional phrase acting as an adjective or adverb) more than once, find another word.

6) Check your spelling by looking, individually, at each word that might be a problem.

7) Make sure that your paper has a title. The title should include both poem titles.

When you're finished proofreading, show your paper to your instructor.

Week 17: Combining Literary Analysis and Biographical Sketch, Part I

Over the next two weeks, you'll work on combining one of your *topoi* (biographical sketch) with literary criticism of a poem. Your aim: to show how some aspect of the poem relates to the writer's life.

Day One: Read

Focus: Reading

Turn to Appendix II. The third poem in the appendix, "The Highwayman," is by the British poet Alfred Noyes, who was born in 1880 and died in 1958. You'll learn more about Noyes when you take notes for your biographical sketch. "The Highwayman," one of his earlier works, was published in 1906.

As before, you'll read the poem four times in a row. It's a long poem, so this may take you a while.

Closely follow these instructions.

STEP ONE: **Read silently**

Read the poem silently and slowly. Stop and look up the meanings and pronunciations of all words you don't know.

STEP TWO: **Read out loud**

Go to a private place and read the poem out loud, at a normal pace. Pronounce each word clearly. Pause at the end of each line so that you can hear the sound of each individual line.

STEP THREE: **Read for punctuation**

Read the poem out loud a second time. This time, ignore the line endings. Instead, pause at each comma; pause for a longer time at semicolons and colons; make the longest pause of all at periods. A dash is a pause that's just a little bit longer than a comma but shorter than a semicolon. A dash shows that the action of the line is still moving energetically forward, even though you're pausing slightly.

If there is no punctuation at the end of a line, read on without pausing. Use your voice to indicate exclamation points.

Be sure to change the tone of your voice slightly when reading direct quotes. Use a slightly different voice for the Highwayman and for the soldiers.

STEP FOUR: **Read for drama**

In your final reading, try to wring every drop of drama out of this poem. You'll read out loud once again. And unless you are a born actor, you'll probably want to do this reading VERY privately.

Here are a few suggestions . . .

Use a creepy, horror-movie voice for lines like "The moon was a ghostly galleon" and for the last two stanzas.

Sway back and forth in rhythm for the lines about the highwayman's skills on horseback (for example, "Riding—riding—riding" and "*Tlot-tlot; tlot-tlot!*"). March in place when King George's men come marching.

Shriek when the highwayman shrieks.

Use a low ominous voice when Tim the ostler appears on the scene.

Use a syrupy, sappy voice when the highwayman starts kissing Bess's hair.

Add anything else you can think of. Try to throw yourself into the poem as fully as possible—even if you feel a little silly.

Day Two: Examine Form

Focus: Understanding meter, rhyme,
and overall structure

Today, you'll study the form of the poem. In each step, you will work independently at first, and then discuss your work with your instructor.

STEP ONE: **Identify the genre of the poem**

Look back at the list of literary terms that you made during Level One of this course. (If you no longer have it on hand, your instructor has a copy.) Can you find the term that identifies the genre of "The Highwayman"? Write your answer below.

When you've identified the genre, tell your instructor what it is. (And if you need help, ask your instructor.)

Genre of "The Highwayman": _____

Features: _____

_____

STEP TWO: **Understand the meter of the poem**

Your next task is to examine the meter of "The Highwayman."

Go through the first stanza now. Try your best to mark each stressed and unstressed syllable, using accent marks and circumflexes the same way you did last week.

Once you've done this, put parentheses around each foot. (Hint: there may be more than one kind of foot in these lines!)

After you finish the first stanza, show it to your instructor before going on.

The wind was a torrent of darkness among the gusty trees,
The moon was a ghostly galleon tossed upon cloudy seas,
The road was a ribbon of moonlight over the purple moor,
And the highwayman came riding—
    Riding—riding—
The highwayman came riding, up to the old inn-door.

Meter: _____

_____

_____

"One kiss, my bonny sweetheart, I'm after a prize to-night,
But I shall be back with the yellow gold before the morning light;
Yet, if they press me sharply, and harry me through the day,
Then look for me by moonlight,
    Watch for me by moonlight,
I'll come to thee by moonlight, though hell should bar the way."

STEP THREE: **Understand the rhyme scheme of the poem**

The rhyme scheme of "The Highwayman" is very regular. Go back to the stanzas in Step Two. Mark the rhyme scheme for both stanzas and then show them to your instructor.

STEP FOUR: **Identify the techniques used in the poem**

Your instructor will help you fill out the following information.

Purpose of irregularities:_____

_____

Onomatopoeia:_____

_____

Alliteration: _____

_____

Metaphors: _____

_____

Similes: _____

_____

Day Three: Think

 Focus: Connecting form and meaning

In today's lesson, your instructor will carry on a dialogue with you. During these dialogues, you'll write brief answers in the spaces below. These answers will help you construct next week's essay.

STEP ONE: **Analyze the poem's use of color**

POSITIVE OCCURRENCES OF RED   **NEGATIVE OCCURRENCES OF RED**

_____   _____

_____   _____

_____   _____

_____   _____

STEP TWO: **Understand the reversals in the poem**

Highwayman/King George's soldiers: _____

_____

_____

_____

_____

_____

Highwayman/Tim: _____

_____

_____

_____

_____

_____

Day/night: _____

_____

_____

_____

_____

Final reversal: _____

_____

Day Four: Review

 Focus: Reviewing the elements of a
biographical sketch

Next week, you'll work on writing a brief analysis of "The Highwayman." The analysis will be combined with a form you learned in the last level of this course: the biographical sketch.

Today, you'll prepare for next week's work by reviewing the elements of a biographical sketch and then reading about the life of Alfred Noyes.

STEP ONE: **Review the *topos***

Last year, you practiced writing biographical sketches. Read through the elements of a biographical sketch now.

Biographical Sketch

Definition: A chronological summary of the important events in a person's life combined with description of aspects of the person

Procedure	Remember
1. Decide on the life events to list in the chronological summary.	1. The main focus can be on the subject's work/accomplishments
2. Choose aspects from the Description of a Person chart to include.	a. Listed chronologically
	b. Listed by subject/topic

A biographical sketch includes elements from another *topos*—the Description of a Person. Read carefully through the elements of personal description now.

Description of a Person

Definition: A description of selected physical and non-physical aspects of a person

Procedure
1. Decide which aspects will be included. They may include:
   Physical appearance
   Sound of voice
   What others think
   Portrayals
   Character qualities
   Challenges and difficulties
   Accomplishments
   Habits
   Behaviors
   Expressions of face and body
   Mind/intellectual capabilities
   Talents and abilities
   Self disciplines
   Religious beliefs
   Clothing, dress
   Economic status (wealth)
   Fame, notoriety, prestige
   Family traditions, tendencies

Remember
1. Descriptions can be "slanted" using appropriate adjectives.
2. An overall metaphor can be used to organize the description and give clues about character.

Last year, you practiced writing a biographical sketch of Marie Antoinette. You'll follow a similar process next week: taking notes, organizing them, and writing. You'll need to make a chronological list of the events in Alfred Noyes's life; you will also need to decide which physical and non-physical aspects of Noyes you will describe.

STEP TWO: **Prepare to take notes**

Prepare now by reading through the following articles and descriptions of Alfred Noyes (1880–1958) and his life. Refer back to the Description of a Person *topos* as you read. Make a tentative decision about which aspects (at least three, but not more than six) of Noyes you will write about. When you have decided, tell your instructor what aspects you have chosen.

Alfred Noyes was born in Wolverhampton, England, to Alfred and Amelia Adams Rawley Noyes. His father was a teacher in Wales, where Noyes drew his early inspiration from the coast and mountains. He was educated at Exeter College, Oxford, but did not finish his degree, concentrating instead on the publication of his first volume of poems, *The Loom of Years* (1902). In 1907 he married an American, Garnett Daniels, and he subsequently spent many years living in the United States. . . . Though Noyes continued to write until his death, this romantic traditionalist, not surprisingly, was out of step with the modernist movement of the 20th century, which he detested for its "haphazardness and comparative literary disrespect," and for which he was rebuked by critics for "his resistance to change and literary evolution."

—George Stade and Karen Karbiener, eds., *Encyclopedia of British Writers, 1800 to Present, Volume* 2 (New York: Facts on File, 2009), p. 356.

Noyes married Garnett Daniels in 1907. Most of his time was spent between the United States and Great Britain. With the publication of more volumes of poetry, his popularity continued to rise. He also served as a Professor of Modern English Literature at Princeton University.

Noyes' wife Garnett Daniels died in 1926 and he converted to Catholicism and married his second wife Mary Angela Mayne Weld-Blundell . . . In 1929 they moved to Lisle Combe, St. Lawrence, Isle of Wight, where Noyes continued his literary activities . . . During World War II, Noyes lived in Canada and America and was a strong advocate of the Allied effort. In 1949 he returned to Britain. Due to his increasing blindness, most of his subsequent works were dictated. His autobiography *Two Worlds for Memory* was published in 1953 . . .

[402] Noyes was a literary conservative who followed the traditional models in the structure and substance of his poetry . . . Alfred Noyes died in 1958 and was buried in the Roman Catholic cemetery at Freshwater, Isle of Wight.

—Mohit K. Ray, ed., *Atlantic Companion to Literature in English* (New Delhi: Atlantic Publishers, 2007), pp. 401–402.

The following obituary and photo of Alfred Noyes appeared in the *New York Times* on June 29, 1958. (June 28 is the date of the poet's death, not the publication date.) The first column, the one beginning LONDON, June 28, appeared on page 1. The remaining text and the photo all appeared on page 68.

Alfred Noyes, Poet, Dies at 77; Noted for 'The Highwayman'

Harold White

Alfred Noyes in study of his home on the Isle of Wight

Alfred Noyes Dead; British Poet Was 77

Special to The New York Times.

LONDON, June 28—Alfred Noyes, poet who probably was best known for his ballad "The Highwayman," died today in a hospital on the Isle of Wight. He was 77 years old.

Mr. Noyes was one of the most prolific, most popular and most traditional of English poets. He wrote mostly of the sea and the country in ballad form, and some of his works were set to music by Sir Edward Elgar. Despite failing eyesight, he continued to work almost until his death.

Many of Mr. Noyes' works had greater success in the United States than Britain. In all, he had visited the United States fifteen times and had lectured in more than 1,000 American cities and towns.

Mr. Noyes' first wife, the for-

Continued on Page 68, Column 5

Continued From Page 1

mer Garnett Daniels, died in 1926. Surviving are his widow, their son and two daughters.

Dramatic Narrative

"The wind was a torrent of darkness, among the gusty trees.
"The moon was a ghostly galleon tossed upon cloudy seas.
"The road was a ribbon of moonlight over the purple moor,
"And the highwayman came riding——
"Riding——riding——
"The highwayman came riding, up to the old inn door."

These lines opened a dramatic narrative whose compelling rhythm and vivid descriptions of sounds, sights and emotions captured the fancy of readers and declaimers of poetry the moment it was published, and still does. In children's books and in poetry anthologies, the thrilling "I'll come to thee by moonlight" promise of the highwayman, and the desperate suicide of "Bess, the landlord's daughter" to warn him, with the shot that killed her, still stirs to tears readers of all ages.

Changing fashions in poetry slowly but relentlessly excluded Alfred Noyes from the ranks of major poets in his later years.

In his early thirties, Mr. Noyes had been hailed as England's leading poet. Nowadays he is best remembered for his early ballads, of which "The Highwayman" was one, and singing lyrics such as are found in "The Barrel-Organ," with its "Come down to Kew in lilac time (it isn't far from London!)"

Conservative Romantic

Mr. Noyes' intense loyalty to Britain's romantic past and his steadfast literary conservatism gave him an early claim to the mantle of Alfred Lord Tennyson. Succeeding appraisals, however, found his work unable to meet the challenging standards of imaginative technique and philosophical insight set by other poets of his turbulent times.

He had two dozen volumes of his poetry published during the first three decades of his career. More recently he shifted his emphasis to the medium of prose and offered works of theology, history and biography that showed the influence of his conversion to the Roman Catholic Church in 1925.

On his first visit to the United States Mr. Noyes was heralded widely for the fact, then considered remarkable, that he supported himself by poetry alone. He later denied with some heat that he "had made poetry pay," but the reputation of a practical craftsman in a generally unprofitable field continued to haunt him.

In physical appearance, too, Mr. Noyes presented a sharp contrast to the traditionally frail and esthetic poet. A first-class oarsman during his college days and a sturdy, active man later, he often struck those he met during his middle years as more like a healthy business man than a devotee of the arts.

Criticized New Trends

Although his philosophical attitudes shifted with the years, the poet's literary orthodoxy was constant. As a young man he was an outspoken critic of his contemporaries who ventured into the field of free verse. Later he consistently decried the trend toward naturalism in literature, singling out Marcel Proust, D. H. Lawrence and James Joyce for special attack.

Mr. Noyes was born Sept. 16, 1880, in Wolverhampton, Staffordshire, England, the son of Alfred and Amelia Adams Rowley Noyes. He wrote his first poetry at the age of 9 and had produced his first epic, a rhymed allegory of several thousand lines, by the time he was 14.

During his education at Exeter College, Oxford, his literary talents went relatively unnoticed, but immediately after his graduation he began to write in London. In 1902, his first volume of poems, "The Loom of Years," appeared.

Although his early volumes were well received, Mr. Noyes' reputation was largely made by "Drake," an epic poem on the British adventurer, which was serialized in Blackwood's Magazine.

First Came Here in 1913

The poet first came to the United States in 1913 with his American-born first wife, on a lecture tour that included appearances at Harvard and Columbia Universities. He remained to become a member of the Princeton University English faculty from 1914 until 1923, with the exception of a period in 1916, when he served with the British Foreign Office in his homeland.

A frequent visitor to the United States between World Wars I and II, Mr. Noyes had homes in London and on the Isle of Wight, where he did much of his later writing on Catholicism. Works in this vein included "The Golden Book of Catholic Poetry," an anthology that he edited; a volume on Horace and a controversial biography of Voltaire that was revised before it gained church acceptance.

Among the poet's best-known works are "Forty Singing Seamen and Other Poems," 1907; "Tales of the Mermaid Tavern," 1913, and "The Torch Bearers," a trilogy on scientific discovery completed in 1930, which included "The Watchers of the Sky," "The Book of the Earth" and "The Last Voyage."

Mr. Noyes was made a Commander of the Order of the British Empire in 1918 for his writing services during the first World War. He held honorary doctorates from Yale and Glasgow Universities.

The following excerpt is from an interview, written by Robert van Gelder, published in the *New York Times,* April 12, 1942, on page BR2. You may not understand all of Alfred Noyes's references, but the interview will definitely give you a sense of his personality.

An Interview With Mr. Alfred Noyes
Who Finds Great Danger in the Literature of This Age

By ROBERT van GELDER

ALFRED NOYES, whose home is on the Isle of Wight, where, as he puts it, he "awaits the call of the Muse," each morning in his study, is in this country on an extensive lecture tour, the profits of which, he said, are going to British refugee children. He is in his sixties, a tall man with thin sandy hair slicked across his head and a most noticeable cupid's bow mouth which he kept half covered with his right hand as he talked of the circumstances surrounding his writing of "The Highwayman."

It had been a matter of environment, he said. The poem had been written in 1903 when he was in his early twenties and "staying in an eighteenth-century house on the edge of the Downs, on a stormy night. The wind rushed through the pine trees and the heather seemed to be blowing away off the edge of the world." * * * "Was there a moon?" "Oh, yes, it was moonlight. The moon and the wind and the setting—the house and the stories of that locality. My poems usually grow out of some sudden picture, or two facts meeting and forming a significant fact. I do not plan what I am to say—the plan forms itself as I write—or it doesn't. Just as so many novelists have said of their novels, that the story never is very good until the characters seize the pen and drive it on. * * *"

on my works—the incident must be forgotten now, I hope so, and I was trying to be funny, don't you see, and answered that poets are born but not paid. In some manner this remark was twisted about, accidentally, and I was heralded as a poet who had succeeded in making poetry pay, and had proclaimed the—the commercial spirit. It was all a mistake, but a mess."

"When the Muse does not call," he said, he reads, "visiting the stream of tradition," the writings "of the men who have carried on civilization for us, who have given us our roots." The great tragedy is that so many of us are rootless and do not realize that this is so "because we have been tricked and bullied and somehow awed by the false intellectuals who for a generation have been smearing with lies and sniggers and sneers the men and the institutions that stand for a continuing tradition, a continuing civilization."

"There is an ugly pathological savour," Mr. Noyes continued, "in the expressions of the pseudo-intellectuals that fills so many of our books and journals and is praised by our critics. The word 'brutal' has become a favorite adjective of praise; do you not see the connection between these rootless writers and the totalitarians in politics? Brutality has become confused with strength in the literary columns as well as in the chambers of Berchtesgaden.

Photo by The New York Times
Alfred Noyes.

through deliberate assault on the

a man balanced, reasonable in all

The poem was not in many school books until about 1920. "Naturally I am delighted that it is in more and more school books each year—it is not declining in favor."

"How does that work—do you receive royalties on each book, each textbook?"

He did not care to talk of that, he said. "I had a most unfortunate experience on my first visit here—in 1911. A reporter asked me something about the royalties

That is not accident. There is a perversion of aim and thought in the world of letters as well as in the political world, make no mistake.

"Think back to Dickens, of the human relationships, the kindly affections that for Dickens made up the real value of life. For D. H. Lawrence, for James Joyce, for Proust, these relationships seem hardly to have existed. A new toughness has been created by our makers of intellectual fashions

human soul. And do not believe that this assault was made by or on behalf of normal minds or normal bodies. There is a cleavage that is very basic between normal men and women and the pseudo-intellectuals who in their consciously obscure poetry and tormented prose attack our heritage and attempt to misshape our future.

"The phrase that I used on the pathological savour of the revolt is not mine, it came from the practical mind of John Buchan,

The following excerpts from a critical article published in 1926 give you some sense of how Alfred Noyes's poetry was regarded by many critics, especially those who taught in universities. The article is on pp. 247–255. Each section is a different excerpt, so don't try to read directly from one into the next!

THE ENGLISH JOURNAL

Volume XV   APRIL 1926   Number 4

THE POETRY OF ALFRED NOYES

EDWARD DAVISON

day. By the time his ambitious "Drake" appeared, in 1906, very soon after he had graduated from Oxford, many of the since-belied reviewers were referring to him as the new Tennyson, one who had come to address the new age with such a poetry as would simultaneously delight the great mass of verse readers and yet win the approval of the litterati of the time. In England there still existed a fairly large public with a fondness for straightforward, singing verse, a public that Kipling had kept alive with very little help from elsewhere. The manner and matter of Alfred Noyes was wholly acceptable to these people. It was in the broad tradition; though it lacked the finer qualities, the sense and insight of Kipling's poetry, it was none the less pleasant and appealing, full of

crude movement and coarse music and meaning that could never
be called obscure. While Robert Bridges was still caviare to the
general, Alfred Noyes captured the popular, ear. Such jingling,
crude pieces as the famous "Barrel Organ" delighted the rough ear
with their jerking tunes.

> Come down to Kew in lilac-time
> In lilac-time, in lilac-time,
> Come down to Kew in lilac-time,
> It isn't far from London;
> And we will wander hand in hand
> With Love in summer's wonderland,
> Come down to Kew in lilac-time,
> It isn't far from London.

This was no better and no worse than it pretended to be. But it
was not poetry, and the fact that so many critics said it was has
had a deleterious effect on the subsequent reputation of the author.
"Drake" with its patriotic appeal and pseudo-epic quality, sealed
his temporary fame. Long critical essays began to appear in some
of the less discriminating periodicals concerning the poet's genius;
he was discussed in the literary histories of the time in a manner
altogether disproportionate to his true deserts. All these expectations were premature, and gradually the English interest began to
wane. The poets, his contemporaries, did not take Alfred Noyes
half so seriously as the majority of his admirers. And then, with

Great War. Here and in most of his work there was too much
rhetoric and too little genuine poetry. His ballad and lyric poems
were padded with fustian between their higher passages. We may
observe in nearly all his earlier books (and the criticism is propor-
tionately true of his later work in many instances) a falling off in
interest whenever the verse lacks a story or refrain to assist its con-
tinuity. Whenever the author lacked some theme independent of
his own imagination he tended to sink into the commonplace. His
poems were crowded with gratuitous roses, moons, and galleons.
He dragged in the picturesque word without stopping to consider
its fitness. Always a facile, though never a subtle metrist, he was
clever enough to disguise his commonplaces in ingenious crudities
of rhythm. The verse, whatever its other defects, never failed
to sing. But the music was never far removed from the barrel-organ tune of the lilac-time poem already quoted. In certain ballad

Week 18: Combining Literary Analysis and Biographical Sketch, Part II

Day One: Take Notes

Focus: Note-taking

Today, you'll prepare to write your biographical sketch of Alfred Noyes.

Remember, a biographical sketch is a combination of character description and chronological narrative. Your sketch will give chronological details of Alfred Noyes's life, but also will include paragraphs that are organized around aspects of Noyes's character, personality, appearance, and accomplishments. Later this week, you'll work on writing a critical analysis of "The Highwayman." Finally, you will combine the two together into a single composition.

STEP ONE: Make up working bibliography

You've practiced taking and organizing notes in several different ways. Today, you'll learn another variation on taking and organizing your notes.

Start out by making a working bibliography. Go through all of the sources in Day Four of Week 17 and list them on a sheet of paper, just as if you were making a bibliography for a finished paper.

Newspaper articles are cited in the following format:

Author last name, author first name. "Title of Article." *Name of newspaper,* date of publication, page range of article.

You will notice that the obituary of Alfred Noyes has no author. The *New York Times* traditionally publishes obituaries anonymously. The obituary should be cited like this:

"Title of Article." *Name of newspaper,* date of publication, page range of article.

and alphabetized by the first word of the title.

Journal articles are cited in the following format:

> Author last name, author first name. "Title of article." *Title of journal* volume: number (date): page range.

When you are finished, show your work to your instructor. If you need help, ask.

STEP TWO: Take notes on chronological events

Now, go through the sources from Week 17, Day Four, and use them to construct a list of chronological events in Alfred Noyes's life. For every event, note the last name of the author. For example:

> Born in Wolverhampton, England (Stade)
> Married Garnett Daniels (1907) (Ray, 401)

Since all of the information from Stade is on a single page, you don't need to list the page number.

If you use the exact phrasing of one of your sources, use quotation marks.

> Visited the U.S. for the first time in 1913 and "was heralded widely for the fact that he supported himself by poetry alone" ("Alfred," 1)

Even though Stade uses the exact phrasing "Born in Wolverhampton, England," this is common knowledge—and also a phrase that any writer would use to express this common knowledge. So it is not necessary to put it in quotation marks. "Heralded widely for the fact that he supported himself by poetry alone," on the other hand, is a sentence that is unique to the article "Alfred Noyes Dead."

You will probably find it easier to do this with a word processing program, since you will need to rearrange events as you go from source to source.

Aim to list at least fifteen but no more than twenty events from Noyes's life.

If you need help, ask your instructor. When you are finished, show your work.

STEP THREE: Take notes on aspects

Your final composition must describe at least two aspects of Alfred Noyes, but no more than five. Now, you will complete your research by taking notes on the aspects you have decided to highlight as part of your biographical sketch.

List each aspect (chosen at the end of last week's work) at the top of a separate sheet of paper. Beneath the aspect, write the notes that give more information about it. You can do this one of two ways:

1) Go through the sources one time each, placing each relevant bit of information beneath the appropriate aspect as you come across it. For example:

Physical appearance	What others think	Mind/intellectual capabilities
	Critics rebuked his "resistance to change and literary evolution" (Stade)	Detested modernism for its "haphazardness" (Stade)
"sturdy, active man" ("Alfred," 68)	Poetry "still stirs to tears readers of all ages" ("Alfred," 68)	"Intense loyalty to Britain's romantic past" ("Alfred," 68)
"more like a healthy business man than a devotee of the arts" ("Alfred," 68)	"early volumes were well received" ("Alfred," 68)	"outspoken critic of his contemporaries" ("Alfred," 68)

2) Go through each source, looking for information about one particular aspect. Then, turn to the next aspect and go through each source a second time (and so on).

Some writers find it easier to research one narrow subject at a time, even if that means you have to reread sources multiple times. Others would rather read each source once, looking for multiple kinds of information. Pick whichever style suits you.

In your final composition, you must describe at least two (and not more than five) aspects of Alfred Noyes. So you'll want to research at least three aspects, in case you don't find enough information to support one of your choices. If you decide to describe Noyes's physical appearance, you can also choose to describe one or both of his portraits. As you are taking notes, also jot down your observations about his portraits. (You can use my sample notes to get you started.)

Take at least four but no more than ten notes on each aspect.

If you need help, ask your instructor for assistance. When you are finished, show your work.

Day Two: Write the Biographical Sketch

 Focus: Writing a biographical sketch that includes aspects of personal description

Over the next two days, you will work on the rough draft of your composition.

STEP ONE: **Draft the chronological narrative**

Using your list of chronological events, write a chronological narrative describing Alfred Noyes's life. You do not have to use every event, but your composition has to be at least three paragraphs and 150 words long. It should not be longer than 300 words.

You must quote directly from at least one of your sources. Also footnote (or endnote) information that does not seem to be common knowledge. There is some room for interpretation here, but (for example), you would want to footnote the information that he wrote his first major epic poem at the age of 14, because that information is only found in one source and does not seem to be widely known. That Noyes married Garnett Daniels, didn't graduate from Exeter, and visited the U.S. for the first time in 1913—all of those facts are common knowledge.

In a footnote, newspaper articles should be cited like this:

"Title," [or Author, "Title,"], *Name of newspaper* (Date), p. #.

Journal articles should appear as

Author name, "Title," in *Name of journal* volume:number (Date), p. #.

Remember two additional rules about footnotes:

1. The first time you cite a source, you write out its information in full; the second time, you just need to use the last name of the author (for the Alfred Noyes obituary, just refer to it as "Alfred Noyes Dead" the second time you use it.)
2. If you cite the exact same source and the exact same page number twice **in a row**, the second time you should just write "Ibid." This is an abbreviation for the Latin word *ibidem*, which means "in the same place."

If you need help, ask your instructor. When you are finished, show your paragraphs to your instructor.

STEP TWO: **Draft the paragraphs describing the aspects of Alfred Noyes**

Now, write one paragraph for each aspect of Alfred Noyes that you have chosen to describe.

You must write at least two paragraphs, each one describing a separate aspect. Each paragraph must be at *least* 35 words long, but no longer than 150 words. You must cite at least one source in each paragraph (although you do not necessarily need to quote directly).

You may do as many as five paragraphs if you're feeling very ambitious—five different aspects!

When you are finished, show your work to your instructor. Your instructor can help you if you have trouble.

STEP THREE: **Combine the narrative and the aspects**

Your final step today is to combine the chronological narrative and the paragraphs describing aspects of Noyes into one composition.

You can choose one of two methods:

1. Put the paragraphs describing the aspects at the end of the chronological narrative.

2. Place each paragraph describing an aspect after a paragraph of the chronological narrative that mentions that aspect.

Once your composition is assembled, you're done for the day. Tomorrow, you'll work on the last major element of the composition—the analysis of "The Highwayman."

Day Three: Write the Analysis

 Focus: Writing about the poem

Today, you'll write a brief critical analysis of "The Highwayman." Your analysis will have three parts: a brief summary of the plot; a description of the poem's structure; and at least one paragraph that deals with a major critical aspect of the poem.

Unless you have trouble, you do not need to show your work to your instructor until the end of the lesson.

STEP ONE: **Write a brief summary of the poem's plot**

Begin by writing a summary of the action in the poem.

Writing a narrative summary is something you practiced again and again in the first level of this course. Treat the poem as a story and summarize its action in 6–10 sentences. Aim for 80–140 words.

Remember that a narrative should have consistent tense throughout.

STEP TWO: **Write a brief description of the poem's structure**

The second part of the critical analysis should deal with the structure of "The Highwayman." Using your notes from Day Two of Week 17, write a paragraph describing at least four of the following structural elements:

> genre
> stanza structure
> refrain
> meter
> rhyme scheme

irregularities
onomatopoeia
alliteration

Quote directly from the poem at least once in your paragraph.
Aim for a total of 100–150 words for this paragraph.

STEP THREE: **Describe one major critical aspect of the poem**

Now, add the final element to your composition by discussing how the form and meaning of the poem interact.

Using your notes from Day Three of Week 17, explain how either the color red or reversals work in the world of the poem. Aim for 75–100 words.

STEP FOUR: **Read through your completed analysis**

Now assemble the three parts into one completed analysis. It should be at least three paragraphs long, around 250 to 400 words in length. Read the analysis out loud to yourself. You will proofread it again tomorrow, but take the time now to cut out any sentences that unnecessarily repeat the same information.

When you are finished, show your work to your instructor.

Day Four: Finalize the Composition

 Focus: Finishing and proofreading a composition

STEP ONE: **Put the entire composition together**

Now it's time to put all of the elements of the composition together.

Insert the three paragraphs of the critical analysis into your biographical sketch. You may decide whether to put it at the end, or whether to insert it after a mention of "The Highwayman" in the sketch. You may also need to add a transition to the first paragraph. Something as simple as adding the phrase, "Alfred Noyes's best-known poem, 'The Highwayman' . . ." to the first sentence may be all that is necessary.

Attach your working bibliography as the Works Cited page. Cut any source that you did not cite in the paper.

STEP TWO: **Write an introduction and conclusion**

Your composition still needs an introduction and a conclusion.

When you first learned about biographical sketches in Level One, you also learned that a biographical sketch should begin with an introductory sentence that gives an overview of who the subject is and why he or she is important. You should recognize this now as an Introduction by Summary: One or more sentences that tell the reader what the composition is like and what its most central conclusions will be. Write an introduction by summary now and attach it to the first paragraph of the composition.

This assignment is long enough so that you can also write a conclusion by summary. You may also choose to write a conclusion by personal reaction. Either conclusion may be a sentence attached to the last paragraph, or a separate closing paragraph.

STEP THREE: **Choose a title**

Title your composition, using the following pattern:

Alfred Noyes: _____

In the blank, write a phrase that you think best describes Alfred Noyes. If you have trouble, ask your instructor for help.

STEP FOUR: **Proofread**

Now proofread your essay, using the following checklist:

1) Make sure that your paper is at least 500 words in length (about 2 1/2 double-spaced typed pages).

2) Check for the required elements: introduction, chronological narrative, description of at least two aspects of Alfred Noyes, critical analysis of "The Highwayman," conclusion, title.

3) Read your paper out loud, listening for awkward or unclear sections and repeated words. Rewrite awkward or unclear sentences so that they flow more naturally.

4) Listen for information that is repeated more than once. Eliminate repetition of ideas.

5) Read through the paper one more time, looking for sentence fragments, run-on sentences, and repeated words. Correct fragments and run-on sentences. Listen for unnecessary repetition. (You will have to repeat the words "poem," "highwayman," "Noyes," etc. multiple times. But listen for other nouns and verbs that you could vary.) If you used a modifier (adverb, adjective, or prepositional phrase acting as an adjective or adverb) more than twice, find another word.

6) Check your spelling by looking, individually, at each word that might be a problem.

7) Check the formatting of your footnotes and your Works Cited page.

When you're finished proofreading, show your paper to your instructor.

Week 19: Explanation by Definition in History: Properties and Function

Day One: Shared and Unique Properties

 Focus: Answering the question "What is it?"

In Weeks 12 through 14 of this course, you studied a new *topos*: *explanation by way of definition*. You learned how to explain the nature of a scientific object or phenomenon.

Over the next two weeks, you'll do the same for a historical object, place, event, or group of people.

For scientific definitions, you learned how to ask three questions:

What are its properties?

How does it function?

Where does it belong?

You will ask the same three questions when you write historical definitions, but your approach to answering them will be slightly different.

STEP ONE: Understand shared and unique properties

Let's start with essential and accidental properties.

In science, you learned that essential properties are those things that *define a thing as the sort or kind that it is*; accidental properties are all of the others. Look at the following properties of a star:

- ball of gas
- nuclear fusion at its core
- held together by gravity

Those are *essential*. If an object in space isn't a ball of gas, or doesn't have nuclear fusion at its core, or isn't held together by gravity, it's not a star. It's something else.

But the star Rigel, in the constellation Orion, is 62 times bigger than our sun, while Proxima Centauri, in the constellation Centaurus, is only 15% of our sun in size. Both of them are still stars, though. Size is *accidental*. It can change from star to star.

How does this work with history?

There is only one *Titanic* or War of 1812. But the *Titanic* shares many qualities with other passenger liners, and even more qualities with ships in general. The War of 1812 was an armed conflict—which means that it is like many, many other wars.

What makes the *Titanic* the *Titanic*, instead of another passenger liner? Size—she was the biggest ship in the world (in 1912). What made the War of 1812 unlike any other of the thousands of wars fought? Time, place, and goals—all of those things were different than the time, place, and goals of other wars.

When you write about history, you will find it more useful to think about properties as *shared* or *unique*. Always try to focus in on the properties that belong to *that particular phenomenon alone* and are not shared with others. Of course you'll also need to discuss properties that are shared—for example, the three-engine system of the *Titanic* (which had been used on an earlier passenger liner) or the combatants in the War of 1812 (the United States and the British Empire, two countries which had fought wars before). But even then, you'll always be asking yourself: What is *unique* about this? What made the *Titanic*'s engines different? What was *new* about the conflict between the United States and Britain?

Remembering this will help your writing to be vivid, engaging, and interesting. Continually asking yourself about the unique properties of a historical phenomenon will keep you from writing boring, bland, generic compositions.

As you look for the shared and unique qualities of a historical phenomenon, you will ask the questions below. Read them out loud to your instructor now. If any of them are unclear, ask for explanations.

What did it look like?
How did it behave?
What did it resemble?
What was it made of?
What sort of structure did it have?
What was its extent in space?
Where did it take place or exist?
What was its extent in time?
Did it repeat or continue into modern times?
    How has it changed over time?

Of course, not all questions will apply to all historical phenomena. For example, the questions "What is it made of?" and "What sort of structure does it have?" would help you in writing a definition of the *Titanic*, but not the War of 1812.

STEP TWO: **Practice the questions about properties**

Read the following description of the ancient Incan city of Machu Picchu, which still exists in ruins today.

Deborah Kops, *Machu Picchu* (Minneapolis: Twenty-First Century Books, 2009), pp. 5–9.

> In the A.D. 1400s, a group of people called the Inca built the small city of Machu Picchu. The city lay northwest of Cuzco, the capital of the great Inca Empire. Machu Picchu stood on a ridge between two peaks in the Andes Mountains of Peru in South America. The ridge rose steeply above tree-covered mountain slopes and the rushing Urubamba River. The builders placed two large temples near the top of the ridge. The site was one of the finest spots in Machu Picchu. From there the Inca enjoyed the beautiful scenery. On clear days, they looked up at the blue sky. And they peered down at the roaring river below.
>
> Examples of the Inca's skills as engineers lay everywhere in Machu Picchu. On one side of the ridge, the Inca found a way to farm the sloping land. They carved it into terraces. These flat areas looked like giant steps covered with soil. Farmers cultivated corn, beans, and potatoes for the residents of Machu Picchu.
>
> On the other section of the ridge, the Inca lived in simple stone houses. Their windows and doorways framed views of distant mountain peaks. Engineers designed fountains to provide residents with water for drinking and bathing. The water came from natural springs. Workers dug channels to direct the spring water to the fountains . . .
>
> By 1573 the Inca had deserted Machu Picchu. They no longer strolled past the fountains, enjoying the sound of trickling water. No one worshipped in the Temple of the Sun. And no one admired the views of tall mountain peaks hidden in the clouds.
>
> The Spanish ruled Peru for almost three hundred years. During that time, people hunting for gold destroyed old Inca buildings. The Spanish used some of the remaining walls to construct churches and palaces. But the Spanish probably never visited Machu Picchu. That beautiful city lay undisturbed for four centuries.

This passage answers many of the questions about properties that you just studied—but not all of the questions. Some of the questions in your list don't really work if you're asking them about a place rather than an object, or a group of people rather than a place.

Determine which of the questions the passage answers, and then answer the relevant questions on the worksheet below. If the question is not answered in the passage, draw a line through it. Otherwise, answer the question.

When you are finished, show your work to your instructor.

What did it look like? _____

_____

How did it behave? _____

_____

What did it resemble? _____

_____

What was it made of? _____

_____

What sort of structure did it have? _____

_____

What was its extent in space? _____

_____

Where did it take place or exist?_____

_____

What was its extent in time? _____

_____

Did it repeat or continue into modern times? _____

_____

How has it changed over time? _____

STEP THREE: **Practice the Qualities Diagram**

As you think about shared and unique qualities, you should add three more questions to the list above. Read these questions out loud now:

What large group of other phenomena can it be assigned to?
What smaller group of other phenomena can it be assigned to?
What qualities does it share with *no other* phenomena?

A historical phenomenon has qualities that are shared with almost all things of its type. The *Titanic* is a boat—so it has many qualities in common with a rowboat tied up at the pier of a fishing pond! (For example: It floats. It has a hull and a bow. It carries people.)

A historical phenomenon also has qualities that are shared with a much smaller group of things. The *Titanic* shares some of its qualities with other ocean liners—but those qualities aren't shared by canoes, submarines, or aircraft carriers. (For example: It was designed to carry paying passengers and to offer luxurious surroundings.)

Finally, a historical phenomenon has qualities that belong only to itself. The *Titanic* was the only ship of its size in the world—it was 882.9 feet long, 92.5 feet across, and 175 high (from the keel to the top of its funnels).

So here's how you would answer these questions:

What large group of other phenomena can it be assigned to? *Boats.*
What smaller group of other phenomena can it be assigned to? *Ocean liners.*
What qualities does it share with *no other* phenomena? *Size.*

To help you think through the relationships between these groups, examine the diagram below.

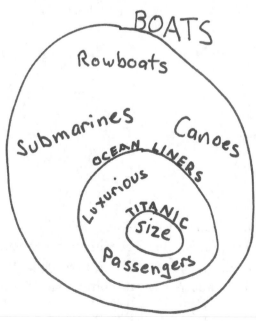

The biggest circle represents the large group *boats*. Ocean liners (like the *Titanic*) are boats. So are rowboats, submarines, and canoes.

The next circle represents the smaller group *ocean liners*. Written within the circle are three characteristics of ocean liners: they are luxurious, they carry passengers, and they are very large in size.

The *Titanic* shares these characteristics with other ocean liners, but in one area the *Titanic* is unique: in her size. The smallest circle represents the unique properties of the *Titanic*.

Why should you draw out a diagram like this? It will help you focus in on the details that should be highlighted in your composition. Obviously, you can't *only* talk about the *Titanic*'s size. You'll also need to focus in on the qualities that the *Titanic* shares with other ocean liners. You'll want to describe the luxurious fittings of the ship, and talk about the number of passengers it could carry. But you won't want to spend very much time in your composition talking about characteristics that the *Titanic* shares with other boats generally. That would produce a bland, uninteresting composition.

There is, of course, more than one way to assign a historical phenomenon to groups. In the diagram above, the large group "boats" is divided into *types* of boats. But you could also divide "boats" according to where they are used, like this:

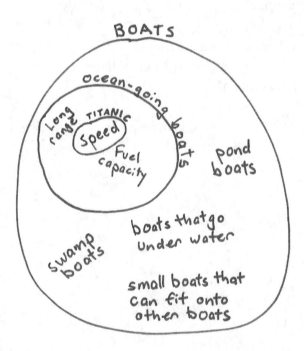

In this diagram, the *Titanic* belongs to the smaller group "ocean-going boats." Ocean-going boats share certain characteristics: they have a long range, they have large fuel capacity, and they are fast. Which quality is unique to the *Titanic*? Speed: the *Titanic* had the ability to get across the ocean and arrive in New York faster than another ocean-going boat. If you were to use this diagram to organize your composition, you would be able to talk not only about speed, but also about the *Titanic's* range and how much fuel the ship carried.

The purpose of these diagrams is to help you focus in on the most important, most distinctive properties of a historical phenomenon. Now, practice drawing up a diagram yourself. Look back at the passage about Machu Picchu. Answer these three questions:

> What large group of other phenomena can it be assigned to?
> What smaller group of other phenomena can it be assigned to?
> What qualities does it share with *no other* phenomena?

Then, construct a diagram like my *Titanic* diagrams illustrating the relationship between the larger and smaller groups.

If you need help, ask your instructor. When you're finished, show your work.

Day Two: Take Notes on Properties

 Focus: Taking notes to answer the question "What is it?"

Today you'll prepare to write an explanation by definition that answers the questions about properties. Your finished composition will be about 120 words, but can be longer if you want.

You'll write about the Inca people, who built Machu Picchu.

STEP ONE: **Read**

Read back through the questions from Day One that you will be answering.

> What did it look like?
> How did it behave?
> What did it resemble?
> What was it made of?
> What sort of structure did it have?
> What was its extent in space?
> Where did it take place or exist?
> What was its extent in time?
> Did it repeat or continue into modern times?
>   How has it changed over time?
> What large group of other phenomena can it be assigned to?
> What smaller group of other phenomena can it be assigned to?
> What qualities does it share with *no other* phenomena?

Then, read through the following passages without stopping to take notes.

Bobbie Kalman, *Peru: The People and Culture* (New York: Crabtree Publishing Company, 2003), pp. 8–9.

(8) The Inca was once the largest civilization in South America. The Incas lived in the Cuzco region of Peru as early as the 1100s, but historians have recorded 1438 as the beginning of their empire. From 1438 to 1532, the Incas expanded their empire across Peru. They were conquered by the Spanish in 1532. The Incas were the most powerful civilization in Peru for less than one hundred years, but they made a lasting impression in that short period . . .

Inca society was based on sharing. People did not work for money. The goods they produced were distributed as people needed them. Young couples received a house and some land for farming. For each child born, they were given more land. Children helped in the fields and at home. Older people were given tasks such as collecting firewood and teaching the children. After a lifetime of working, elderly Incas were provided with food and clothing.

Charles Williams Mead, *The Musical Instruments of the Inca* (Washington, D.C.: The American Museum of Natural History, 1903), p. 59.

(59) The quipu is a fringe consisting of a main cord with other cords of various colors hanging from it. In the fringe knots of different kinds were tied. The ancient [Inca], having no written language, made use of the quipu to keep their accounts and possibly to record historic incidents. By the color of the cord, the kind of knot, the distance of the knots from the main cord and from each other, many facts could be recorded and preserved. The maker of a quipu had a system which was to a great extent arbitrary, and which had to be explained when the quipu was placed in the keeping of another.

Clements Robert Markham, *The Incas of Peru* (New York: E. P. Dutton and Co., 1910), pp. 78, 121–122, 137–138.

(78) The land of the Incas was 250 miles in length by 60 in width. It is bounded on its western side by the river Apurimac, "chief of the speaking waters," dashing down a profound ravine with precipitous sides. On the east was the Vilcamayu, "the sacred river," flowing from the "sacred lake" at the foot of the lofty snow peak which is visible from Cuzco, rising majestically into the azure sky . . .

(121) We see the Incas in the pictures at the church of Santa Ana at Cuzco. The . . . forehead [was] high, the nose slightly aquiline, the chin and mouth firm, the whole face majestic, refined, and intellectual. The hair was carefully arranged . . . (122) The tunic and mantle varied in colour, and were made of the finest . . . wool. In war the mantle was twisted and tied up, either over the left shoulder or round the waist. On the breast the Incas wore a circular golden breastplate representing the sun, with a border of signs for the months. The later Incas wore a very rich kind of brocade, in bands sewn together, forming a wide belt.

(137) It was the wise policy of the Incas to try to establish one language throughout their vast dominions, and they had an excellent instrument for their purpose. Their language was called *Runa-simi,* literally 'the man's mouth,' or, as we should say, the man's tongue or the human speech . . . (138) The *Runa-simi* is a rich and flexible language.

John Hemming, *The Conquest of the Incas* (New York: Harcourt, Inc., 1970), pp. 60–61.

Ordinary Indians in Inca times wore a standard uniform and were forbidden any variations. They were issued with their clothes from common stores and wore them day and night. When sleeping, the Indians, then as now, removed only their outer garments. Their clothes—one suit for everyday wear, one for festivals—were constantly darned but rarely washed. Men wore a breechclout: a piece of cloth passed between the legs and fastened to a belt in front and behind. Above they (61) wore a white sleeveless tunic, a straight-sided sack with openings for the head and bare arms, hanging down almost to the knees: this gave them the appearance of Romans or medieval pages. Over the tunic they wore a large rectangular cloak of brown wool, knotted across the chest or on one shoulder. The women wore a long belted tunic, rather Grecian, hanging to the ground but slit to expose the legs when walking.

Gary Underwood, *Spirit of the Incas* (Clayton South, Australia: Blake Education, 2006), pp. 6–8.

(6) The Incas were a Native American population who lived in South America many centuries ago. My family is descended from the Incas. People who are descended from the Incas make up almost 45 percent of the population of the Andes region. They speak Quechua, which is the Incan language, and live in close-knit communities. Their main work is farming and herding . . .

(7) The Incas controlled a great empire in South America from the twelfth to the early sixteenth century.

The empire centered on the Andes. It included areas in modern-day
Peru, Ecuador, Chile, Bolivia and Colombia. . . .

(8) When the Spanish conquered the Incas, they tried to outlaw the
Incan religion and customs. However, many traditions managed to survive.
They have been passed on to us today.

STEP TWO: **Take notes**

Now you'll take notes for your own description. On your own paper, write each question and
then look for the answers to that question in the passages provided. You can change the word
it to *they* or *he* in the question since you are studying a group of people rather than an object or
event. Jot down the answers, and be sure to record the author and page number of the passage
where you found specific pieces of information.

Only try to answer the first ten questions. Leave the last three questions for the next step.
Here is an example of how some of your answers might look:

What did they resemble?
**clothing "gave them the appearance of Romans or medieval pages," or
"rather Grecian" (Hemming, p. 61)**

If the question does not apply to your topic, you do not need to write it down or answer it.
For every other question, you should aim to have at least two answers. Take at least three notes
from each author.

When you are finished, show your work to your instructor.

STEP THREE: **Diagram**

Now, return to the last three questions and try to answer them.

What large group of other phenomena can the Inca be assigned to?
What smaller group of other phenomena can the Inca be assigned to?
What qualities do the Inca people share with *no other* phenomena? (You can provide more
than one answer to this question.)

When you've answered the questions, try to construct a diagram showing the larger group, the
smaller group, and the qualities that only the Inca have.

If you get frustrated, ask your instructor for help. When you're finished, show your work.

Day Three: Write About Properties

> Focus: Writing answers to the question
> "What is it?"

Today you will organize your thoughts and write a composition about the Inca people based on the notes that you took about their properties. Your composition will be two paragraphs long.

Although you may check your work with your instructor at any time, you do not have to show it until you've finished the final proofreading in Step Five.

STEP ONE: **Organize**

You may choose to organize your composition in one of the following ways:

Paragraph I. The Inca Empire (where, when, etc.)
Paragraph II. The Inca people (appearance, behavior, etc.)

OR

Paragraph I. Incan people in the past
Paragraph II. Incan influence in modern times

Whichever organization you choose, be sure to spend at least three sentences discussing the property or properties that you identified as unique to the Inca.

Divide your notes now so that they fall into two groups.

STEP TWO: **Write**

Now use your organized notes to write a description of the Inca people. Follow these guidelines:

1) The description should have at least two paragraphs and be at least 120 words in length. Longer is just fine.
2) Cite at least three of your sources.
3) Answer at least five of the questions.
4) Use at least one direct quote.
5) Use at least one simile or metaphor from your own imagination.
6) Write at least three sentences dealing with the quality or qualities you've identified as unique to the Incas.

Remember: you do *not* have to use all of the quotes and answers you've collected! Nor is it necessary for you to answer every question.

STEP THREE: **Assemble the Works Cited page**

Title a separate piece of paper "Works Cited." List the sources you used in alphabetical order.

STEP FOUR: **Title your description**

Now choose a descriptive title for your composition. The title should *not* simply be "The Incas"! If you need to review, look back at Week 12, Day 4.

STEP FIVE: **Proofread**

Before handing your paper to your instructor, go through the following proofreading steps.

1) Check to make sure that your paper has followed the guidelines in Step One.
2) Read your paper out loud, listening for awkward or unclear sections and repeated words. Rewrite awkward or unclear sentences so that they flow more naturally.
3) Read through the paper one more time, looking for sentence fragments, run-on sentences, and repeated words. Correct fragments and run-on sentences. Replace repeated words that sound monotonous; use your thesaurus if necessary.
4) Check the format of your footnotes and Works Cited page.
5) Check your spelling by looking, individually, at each word that might be a problem.

When you are finished, give your paper to your instructor for evaluation.

Day Four: Understand Function

Focus: Answering the question,
"How does it work?"

Remember, a fully-developed definition answers three questions:
>*What is it?* [Shared and unique properties]
>*How does it work?* [Function]
>*Where does it belong?* [Genus]

Now that you've learned how to write about the properties of a historical phenomenon, you'll learn about function.

STEP ONE: **Understand how to explain function in history**

When you learned how to write about the function of a scientific phenomenon, you answered three major questions:

> *How does it work or behave?*
> *Who/what needs it or uses it?*
> *For what purposes?*

For a historical phenomenon, you have to add one more question:

> *What was its significance?*

When you explain *significance*, you explain how a historical object, event, place, or people group affected the world around it and after it.

Read the following description of the submarine *Turtle*, built in 1775 by the American submarine inventor David Bushnell. (Notice the mention of the *Nautilus* in the last paragraph of the reading; you may remember reading about the *Nautilus* back in Week 2 of this course.)

> A line can be drawn from the first American submarine inventor, David Bushnell, to the precursor of all modern U.S. submarine designers, John P. Holland. Bushnell seems to have inspired Robert Fulton. Fulton's successful experiments probably inspired craft used by both sides during the Civil War. Their successes led to the foundation of the Naval Torpedo Station at Newport in 1869. . . .

> In 1775, Bushnell designed and built the submersible *Turtle* for the specific purpose of breaking the British blockade of New York harbor . . . *Turtle* had slight positive buoyancy and normally floated with 6–7 in. of conning tower above the surface. To submerge, the operator used a foot pedal to flood the bilges. He could eject water by means of a pump. Once the boat was at near-neutral buoyancy, depth could be adjusted by turning a vertical (haul-down) screw, apparently the first to be designed for a submarine. She was propelled by a second screw, mounted in her bow and operated by a hand or by foot pedal. For safety, she could jettison her 200-lb lead keel (there were also 700 lb of fixed lead ballast). Alternatively, her operator could surface completely by pumping out the bilges. When near the surface, the operator could breathe through a tube, which closed automatically when *Turtle* submerged . . .

> Bushnell's *Turtle* was the first American submarine.

> —Norman Friedman, *U.S. Submarines Since 1945: An Illustrated Design History* (Annapolis: U.S. Naval Institute, 1994), pp. 11–12.

This passage answers all four questions about function. It gives a detailed description of how the *Turtle* worked. It explains who/what used it—the Americans, during the Revolutionary War. It tells the reader what purpose the *Turtle* served: it was intended to help break the British blockade of New York harbor. And, finally, it tells you what the significance of the *Turtle* is. The *Turtle* was "the first American submarine." And not only was the *Turtle* the first American submarine, but its design led to the work of later submarine inventors and, finally, to the establishment of the Naval Torpedo Station.

Historical significance often involves superlative words such as "first," "last," "largest," "greatest," and "most influential." You may also see phrases such as "led to," "inspired many," "changed the course of," and "is still." Read the statements of historical significance below:

OBJECT
Magna Carta is still invoked today by politicians, and is still sometimes cited in judgements in courts of law.
> Claire Breay, *Magna Carta: Manuscripts and Myths* (London: British Library, 2002), p. 48.

EVENT
The second siege of Constantinople changed the course of history.
> M. P. Cosman and L. G. Jones, *Handbook to Life in the Medieval World* (New York: Facts on File, 2003), p. 47.

PLACE
Odessa was probably the most influential place for the development of modern Hebrew literature.
> Marcel Cornis-Pope and John Neubauer, *History of the Literary Cultures of East-Central Europe* (Philadelphia: J. Benjamins Pub., 2006), p. 194.

PEOPLE
The Athenians, rather than the Egyptians, were the greatest artists, the bravest soldiers, and the creators of the "noblest polity" in the ancient world.
> Lynn Parramore, *Reading the Sphinx* (New York: Palgrave Macmillan, 2008), p. 3.

Each statement is part of a discussion of *function*.

Underline the phrases that point to the historical significance of the phenomenon discussed. When you are finished, show your work to your instructor.

STEP TWO: Examine the questions about function

When you studied function in science, you found good, complete answers to the questions about function by asking a series of more focused questions. The same is true for function in history.

Of course, you wouldn't ask *all* of these questions for any one phenomenon. But a selection of them will help you find the details that belong in your definition.

Read these questions out loud to your instructor now. If any of them confuse you, ask your instructor for explanations.

How did it work, behave, or unfold?
    Will a descriptive sequence help the reader understand how it worked?
        What would the sequence describe?
    Was its behavior predictable or unpredictable?
    Did it work/behave differently under different circumstances?
        At different times?
    Can its behavior or sequence be divided into phases?
        What separates the phases?
    Was there a cause or trigger for the event?
    What was the time frame for its behavior or significance?
    Where did the behavior take place?
Who/what needed it, used it, or was affected by it?
    What effects did it have on the surrounding events/people?
    What events led up to it?
    What events occurred because of it?
For what purposes or reasons?
    Is there more than one purpose or reason?
    Did the purpose or reason change at different times?
    Was the purpose or reason dependent on any other conditions?
What is its significance? Why do we remember it?
    What did it change?
    Did it create/become a major turning point?
    Did later phenomena use it or depend on it?

STEP THREE: **Analyze**

Go back to the paragraphs about the *Turtle* now. Using the list of questions below, try to determine which of the questions about function are answered in the passage. If the question is not addressed in the paragraphs, draw a line through it. If it is, write the answer to the question in your workbook next to the question.

How did it work, behave, or unfold?
    Will a descriptive sequence help the reader understand how it worked?
        What would the sequence describe?
    Was its behavior predictable or unpredictable?
    Did it work/behave differently under different circumstances?
        At different times?

Can its behavior or sequence be divided into phases?
>   What separates the phases?

Was there a cause or trigger for the event?

What was the time frame for its behavior or significance?

Where did the behavior take place?

Who/what needed it, used it, or was affected by it?
>   What effects did it have on the surrounding events/people?

>   What events led up to it?

>   What events occurred because of it?

For what purposes or reasons?
>   Is there more than one purpose or reason?

>   Did the purpose or reason change at different times?

>   Was the purpose or reason dependent on any other conditions?

What is its significance? Why do we remember it?
>   What did it change?

>   Did it create/become a major turning point?

>   Did later phenomena use it or depend on it?

Week 20: Explanation by Definition in History: Genus

You've learned how to answer two of the three questions in a historical definition:

What is it? [Shared and unique properties]

How does it work? [Function]

There's only one question left.

Where does it belong? [Genus]

This week, you'll learn about genus, and then practice putting together a composition that answers questions about both function and genus.

Day One: Understand Genus in History

Focus: Answering the question
"Where does it belong?"

STEP ONE: Understand genus

When you answer the question "Where does it belong?" for a historical phenomenon, you must first think about its properties and the way it functions. Then, think about other objects, events, places, or groups of people that share these properties or this function. Then, ask yourself, "What larger group does this belong to? What other objects or phenomena have these properties, or function in this way?"

You began to do this back when you examined properties. When you made your Qualities Diagram, you thought about the *largest* group that your subject belonged to, and then tried to identify a smaller group as well. That assignment was intended to help you focus in on the unique qualities of your subject—the properties that *no other* historical phenomena shared. When you think about genus, you focus in more on the properties that your subject has in common with other events, places, objects, or people groups.

Think back to last week's example, the *Titanic*. I placed the *Titanic* in the large group "boats," and then put it into the smaller group "ocean liners." I then pointed out that I would want to pay special attention to the *Titanic*'s size, since that was the property that set the *Titanic* apart from other ocean liners.

But if I were to write a paragraph defining the genus of the *Titanic,* I would want to point out all of the features that the *Titanic* had in common with other luxury ocean liners of its time:

gourmet meals and private rooms for first-class passengers

a steerage class

running water and bathtubs

a "promenade deck" where passengers could stroll

use of radios ("wireless telegraphs") in the control room

a crow's nest lookout

coal-fueled

and so on.

Take a minute to review what you learned about genus when you wrote a scientific definition:

> What's the purpose of identifying genus?
>
> Grouping your object (or phenomenon) together with others forces you to think about *why* you're defining it—what the ultimate point of your essay will be. When you write about volcanoes, are you focusing in on a volcano as just one of the many things that happen at the edges of the earth's plates—simply another example of what shifts in the earth's crust bring about? Or will you present the volcano as one of the most destructive forces in nature—an explosive phenomenon that destroys everything it touches?
>
> Like the questions you've asked about properties and function, questions about genus force you to think more deeply about what you're writing. (And that's why writing is such hard work—because you have to *think* in order to do it well.)

If I group the *Titanic* together with other ocean liners, my composition will tend to focus in on how luxurious the ship was—because the *Titanic* had every feature of an ocean liner, except bigger, better, and fancier. But if I group the *Titanic* with other ocean-going boats, I might end up writing more about its size and speed—because size and speed are what an ocean-going boat needs in order to get across the Atlantic or Pacific.

STEP TWO: **Examine the questions about genus**

The questions about genus in history are similar to the questions you studied for scientific definitions. Read through the questions again slowly and carefully.

What other objects, events, people, or places can it be grouped with?
What are the qualities that lead you to group them together?
What name can you give this group?
In what significant ways is it different from the others in its group?

Here's how those questions might be answered for the *Titanic:*

What other objects, events, people, or places can it be grouped with? *Other ocean liners, particularly the other ocean liners built by the White Star Line company*
What are the qualities that lead you to group them together? *Built to carry hundreds of passengers across the ocean from Europe to America; powered by coal-fired steam engines; included living quarters, bathrooms, and dining rooms for the passengers*
What name can you give this group? *Ocean liners OR White Star ocean liners*
In what significant ways is it different from the others in its group? *Larger; more luxurious; fewer life boats*

STEP THREE: **Read**

Read the following two paragraphs carefully. The Krak des Chevaliers is a castle that was built by Crusaders in the twelfth century, just east of the Mediterranean Sea.

> Krak des Chevaliers is . . . the most impressive of the castles built in the Middle East during the Crusades . . . It is also a prime example of the way in which Muslim military architecture was adopted almost entirely unchanged by the West.
>
> This castle was one of five built to safeguard the strategic Homs Gap in Syria. Its three key features are its location on what was already a natural strongpoint, its huge size and massive construction, and its use of concentric rings, studded with circular defensive towers around its keep, the heart of the castle. The site itself is formidable—a mountainous spur of rock, from which the ground slopes steeply. The gatehouse in the outer curtain wall leads to a typical Crusader device, the "bent entrance": assuming they had been able to storm the outer wall, attackers were then forced to follow a winding path where they were subject to further enemy fire . . . The principal function of castles such as this was not merely to secure conquered territory but to resist attack while supporting a huge garrison . . . But having successfully resisted 12 sieges, the Krak finally fell, in 1271, through treachery.
>
> —Jonathan Glancey, *Eyewitness Companions: Architecture*
> (New York: DK Publishing, 2006), p. 239

STEP FOUR: **Analyze**

Using the list of questions below, try to determine which of the questions about genus are answered in the passage. If the question is not addressed in the paragraphs, draw a line through it. If it is, write the answer to the question in your workbook next to the question itself.

What other objects, events, people, or places can it be grouped with?

What are the qualities that lead you to group them together?

What name can you give this group?

In what significant ways is it different from the others in its group?

When you are finished, show your answers to your instructor.

Days Two through Four: Take Notes on Function and Genus, Write about Function and Genus

 Focus: Researching and writing about the questions "How does it work?" and "Where does it belong?"

Over the next three days, you will take notes about function and genus and write a brief composition answering the questions about both. You will write about the *Dred Scott* case, an important court case that took place just before the Civil War.

Instead of dividing the work up into days, I have listed the steps below. You can decide whether it makes more sense to take notes over two days and write on the third, or to take notes on one day and spend two days writing. (Or some other division.)

The steps you'll take are:

Step One: Review the questions about function and genus
Step Two: Read
Step Three: Take notes
Step Four: Organize your notes
Step Five: Write the essay
Step Six: Introduction and conclusion

Step Seven: Title and Works Cited page
Step Eight: Proofread

Note that court cases are italicized. When Dred Scott, the person, is mentioned, the name will be in plain (Roman) type. When the court case is mentioned, it will be referred to as *Dred Scott*.

STEP ONE: **Review the questions about function and genus**

Read the following questions about function and genus out loud, paying close attention to each one.

Function: How does it work?
　　How did it work, behave, or unfold?
　　　　Will a descriptive sequence help the reader understand how it worked?
　　　　　　What would the sequence describe?
　　　　Was its behavior predictable or unpredictable?
　　　　Did it work/behave differently under different circumstances?
　　　　　　At different times?
　　　　Can its behavior or sequence be divided into phases?
　　　　　　What separates the phases?
　　　　Was there a cause or trigger for the event?
　　　　What was the time frame for its behavior or significance?
　　　　Where did the behavior take place?
　　Who/what needed it, used it, or was affected by it?
　　　　What effects did it have on the surrounding events/people?
　　　　What events led up to it?
　　　　What events occurred because of it?
　　For what purposes or reasons?
　　　　Is there more than one purpose or reason?
　　　　Did the purpose or reason change at different times?
　　　　Was the purpose or reason dependent on any other conditions?
　　What is its significance? Why do we remember it?
　　　　What did it change?
　　　　Did it create/become a major turning point?
　　　　Did later phenomena use it or depend on it?

Genus: Where does it belong?
　　What other objects, events, people, or places can it be grouped with?
　　What are the qualities that lead you to group them together?
　　What name can you give this group?
　　In what significant ways is it different from the others in its group?

STEP TWO: **Read**

Read through the following passages without stopping to take notes.

Karen Price Hossell, *The Emancipation Proclamation* (Chicago: Heinemann Library, 2006), p. 11.

Dred Scott was a slave who was born in Virginia. When he was about thirty, his master died and Scott was sold to a military surgeon named Dr. John Emerson. Scott traveled with Dr. Emerson as he moved from one military post to another. Some of the states they lived in were free territories such as Illinois and Wisconsin. Because slavery was not legal in those states, Scott wondered whether he was still legally a slave when he lived there, but he did not ask for his freedom. After Dr. Emerson died, though, a lawyer helped Scott file a case against Emerson's widow saying that because he had lived in territories that did not have slaves, he should be free. The case went to the United States Supreme Court in 1857. All Americans were interested in the outcome of the case, because it could change slavery forever.

But the Chief Justice of the Supreme Court, Roger B. Taney, supported slavery. He and the other justices decided that slaves were still slaves even when they lived in free territories. They also said that black people, whether they were slaves or not, could never become United States citizens. Additionally, they decided that the laws that banned slavery in certain United States territories were unconstitutional. Scott died only a few months after this decision, still a slave.

Jason Skog, *The Dred Scott Decision* (Mankato, Minn.: Compass Point Books, 2006), pp. 6–8.

(6) Through various laws and compromises during the first half of the 19th century, Congress had taken different actions regarding slavery. It sometimes banned slavery in federal territories; it sometimes allowed slavery in federal (7) territories; and it sometimes left it up to the citizens of a territory to decide.

For example, the Missouri Compromise of 1820 allowed Missouri to enter the Union as a slave state. But it banned slavery in certain federal territory north of Missouri's border. In 1854, Congress reversed that decision and allowed slavery in territory where it had been banned by the Missouri

Compromise. And now, in 1857, the Supreme Court was about to decide Dred Scott's fate, along with the fate of slaves throughout the country.

(8) . . . By a vote of 7 to 2, the Supreme Court decided that Scott and his family were still slaves.

But the court's decision had a much wider effect than just on Dred Scott. The court's interpretation of the law resulted in two major findings: First, that no person of African ancestry, whether free in the North or enslaved in the South, could be a U.S. citizen; and second, that Congress could not ban slavery in the federal territories, and any attempt to do so would be unconstitutional.

Sharon Cromwell, _Dred Scott v. Sandford: A Slave's Case for Freedom and Citizenship_ (Mankato, Minn.: Compass Point Books, 2009), pp. 15–17.

(15) Dred Scott's lawsuit was not the first of its kind. In a similar case in 1824 called _Winny v. Whitesides_, a slave named Winny won her freedom from her owner, Phoebe Whitesides, when the Missouri Supreme Court ruled in her favor. Whitesides had taken Winny from Kentucky, slave state, to the Indiana Territory, where slavery was banned. Later the Whitesides settled in Missouri Territory, and there Winny sued to attain her freedom.

The opinion of the court's majority was that a slave owner who took a slave into a free territory "and by the length of his residence there indicates an intention of making that place his residence & that of his slave gives a jury reason to believe that his slave has become a free man." The legal term "once free, forever free" came from the Winny case and similar court rulings. In other cases, courts in Missouri, Kentucky, and Louisiana had often freed slaves who had lived in free states or territories.

(16) Earlier legal cases did not sway the Supreme Court's decision in the _Dred Scott_ case. Instead the high court found that the idea of "once free, forever free" was invalid. The Supreme Court often makes (17) decisions that overrule decisions of lower courts, and that is what happened in the case of Dred Scott.

Ethan Greenberg, _Dred Scott and the Dangers of a Political Court_ (Lanham, Md.: Lexington Books, 2009), p. 2.

The _Dred Scott_ decision demonstrated to most neutral observers (although there were, admittedly, very few neutral observers at the time) that the Supreme Court was firmly committed to the defense of slavery. The decision appeared to be an attempt by the Court to resolve in favor of slavery the most hotly disputed political issue of the day—the future of slavery in the territories that made up the great American West. Not surprisingly, *Dred Scott* was met by a firestorm of criticism, protest and resistance. Many contemporaries believed, and most historians now agree, that the *Dred Scott* decision and its aftermath were important steps on the road that led to the Civil War.

History has not been kind to the *Dred Scott* decision. It is widely regarded as "the worst ever by the Supreme Court."

Carol Berkin et al., *Making America: A History of the United States, Vol. 1: To 1877*, brief 5th ed. (Boston: Wadsworth, 2011), p. 311.

. . . the Court's decision in *Dred Scott v. Sandford* declared that because no state at the time the Constitution was ratified had included African Americans as citizens, then no one of African descent could become a citizen of the United States. Ever! It would take the Thirteenth, Fourteenth, and Fifteenth Amendments to the Constitution to remove the legal justification behind the Court's opinion, but even these did not reverse the racism underlying the decision. The *Dred Scott* case and the amendments designed to correct the constitutional defects that led to it still play a key role in dozens of cases in the nation's courts each year.

Now that you've read through the sources, go through the questions one more time. Using the list below, cross out the questions that you won't be able to answer for the *Dred Scott* case. When you've finished, check your work with your instructor.

Function: How does it work?
　How did it work, behave, or unfold?
　　Will a descriptive sequence help the reader understand how it worked?
　　　What would the sequence describe?
　　Was its behavior predictable or unpredictable?
　　Did it work/behave differently under different circumstances?
　　　At different times?
　　Can its behavior or sequence be divided into phases?
　　　What separates the phases?
　　Was there a cause or trigger for the event?
　　What was the time frame for its behavior or significance?
　　Where did the behavior take place?
　Who/what needed it, used it, or was affected by it?
　　What effects did it have on the surrounding events/people?
　　What events led up to it?
　　What events occurred because of it?
　For what purposes or reasons?

Is there more than one purpose or reason?

Did the purpose or reason change at different times?

Was the purpose or reason dependent on any other conditions?

What is its significance? Why do we remember it?

What did it change?

Did it create/become a major turning point?

Did later phenomena use it or depend on it?

Genus: Where does it belong?

What other objects, events, people, or places can it be grouped with?

What are the qualities that lead you to group them together?

What name can you give this group?

In what significant ways is it different from the others in its group?

STEP THREE: **Take notes**

Just as you did when you took notes to write definitions in science, organize your notes as you take them. On your own paper, write each question that you didn't cross out. Then, look for answers to the questions in the passages.

As you learned in Week 18 when you wrote about Alfred Noyes, you can choose to do this in one of two ways:

1) Go through the sources one time each, placing each relevant bit of information from each source beneath the appropriate question as you go.

2) Pick the first question and go through all five sources, looking for answers. Do the same for the second question, and then the third, and so on.

There is a lot of information in these passages. Try not to be overwhelmed by it all. Some questions, such as "What name can you give this group?" will only need one answer or note. Some questions, such as "What events led up to it?" will require several notes.

A descriptive sequence is particularly helpful in historical events. You may find it helpful to number the different events that took place in the *Dred Scott* case, like this:

Will a descriptive sequence help the reader understand how it works?

1. Dred Scott was sold as a slave to Dr. John Emerson (Hossell)

2.

3.

4.

. . . and so on.

When you answer the questions "Who/what needed it, used it, or was affected by it? What effects did it have on the surrounding events/people?" you might want to organize your notes like this:

Who was affected by it?   **What effects did it have?**
Dred Scott   died still a slave (Hossell)

You might also want to number and place in chronological order the events leading up to the decision.

When you are finished, show your work to your instructor.

STEP FOUR: **Organize your notes**

Read back through the notes that you took on the passages. Before you begin to write, do two things:

1. You may not have found good or complete answers to some of the questions. If so, you can decide not to answer them; remember, you don't need to address *every* question in your composition. Cross out any questions that you decide not to answer now.

2. Decide what order you'll answer the questions in. Put your notes in that order now. If you need help doing this, ask your instructor.

STEP FIVE: **Write**

Now you are ready to write your composition.

Using your notes, write at least four paragraphs and 200 words about the *Dred Scott* case. (If you want to write a longer composition with more paragraphs, you can, but don't go beyond 500 words!) In the next step, you will add an introduction and conclusion to this composition.

Cite at least three of your sources as you write. Quote directly from at least one of the sources.

Be sure that you answer some of the questions about function *and* some of the questions about genus.

You do not need to show your essay to your instructor until you have proofread it in Step Eight.

STEP SIX: **Introduction and conclusion**

You must write both an introduction and a conclusion to your composition.

Your introduction and conclusion cannot *both* be one sentence long. If you write a one-sentence introduction, you must write a longer conclusion, and vice versa. Remember: a one-sentence introduction or conclusion can be added to the first or last paragraph of your composition, but a two- or three-sentence introduction or conclusion can stand on its own as an independent paragraph.

Below, you will find some guidance and additional information. Pick one type of introduction and another type of conclusion. When you've finished writing your introduction and conclusion, insert them into your composition.

If you need help, ask your instructor.

Introduction by Summary: State one or two vital facts about the case—or sum up its significance. Your goal is to pique the reader's interest, rather than give away all of the important details about *Dred Scott*.

Introduction by History: This should give historical background that comes *before* the events in the composition. Use the information below to write two or three sentences that give a broader history of the *Dred Scott* case.

Cory Gideon Gunderson, *The Dred Scott Decision* (Edina, Minn.: Abdo Publishing Company, 2004), pp. 4–6.

> In 1619, almost 200 years before Dred Scott's birth, the first Africans were brought to Jamestown, Virginia. Some were likely indentured servants. They worked for their masters for a specified number of years, after which they were freed. Others were slaves who were purchased by colonists . . .
>
> In the South, most citizens considered the right to own slaves no different than the right to own any other kind of property. In the North, attitudes toward slavery varied. Some people, such as the Quakers in Germantown, Pennsylvania, were very vocal in their protest of the practice. Their Christian beliefs led them to view ownership of another human being as immoral.
>
> Other Northerners didn't give slavery much consideration. That's because the North's economy depended on slavery less than the South's economy did. Industries, which were much more prevalent in the North, could hire European immigrants at a low cost. And in the North, farms were smaller than those in the South. That meant Northern farmers could manage their land without the need for slaves.
>
> In the South, however, large plantations were common. Many people were needed to work them.

Introduction by Anecdote: Use the following information to visualize the day of the *Dred Scott* decision. Write your own anecdote to describe the court scene as if you were there.

Corinne J. Naden and Rose Blue, *Dred Scott: Person or Property?* (Tarrytown, N.Y.: Benchmark Books, 2005), p. 66.

> At the time the courtroom was the old Senate chamber. (The Supreme Court did not get its own building until 1935.) The *New York Tribune* called

it "a potato hole of a place . . . a queer room of small dimensions and shaped overhead like a quarter section of a pumpkin shell." It was heated by fireplaces and tended to be dark.

Jason Skog, *The Dred Scott Decision* (Mankato, Minn.: Compass Point Books, 2006), p. 4.

> It was a cool, sunny morning in Washington, D.C., on March 6, 1857. The courtroom deep within the nation's Capitol was crammed with curious spectators and members of the press. Whispers went through the crowd as the nine justices in black robes entered the room at 11 A.M. The audience and the nation were eager to hear the Supreme Court's ruling on whether a slave named Dred Scott was a free man.

Conclusion by Summary: Write one or more sentences summing up the significance of the case. (You should already have covered the important facts in the body of the composition.)

Conclusion by Personal Reaction: Would history have been different if the *Dred Scott* case had never happened? Or: How would you have felt if you had been in the courtroom on the day of the case? Or: What do you personally feel about the Supreme Court's decision?

Conclusion by Question: Ask if the reader agrees with the significance of the case, or what the reader's reaction was to the case. OR: Ask an open-ended question about how history might have turned out without the *Dred Scott* case.

STEP SEVEN: **Title and Works Cited page**

Read the following titles of books about the *Dred Scott* case. Notice that each title has the topic, and then a colon (:), followed by a descriptive phrase.

> *Dred Scott v. Sandford: A Slave's Case for Freedom and Citizenship*
> *The Dred Scott Case: Slavery and Citizenship*
> *Dred and Harriet Scott: A Family's Struggle for Freedom*
> *The Dred Scott Decision: Law or Politics?*

The first part of each title is known as the *main title*. The phrase after the colon is the *subtitle*.

Model your title on the examples above. Your main title can be either "The *Dred Scott* Case" or "*Dred Scott.*" (Or, referring to the man himself, "Dred Scott.") Place a colon after your main title. For your subtitle, write a descriptive phrase that sums up the main point or the most important section of your composition.

Title a separate piece of paper "Works Cited." List your sources in alphabetical order.

STEP EIGHT: **Proofread**

Before you hand your paper to your instructor, follow these proofreading steps.

1) Make sure that your paper is at least 225 words in length.

2) Check for the required elements: title and subtitle separated by a colon, Works Cited page, introduction and conclusion (at least one of these should be longer than 1 sentence), at least three sources cited, and at least one direct quote.

3) Read your paper out loud, listening for awkward or unclear sections and repeated words. Rewrite awkward or unclear sentences so that they flow more naturally.

4) Listen for information that is repeated more than once. Eliminate repetition of ideas.

5) Read through the paper one more time, looking for sentence fragments, run-on sentences, and repeated words. Correct fragments and run-on sentences. Listen for unnecessary repetition. (You will have to repeat the words "slavery" "slaves" "court" etc. multiple times. But listen for other nouns and verbs that you could vary.) If you used a modifier (adverb, adjective, or prepositional phrase acting as an adjective or adverb) more than twice, find another word.

6) Check your spelling by looking, individually, at each word that might be a problem.

7) Check the formatting of your footnotes and your Works Cited page.

When you're finished proofreading, show your paper to your instructor.

WEEK 21: EXPLANATION BY DEFINITION PROJECT IN HISTORY

After you studied explanations by definition in science, you wrote your own definition on a topic of your choice. Now you'll do the same in history.

Your composition will need to be at least 500 words in length (usually, about two double-spaced typed pages of text). That includes your introduction and conclusion, but not your Works Cited page.

As before, instead of breaking your tasks down into four days, I'm going to give you a suggested amount of time to spend on each step, and let you (and your instructor) decide how many days to spread them out over.

Remember: these are only *suggested* times! It's fine to take more than a week to work on this assignment. It's also perfectly fine to switch topics after you begin, even if this slows you down.

Here's an overview of the steps:

Step One: Review the *topos*	20–30 minutes
Step Two: Brainstorm a topic	45–60 minutes
Step Three: Pre-reading	Time for library visit, plus 1–3 hours for reading
Step Four: Take notes	2–4 hours
Step Five: Draft the composition	2–4 hours
Step Six: Finalize the composition	1–3 hours

Before you start on Step One, read through the entire week's lesson.

Although you don't need to show your work to your instructor after each step, ask for help whenever you need it. Your instructor may ask to see your work at any time. Always be ready to show it.

STEP ONE: **Review the *topos* (20–30 minutes)**

Before you start to look for a topic, review the questions you'll be trying to answer.

On a sheet of paper, copy down the following *topos* and place it into the Reference section of your Composition Notebook.

Explanation by Definition: Historical Object, Event, Place, or People Group

Definition: An explanation of properties, function, and genus

Procedure

1. Answer the following questions:

Shared and Unique Properties

What did it look like?

How did it behave?

What did it resemble?

What was it made of?

What sort of structure did it have?

What was its extent in space?

Where did it take place or exist?

What was its extent in time?

Did it repeat or continue into modern times?

    How has it changed over time?

What large group of other phenomena can it be assigned to?

What smaller group of other phenomena can it be assigned to?

What qualities does it share with *no other* phenomena?

Function

How did it work, behave, or unfold?

    Will a descriptive sequence help the reader understand how it worked?

        What would the sequence describe?

    Was its behavior predictable or unpredictable?

    Did it work/behave differently under different circumstances?

        At different times?

    Can its behavior or sequence be divided into phases?

        What separates the phases?

    Was there a cause or trigger for the event?

    What was the time frame for its behavior or significance?

    Where did the behavior take place?

Who/what needed it, used it, or was affected by it?

    What effects did it have on the surrounding events/people?

    What events led up to it?

    What events occurred because of it?

For what purposes or reasons?

    Is there more than one purpose or reason?

    Did the purpose or reason change at different times?

    Was the purpose or reason dependent on any other conditions?

What is its significance? Why do we remember it?

Remember

1. Not all questions need to be answered.

2. Answers to genus and properties may overlap.

3. Always try to explain significance.

What did it change?

Did it create/become a major turning point?

Did later phenomena use it or depend on it?

Genus

What other objects, events, people, or places can it be grouped with?

What are the qualities that lead you to group them together?

What name can you give this group?

In what significant ways is it different from the others in its group?

STEP TWO: Brainstorm a topic (20–30 minutes)

Once again, it's time to brainstorm!

Back in Week 8, you learned to ask four questions for topics in history: When? Where? What? Who? Each one of these questions points you in the direction of a historical event, object, place, or group of people—the four things you've been studying how to define.

When? Event

Where? Place

What? Object

Who? Group of people

As you prepare to research your historical definition, you'll adapt the brainstorming techniques you used in Week 8 to help you find a topic. (If you don't remember that lesson, turn back to Week 8 and read through the instructions for Day One now.)

Follow these instructions:

1. Write the words EVENT, PLACE, OBJECT, and GROUP OF PEOPLE along the long side of a piece of paper.

Under the heading EVENT, write at least three words or phrases describing events that happen over a period of time—battles, wars, revolutions, cultural eras (for example, the Great Depression).

Under the heading PLACE, write at least three geographical designations: countries, cities, rivers, mountains, even continents.

Under the heading OBJECT, write down at three three *things* that people have used in history. These should be the sorts of objects that historians study and archaeologists dig up; they can be very small (compasses or sextants used in navigation, say) or very large (windmills or blimps).

Under the heading GROUP OF PEOPLE, write down at least three different people groups or nations (e.g., "nomads" or "The French" or "peasants").

2. Circle one name or phrase in each column that seems potentially the most interesting to you. Now, choose three of the four circled names or phrases for further investigation. You should end up with a total of three brainstorming maps.

a. If you chose the circled term from the EVENT column, write it in the middle of a second blank sheet of paper. Now ask yourself: Where did it take place? Who was involved? What objects were important to/used in the event? Try to come up with at least two answers for each question. For a brief event, such as the Battle of Hastings, there may be only one "where" answer. (However, if you were to investigate, you would find out that different phases of the battle took place on different parts of the slope and crest of Senlac Hill, so you could put "Slope of hill" and "Crest of hill" as different locations.)

Use different colored pens or pencils to write the answers in a brainstorming map around your central term.

b. If you chose the circled term in the PLACE column, ask yourself: When was this place important? What objects were central to the place, or used in/nearby/in order to explore/conquer/farm/sail on it? What group of people is identified with it?

c. If you chose the circled term in the OBJECT column, ask yourself: Who built or used it? When was it used? Where?

d. If you chose the circled term in the GROUP OF PEOPLE column, ask yourself: Where did they live and/or flourish? What is the best-known event in their past? What object is most identified with them, or most important to them?

3. Because you are writing a definition, you do not need to complete the final brainstorming step of defining the subject area. It's already defined: you're writing a definition! But these brainstorming maps should give some idea of which object or phenomenon is best suited to an explanation by definition. Pick the map that turned out the best—the one that you found the most information on, or that you found the most interesting.

STEP THREE: **Pre-reading (Time for library visit, plus 1–3 hours for reading)**

Now you'll use your brainstorming map to help you locate titles for pre-reading.

You should aim to end up with at least three sources that give you valuable information about your topic. Follow the same sequence as in Week 15:

1. Make an initial list of titles to look for, using your local library's online catalog. Search for several different terms from your brainstorming map.

2. Take your brainstorming map with you and visit the library. Locate your chosen titles. Glance at the titles on either side on the shelf to see if they look useful. Pull six to eight books off the shelf and examine them. Use the indices to make sure that each book addresses your topic. Remember: you need information about properties *and* function. You can determine an appropriate genus yourself.

3. Try to bring home at least four books that relate to your subject.

4. Read the chapters or sections of each book that relate to your topic. Don't take notes yet; instead, use bookmarks or Post-It Notes to mark pages that you might want to use.

STEP FOUR: Take notes (2–4 hours)

Using proper form, take notes from at least three of your books. The number you will take will vary; try not to take more than 20 notes from any one book.

Take notes in the way suggested in last week's work: As you take your notes, organize them by the question that they answer. This will be easier if you go through the Explanation by Definition in History chart first and cross out the questions that don't apply to your particular topic.

Be sure that your notes answer at least four of the questions under Properties, and at least three to four of the questions under Function.

Whenever you find a piece of information that might help you place your subject into a group, list it under Genus. You'll probably want to put the *same* information into either Properties or Function; it's perfectly fine to duplicate your notes for Genus. You *must* discuss Genus in your final composition.

STEP FIVE: Draft the composition (2–4 hours)

Using your ordered notes, write your composition.

When you wrote your first original description in Week 15, I told you to follow this order:

> First, describe the properties of your subject (in any order that you choose). Then, describe the function. Finally, identify the genus.

For this composition, I'm not going to assign you any particular order. Instead, make sure that you address at least four of the questions for properties and at least four of the questions for function.

You must also spend at least two to three sentences placing your subject into a group and explaining how it is different from the other members of that group. You might find it useful to see an example; here is how I would have addressed genus in the *Dred Scott* composition from last week.

> Other court cases, including *Winny v. Whitesides* as well as many others, had granted freedom to the slave. But the *Dred Scott* case did not. Instead, the case reversed the decisions of other courts—and divided the nation.

In three sentences, I defined the group to which *Dred Scott* belonged (other court cases about slaves) and then said how it was different (it did not grant freedom, it reversed the other decisions, it divided the nation).

You should have at least four paragraphs.

Quote directly from at least two of your sources. Make sure to footnote all direct quotes and anything which is not common knowledge.

Check your *topoi* chart one more time to make sure that you have included the required elements.

Since your complete composition, including introduction and conclusion, should be at least 500 words long, aim to have at least 450 words in this initial draft.

STEP SIX: **Finalize the composition (1–3 hours)**

1. Review the Introductions and Conclusions chart in the Reference section of your Composition Notebook. Choose one kind of introduction and another kind of conclusion. Write your introduction and conclusion. Make sure that you have at least 500 words total.

2. Choose a main title and a subtitle, separating the two with a colon. If necessary, look back at Week 20, Step Seven to review the format.

3. Assemble your Works Cited page.

4. Proofread, using the seven steps outlined in last week's assignment (Step Eight).

When your composition is finished, show it to your instructor.

WEEK 22: INTENSIVE COPIA REVIEW AND PRACTICE

You've spent most of the past few weeks researching and writing. Now it's time for a change of pace. This week, you'll review all of the copia skills you've learned so far, master a new kind of sentence transformation, and then put your knowledge of copia to use by transforming a piece of classic prose.

Day One: Copia Review, Part I

Focus: Reviewing skills in sentence transformation

Read the examples and complete the exercises below. If you need more review, go back to the lesson listed and reread the explanations. If you are still confused, ask your instructor for help.

Remember: your transformed sentences might sound better than the original—and they might sound a lot worse. You won't know until you try the transformations and then read the sentences out loud.

STEP ONE: Transforming nouns into descriptive adjectives and vice versa

Full explanation found in Week 1, Day 4. The sentences in this exercise are taken from *The Portrait of a Lady*, by Henry James.

Example:

The <u>old-world</u> quality in everything that she now saw had all the charm <u>of strangeness</u>.

```
   ADJ       N              N     PREP   OP
old-world quality    →    quality of old-worldness
```

```
     N    PREP  OP              ADJ    N
charm of strangeness  ⟶  strange charm
```

The quality <u>of old-worldness</u> in everything she now saw had a <u>strange</u> charm.

Remember that it may sometimes it may be necessary to alter the wording of the sentence slightly (above, I did not write "had all the strange charm"). Also, your prepositional phrases will probably all include the preposition "of." This is the most natural preposition to use, and there's no need for you to struggle to find different prepositions instead.

Exercise:

   On your own paper, rewrite the following sentences by changing descriptive adjectives to nouns in prepositional phrases *or* vice versa. You will need to locate the descriptive adjectives and nouns to be transformed—but if you can't find them, ask your instructor.

   A *sally* is a clever remark.

Ah, we too are a lovely group!
He had a narrow, clean-shaven face, with features evenly distributed and an expression of placid acuteness.
It was an awkward beginning for a clever man.
For this extravagant sally his simple visitors had no answer.
That she was a brave musician we have already perceived.
Isabel sat there a long time, under the charm of their motionless grace.
Isabel moved away and stood looking into the sunny stillness of the garden.
A cold, cruel rain fell heavily.
The father caught his son's eye at last and gave him a mild, responsive smile.

STEP TWO: **Transforming infinitives into participles and vice versa**

Full explanation found in Week 2, Day 4. The sentences in this exercise are taken from *Things Fall Apart,* by Chinua Achebe.

Example:

The headmaster blew the whistle <u>to call</u> the assembly to order.

```
        INF          PART
     to call  ⟶  calling
```

The headmaster blew the whistle, <u>calling</u> the assembly to order.

The horse started <u>galloping</u> wildly away.

PART   INF
galloping → to gallop

The horse started to gallop wildly away.

Exercise:

Rewrite the following sentences on your own paper, changing infinitives to participles and vice versa. Remember that you may need to add a comma when you change an infinitive into a participle, or delete a comma when a participle becomes an infinitive.

The next morning the crazy men actually began to clear a part of the forest and to build their house.

The troublesome nanny-goat sniffed about, eating the peelings.

At such times, in each of the countless thatched huts of Umuofia, children sat around their mother's cooking fire telling stories.

At night the messengers came in to taunt them and to knock their shaven heads together.

That night the Mother of the Spirits walked the length and breadth of the clan, weeping for her murdered son.

The elders sat in a big circle and the singers went round singing each man's praise as they came before him.

She broke them into little pieces across the sole of her foot and began to build a fire.

As soon as he heard of the great feast in the sky his throat began to itch at the very thought.

STEP THREE: Changing main verbs into infinitives

Full explanation found in Week 2, Day 4. Remember: when you change a main verb to an infinitive, you will then need to add another main verb—which means you'll add new meaning to the sentence.

The sentences in this exercise are adapted from *The Red Badge of Courage,* by Stephen Crane. The original sentences all contain main verbs plus infinitives; I have changed Crane's infinitives to main verbs and cut out Crane's original main verbs. When you're finished, your instructor will show you Stephen Crane's actual sentences.

To help you with these sentences, I've underlined the verbs that need to be changed back to infinitives.

Example:

He <u>remained</u> on his guard.

> MAIN VERB   INF
> remained ⟶ to remain

He resolved to remain on his guard.
He continued to remain on his guard.
He hoped to remain on his guard.

Exercise:

Rewrite the following sentences on your own paper, changing each underlined verb to an infinitive and adding a new main verb.

Ma, I'<u>m enlisting</u>.
She <u>milked</u> the brindle cow.
The army had done little but sit still and <u>keep</u> warm.
He <u>proved</u> mathematically to himself that he would not run from a battle.
Previously he <u>had</u> never <u>wrestled</u> too seriously with this question.
He <u>admitted</u> that as far as war was concerned, he knew nothing of himself.
He sprang from the bunk and <u>paced</u> nervously to and fro.

Day Two: Copia Review, Part II

 Focus: Reviewing skills
in sentence transformation

Continue to read the examples and complete the exercises below. Remember: If you need more review, go back to the lesson listed and reread the explanations.

STEP ONE: Transforming indirect objects into prepositional phrases and vice versa

Full explanation found in Week 3, Day 4.

Example:

                 S   V   IO   DO
The fastidious gardener gave his poodle a pedicure.

→   S   V   DO   PREP   OP
The fastidious gardener gave a pedicure to his poodle.

Exercise:

In the following sentences, change indirect objects to prepositional phrases. In sentences that do not have indirect objects, find the prepositional phrase that can be transformed into an indirect object and rewrite the sentence.

The wolf gave Romulus and Remus her milk.
The woodpecker also brought food to the twins.
The starving Esau sold Jacob his birthright in exchange for a bowl of soup.
From debtor's prison, Paul Bunyan wrote letters to his friends and family.
The waters of the River Styx almost granted Achilles immortality.
The bear gave her cub the newly caught salmon.

STEP TWO: Transforming active verbs into passive verbs and vice versa

Full explanation is found in Week 3, Day 4. Remember that when you change a passive verb into an active verb, you may have to create a new subject for the verb—although you may find the subject in a prepositional phrase following the verb (or elsewhere in the sentence).

When you change an active verb into a passive verb, the subject will have to be placed in a prepositional phrase that modifies the verbs.

The sentences in this exercise are adapted from Bobbie Kalman's *Peru: The People and Culture*.

Example:

As the Inca Empire grew, neighboring cultures and peoples were absorbed.

PASSIVE VERB		NEW SUBJECT	ACTIVE VERB
were absorbed	→	it	absorbed

As the Inca Empire grew, it absorbed neighboring cultures and peoples.

The nearby nations feared the Inca.

SUBJECT	ACTIVE VERB		SUBJECT	PASSIVE VERB	PREP PHRASE
nearby nations	feared	→	Inca	were feared	by nearby nations

Exercise:

Read the following sentences. If the verb is active, change it to passive. If it is passive, change it to active and invent a new subject.

The founder of the Inca dynasty, Manco Capac, led his people to the site of the present-day city of Cuzco.

The Incas expanded their empire across Peru.

They were conquered by the Spanish in 1532.

The Incas made a lasting impression during the short period when they flourished.

Inca society was based on sharing.

Older people were given tasks such as collecting firewood.

After a lifetime of working, elderly Incas were provided with food and clothing.

STEP THREE: Added and intensified adjectives

Full explanation found in Week 4, Day 4. The sentences in this exercise are adapted from *The Call of the Wild*, by Jack London.

Examples:

Added Adjective

They did not see the <u>instant</u> transformation.

→   They did not see the <u>instant and terrible</u> transformation.

Intensified Adjective

He broke from a <u>sad</u> contemplation.

→   He broke from a <u>mournful</u> contemplation.

Exercise:

Rewrite the following sentences by intensifying each underlined adjective *and* adding a second adjective. You will also need to add a comma or the word "and." Use a thesaurus if you need to.

The first sentence has been done for you as an example. Notice that the generic adjective "scary" has been changed to the intensified adjective "terrifying," and another adjective, "irresistible," has been added. The second adjective does not have to be a synonym for the first, but it should be consistent with the meaning of the sentence.

When you are finished, show your work to your instructor, who has the original versions of the sentences for you to compare to your own.

They were mere skeletons, draped loosely in draggled hides, with blazing eyes and slavered fangs. But the hunger-madness made them <u>scary</u>.
But the hunger-madness made them <u>terrifying, irresistible</u>.

When he flung himself against the bars, <u>shaking</u>, they laughed at him and taunted him.
He sprang back, <u>growling</u>, fearful of the unseen and unknown.
The hair hung down, <u>not nice</u>, or matted with dried blood where Hal's club had bruised him.
Thirty or forty huskies ran to the spot and surrounded the combatants in an <u>interested</u> circle.
Then they became friendly, and played about in the <u>nice</u> way with which fierce beasts belie their fierceness.
Buck hurried on, swiftly and stealthily, every nerve <u>working</u>, alert to the multitudinous details which told a story—all but the end.
Also, they held it a mercy, since Dave was to die anyway, that he should die in the traces, <u>happy</u>.
Buck staggered over against the sled, <u>tired</u>, sobbing for breath.

Day Three: Copia Review, Part III

 Focus: Reviewing skills in simile, metaphor, and descriptive phrases

In 322 BC Aristotle wrote in *De Poetica,* "The greatest thing by far is to be a master of metaphor. It is the one thing that cannot be learned from others; it is also a sign of genius, since a good metaphor implies an eye for resemblance."

So, if metaphor can't be learned, how can you become a master (and genius)? Through practice. Today, you'll be practicing both metaphor and simile.

STEP ONE: **Identifying metaphor and simile**

If you need to review metaphor and simile, look back at Week 5, Day 4, and Week 6, Day 4.

Underline the metaphors and similes in the following sentences. Mark each metaphor with an *M* and each simile with an *S*. Draw an arrow from the metaphor or simile to the word it describes by comparison.

The fog comes / on little cat feet.
(Carl Sandburg, "The Fog")

Sometimes a piece of sun / burned like a coin in my hand.
(Pablo Neruda, "Clenched Soul")

Lost in the forest, I broke off a dark twig / and lifted its whisper to my thirsty lips.
    (Pablo Neruda, "Lost in the Forest")

He was very tall and strong, with a face as big as a ham.
    (Robert Louis Stevenson, *Treasure Island*)

I took him by the waist as if he had been a sack of bran, and, with one good heave, tumbled
him overboard.
    (Robert Louis Stevenson, *Treasure Island*)

I remember observing the contrast the neat, bright doctor, with his powder as white as snow,
and his bright, black eyes and pleasant manners, made with the coltish country folk, and above
all, with that filthy, heavy, bleared scarecrow of a pirate of ours.
    (Robert Louis Stevenson, *Treasure Island*)

His broad, permanently scowling face was composed of three downward curves, something like
the insignia of a sergeant's stripes.
    (Gregory David Roberts, *Shantaram*)

My mind was muddy water, and one idea splashed up from it.
    (Gregory David Roberts, *Shantaram*)

Arms, legs, and heads crushed in on one another as we hunkered down in terror while the
mortars tore up the rocky ground outside as if it was papier-mâché.
    (Gregory David Roberts, *Shantaram*)

STEP TWO: Transforming words into metaphors or similes

The sentences below all originally contained figurative language. Change the underlined
word(s) to metaphors or similes as directed. When you are finished, show your work to your
instructor, who has the original sentences for you to compare with yours.

    The key to writing good metaphor and simile is originality. Instead of using familiar
phrases such as "hot as fire" or "as light as a feather," use your own experiences. What incred-
ible heat have you experienced? Maybe you'd write "as hot as asphalt in August." Don't be
afraid to try unusual, surprising, or even awkward metaphors and similes—that's what practice
is for.

Exercise, Part 1: Substituting metaphors for words and phrases

Invent and then substitute a metaphor for each of the words or phrases underlined.

Example:
Her face was <u>radiant</u>.   →   Her face was <u>a brown moon that shone on me</u>.
(Maya Angelou, *I Know Why the Caged Bird Sings*)

<u>Clouds</u> form endless patterns.
(Leslie Parrott, *The First Drop of Rain*)

But most miraculously did we escape, how we can scarcely say, the swell passed under, and we all but capsized, as we slid from the back of the <u>huge wave</u>.
(*Maryland Colonization Journal*)

In the evening, a brilliant display of fireworks suddenly illuminated the heavens. It was a <u>colorful masterpiece</u>.
(Gustave Flaubert, *Madame Bovary*)

I was trying to fight down the fear that <u>rose within me</u>.
(Gregory David Roberts, *Shantaram*)

There is <u>shine</u> in her hair.
(Oscar Wilde, *An Ideal Husband*)

I am <u>a lost, aimless man</u>.
(Oscar Wilde, *An Ideal Husband*)

Exercise, Part 2: Substituting similes for adverbs
Invent and then substitute a simile for each of the underlined adverbs.

Example:

He laughed <u>harshly</u>.   →   He laughed <u>like the screech of a rusty hinge</u>.
(James Whitcomb Riley, "The Nine Little Goblins")

[Alessandro] would have drawn near to her <u>quickly</u>.
(Helen Hunt Jackson, *Ramona*)

Down he sat / <u>Slowly</u>.
(Elizabeth Barrett Browning, "Aurora Leigh")

The horse darted away <u>speedily</u>.
　　(Mark Twain, *Roughing It*)

At first, Mowgli would cling <u>warily</u>, but afterward he would fling himself through the branches <u>boldly</u>.
　　(Rudyard Kipling, "Mowgli's Brothers")

In vain he kick'd, and swore, and writhed, and bled, / And howl'd for help <u>wildly and desperately</u>.
　　(Lord Byron, "Don Juan")

Sleep she <u>soundly</u>.
　　(Shakespeare, *Merry Wives of Windsor*)

Keimer stared <u>helplessly</u>.
　　(Benjamin Franklin's Autobiography)

STEP THREE: **Substituting descriptive phrases for single words**

You can also substitute a descriptive phrase for a single word. Back in Week 13, you learned that Erasmus substituted phrases for the noun "letter," like this:

S	V	DO
<u>letter</u>	<u>pleased</u>	me

S	V	DO
<u>words from your pen</u>	<u>brought</u>	joy

S	V	DO
<u>pages I received from you</u>	<u>sent</u>	light

S	V	IO	DO
<u>pearls of wisdom</u>	<u>gave</u>	me	pleasure

The very last phrase, "pearls of wisdom," is a metaphor. But the other two phrases substituted for "letter" are not. They are simply descriptions of what a letter is.

　　In today's last exercise, you'll think up descriptive phrases to substitute for words or simple phrases. Here's an example for you to look at, from Ernest Hemingway's classic story *The Old Man and the Sea:*

Nothing showed on the surface of the water but <u>a sea creature</u>.

→   Nothing showed on the surface of the water but <u>the purple, formalized, iridescent, gelatinous bladder of a Portuguese man-of-war</u>.

The second sentence is what Hemingway actually wrote. Instead of the simple phrase "sea creature," he wrote a specific, colorful description of the sea creature itself.

In the sentences below, substitute a descriptive phrase for the underlined words. You can use a metaphor if you think of a good one, but think carefully about what the underlined words *represent*. Is there another way to describe or define it?

This will be a challenging assignment. Do your best, and if you draw a total blank, ask your instructor.

Beneath all that silence and placidity <u>the great whale</u> was writhing and wrenching in agony!
(Herman Melville, *Moby Dick*)

In the fourth seat at my left sat <u>Abraham Lincoln</u>.
(William Eleroy Curtis, *The True Abraham Lincoln*)

<u>A cat</u> would then roll about on the ground, emitting large wads of hair and horrible screams and air-rending hisses.
(William Jordan, *A Cat Named Darwin*)

"The Home Secretary," he said between gasps as he drank the <u>coffee</u>, "is indiscreet in his correspondence and is generally a most careless man."
(Edgar Wallace, *The Four Just Men*)

Men, women, and children were <u>fishermen</u>.
(Norman G. Owen, *The Emergence of Modern Southeast Asia: A New History*)

Day Four: Varying by Equivalence

 Focus: Turning positives into negatives
and vice versa

STEP ONE: Understand varying by equivalence

Have you ever asked someone if she was sad, and received the reply: "Well, I'm not happy"? This is a literary technique, called *varying by equivalence*.

Imagine that you're cooking and need to add three eggs to a recipe. You've got four in a carton, so subtract one egg, put it back in the fridge, and use the rest. How many eggs will you end up using?

> *four, minus one*

But imagine now that you've only got two eggs. To make your brownies, you'll need to run next door and borrow an egg from a friend. How many eggs will you put into the batter?

> *two, plus one*

"Four minus one" and "two plus one" are *equivalent.* Both of them come out to the same number: three. But they have slightly different shades of meaning. "Four minus one" means that you've got a leftover egg to eat for breakfast. "Two plus one" means that you've got to give an egg back to your friend as soon as you go shopping.

When you write, you can use *equivalent expressions* to say the same thing in two different ways. Study the chart below:

Positive Statements	Negative Statements
He was in the first place	He was not among the last
There is much deceit	There is no lack of deceit
Her hearing is excellent	She is not at all deaf
I approve	I am unable to disapprove

Each positive statement can be phrased as a negative—and vice versa. This is called *varying by equivalence.*

Varying by equivalence can make your writing more colorful, exact, and even funny. In the play *Hamlet,* Shakespeare writes, "They have a plentiful lack of wit." He means, "They are not witty." By rephrasing this negative expression into a positive one, he delivers a much more effective (and entertaining) insult.

Stating something first positively and then negatively—or vice versa—is a strategy often used by speechwriters. Does this sound familiar?

"Ask not what your country can do for you—ask what you can do for your country."

That comes from a speech that President John F. Kennedy made in January of 1961. First, he told us what *not* to ask. Then, he told us *what* to ask. The negative came first; then, the positive.

One caution: Be careful when you vary by equivalence that you do not change the meaning of the sentence. For example, if you are given the positive phrase "first place," you can rewrite it as "not among the last"—after all, the first-place winner is certainly not among the last to cross the finish line. But if you are given the negative statement "He was not among the last," you can't just rewrite it as "He was in the first place." "Not among the last" might mean second, or third, or fourth. You'd need some more information before writing "He was among the winners!"

STEP TWO: **Practice changing positives into negatives and vice versa**

Fill in the chart below, changing positives into negatives and vice versa. You don't have to get too creative (although you can if you want)—this is just to get you comfortable with the idea.

Positive: Negative:

The weather was cold   _____

_____   He was not intelligent

I hope you are well   _____

She paid attention to him   _____

_____   They didn't sing well

The ship was sinking   _____

_____   I could not find even one clean sock

_____   There was no scarcity of pigeons

STEP THREE: **Add to the Sentence Variety chart**

Add the following principle and illustration to the Sentence Variety chart.

positive statement ⟷ negative statement   Her eyesight is excellent.
                                               She is not at all shortsighted.

                                               I am never unhappy.
                                               I am always filled with joy.

STEP FOUR: **Use the skill of varying by equivalence**

The sentences below are adapted from Jane Austen's classic novel *Pride and Prejudice*. On your own paper, rewrite each underlined word, phrase, or statement so that positives become negatives and negatives become positives—just as Jane Austen first wrote them.

When you are finished, ask your instructor to show you Austen's original sentences. How close were you?

Bingley was <u>not contented</u>; his sisters declared that they were <u>not merry</u>.

His apparent partiality <u>was no longer present</u>, his attentions <u>did not continue</u>, he was <u>Elizabeth's admirer no more</u>.

It was <u>seldom</u> that she could turn her eyes on Mr. Darcy himself.

<u>At once</u> her mother gave her to understand that the probability of their marriage was <u>not at all unpleasant</u> to her.

In spite of her <u>lack of liking</u>, she <u>was completely aware of</u> the compliment of such a man's affection.

My <u>not negative</u> opinion, once lost, is lost <u>for not a brief period of time</u>.

She was a <u>never wavering</u> talker.

Conceal the <u>less than mirthful</u> truth as long as it is possible.

WEEK 23: OUTLINING AND REWRITING, PART I

Over the next two weeks, you'll return to outlining (something that you haven't done since Week 12) and refresh your outlining skills. You'll also try something new. After outlining and analyzing an essay, you'll try your hand at rewriting the essay—using your outline, but not looking at the original.

Why?

Rewriting a classic essay is yet another way to build up your writing. When the American statesman Benjamin Franklin was a young man, he realized that his writing "fell far short in elegance of expression, in method, and in perspicuity" (by which he meant "clearness of expression"). In his *Autobiography,* Franklin tells us what he did to improve his writing skills. The *Spectator* was a popular newspaper, containing essays and opinion pieces, published in Britain beginning in 1711.

> About this time I met with an odd volume of the *Spectator.* It was the third. I had never before seen any of them. I bought it, read it over and over, and was much delighted with it. I thought the writing excellent, and wished, if possible, to imitate it. With this view I took some of the papers, and making short hints of the sentiment in each sentence, laid them by a few days, and then, without looking at the book, tried to complete the papers again, by expressing each hinted sentiment at length, and as fully as it had been expressed before, in any suitable words that should come to hand. Then I compared my *Spectator* with the original, discovered some of my faults, and corrected them . . . By comparing my work afterwards with the original, I discovered many faults and amended them; but I sometimes had the pleasure of fancying that, in certain particulars of small import, I had been lucky enough to improve the method or the language, and this encouraged me to think I might possibly in time come to be a tolerable English writer, of which I was extremely ambitious.
>
> —*The Autobiography of Benjamin Franklin,*
> Part I, "Parentage and Boyhood"

In your own efforts to be "a tolerable English writer," you'll try out Franklin's method.

Day One: Read

 Focus: Reading and understanding a
comparison-contrast essay

STEP ONE: **Read**

Read through the following excerpt from the essay "A Brother of St. Francis," by the Irish writer Grace Rhys. Rhys was born in 1865 and wrote novels, short stories, and essays. This essay was originally published as part of the collection of essays *About Many Things* (London: Methuen, 1920).

The title refers to St. Francis of Assisi, the Italian monk who founded the Franciscan Order. St. Francis is traditionally identified with love for animals and the care of nature.

Some of Rhys's vocabulary and references may be challenging for you. On this first reading, don't worry if you don't understand some of the words or sentences. Just read slowly and carefully all the way through to the end.

— — —

A Brother of St. Francis

by Grace Rhys

When talking to a wise friend a while ago I told her of the feeling of horror which had invaded me when watching a hippopotamus.

"Indeed," said she, "you do not need to go to the hippopotamus for a sensation. Look at a pig! There is something dire in the face of a pig. To think the same power should have created it that created a star!"

Those who love beauty and peace are often tempted to scamp their thinking, to avoid the elemental terrors that bring night into the mind. Yet if the fearful things of life are there, why not pluck up heart and look at them? Better have no Bluebeard's chamber in the mind. Better go boldly in and see what hangs by the wall. So salt, so medicinal is Truth, that even the bitterest draught may be made wholesome to the gentlest soul. So I would recommend anyone who can bear to think to leave the flower garden and go down and spend an hour by the pigstye.

There lies our friend in the sun upon his straw, blinking his clever little eye. Half friendly is his look. (He does not know that I—Heaven forgive me!—sometimes have bacon for breakfast!) Plainly, with that gashed mouth, those dreadful cheeks, and that sprawl of his, he belongs to an older world; that older world when first the mud and slime rose and moved, and, roaring, found a voice; aye, and no doubt enjoyed life, and in harsh and fearful sounds praised the Creator at the sunrising.

To prove the origin of the pig, let him out, and he will celebrate it by making straight for the nearest mud and diving into it. So strange is his aspect, so unreal to me, that it is almost as if the sunshine falling upon him might dissolve him, and resolve him into his original element. But no; there he is, perfectly real; as real as the good Christians and philosophers who will eventually eat him. While he lies there let me reflect in all charity on the disagreeable things I have heard about him.

He is dirty, people say. Nay, is he as dirty (or, at least, as complicated in his dirt) as his brother man can be? Let those who know the dens of London give the answer. Leave the pig to himself, and he is not so bad. He knows his mother mud is cleansing; he rolls partly because he loves her and partly because he wishes to be clean.

He is greedy? In my mind's eye there rises the picture of human gormandisers, fat-necked, with half-buried eyes and toddling step. How long since the giant Gluttony was slain? or does he still keep his monstrous table d'hote?

The pig pushes his brother from the trough? Why, that is a commonplace of our life. There is a whole school of so-called philosophers and political economists busied in elevating the pig's shove into a social and political necessity.

He screams horribly if you touch him or his share of victuals? I have heard a polite gathering of the best people turn senseless and rave at a mild suggestion of Christian Socialism. He is bitter-tempered? God knows, so are we. He has carnal desires? The worst sinner is man. He will fight? Look to the underside of war. He is cruel? Well, boys do queer things sometimes. For the rest, read the blacker pages of history; not as they are served up for the schoolroom by private national vanity, but after the facts.

If a cow or a sheep is sick or wounded and the pig can get at it, he will worry it to death? So does tyranny with subject peoples.

He loves to lie in the sun among his brothers, idle and at his ease? Aye, but suppose this one called himself a lord pig and lay in the sun with a necklace of gold about his throat and jewels in his ears, having found means to drive his brethren (merry little pigs and all) out of the sun for his own benefit, what should we say of him then?

No; he has none of our cold cunning. He is all simplicity. I am told it is possible to love him. I know a kindly Frenchwoman who takes her pig for an airing on the sands of Saint-Michel-en-Grève every summer afternoon. Knitting, she walks along, and calls gaily and endearingly to the delighted creature; he follows at a word, gambolling with flapping ears over the ribs of sand, pasturing on shrimps and seaweed while he enjoys the salt air. Clearly, then, the pig is our good little brother, and we have no right to be disgusted at him. Clearly our own feet are planted in the clay.

STEP TWO: **Discuss**

Go back through the essay now and underline any vocabulary words, sentences, or references that you didn't understand on your first reading. When you're finished, discuss the essay with your instructor.

STEP THREE: **Reread**

Now that you have discussed the essay, go back through and read it from beginning to end a second time, just as carefully.

Day Two: Outlining

Focus: Creating a two-level outline

STEP ONE: **Summarize**

Before you begin outlining the paragraphs of the essay, make sure that you understand its overall form and meaning.

In order to do this, you'll need to answer three questions:
1) What technique does Grace Rhys use in the essay?
2) What is she telling us about pigs?
3) What is she telling us about ourselves?

If you're able to answer, write one sentence answering each question on your own paper. If not, ask your instructor for help.

STEP TWO: **Two-level outline**

Now, write out a two-level outline of the essay. Make use of the helps in the copy below. The paragraphs are divided into groups, separated by the sign ◉; assign a Roman numeral to each group.

If you need more assistance, ask your instructor how many subpoints belong to each Roman numeral.

If you *still* need help, tell your instructor.

When talking to a wise friend a while ago I told her of the feeling of horror which had invaded me when watching a hippopotamus.

"Indeed," said she, "you do not need to go to the hippopotamus for a sensation. Look at a pig! There is something dire in the face of a pig. To think the same power should have created it that created a star!"

Those who love beauty and peace are often tempted to scamp their thinking, to avoid the elemental terrors that bring night into the mind. Yet if the fearful things of life are there, why not pluck up heart and look at them? Better have no Bluebeard's chamber in the mind. Better go boldly in and see what hangs by the wall. So salt, so medicinal is Truth, that even the bitterest draught may be made wholesome to the gentlest soul. So I would recommend anyone who can bear to think to leave the flower garden and go down and spend an hour by the pigstye.

There lies our friend in the sun upon his straw, blinking his clever little eye. Half friendly is his look. (He does not know that I—Heaven forgive me!—sometimes have bacon for breakfast!) Plainly, with that gashed mouth, those dreadful cheeks, and that sprawl of his, he belongs to an older world; that older world when first the mud and slime rose and moved, and, roaring, found a voice; aye, and no doubt enjoyed life, and in harsh and fearful sounds praised the Creator at the sunrising.

To prove the origin of the pig, let him out, and he will celebrate it by making straight for the nearest mud and diving into it. So strange is his aspect, so unreal to me, that it is almost as if the sunshine falling upon him might dissolve him, and resolve him into his original element. But no; there he is, perfectly real; as real as the good Christians and philosophers who will eventually eat him. While he lies there let me reflect in all charity on the disagreeable things I have heard about him.

He is dirty, people say. Nay, is he as dirty (or, at least, as complicated in his dirt) as his brother man can be? Let those who know the dens of London give the answer. Leave the pig to himself, and he is not so bad. He knows his mother mud is cleansing; he rolls partly because he loves her and partly because he wishes to be clean.

He is greedy? In my mind's eye there rises the picture of human gormandisers, fat-necked, with half-buried eyes and toddling step. How long since the giant Gluttony was slain? or does he still keep his monstrous table d'hote?

The pig pushes his brother from the trough? Why, that is a commonplace of our life. There is a whole school of so-called philosophers and political economists busied in elevating the pig's shove into a social and political necessity.

He screams horribly if you touch him or his share of victuals? I have heard a polite gathering of the best people turn senseless and rave at a mild suggestion of Christian Socialism. He is bitter-tempered? God knows, so are we. He has carnal desires? The worst sinner is man. He will fight? Look to the underside of war. He is cruel? Well, boys do queer things sometimes. For the rest, read the blacker pages of history; not as they are served up for the schoolroom by private national vanity, but after the facts.

If a cow or a sheep is sick or wounded and the pig can get at it, he will worry it to death? So does tyranny with subject peoples.

He loves to lie in the sun among his brothers, idle and at his ease? Aye, but suppose this one called himself a lord pig and lay in the sun with a necklace of gold about his throat and jewels in his ears, having found means to drive his brethren (merry little pigs and all) out of the sun for his own benefit, what should we say of him then?

No; he has none of our cold cunning. He is all simplicity. I am told it is possible to love him. I know a kindly Frenchwoman who takes her pig for an airing on the sands of Saint-Michel-en-Grève every summer afternoon. Knitting, she walks along, and calls gaily and endearingly to the delighted creature; he follows at a word, gambolling with flapping ears over the ribs of sand, pasturing on shrimps and seaweed while he enjoys the salt air. Clearly, then, the pig is our good little brother, and we have no right to be disgusted at him. Clearly our own feet are planted in the clay.

Day Three: Rewriting

Focus: Rewriting a classic essay
from an outline

Today, you'll use the outline you created to rewrite Grace Rhys's essay in your own words.

STEP ONE: Reread

Read "A Brother of St. Francis" again, carefully, from beginning to end.

STEP TWO: Understand the model

Before you start writing, take another look at the structure of "A Brother of St. Francis." A sample outline of the passage is on the left; a description of the elements of the essay is on the right. Read through both of them carefully.

I.	Introduction	Two-part introduction
	A. Anecdote	Personal anecdote
	B. Command to the reader	Direct statement to reader
II.	The pig	Description of the main subject
	A. Appearance	Major aspect
	B. Mud	Second major aspect
III.	Comparison of pig and man	Comparison of main subject and
	A. Dirty	another subject
	B. Greedy	Six aspects compared
	C. Pushy	
	D. Screams and fights	
	E. Worries the wounded	
	F. Lies around while others work	
IV.	Conclusion	Two-part conclusion
	A. The pig	Conclusion by personal reaction
	B. Ourselves	(Final statement)

Let's look at each one of these elements in turn.

First, notice that Rhys's introduction and conclusion have the same structure. Each one starts with a story (her conversation with her friend in the introduction, a story *about* another friend in the conclusion) and then ends with a direct statement to the reader. This is another version of the Introduction by Anecdote; at the end of her story, Rhys exhorts the reader to think carefully, to consider the pig without fear.

Second, Rhys goes on to introduce her main subject, the *thing* to which she will compare another *thing*: the pig. She introduces the pig by describing in detail two major aspects of the pig: its appearance, and its habits. (Those might sound familiar to you from your biographical sketch *topos*.)

Third, Rhys compares six details about a pig's behavior with details about the same behavior in humans. This is the main part of the essay—the comparison and contrast. (There is more comparison than contrast—she finds pigs and people to be very similar!).

Finally, Rhys writes a conclusion which is very effective because it has different content, but the same structure as the introduction. She uses the form of a Conclusion by Personal Reaction by first telling a story that she's heard, and then explaining to the reader what she's learned by taking her own advice and considering the pig—that we too have "feet of clay" (meaning that we too are tempted to behave like animals).

STEP THREE: **Rewrite**

Now that you've got a little more understanding about the structure of Grace Rhys's essay, use your outline to write your own version of her piece without glancing back at it even once.

This is not an exercise in memorization! You are not supposed to reproduce her words exactly. Remember, Franklin said that his effort was to express the ideas in the original piece

"as fully as it had been expressed before, in any suitable words that should come to hand."
You can and should use your own words. I'm also going to give you a break: your essay doesn't
need to be "as fully" expressed as the original. It can be shorter. Use these guidelines for each
section.

Section	Rhys's word count	Your word count
I.	172 words	At least 70 words
II.	183 words	At least 70 words
III.	342 words	At least 125 words
IV.	110 words	At least 50 words

Just to help you out, here's my stab at rewriting the introductory anecdote without looking
back:

> Not long ago, I was talking to a friend about my fear of hippopota-
> muses. She said, "Forget about the hippopotamus. Look how terrifying pigs
> are!" She was right. I didn't want to think carefully about a pig.

Compare this with the original opening paragraphs.

> When talking to a wise friend a while ago I told her of the feeling of
> horror which had invaded me when watching a hippopotamus.
> "Indeed," said she, "you do not need to go to the hippopotamus for
> a sensation. Look at a pig! There is something dire in the face of a pig. To
> think the same power should have created it that created a star!"

As you can see, I used my own words, and left out the whole observation that stars and
pigs were created by the same power. But I retell the same conversation that Grace Rhys does.
Since you've never tried to do this before, it may seem difficult and unnatural. If you have
no idea at all what to write, ask your instructor for help.
When your composition is finished, show it to your instructor.

STEP FOUR: **Compare**

Read your essay out loud.
Then, read the original essay out loud.
You don't have to make any huge conclusions about how they compare. Just listen to how
each essay sounds.

Day Four: Copia Exercise
Sentence Transformation

 Focus: Practicing skills in sentence transformation

STEP ONE: **Review**

Read carefully through your Sentence Variety chart and pay close attention to the examples. You should have nine different types of transformation on the chart.

STEP TWO: **Transform**

Pick five sentences from your rewrite of "A Brother of St. Francis." Using five of the techniques on the Sentence Variety chart, transform each sentence. Read the original sentences and the transformed sentences out loud to your instructor. Decide together which sentences sound best.

Insert the best sentences back into your composition. Does this improve the sound of your essay?

If you have trouble finding sentences to transform, make use of the following tips as you look through your work.

To transform descriptive adjectives into nouns, look for adjectives that come right before the nouns they modify. Or, look for prepositional phrases beginning with "of" and see if they can be turned into descriptive adjectives.

To transform active verbs into passive, look for sentences with action verbs and direct objects.

Look for sentences with indirect objects to transform into objects of a preposition.

To transform a participle into an infinitive, look for an -ing word following an action verb.

To transform a main verb into an infinitive, pick a strong verb and see whether you are able to add one of the following verbs to it:

VERBS THAT ARE OFTEN FOLLOWED BY INFINITIVES

agree	aim	appear	arrange	ask	attempt
beg	begin	care	choose	consent	continue
dare	decide	deserve	dislike	expect	fail
forget	get	hesitate	hope	hurry	intend
leap	like	love	ought	plan	prefer
prepare	proceed	promise	refuse	remember	start
strive	try	use	wait	want	wish

To intensify an adjective, look for descriptive adjectives that either come before a noun or follow a linking verb.

To change a word into a phrase, metaphor, or kenning, look for strong and interesting nouns.

To change a positive statement to a negative statement, look for a strong statement. Then use your thesaurus to find antonyms for the nouns and verbs in the statement.

If you have trouble, ask your instructor for help.

Week 24: Outlining and Rewriting, Part II

Day One: Read

 Focus: Reading and understanding an essay of definition

STEP ONE: Read

Read through the following slightly condensed essay "A Few Words on Christmas," by Charles Lamb. Lamb was an English writer who lived 1775–1834 (which means that when he died, Charles Dickens was twenty-two years old). He is best known for *Tales from Shakespeare,* a children's book retelling the stories of Shakespeare's plays. Lamb co-wrote *Tales from Shakespeare* with his younger sister, Mary.

This essay was first published in *The London Magazine* in 1822.

Like last week's essay, this essay might contain some challenging vocabulary and unfamiliar references. Don't worry if you don't understand every sentence; just read slowly and carefully through to the end.

- - -

A Few Words on Christmas

by Charles Lamb

Close the shutters, and draw the curtains together, and pile fresh wood upon the hearth! Let us have, for once, an innocent *auto de fé*. Let the hoarded corks be brought forth, and branches of crackling laurel. Place the wine and fruit and the hot chestnuts upon the table. And now, good folks and children, bring your chairs round to the blazing fire. Put some of those rosy apples upon your plates. We'll drink one glass of bright sherry "to our absent friends and readers," and then let us talk a little about Christmas.

301

And what is Christmas?

Why, it is the happiest time of the year. It is the season of mirth and cold weather. It is the time when Christmas-boxes and jokes are given; when mistletoe, and red-berried laurel, and soups, and sliding, and school-boys, prevail; when the country is illuminated by fires and bright faces; and the town is radiant with laughing children. Oranges, as rich as the fruit of the Hesperides, shine out in huge golden heaps. Cakes, frosted over (as if to rival the glittering snow) come forth by thousands from their ovens: and on every stall at every corner of every street are the roasted apples . . .

And *this* night is Christmas Eve. Formerly it was a serious and holy vigil. Our forefathers observed it strictly till a certain hour, and then requited their own forbearance with cups of ale and Christmas candles, with placing the *yule log* on the fire, and roaring themselves thirsty till morning. Time has altered this. We are neither so good as our forefathers were—nor so bad. We go to bed sober; but we have forgotten their old devotions. Our conduct looks like a sort of compromise; so that we are not worse than our ancestors, we are satisfied not to be better: but let that pass . . .

One mark and sign of Christmas is the *music*; rude enough, indeed, but generally gay, and speaking eloquently of the season. Music, at festival times, is common to most countries. In Spain, the serenader twangs his guitar; in Italy, the musician allures rich notes from his Cremona; in Scotland, the bagpipe drones out its miserable noise; in Germany, there is the horn, and the pipe in Arcady. We too, in our turn, have our Christmas "*Waits*," who witch us at early morning, before cock-crow, with strains and welcomings which belong to night. They wake us so gently that the music seems to have commenced in our dreams, and we listen to it till we sleep again. Besides this, we have our songs, from the young and the old, jocose and fit for the time. What old gentleman of sixty has not his stock—his one, or two, or three frolicksome verses. He sings them for the young folks, and is secure of their applause and his own private satisfaction. His wife, indeed, perhaps says "Really, my dear Mr. Williams, you should *now* give over these, &c."; but he is more resolute from opposition, and gambols through his "Flowery Meads of May," or "Beneath a shady bower," while the children hang on his thin, trembling, untuneable notes in delighted and delightful amazement . . .

Leaving now our *eve* of Christmas, its jokes, and songs, and warm hearths, we will indulge ourselves in a few words upon CHRISTMAS DAY. It is like a day of victory. Every house and church is as green as spring. The laurel, that never dies—the holly, with its armed leaves and scarlet berries—the mistletoe, under which one sweet ceremonial is (we hope still) performed, are seen. Every brave shrub that has life and verdure seems to come forward to shame the reproaches of men, and to show them that the earth is never dead, never parsimonious. . . .

Hunger is no longer an enemy. We feed him, like the ravenous tiger, till he pants and sleeps, or is quiet. Everybody eats at Christmas. The rich feast as usual; but the tradesman leaves his moderate fare for dainties. The apprentice abjures his chop, and plunges at once into the luxuries of joints and puddings. The school-boy is no longer at school. He dreams no more of the coming lesson or the lifted rod; but mountains of jelly rise beside him, and blanc-mange, with its treacherous foundations, threatens to overwhelm his fancy; roods of mince pies spread out their chequered riches before him . . . Even the servant has his "once a year" bottle of port; and the beggar his "alderman in chains."

Oh! merry piping time of Christmas! Never let us permit thee to degenerate into distant courtesies and formal salutations. But let us shake our friends and familiars by the hand, as our fathers and their fathers did. Let them all come around us, and let us count how many the year has added to our circle. Let us enjoy the present, and laugh at the past. Let us tell old stories and invent new ones—innocent always, and ingenious if we can. Let us not meet to abuse the world, but to make it better by our individual example. Let us be patriots, but not men of party. Let us look *of the time*—cheerful and generous, and endeavour to make others as generous and cheerful as ourselves.

STEP TWO: **Discuss**

Go back through the essay now and underline any vocabulary words, sentences, or references that you didn't understand on your first reading. When you're finished, discuss the essay with your instructor.

STEP THREE: **Reread**

Now that you have discussed the essay, go back through and read it from beginning to end a second time, just as carefully.

Day Two: Outlining and Analyzing

 Focus: Understanding the structure of the essay

STEP ONE: **Two-level outline**

Begin today's work by writing out a two-level outline of the essay.

> Use this model:
> I.
> II.
> III.
> > A.
> > B.
> IV.
> > A.
> > B.
> V.

Write your outline on your own paper, or use your word processor. If you are writing on paper, leave plenty of room after each major point and subpoint—you'll be returning to this sheet of paper in the second and third steps of today's work.

See if you can figure out where to divide the essay into major points and subpoints. If you need help, ask your instructor.

When you are finished, check your outline with your instructor.

STEP TWO: **Three-level outline**

Now go back to the sections of the essay covered by the Roman numerals III and IV on your outline. Each of those major points has subpoints.

Beneath each subpoint, find the correct number of supporting details, as indicated below. Insert them into your outline. Ask for help if necessary; when you are finished, show your outline to your instructor.

> III.
> > A. (2 supporting details)
> > B. (3 supporting details)
> IV.
> > A. (2 supporting details)
> > B. (4 supporting details)

STEP THREE: **Analysis**

You'll finish today's work by looking at the remaining three paragraphs of the essay: the introduction, the definition, and the conclusion. Rather than outlining these paragraphs, you will try to identify the elements of introductions, conclusions, and definitions that they include.

Carry out the instructions below.

1. Reread the first paragraph of Charles Lamb's essay. Examine the types of introductions on your Introductions chart. Which type of introduction does Lamb use? Write the name of the type on your outline, following the Roman numeral I.

2. Reread the last paragraph of the essay. Examine the types of conclusions on your Conclusion chart. What type of conclusion is closest to Lamb's? Write the name of the type on your outline, following the Roman numeral V.

3. Turn to the chart that describes Explanation by Definition: Historical Object, Event, Place, or People Group. Read through the questions. Then, look carefully at the two paragraphs (the first is only one line long) that belong to Roman numeral II. In your opinion, does Lamb define Christmas by focusing on its properties, its function, or its genus? Write your answer on your outline, following the Roman numeral II.

When you are finished, show your work to your instructor.

Day Three: Rewriting

Focus: Rewriting a classic essay
from an outline

Today, you'll use the outline you created to rewrite Charles Lamb's essay in your own words.

STEP ONE: **Reread**

Read "A Few Words on Christmas" again, carefully, from beginning to end.

STEP TWO: **Understand the model**

Before you start writing, take another look at the structure of "A Few Words on Christmas." A sample outline of the passage is on the left; a description of the elements of the essay is on the right. Read through both of them carefully.

I.   **Introduction**   Introduction by anecdote in first person
       Introduction by Anecdote   plural, including both writer and reader

II. **Definition of Christmas**
       Function   Definition of the phenomenon

III. **Christmas Eve**   Division of phenomenon into two phases
     A. **Christmas Eve customs**   Aspects of the first phase
         1. Formerly, serious and holy vigil   using comparison and contrast
         2. Now, sober but no devotions
     B. **Music**
         1. In other countries
         2. The waits in England
         3. Our own songs

IV. **Christmas Day**   Aspects of the second phase
     A. **Decorations OR Visual signs**
         1. Houses and churches
         2. The plants used
     B. **Food**
         1. Rich and tradesmen
         2. Apprentices
         3. School-boy
         4. Servant and beggar

V.   **Conclusion**   Conclusion by personal reaction in first
       Conclusion by Personal Reaction   person plural, including both writer and
                                              reader

Let's look at each one of these elements in turn.

First: Just like Grace Rhys, Charles Lamb is careful to make his introduction and his conclusion resemble each other. Both of them are personal (a personal anecdote, and a personal opinion), and both of them are written in the first person plural.

Second, Lamb gives a brief definition of the event he is about to talk about.

Third, Lamb goes on to divide the event into two phases: Christmas Eve and Christmas Day. He then goes on to discuss important aspects of each phase. In his paragraphs about Christmas Eve, he also uses comparison and contrast—he contrasts old Christmas Eve customs with new Christmas Eve customs, and he also compares the music in England to the music in other countries.

STEP THREE: **Rewrite**

Now rewrite Lamb's essay, in your own words, using *only* your outline. Don't look at the essay itself as you write!

Like your Rhys essay, your version of "A Few Words on Christmas" can be shorter than the original. Use these guidelines as a minimum word count for each section:

Section	Lamb's word count	Your word count
I.	94	35
II.	111	50
III.	328	120
IV.	222	75
V.	128	50

If you get completely stuck, ask your instructor for help.

When your composition is finished, show it to your instructor.

STEP FOUR: **Compare**

Read your essay out loud.

Then, read the original essay out loud.

You don't have to make any huge conclusions about how they compare. Just listen to how each essay sounds.

Day Four: Copia Exercise
Figurative Language

Focus: Practicing skills in
figurative language

STEP ONE: **Examine plain and figurative language**

Charles Lamb was a writer of his time. In the eighteenth century, metaphors, similes, and other word pictures were an essential part of any good writer's vocabulary. Lamb's essays and stories are packed with figurative language—so much so that we might find them hard to read. In modern times, good writers usually write straightforward, clean prose, with word pictures used sparingly—for emphasis, not as a regular way of expression.

Neither one of these ways of writing is good or bad; they are simply different. Modern writing (spare, clean, and bare) can be improved with a few techniques from the eighteenth century. And, if you ask me, Charles Lamb's writing would be much improved with a little more sparsity and cleanliness.

Today, you'll take a series of sentences from Charles Lamb's ornate essay and change them around. For each, you'll first rewrite the sentence in plain, straightforward prose, with no word picture. You'll then turn your plain sentence back into an expression with a metaphor or simile—but one drawn from your world, that makes sense to you.

Here's how I would handle Lamb's strange first metaphor, about the *auto de fé*. (What a bizarre metaphor for an essay about Christmas!)

Let us have, for once, an innocent *auto de fé*.
Let us have a welcoming, warm Christmas fire in the hearth.
Let us have, for once, an innocent sea of fire and brimstone.
Let us have, for once, a harmless wildfire.

First, I turned Lamb's metaphor back into a straightforward statement. Then I thought to myself: What is made out of fire, but isn't an innocent fire burning in a living room fireplace? Wildfire—forest fires—burn wood, but aren't innocent. And hell is pictured as a sea of fire and brimstone. I tried substituting both of those for "warm Christmas fire in the hearth."

I don't think either of my metaphors is very good, by the way. But I also think Lamb's is weird and unnecessary. If I were writing this essay, I'd choose the straightforward statement in place of the other three.

STEP TWO: **Transform Charles Lamb's sentences**

On your own paper, rewrite each of the following sentences twice—once as a plain statement with no figurative language, and once with a metaphor or simile of your own choosing. Read all three sentences and, for each, pick your favorite. What sounds best to your ear—the plain statement, Lamb's figurative language, or your own imaginative effort?

Oranges, as rich as the fruit of the Hesperides, shine out in huge golden heaps.
Cakes, frosted over (as if to rival the glittering snow) come forth by thousands from their ovens.
It is like a day of victory.
Every house and church is as green as spring.
Hunger is no longer an enemy.
We feed him, like the ravenous tiger, till he pants and sleeps, or is quiet.
Mountains of jelly rise beside him.
Roods of mince pies spread out their chequered riches before him.

When you are finished, show your sentences to your instructor.

Week 25: Independent Composition: Modeled on A Classic Essay

This week, you'll do something different—you'll write an essay based on one of the two models you've examined in the past two weeks. Using the frame provided by either Grace Rhys or Charles Lamb, you'll fill it with your own original content.

Your composition will need to be at least 450 words in length (usually, about two double-spaced typed pages of text).

As I've been doing for these independent writing projects, I will give you a suggested amount of time to spend on each step, rather than breaking your tasks down into four days. Remember: these are only *suggested* times! You and your instructor can decide how many days to devote to the assignment—three days, four days, or even more if necessary. Remember that it's perfectly fine to switch topics after you begin, even if this slows you down.

Here's an overview of the steps:

Step One: Understand the assignment	20–30 minutes
Step Two: Brainstorm a topic	45–60 minutes
Step Three: Pre-writing	2–3 hours
Step Four: Draft the composition	3–6 hours
Step Five: Sentence revision	1 hour
Step Six: Proofread and title	30–60 minutes

Before you start on Step One, read through the entire week's lesson.

Although you don't need to show your work to your instructor after each step, ask for help whenever you need it. Your instructor may ask to see your work at any time. Always be ready to show it.

STEP ONE: Understand the assignment (20-30 minutes)

Read through the following two assignments and choose one of them. Be sure to read all the way to the end of Step One before you decide.

1) Comparison Essay, Based on Grace Rhys's "A Brother of St. Francis"

Your task: Compare two different things, showing that one is better than its reputation and the other is worse.

You can follow Rhys closely and compare human beings to another animal (not a pig). You can show that human beings are no better than this animal—or you can concentrate on showing that the animal is far, far nobler and more interesting than people. You can compare human beings to something else that isn't an animal. Or you can compare two things that are different from each other—any two things.

Your limitation: You have to have the same basic intention as Grace Rhys. Of the two subjects that you pick to compare, one of them has to have a much more positive, important, or valued character than the other. And you have to show that the less valued subject is nobler than most people think, while the more valued subject is less wonderful than its reputation. (For example, imagine that you're going to write about food. Compare Cracker Jack and broccoli. Show that Cracker Jack has many wonderful qualities—and that broccoli is not as great as people think.)

The structure of your essay must follow this pattern:

Two-part introduction
    Personal anecdote
    Direct statement to reader
Description of the main subject
    Major aspect of main subject described
    Second major aspect of main subject described
Comparison of main subject and another subject
    Three to six aspects of both subjects compared
Two-part conclusion
    Conclusion by personal reaction
    Final statement

2) Definition and Description Essay, Based on Charles Lamb's "A Few Words on Christmas"

Your task: Define and describe a special event that you have experienced.

You can describe a yearly holiday (although not Christmas). You can describe a family tradition—a visit to the State Fair, a yearly beach vacation. Or you can describe an event that you loved and remember fondly—a special trip that you took with your parents, the greatest birthday party you ever had, the time you won a competition.

Your limitation: Your essay has to be positive; it has to show the *wonderfulness* of the event, and it has to invite/exhort/encourage others to experience it or plan a similar experience.

The structure of your essay must follow this pattern:

Introduction by anecdote
  Written in the first person plural, including both writer and reader
Definition of the event
Division of the event into two phases
  Description of aspects of the first phase, using comparison and contrast
  Description of aspects of the second phase
Conclusion by personal reaction
  Written in the first person plural, including both writer and reader

GENERAL INSTRUCTIONS FOR BOTH ESSAY TYPES

Choose a topic that won't require you to do a lot of extra research and reading. Your focus in this essay should be on reproducing the structure of one of these classic essays, but pouring your own ideas and experiences into it. If you do need to quote and footnote a piece of information, you may—but it is fine to write this essay with no footnotes whatsoever.

Even if the model feels unnatural and strange to you, concentrate on expressing your own experiences and ideas, using your own vocabulary. Sticking to the framework of the model will expand your abilities by forcing you to develop an idea in a new way—one you would probably never have come up with on your own.

STEP TWO: **Brainstorm a topic (45–60 minutes)**

To find a topic, you'll need to brainstorm—but your brainstorming will look a little different, depending on which model you choose.

If you find that you're completely stuck on your topic, switch to the other model and try brainstorming that one instead.

You can ask your instructor for help if you need it.

1) For Comparison Essay, Based on Grace Rhys's "A Brother of St. Francis"

a) First, jot down as many things as you can think of on a sheet of paper. To get you started, think about the following categories:

> *Kinds of animals*
> *Types of food*
> *Pastimes and entertainments*
> *Sports*
> *Hobbies*
> *Books and movies*
> *Famous historical events*
> *Kinds of jobs (or careers)*

b) Next, draw a line down the middle of a piece of paper. On one side, write "Positive." On the other, write "Negative." Under the heading "Positive," write down the names of everything you came up with that has a positive reputation or connotation (it won an Oscar, it is cute and fluffy, it's good for you, it has prestige). On the other side of the paper, write down everything that has a negative reputation or connotation (it lost millions at the box office, it's a predator, only losers are associated with it). If something is neutral, leave it off the list.

Here an example of how a few categorizations might work:

POSITIVE	**NEGATIVE**
Lemurs	*Vultures*
Being a doctor	*Being a garbage collector*
The Civil Rights movement	*The Black Hole of Calcutta*

c) Using your lists, choose two things to compare. The *negative* subject will be your main subject (like Rhys's pig). The *positive* subject will be the thing that you compare it to (in Rhys's essay, human beings).

2) Definition and Description Essay, Based on Charles Lamb's "A Few Words on Christmas"

a) Begin by writing down the names of as many holidays and special occasions as you can.

b) Write down brief phrases or sentences describing special events in your past (trips, events, family outings) that stand out in your memory.

c) Look back through your list. Try to remember, right off the top of your head, three or four specific, colorful descriptive details about each one. Choose the event or holiday that is the most well-defined and vivid in your mind.

STEP THREE: **Pre-writing (2–3 hours)**

Before you start working on your actual essay, you need to go through each required element and make sure that your topic is going to work for you. Plus, giving yourself time to do pre-writing will make the drafting of the composition much simpler, and will allow you to concentrate on making your prose read smoothly and beautifully.

For an essay based on your own personal thoughts and reactions, the pre-writing step is like the note-taking step when you write an essay based on research. It gives you the raw material to turn into a composition. You should never plunge directly into drafting an essay without giving yourself plenty of notes to work with, rearrange, and juggle.

Follow the directions below for the essay of your choice.

1) Comparison Essay, Based on Grace Rhys's "A Brother of St. Francis"

Keep in mind your task: You must compare two things, showing that one is better than its reputation, and the other is worse.

On your own paper, jot down phrases and sentences that address the following questions and suggestions. You may find it helpful to glance back at Rhys's original essay in Week 23 as you work.

Two-part introduction

Personal anecdote. *What story will you retell or invent in order to introduce your main subject—your negative subject? This story should highlight the negative aspects of the subject—why people think poorly of it.*

Direct statement to reader. *Exhort the reader to re-examine or re-think his or her original reaction.*

Description of the main subject

Major aspect of main subject described. *This does not have to be specifically either negative or positive, but it should be something that is absolutely characteristic of your subject—something that makes it what it is. You can use the Explanation by Definition chart in your topoi reference section to help you brainstorm.*

Second major aspect of main subject described. *Same instructions as above—but this could be a slightly less central property or aspect of the subject—perhaps personal appearance or something else that will draw the reader into a deeper consideration of what the subject is.*

Comparison of main subject and another subject

Three to six aspects of both subjects compared. *In order to prepare for this step, you'll need to borrow techniques that you first practiced in Week 5, when you learned about comparison and contrast. Jot down as many aspects of each subject as you can think of, and then circle those that are similar. Remember, your goal is to show the similarity between the two subjects, just as Rhys showed the similarities between pigs and people by highlighting their behavior.*

Two-part conclusion

Conclusion by personal reaction. *This should be a story or anecdote that—in contrast to the opening story—highlights something that is good, positive, or lovable about the main subject.*

Final statement. *Can you explain what difference it will make to the reader if he or she can change the way he or she thinks about the main subject? Or can you make a statement about how he or she should* view *the main subject?*

2) Definition and Description Essay, Based on Charles Lamb's "A Few Words on Christmas"

Keep in mind your task: You must define and describe a special event that you have experienced.

On your own paper, jot down phrases and sentences that address the following questions and suggestions. You may find it helpful to glance back at Lamb's original essay in Week 24 as you work.

Introduction by Anecdote

Written in the first person plural, including both writer and reader. *Can you imagine a scene that takes place during the event? What do you see, smell, hear, taste, feel? Now, can you invite the reader to join you in sensing the same things?*

Definition of the event. *What characterizes the event? What behaviors take place during it? What do you see, hear, smell, feel, taste, or do during the event? How long does it last? Who takes part in it? Try to answer these and any other useful questions from your Explanation by Definition chart. The most central qualities of the event belong here. Others that you come up with can be addressed in the "Description of aspects of the second phase" below.*

Division of the event into two phases. *Some holidays, like Christmas, have both an "eve" and a "day." But even if your event doesn't fall into this pattern, you can divide it into a before/after, before/during, or during/after. What divisions work best? What characterizes each part of the division?*

Description of aspects of the first phase, using comparison and contrast. *Do different people observe/celebrate this part of the event in different ways? Are these people separated by age, experience, gender, nationality? What makes them different, and how are their reactions different?*

Description of aspects of the second phase. *Here, you should describe at least two of the aspects you came up with but did not use in the Definition of the Event, above. If necessary, spend a little more time brainstorming, using the Explanation by Definition questions.*

Conclusion by Personal Reaction

Written in the first person plural, including both writer and reader. *This should not be a scene or a story; more of an exhortation to the reader to join you in making the most of this event or another like it in the future. Remember to use "we" and "us" as you make your notes. What part of the event would benefit others the most? How would it change them?*

STEP FOUR: Draft the composition (3–6 hours)

Using your pre-writing notes and keeping an eye on the model that you're following, write your composition. Remember: you're aiming for at least 450 words. Your composition must include the elements listed in Step One, but you can decide where your paragraphs should end and begin.

STEP FIVE: Sentence revision (1 hour)

Read back through your composition now. If you have not already used at least one metaphor and at least one simile, find a place for both of these now. Add them in.

Once you have made sure that your essay contains both a metaphor and a simile, look back at your Sentence Variety chart. You must use at least *two* additional techniques (not including metaphor and simile!) to transform at least two of your original sentences.

Your goal here is to make your sentences sound more lyrical and beautiful, not to make them more awkward. Read your original and transformed sentences out loud to make sure that you have improved them.

If you have difficulty finding sentences to transform, look back at the guidelines given to you in Week 23, Day Four.

STEP SIX: **Proofread and title (30–60 minutes)**

Proofread your paper, using the following steps.

1) Make sure that your paper is at least 450 words in length.

2) Check to make sure that all of the elements listed in the model are also in your paper.

3) Read your paper out loud, listening for awkward or unclear sections and repeated words. Rewrite awkward or unclear sentences so that they flow more naturally.

4) Listen for information that is repeated more than once. Eliminate repetition of ideas.

5) Read through the paper one more time, looking for sentence fragments, run-on sentences, and repeated words. Correct fragments and run-on sentences. Listen for unnecessary repetition. If you used a modifier more than twice, find another word.

6) Check your spelling by looking, individually, at each word that might be a problem.

When your paper is completely proofread, give it a title—once again, following the example of your models.

Grace Rhys titled her essay using a descriptive phrase/metaphor for the pig: "A Brother of St. Francis." If you wrote an essay modeled after Rhys's work, title it by thinking of a descriptive phrase/metaphor that applies to your main subject.

Charles Lamb titled his essay very literally: it is "A Few Words on" the topic of Christmas. If you wrote a composition like Lamb's, give it the same kind of title—but you have to think of a different way to say "a few words."

Once you've titled your essay, give it to your instructor for evaluation.

WEEK 26: EXPLANATION BY TEMPORAL COMPARISON IN HISTORY

Day One: Introduction to Temporal Comparisons

 Focus: Understanding how to compare something to itself at different points in time

This week, you'll return to the idea of comparison and contrast—with a twist.

STEP ONE: **Understand the concept of temporal comparison**

Look at the following photos:

Now, look back at these two portraits, taken from Week 18 of this course.

What do the two sets of pictures have in common? Both of them show the same place or person at different points in time. The first set of photos shows a store building in Porter County, Indiana, in 1917—before and after a tornado blew through the town. The portraits show the author Alfred Noyes. The first portrait is of Noyes as a middle-aged writer; the second is of Noyes as an old man, shortly before his death.

You can use writing to present the same sort of "before and after" depictions of objects, events, places, or people. When you describe the properties of one thing at two different points in time, you are writing a *temporal comparison*. You are comparing something to itself at another point in time.

Look at this example of temporal comparison, from a two-volume biography of Mary, Queen of Scots.

> She came into England at the age of twenty-five, in the prime of womanhood, the full vigour of health, and the rapidly ripening strength of her intellectual powers. She was there destined to feel in all its bitterness that "hope delayed maketh the heart sick." Year after year passed slowly on,

and year after year her spirits became more exhausted, her health feebler, and her doubts and fears confirmed, till they at length settled into despair. Premature old age overtook her, before she was past the meridian of life; and for some time before her death, her hair was white. . . . Yet, during the whole of this long period . . . Mary retained the innate grace and dignity of her character, never forgetting that she had been born a queen.

—H. G. Bell, *Life of Mary Queen of Scots*, Vol II
(Edinburgh: William Brown, 1890), p. 181.

This contrasts the qualities of the young Mary (in her prime, in full health, her intellect strengthening) with the older Mary (exhausted spirits, feeble health, despairing, white-haired). It also tells you what stayed the same: "the innate grace and dignity of her character."

A comparison in time highlights how a single object, event, place, or person has *changed*, through pointing out both the things that have shifted over time. It can also point out what things have stayed the same.

STEP TWO: Analyze paragraphs of temporal comparison

Now you'll look in more detail at how a brief temporal comparison is constructed.

For each of the comparisons below, fill out the chart by writing down all the ways in which the historical phenomena differ at earlier and later dates. If you need help, ask your instructor.

The first chart has been started for you.

1) This paragraph is about the famous II Army Corps of the United States; the Corps fought against the Confederate States during the American Civil War.

The II Corps had been fought out and used up. It had been the most famous corps in the army. It had stormed Bloody Lane at Antietam, it had taken 4,000 casualties at Gettysburg, and it had broken the Bloody Angle at Spotsylvania. But now it was all shot to pieces, and instead of being the army's strongest fighting unit, it was the weakest. Nothing but a long period of recruiting, drill, and discipline would bring it up to its old level.

—Bruce Catton, *A Stillness at Appomattox*
(New York: Anchor Books, 1990), p. 212.

II Army Corps before	II Army Corps after
Most famous in the army Stormed Bloody Lane at Antietam	Fought out and used up

2) This compares the ancient Olympics with the modern version.

People often deplore the modern Olympics for their corruption or supposed inferiority when compared to their ancient counterpart—rather unfairly, I believe. In essence, the two are the same. The modern Olympics, too, represent the pinnacle of excellence and prestige, and in most significant ways they are not much different from the ancient version. The principal difference, I think, is how much the modern Olympics dwarf their ancient ancestor in size. At Sydney 2000, more than 10,000 athletes from 200 countries competed in 300 events. That's big. In the heyday of the ancient Olympics, for example, the fifth century BC, there was a total of 14 events and perhaps up to 300 or so competitors. In antiquity, perhaps as many as 40,000 spectators could watch the games. Because of modern electronic communication, the whole world watches today's Olympics, which have become the greatest show on earth. Almost anywhere on earth one can view them on television, and almost everywhere on earth people *do* view them.

> —David C. Young, *A Brief History of the Olympic Games* (Oxford: Blackwell Publishing, 2004), pp. 138–139.

Ancient Olympics	Modern Olympics

3) These three paragraphs compare conditions before and after the nineteenth-century Industrial Revolution.

Before the Industrial Revolution, many families made their own furniture, clothes, and shoes. All these crafts were handmade, and because the process was slow, craftspeople produced very few items. This in turn made these items very expensive. Only people with enough money could afford to buy things they needed from craftspeople.

The situation dramatically changed when new devices and machines started to replace hand labor. With the help of new devices, craftspeople could produce more goods at a lower price. In addition, the development of bigger machines gave rise to factories. Thus from making goods by hand in small shops or homes, people moved to making them in factories and later on assembly lines. These changes made goods more affordable to a greater number of people.

. . . [D]uring the Industrial Revolution, millions of people abandoned a traditional life in the countryside and moved to cities, which created a specialized and interdependent economic life and made an urban worker more dependent on the will of the employer than the rural worker had been.

—Carl E. Van Horn and Herbert A. Schaffner, eds., *Work in America: An Encyclopedia of History, Policy, and Society* (Santa Barbara, Calif.: ABC-CLIO, Inc., 2003), p. 285.

Before the Industrial Revolution	During and After the Industrial Revolution

STEP THREE: Understand the place of a brief temporal comparison in the Description of a Person

Look again at the paragraph about Mary Queen of Scots. Read it carefully and then read through the list of qualities that the writer compares and contrasts.

She came into England at the age of <u>twenty-five</u>, in the <u>prime of womanhood</u>, the full <u>vigour of health</u>, and the rapidly ripening <u>strength of her intellectual powers</u>. She was there destined to feel in all its bitterness that "hope delayed maketh the heart sick." Year after year passed slowly on, and year after year her spirits became more exhausted, her <u>health feebler</u>, and her <u>doubts and fears</u> confirmed, till they at length settled into despair. <u>Premature old age</u> overtook her, before she was past the meridian of life; and for some time before her death, her <u>hair was white</u> . . . Yet, during the whole of this long period . . . Mary retained the innate <u>grace and dignity</u> of her character, never forgetting that she had been born a queen.

—H. G. Bell, *Life of Mary Queen of Scots*, Vol II
(Edinburgh: William Brown, 1890), p. 181.

Age   (twenty-five, prime of womanhood, premature old age)
Health   (vigour of health, health feebler)
Intellect   (strength of intellectual powers, doubts and fears)
Appearance   (hair was white)
Character   (grace and dignity)

Now, examine the Description of a Person from your list of *topoi*.

Description of a Person

Definition: A description of selected physical and non-physical aspects of a person

Procedure

1. Decide on which aspects will be included. They may include:

   Physical appearance
   Sound of voice
   What others think
   Portrayals
   Character qualities
   Challenges and difficulties
   Accomplishments
   Habits
   Behaviors
   Expressions of face and body
   Mind/intellectual capabilities
   Talents and abilities
   Self disciplines
   Religious beliefs
   Clothing, dress
   Economic status (wealth)
   Fame, notoriety, prestige
   Family traditions, tendencies

Remember

1. Descriptions can be "slanted" using appropriate adjectives.
2. An overall metaphor can be used to organize the description and give clues about character.

In comparing the young Mary to the older Mary, the writer mentions her physical appearance, her character qualities, challenges, and difficulties she faced (premature aging, decline in her health), and her intellectual capabilities.

This paragraph about Mary Queen of Scots is one part of a longer description of Mary. As you can see, the writer chooses aspects of Mary and then compares them at different points in time. The paragraph of temporal comparison becomes a small part of a longer composition—a Description of a Person.

On your Description of a Person chart, add a third point under the heading "Remember." The point should be:

> **3. The description can include one or more paragraphs of temporal comparison (the comparison of aspects at different points in time)**

STEP FOUR: Understand the place of a brief temporal comparison in an Explanation by Definition

A brief temporal comparison can also be used in an explanation by definition, as a way of exploring any of the three areas that a definition involves—properties, function, genus.

Look back at the three charts you made in Step Two. On the lines below, jot down the questions that are answered about properties, function, and/or genus in each chart.

II Army Corps: _____

_____

_____

_____

Olympics: _____

_____

_____

_____

Industrial Revolution: _____

_____

_____

_____

When you are finished, check your answers with your instructor. Ask for help if you need it. Finish up today's work by adding the following to the Explanation by Definition: Historical Object, Event, Place, or People Group chart, in the "Remember" column:

4. The definition can include one or more paragraphs of temporal comparison (the comparison of properties, function, and/or genus at different points in time)

Day Two: Writing Brief Temporal Comparisons, Part I

 Focus: Using visual observation to compare changes over time

Over the next two days, you'll practice writing several kinds of brief temporal comparisons.

STEP ONE: **Observe a set of portraits**

Look carefully at these two photographs. The first shows the British statesman Winston Churchill in 1895, at the age of twenty-one; he is wearing the uniform of a British cavalry officer (his unit was called the 4th Queen's Own Hussars). The second shows Churchill in 1943, during an interview in Canada; he is sixty-nine years old and is partway through his first term as Prime Minister of the United Kingdom.

On a piece of notebook paper, make two columns. At the top of one column, write "Young Churchill." At the top of the other, write "Old Churchill." As you examine the photographs, jot down words and phrases that describe them.

Since you're relying entirely on visual observation, you can only address the following aspects in the Description of a Person directly:

> Expressions of face and body
> Clothing, dress

You'll also want to describe the shape of Churchill's face, his hair, his weight, the shape of his nose and mouth—all the things that you would include if you were describing a person to someone else and wanted your description to be recognizable.

But you can also *speculate* about other things based on your interpretation of Churchill's appearance: his stance, his expression, the look in his eyes, etc. As you take notes, choose one or more of the following and write down words and phrases that you think *might* describe them for both the young and the old Churchill.

> Character qualities
> Mind/intellectual capabilities
> Talents and abilities

If you have difficulty, ask your instructor for help.

You should end up with 6–10 observations in each column. Show your work to your instructor when you are finished.

STEP TWO: Write about a set of portraits

Using your lists and referring back to the portraits, write one or two brief paragraphs contrasting the young Churchill to the older Churchill. Aim to have between 50 and 100 words.

Your paragraphs will probably flow more smoothly if you write a paragraph about young Churchill and then another about the older Churchill (the subject-by-subject method of comparison). However, you can also do a point-by-point comparison, where you compare the physical appearance of the two versions of Churchill, then the character of young vs. old, then the expressions of each, and so forth. If you do this, you have to try to avoid repeating "The young Churchill . . . the old Churchill" over and over again.

When your description is finished, show it to your instructor.

STEP THREE: Produce a slanted version of the description

In the first level of this course (Week 17), you learned that a personal description can be slanted, or biased. The words that you choose as you write your description can incline the reader to like or dislike, respect or despise the subject.

Read the following description of the Mughal emperor Akbar, written by his son Jahangir:

> In his august personal appearance he was of middle height, but inclining to be tall; he was of the hue of wheat; his eyes and eyebrows were black, and his complexion rather dark than fair; he was lion bodied, wth a broad chest, and his hands and arms long . . . His august voice was very loud, and in speaking and explaining had a peculiar richness.[43]

Jahangir greatly admired his father; you can tell this by the words he chooses. With your pencil, underline the words "august," "wheat," "lion-bodied," "broad," "long," and "richness." These are nouns and adjectives with positive connotations. If Jahangir had written that his father was "of the hue of clay" or that he was "jackal-bodied," you would have an entirely different picture of Akbar.

Compare Jahangir's words with the following description of the emperor Nero, written by the Roman historian Suetonius:

> He was well-proportioned, but his body was spotted and malodorous . . . His features were pretty rather than pleasing, with eyes that were blue, but dull. His neck was heavy and his stomach hung over his skinny legs.[44]

If Suetonius had described Nero's features as "fine-cut," his neck as "strong," and his legs as "trim," you would take away an entirely different (and much more positive) impression of the emperor.

Using your thesaurus, rewrite your brief description so that the reader gets a positive impression of the young Churchill and a negative impression of the older Churchill—or vice versa. Remember that the same quality can often be described with negative *or* positive words. Here are a few options to get you started—but be sure to choose some words of your own as well.

POSITIVE	NEGATIVE
determined	obstinate
solid	corpulent
cheeks	jowls
confident	arrogant

When you are finished, show your work to your instructor.

---

43. John F. Richards, *The Mughal Empire* (Cambridge University Press, 1995), pp. 44–45.

44. Eric R. Varner, *Mutilation and Transformation: Damnatio Memoriae and Roman Imperial Portraiture* (Brill, 2004), p. 47.

Day Three: Writing Brief Temporal Comparisons, Part II

 Focus: Using written descriptions to compare changes over time

STEP ONE: **Read about a place at two different points in time**

Read the following brief descriptions of Lake Chad, a lake which has varied enormously in size and depth for centuries.

> North Africa's Lake Chad was once as large as Lake Erie in North America, but 50 years of drought combined with over-pumping of lake water for irrigation has reduced the lake's size to 5% of its 1960 size. The lake's now dry bed is "pumping dust everywhere, all year long, almost every day." It is blown, depending on the season, to Europe, the United States, and elsewhere.[45]

> After a period of high inflows [heavy rains and water draining into the lake] in the 1960s, the lake occupied an area of 23,500 square kilometers. By the 1990s . . . its surface area had shrunk to about 1350 square kilometers, so that the lake only occupied a small are in the south of its original basin.[46]

> Lake Chad, once one of the largest on the Earth, has been dramatically decreasing since the 1960s . . . Since 1963, the lake has shrunk to nearly a twentieth of its original size, due both to climactic changes and to high demands for agricultural water . . . About 50% of the decrease in the lake's size since the 1960s is attributed to human massive water use, with the remainder attributed to . . . a significant decline in rainfall . . . The changes in the lake have contributed to potable water shortages, collapsed fisheries, soil salinization, and increasing poverty through the region. Another ecological problem is related to the invasive plant species which currently cover about 50% of the remaining surface of Lake Chad.[47]

---

45. Marquita K. Hill, *Understanding Environmental Pollution*, 3rd ed. (Cambridge University Press, 2010), p. 147.

46. Julie J. Laity, *Deserts and Desert Environments* (Wiley-Blackwell, 2008), p. 116.

47. Jacques C. J. Nihoul et al., eds., *Dying and Dead Seas: Climatic Versus Anthropic Causes* (Kluwer Academic Publishers, 2003), pp. 27, 29.

Lake Chad is [now] very shallow . . . averaging 1.5 m. [4.9 ft] in depth. It is fringed by a zone of swampy vegetation dominated by reeds. Water plants often form dense thickets or floating mats even in the center of the lake. Local inhabitants use the stems of papyrus as material for canoe making. There are many small islands formed by the invasion of moving sand dunes near the northeastern coast; some of them are inhabited and utilized as bases for fishing.[48]

At such times [when the lake was higher] there was extensive open water . . . and belts of aquatic vegetation fringing the shores were narrow or absent.[49]

Its surface area measured 10,000 square miles (25,000 square kilometers) in 1963 but had shrunk to 839 square miles (1,350 square kilometers) by 2001, causing the lake to become one-twentieth of its original size . . . Fish quantities . . . are significantly decreasing . . . however, the shrinkage of Lake Chad has created more farmland, land that is fed by the lake when its boundaries expand during rainy weather. Leftover fish manure fertilizes this farmland, adding to fertility, and this combination allows farmers to survive three-month drier periods . . . [so that] people living by the lake are effectively fed by agriculture.[50]

[The following is from a nineteenth-century eyewitness description of Lake Chad.]

This remarkable lake . . . covers an area of about 10,000 square miles . . . Its elevation above the sea is about 800 feet, with a depth of about fifteen feet. Its surface is dotted by a large number of islands . . . [T]he tribes living on the borders of this lake [live primarily on] . . . fish, which they catch in the lake and dry in the sun.[51]

STEP TWO: **Observe contrasts**

On a piece of notebook paper, make two columns. At the top of one column, write "Lake Chad Before 1960s." At the top of the other, write "Lake Chad Now." Go back through the paragraphs above and jot down words and phrases that describe Lake Chad in the appropriate columns.

---

48. Rongxing Guo, *Territorial Disputes and Resource Management: A Global Handbook* (Nova Science Publishers, 2007), p. 79.
49. Graham Connah, *Three Thousand Years in Africa: Man and His Environment in the Lake Chad Region of Nigeria* (Cambridge University Press, 1981), p. 23.
50. R. W McColl, *Encyclopedia of World Geography*, Vol. 1 (Facts on File, 2005), p. 162.
51. Donald Mackenzie, *The Flooding of the Sahara* (Sampson Low, Marston, Searle & Rivington, 1877), p. 152.

You should end up with six to ten observations in each column. Show your work to your instructor when you are finished.

STEP THREE: Write about a place at two different points in time

Using your chart, write the same sort of description as in the last assignment—one or two paragraphs contrasting Lake Chad before the 1960s with Lake Chad today. You have a little bit more information than you did for the Churchill assignment, so aim for 75–125 words.

For the purposes of this assignment, it isn't necessary for you to footnote your information. Try not to use the exact words of your sources, but the information in the source paragraphs is definitely general knowledge.

As with the last assignment, you will probably find it easier to write first about Lake Chad before the 1960s, and then cover the same aspects for Lake Chad now. But you can also write point by point (size then, size now; depth then, depth now; vegetation then, vegetation now; etc.) as long as you can avoid repeating "then" and "now" or similar phrases over and over again.

When you are finished, show your work to your instructor.

STEP FOUR: Add vivid metaphors and/or similes

When you first began writing descriptions of places in the first level of this course (Week 10), you learned that effective descriptions use figurative language—vivid metaphors and interesting similes.

Here are examples of both, drawn from Charles Dickens's classic novel *Oliver Twist*.

> The snow lay on the ground, frozen into a hard thick crust; so that only the heaps that had drifted into by-ways and corners were affected by the sharp wind that howled abroad: which, <u>as if expending increased fury on such prey as it found</u>, caught it savagely up in clouds, and, whirling it into a thousand misty eddies, scattered it in air.

> The old smoke-stained storehouses on either side rose heavy and dull from the dense mass of roofs and gables, <u>and frowned sternly upon</u> water too black to reflect even their lumbering shapes.

In the first example, Dickens uses a simile (introduced by *as if*) to compare the wind to a bird of prey. In the second, he uses a metaphor—he speaks of the storehouses as though they were old angry men staring down into the water.

Go back to your description and try to invent one simile and one metaphor. Insert them into your description. Does it sound more interesting—or does the new language sound forced? You won't always improve a piece of writing by including metaphors and similes, but you won't know until you make the experiment.

Day Four: Introduction to Longer Temporal Comparisons

> Focus: Understanding the use of temporal comparison as an organizing theme

A temporal comparison can be a useful element in a longer composition, but it can also stand on its own as an independent piece. Today, you'll look at an essay-length temporal comparison and analyze its elements.

STEP ONE: **Read**

The following essay, "By Post to Peace," was written by Karl Krueger and first appeared in *The Rotarian* (January 1938, pp. 38–39). It describes how the postal system changed from its beginnings up until 1938. Read it carefully.

— — —

When you stick a 3-cent stamp on a letter and drop it in a box, you give the missive wings that will whisk it from Alaska to Argentina—or from any point to any other point in the Americas. A 5-cent stamp will speed your letter from Texas to Tibet—or from any point on the American Continents to any point on any other continent (save the unpeopled ones), and vice versa. You will not worry about safe delivery . . . and you need not. The mail has a knack for getting through . . .

How long has this quick, cheap, sure mail service to all parts of the world existed? Well, for approximately 65 years. A German named Heinrich von Stephan started it all with his personal achievement, the International Postal Union. But let's return to that later.

Perhaps the world's first postmen were the swift runners who shuttled between the monarchs of southwest Asia, carrying clay tablets on which were inscribed the confidences of the kings. The posts of the Persian Empire under the kings who followed Cyrus are a significant early example. The Romans developed their postal services to a fine precision, but these, with their empire, collapsed.

For at least two millenniums the terms "post office" and "post roads" have been in use. The Bible makes such reference. In the Book of Esther one may read how from India to Ethiopia to a hundred and twenty-seven provinces King Ahasuerus sent letters by posts on horseback. Assyrian and Egyptian records refer to postal services, and the Aztecs had a system of parcel post—for royal purposes.

As Europe emerged from the fog of the Dark Ages, merchants set up private posts. Governments duly saw in them a source of power and revenue and took them over.

The first post office for the general public was established on the Continent of Europe in the 16th Century. Public posts followed soon in England and here made the fastest progress, establishing the first low rates for delivery service.

The growing communication between nations complicated the problem of mails—and treaties between nations, such as those between England and France providing prompt delivery, had to suffice for a time.

But, to leap forward over a few centuries, let's turn again to von Stephan. While on his job as first director of posts for the North German Confederation, he began to ponder some of the inscrutables of postal service as it then went in the world. Postage on a letter from Berlin to New York, he noted, was 90 cents if it was sent by a German steamer; $1.25 if it crossed on a British boat. Postage on a letter from Berlin to Rome was 68 cents via Switzerland; 90 cents through France. He saw that letters to Russia could go by more than a dozen different routes, with almost that many different postage rates. The confusion challenged the pragmatic von Stephan.

So, as one man who wanted to do all other men a good turn, he suggested the calling of an International Congress to consider a few proposals. It met in 1874 in Berne, Switzerland, and in but a few weeks adopted *all* his proposals. The meeting resulted in the formation of the International Postal Union, which, in 1878, became the Universal Postal Union. Fundamentally, the agreement which von Stephan wrote for Europe and the United States serves every country in the world today.

Four items on which the delegates to that original Congress found they could agree and which then covered the field were:

1. Uniformity of postage rates and units of weight.

2. Classification of correspondence, letters, postcards, printed papers.

3. Definite payments to railroad and steamship lines of countries other than that of origin.

4. Universal adoption of a system of registration and compensation . . .

In practice, the principles now mean this:

Your 5 cents for an overseas letter go to the office where you buy the stamp. Each country delivers your letter free and without recording its passage. Your letter may have to pass through many hands in dozens of countries, yet it is sent on swiftly toward its destination . . . without question.

STEP TWO: **Outline**

There is more than one way to outline this passage "correctly." Your assignment is to pay particular attention to the comparisons in the passage by making an outline on your own paper that fits the model below. You may copy the points in bold type directly into your own outline. If a point is in italics, it is telling you the *type* of information that you need to use to fill in the outline.

I.   **Introduction**
   A. **The mail in 1938**
      1. *One kind of mail*
      2. *Another kind of mail*
      3. *A characteristic of the mail*
   B. *An aspect of the mail system's history*
      1. *Observation about length of time*
      2. *Founder*
II. **Ancient mail systems**
   A. *Type of early postal system*
   B. *Type of early postal system*
   C. *Type of early postal system*
   D. *Type of early postal system*
   E. **Other postal systems**
III. **Medieval mail systems**
   A. *One kind of system*
   B. *Another kind of system*
      1. *A place where it was*
      2. *A place where it was*
   C. *Another feature of the medieval systems*
IV. **Heinrich von Stephan's changes**
   A. *Overall title for things he noticed*
      1. *One type of thing he noticed*
      2. *Another type of thing he noticed*
   B. *Thing he spearheaded*
      1. *First detail about what he spearheaded*
      2. *Second detail about what he spearheaded*
   C. *Result*
      1. *First detail of result*
      2. *Second detail of result*
      3. *Third detail of result*
      4. *Fourth detail of result*
V. *Current condition*
   A. *One type of detail about current condition*
   B. *Another type of detail about current condition*

If you need help, ask your instructor. When you're finished with your outline, show it to your instructor.

STEP THREE: **Analyze**

During this step, your instructor will carry on a dialogue with you.

STEP FOUR: **Write down the pattern of the *topos***

Finish up today's lesson by copying the following onto a blank sheet of paper in the Reference section of your Composition Notebook. You'll come back to this *topos* next week and examine it further.

Temporal Comparison: History

Definition: A comparison between the earlier and later stages of the same historical phenomenon

Procedure	Remember

1. Begin with a brief introduction to the phenomenon.
  a. May include a summary of its current state
  b. Can briefly mention important aspects
2. Describe at least one earlier stage of its development.
  a. Properties
  b. Function
  c. Genus
3. Describe the transition to its current form.
  a. May involve a chronological narrative of historical events
  b. May involve a historical sequence
4. Describe the current form of the phenomenon.
	1. Can include more than one earlier stage of development

Week 27: Temporal Comparisons in History and Science

Day One: Take Notes for a Temporal Comparison

 Focus: Taking notes on a subject
at two points in time

Today you will prepare to write your own version of a longer temporal comparison in history. You'll be taking notes about how the city of Chicago changed from the early 1800s to the early 1900s.

STEP ONE: **Review the *topos***

Before you begin your note-taking, review the form of the comparison by reading carefully through the Temporal Comparison: History *topos* in your reference notebook.

With the definition in mind, read through the following excerpt from a longer temporal comparison in history, written by an educator who went back to her old primary school for a visit.

> Are schools better today than the ones we attended? We can specu-
> late on this . . . I had such an opportunity when I received an invitation
> extended by one of my students who is teaching "my old school" to attend a
> second-grade production . . .
>
> More than 30 years have passed since I left Public School #86 for
> junior high. As a visitor to the school, I was allowed, indeed required, to use
> the main entrance. Neatly handwritten signs announcing student events
> suggested students now used this lobby, which was previously off-limits.
> The austere white marble and plaster walls seemed less forbidding with
> these additions.

337

When I approached the auditorium, I noticed the dark red velvet drapes had been replaced with light green ones—but the chandeliers that had lighted the room were the same, as were the hard wooden seats. Lincoln's and Washington's formal portraits were replaced with contemporary posters and student art work. The starched white cotton middy shirts and red ties had given way to colorful, casual dress. While the audience was getting settled, some adults prevailed on students to "keep quiet," as my teachers did. Most, however, allowed children to talk to classmates and wave to arriving friends . . .

Reflecting on this recent visit, I think the school has improved markedly. Principally I attribute this to the changed roles for the children and their teachers . . .

—From "School Days—Then and Now," by Rita S. Brause. In *Anthropology & Education Quarterly* (18:1, Mar., 1987), pp. 53–55.

Notice that Rita Brause begins by introducing you to the phenomenon of her school (in the original, the introduction is much longer) and then goes on to describe both earlier and later stages in its development. However, instead of describing the school as she knew it, talking about its transition, and then describing it again as it is in the present day, she goes back and forth between the earlier and later versions of the school, like this:

Entrance lobby in my day	compared to	Entrance lobby now
Drapes in my day	compared to	Drapes now
Chandeliers in my day	compared to	Chandeliers now

and so on. When she finishes making her comparisons, she then begins to write about *why* the transition to the current form of the school happened ("I attribute this to the changed roles . . ."). I didn't include this part of the essay because it is full of academic language—the writer is a professor at Fordham University.

What should you take away from this? When you're writing a temporal comparison, you can either organize your thoughts subject by subject or point by point—just as when you're doing a regular Explanation by Comparison/Contrast. In a subject-by-subject comparison, Rita Brause would spend a page or two describing her school as it was when she attended it, and then spend another page or so describing all the same aspects about the school in the present day. In her point-by-point comparison, she goes back and forth, describing each aspect of the school then and now.

On your Temporal Comparison: History chart, write

2. Can either be organized point by point or subject by subject

in the Remember column.

STEP TWO: **Read**

Read through the following excerpts about the city of Chicago both before and after the Great Fire of 1871 without stopping to take notes.

George Edwards Plumbe, *Chicago: The Great Industrial and Commercial Center of the Mississippi Valley* (Chicago: The Civic-Industrial Committee of the Chicago Association of Commerce, 1912), pp. 12–15.

(12) Moses Kirkland in his "History of Chicago," page 119, says: "At the beginning of that year (1848) Chicago had neither railroads nor canal nor any other means of communication with the outer world than by wheeled vehicles and vessels on Lake Michigan . . . It could boast of no sewers nor were there any sidewalks except a few plans here and there, nor paved streets. The streets were merely graded to the middle, like country roads, and in bad weather, were impassable. A mud hole deeper than usual would be marked by signboards with the significant notice thereon, 'No bottom here, the shortest road to China.' There was no gas, and water continued to be supplied from carts by the bucketful. There were no omnibuses, (13) cabs nor horse cars, nor cars of any kind, much less telegraph and telephones. Wabash Avenue, between Adams and Jackson Streets, was regarded as out of town, where wolves were occasionally seen prowling about."

The era of railroad construction in the West immediately followed this increased population and multiplication of industrial enterprises. The Galena and Chicago Union Railroad was opened to Elgin in January, 1850; to Belvidere, December 3rd, 1852, and to Freeport in 1853. The Chicago and Burlington Railroad was opened to Burlington, Iowa, in 1855, and to Quincy, Ill., in 1856. The first road to enter Chicago from the East was the Lake Shore and Michigan Southern in February, 1852, and the Michigan Central Railroad in May of the same year. Next came the Chicago, Rock Island and Pacific, which was completed to Joliet in 1853 and to Rock Island in 1854. In rapid succession came the Chicago and Alton, the Chicago and Milwaukee, and the Pittsburgh, Ft. Wayne and Chicago. . . .

The following table shows the growth of the city in population. In 1823 Chicago is described as "a village in Pike County containing (15) 12 or 15 houses, and about 60 or 75 inhabitants." The first government census was taken in 1840, which gives the earliest official data as to population.

1835	3,297	1880	503,185
1840	4,470	1890	1,099,850
1850	29,963	1900	1,689,575
1860	109,260	1910	2,185,283
1870	298,977	1920	2,284,378

Ballard C. Campbell, ed., *Disasters, Accidents and Crises in American History* (New York: Infobase Publishing, 2008), pp. 127–128.

(127) On the night of October 8, 1871, fire broke out in a busy neighborhood of Chicago in a cattle barn owned by Patrick and Catherine O'Leary at 137 West DeKoven Street. Fanned by strong winds and fed by structures left tinder-dry in the wake of a four-month drought, the fire marched uncontrollably through the "Queen of the West," as the city was known . . . (128) The flames spread through the downtown area throughout the following day, destroying homes, churches, factories, warehouses, and municipal buildings and driving terrified residents before it . . . For 30 hours, the blaze consumed nearly everything in its path, flickering out only after reaching the city limits and thus running out of fuel by the early morning of October 10. With an estimated 300 dead, 90,000 homeless, and some 18,000 destroyed buildings across 2,000 acres, the Queen of the West lay in ruins . . . Chicago proved itself a remarkably resilient community. Within hours of the fire's end, a massive rebuilding effort was under way. A year later, $40 million worth of new buildings had already been erected, and the city had extended its boundaries into Lake Michigan by using refuse from the disaster as landfill.

Dennis H. Cremin & Elan Penn, *Chicago: A Pictorial Celebration* (New York: Sterling Publishing Co., Inc., 2006), p. 7.

To the astonishment of the world, Chicago rebuilt quickly after the fire, asserting its resourcefulness and resolve as it began creating a new city upon the still-smoldering ashes of the old. During this time and up through the 1890s, the city experienced a period of unprecedented economic growth and expansion, becoming the national capital of such iconic industries as animal slaughtering, meat packing, and shipping. The city became known as "the hog butcher to the world," a role exemplified by the Union Stock Yards entrance.

At the same time, Chicago was gaining a reputation as the creator of the first skyscrapers. This history is found in many early structures, including the Monadnock Building, one of the first buildings to demonstrate

Chicago's ability to be an innovator in the field of architecture. This ability would become one of the city's hallmarks in the years to come, as some of the world's most innovative architects chose Chicago as their playground.

Donald L. Miller, *City of the Century: The Epic of Chicago and the Making of America* (New York: Simon & Schuster, 1996), p. 177.

Three decades after a great part of [Chicago] was consumed by firestorms, it had an infrastructure of urban services that was the marvel of the world—fourteen hundred miles of paved streets, thirty-eight thousand street lamps (many of them powered by electricity), almost a thousand miles of streetcar lines, a fleet of 129 fire engines, a waterworks that pumped 500 million gallons of water a day, a system of fifteen hundred miles of sewers, a Sanitary and Ship Canal that was the biggest American engineering project of the 1890s, over two thousand acres of landscaped parks, and twenty and more of the tallest, most impressively constructed buildings on earth . . .

The fire leveled the central business district but did not destroy integral parts of Chicago's great Prairie Exchange Engine—the stockyards and new packing plants on the South Side, the eighteen trunk lines connecting the city to the nation, twenty miles of wharfage, lumberyards, and mills along the river, two-thirds of the city's grain elevators, and that part of its new factory district to the west of Mrs. O'Leary's barn.

STEP THREE: **Take notes**

Spend the rest of your work time today taking notes about Chicago.

You'll find it easier to write your composition if you organize your notes as you take them. Use three different headings, either on three sheets of paper or as three columns on a single page:

Chicago in the Early 1800s

Chicago in the Late 1800s/Early 1900s

What Led to the Change?

Now, go back through the passages and take notes from each source. Just as you did with the Dred Scott piece, you can do this in one of two ways:

1) Go through the sources one time each, placing each relevant bit of information from each source beneath the appropriate question as you go.

2) Pick the first heading and go through all four sources, looking for answers. Do the same for the second heading, and then the third.

Take at least two notes from each passage, and at least 12 notes in total. When you are finished, show your work to your instructor.

Day Two: Write a Temporal Comparison in History

 Focus: Writing about a subject at different points in time

STEP ONE: **Write**

Using your notes, write the rough draft of a composition that compares Chicago in the early 1800s to Chicago in the late 1800s/early 1900s and later. Follow the pattern of the Temporal Comparison: History on your *topoi* chart:

1) Begin with a brief introduction to the city of Chicago. You can decide whether this will describe Chicago in the present day (this might require you to look up a few more facts) or in the 19th century.

2) Describe Chicago in the early 19th century.

3) Describe the Great Fire briefly, including a short chronological narrative of historical events.

4) Describe Chicago in the late 19th/early 20th century more fully.

For this essay, use the subject-by-subject rather than point-by-point approach.

Your composition must be at least 150 words in length, and should be divided into at least two or three paragraphs.

Cite at least three sources, using at least one direct quote.

You can show your draft to your instructor if you need help, but you do not *have* to show your work until after you've proofread it in Step Three.

STEP TWO: **Title and Works Cited page**

Choose a title for your essay. Include the main subject (Chicago) as well as a phrase describing the time frame that you cover in your composition.

Title a separate piece of paper "Works Cited." List the sources used in alphabetical order.

STEP THREE: **Proofread**

Proofread your paper, following these guidelines.

1) Make sure that your paper is at least 150 words in length and at least two paragraphs.

2) Check for the required elements: descriptive title, introduction to Chicago, description of Chicago in the early 1800s, description of the city after the fire, description of the fire as the

transition point; also a Works Cited page, at least three sources cited, and at least one direct quote.

3) Read your paper out loud, listening for awkward or unclear sections and repeated words. Rewrite awkward or unclear sentences so that they flow more naturally.

4) Listen for information that is repeated more than once. Eliminate repetition of ideas.

5) Read through the paper one more time, looking for sentence fragments, run-on sentences, and repeated words. Correct fragments and run-on sentences. Listen for unnecessary repetition. If you used a modifier (adverb, adjective, or prepositional phrase acting as an adjective or adverb) more than twice, find another word.

6) Check your spelling by looking, individually, at each word that might be a problem.

7) Check the formatting of your footnotes and your Works Cited page.

When you're finished proofreading, show your paper to your instructor.

Day Three: Introduction to Temporal Comparison in Science, Part I

 Focus: Understanding the first kind of temporal comparisons in science

All things in nature change over time. In fact, a large part of science is the study of why, and how, things change.

When you describe the changes that have happened to a scientific object or phenomenon over time, you are writing a temporal comparison. There are two major kinds of temporal change in science: regular changes that are part of repeating life cycles, and changes that are *not* part of regular growth and development.

Over the next few days, you'll analyze and practice both kinds of comparison.

STEP ONE: Read: Temporal comparison of changes due to repeating life cycles

Read through the following five paragraphs carefully. The author is providing you with an Explanation by Definition; in the course of the essay, he will answer a series of questions about properties and function.

> Frogs are mainly juice. If they try to make more than a short journey away from moisture, in a drought, they will perish for want of water; and then their bodies will dry away. The frog's bones are so soft that he scarcely leaves any skeleton.

A frog meets with remarkable changes during his natural life. He begins as an egg and hatches out as a fish. That is, a tadpole, or polliwog, at first has gills, breathing water alone. In his early days, however, the tadpole soon loses the outside part of his gills and breathes air; so that he has to come to the surface of the water every few minutes, like a porpoise, to get a fresh gulp of breath.

During the first part of his career, he swims by sculling with his long tail. After a while his legs begin to grow out, his tail becomes shorter and shorter, and when he is a complete frog, he has no tail at all, but swims by kicking. When half frog and half tadpole, he still has a good deal of tail, and, in addition, big hind legs and mere sprouts for fore legs; so that he is a very funny-looking fellow. A bullfrog-tadpole at this stage seems "neither of heaven nor of earth."

Again, the tadpole eats water-plants; but when he becomes a frog, he feeds on animal life. Tadpoles eat the green moss or "scum" that we see so often on logs and plants in a stagnant pool, and they show a good appetite for soft, decaying water-growths. The fouler the pool, the happier the tadpoles. As they are numerous, and thus devour a great amount of matter that would make it very unhealthful to live near a stagnant pond, they are really useful creatures . . .

The frog does not breathe air into lungs, as do most animals, for he has nothing to draw it with. He has no ribs, no diaphragm, and no real lungs; but a kind of sack instead. He takes in a mouthful of air, and then *swallows* it by means of muscles in the throat; but it goes into the air-sack, and not into the stomach. It is just as necessary for a frog to shut his mouth to take a breath, as it is for us to close the mouth with the lips or tongue in order to swallow. This explains why a frog can be suffocated to death if his mouth is kept *open* in some way.

—Harold W. Chamberlain, "Queer Things about Frogs," in *St. Nicholas* 20:I (November 1892–April 1893), pp. 837–838.

STEP TWO: Analyze: Temporal comparison of changes due to repeating life cycles

Using your Explanation by Definition: Natural Object or Phenomenon chart, go back through the composition. In the spaces provided below, write which question(s) each paragraph of the essay answers.

When you are finished, show your work to your instructor.

Paragraph #1: _____

_____

_____

Paragraph #2: _____

_____

_____

Paragraph #3: _____

_____

_____

Paragraph #4: _____

_____

_____

Paragraph #5: _____

_____

_____

STEP THREE: **Discuss**

Your instructor will carry on a short conversation with you.

Sequence: Natural Process

process by which tadpole becomes frog

tadpole   ⇒ ⇒ ⇒ ⇒ ⇒ ⇒ ⇒ ⇒ ⇒ ⇒ ⇒ ⇒ ⇒ ⇒ ⇒   frog

Explanation by Definition, Using Temporal Comparison

how baby tadpoles breathe | how older tadpoles breathe

how tadpoles swim | how half-grown frogs swim | how grown frogs swim

what tadpoles eat | what frogs eat

STEP FOUR: **Add to the *topos***

In the "Remember" column of your Explanation by Definition: Natural Object or Phenomenon chart, add the following:

> **3. Temporal comparison (describing the same thing at two different points in time) can be used to develop your answers**

Day Four: Writing a Temporal Comparison in Science, Part I

 Focus: Writing temporal comparisons of changes due to repeating life cycles

Like frogs, stars have a regular life cycle: birth, youth, maturity, age, death. Today, you'll write a brief temporal comparison of your own, describing a star at two different points in time: youth and old age.

STEP ONE: **Read**

Read carefully through the following paragraphs of information.

> Both visible- and radio-wavelength observations detect dense disks of gas and dust orbiting young stars. For example, at least 50 percent of the stars in the Orion Nebula are surrounded by such disks. A young star is detectable at the center of most disks, and astronomers can measure that the disks contain many Earth masses of material in a region a few times larger in diameter than our solar system. . . . Evidently, disks of gas and dust are a common feature around stars that are forming.
> —Dana Backman and Michael A. Seeds, *Universe: Solar System, Stars, and Galaxies* (Boston: Cengage Learning, 2011), p. 158.

. . . [B]ecause the surface of the young star is hot it is radiating energy out into space. Instinctively we might think that since it is losing energy by radiation it should cool down but, paradoxically, it does the exact opposite and heats up . . . The temperature is not uniform throughout the young star since it is much cooler on the outside than internally . . . At the centre the internal temperature has risen to 15 million K, at which stage nuclear processes take place in the interior that transform hydrogen to helium . . . Since new stars consist mainly of hydrogen they have an abundance of fuel . . . for a considerable time.

—M. M. Woolfson, *Materials, Matter & Particles: A Brief History* (London: Imperial College Press, 2010), pp. 293–294.

Corona: The extremely tenuous outermost part of a star's atmosphere . . . Young stars, such as those in the Orion nebula or the Pleiades, rotate faster than older stars of the same spectral type; they too have powerful X-ray emitting coronae.

—John Daintith and William Gould, *Astronomy* (New York: Facts on File, 2006), p. 98.

Some nebulae associated with young stars are blue . . . [as a] result of blue light from the young hot stars being scattered by clouds of dust. . . . A few nebulae mark the locations of stars in old age, 'red giant' stars which have shed their outer layers to form glowing rings of gas, sometimes misleadingly called planetary nebulae (they have nothing to do with planets). . . .

—David Ellyard and Wil Tirion, *The Southern Sky Guide* (Cambridge: Cambridge University Press, 1992), p. 18.

As hydrogen in a star's core is converted into helium, the core begins to contract and heat up. This heats the surrounding shell of hydrogen and causes the fusion of the hydrogen in the shell to proceed more rapidly. The rapid release of energy . . . causes the star to expand, cool down, and enter the red-giant phase . . . During the red-giant phase, a star varies in temperature and brightness . . . The star becomes very unstable, and the outer layers are blown off, forming a beautiful planetary nebula . . . Despite its name, a planetary nebula has absolutely nothing to do with planets. The name came about because the first fuzzy photographs of planetary nebulae looked to astronomers something like faint, distant planets.

—James T. Shipman, Jerry D. Wilson, and Aaron Todd, *An Introduction to Physical Science,* 12th ed. (Boston: Houghton Mifflin, 2009), p. 514.

It may seem strange that a star can decrease its surface temperature and at the same time increase its luminosity . . . The key to understanding this apparent contradiction is to realize just how large the red giant becomes. The Sun, at this stage in its life as a giant, will have expanded so that it encompasses the orbit of Mercury! It is true that each square meter of the Sun's cooler surface will emit less radiation, but the surface will have become so tremendously large that the total radiation emitted will be greater than before . . .

[T]he helium-burning process that provides much of the energy for red giants is unstable and varies greatly in response to small changes in temperature. As a result, a red giant undergoes instabilities.

—Theo Koupelis, *In Quest of The Universe*, 6th ed., (Sudbury, Mass.: Jones & Bartlett Learning, 2011), pp. 400, 402.

STEP TWO: **Chart**

Divide your own paper into two columns. At the top of the left-hand column, write "Young star." At the top of the right-hand column, write "Old star."

Go back through the paragraphs from Step One and write descriptive information about young stars in the left column; information about old stars goes in the right column. Remember that you are not writing details about *sequences*. You don't need to write down information about *how* a star moves from youth into old age; this will not be part of your final composition.

For the purposes of this assignment, don't worry about noting down the source for each piece of information.

The beginning of your chart might look like this:

Young star	Old star
Orbited by a disk of gas and dust	Red giants Shed outer layers become glowing rings of gas ("planetary nebulae")

Aim to have at least five pieces of information under each heading.

When you are finished, show your work to your instructor.

STEP THREE: **Write**

Using the information in your chart, write a point-by-point comparison of a young star and an old star.

You will probably find it helpful to begin by locating parallel pieces of information. For example, in the chart above, "Orbited by a disk of gas and dust" and "Shed outer layers become glowing rings of gas" are parallel—both of them describe the relationship of the star to outlying layers of gas. You should discuss these two points in the same paragraph.

The composition can be brief; aim for at least a hundred words. You'll probably want to divide the composition into at least two paragraphs. Avoid one-sentence paragraphs, though!

Your biggest challenge will be to avoid repeating "young star" and "old star" over and over again. Try to think of ways to vary your sentence structure.

When your work is finished, show it to your instructor.

WEEK 28: TEMPORAL COMPARISONS IN SCIENCE

Day One: Introduction to Temporal Comparison in Science, Part II

 Focus: Understanding the two kinds of temporal comparison in science

STEP ONE: **Write down the pattern of the *topos***

In last week's work, you began to learn about the different ways that a temporal comparison in science can be constructed. These comparisons often occur as part of a longer composition, but could also stand alone as brief independent essays.

By way of review, copy the following onto a blank sheet of paper in the Reference section of your Composition Notebook.

Temporal Comparison: Science

Definition: A comparison between the earlier and later stages of the same natural object or phenomenon

Procedure

1. Compare aspects of the subject at different stages of a regular life cycle
2. Can either be organized point by point or subject by subject

Remember

1. Often occurs as part of a longer composition

STEP TWO: **Read: Temporal comparison of natural changes**

Read through the following two excerpts carefully. The first describes the Great Red Spot, a storm in Jupiter's atmosphere so large that it can be seen from Earth. The second describes a glacier which once covered the land that is now Wisconsin.

Though the Great Red Spot has remained active throughout at least the last 170 years, it does change visibly through time. The spot did not become truly prominent until the 1880s, which is when it developed its deep red color. Since then the color has continued to fluctuate, varying from deep red to pale salmon or buff, or even disappearing completely, leaving what is then called the Red Spot hollow. The Great Red Spot is now about 15,000 miles (24,000 km) in the east-west dimension by 8,750 miles (14,000 km) in the north-south dimension. Though even the current Great Red Spot is far larger than the planet Earth, which has a diameter of about 8,125 miles (13,000 km), the spot has been as large as 25,000 miles (40,000 km) in its east-west dimension. In addition to changing size, the spot wanders in position. Over a regular 90-day period, the Spot moves 1,250 miles (2,000 km) north and then 1,250 miles (2,000 km) south of its average latitude. The Great Red Spot also moves in longitude and over the last hundred years has completed about three circuits back and forth around the planet.

—Linda T. Elkins-Tanton, *Jupiter and Saturn*
(New York: Chelsea House, 2006), pp. 50–51.

As the glacier advanced, it pried up bedrock, captured huge boulders, and pushed nearly everything out of its way. It pulverized, scraped, scoured, and bulldozed. Like a huge vacuum cleaner, it picked up massive amounts of dust, dirt, and debris. In northern Wisconsin, the glacier reached a thickness of nearly two miles, and at the spot where the state capitol now stands, the glacier towered sixteen hundred feet into the air . . .

Then . . . the sun began to win its battle with the great continental glacier. Warmer, dryer weather shut off the cold and snow that powered the massive ice machine in its 1,000-mile advance from the north. The glacier ground to a halt just ten miles southwest of Madison's Isthmus. Each spring the brow of the great glacier began to glisten. Beads of water coalesced into tiny streams like nervous perspiration from a sentient being awaiting its imminent demise. The snout of the glacier began to drip.

During the heat of the summer the hungry sun and thirsty wind caused tiny streams to form atop the glacier. Soon they converged into rivers whose raging currents cut deep furrows in the top and along the leading edge of the glacier . . . [T]he once invincible glacier, its surface now deeply lined, retreated to Canada, melting at the rate of about 1,000 feet per year.

—David V. Mollenhoff, *Madison: A History of the Formative Years*
(Madison: The University of Wisconsin Press, 2003), pp. 3–4.

STEP THREE: **Analyze: Temporal comparison of natural changes**

How is the Great Red Spot of Jupiter different from a frog?

I'm sure that plenty of differences come to your mind. But here's the one I want you to think about: Frogs go through the same transformation again and again. Millions of tadpoles have breathed with gills and eaten pond scum, before turning into frogs that breathe air and eat animal life. The descriptions in "Queer Things about Frogs" could apply to almost any tadpole-to-frog transformation.

But the Great Red Spot of Jupiter goes through a unique series of changes. Nothing except the Great Red Spot itself can be described in exactly this way. There are many natural phenomena which change over time—but do not go through a predictable, regular "life cycle."

Read carefully through the chart below:

Earlier Great Red Spot
1. Developed deep red color 1880s
2. 25,000 miles east to west

Current Great Red Spot
1. 15,000 miles east to west

Ongoing Changes
1. Color fluctuates
2. Moves 1,250 miles north-south
3. Moves in longitude

You will see that the author describes the Great Red Spot at two different points in time—in its earliest form, when it had just developed its deep red color and was 25,000 miles across; and in its current form, when it has shrunk to 15,000 miles across. The author also adds an additional set of descriptions: The Great Red Spot changes color and location constantly. These changes are *cyclical*. They happen over and over again—but they happen only to the Great Red Spot, not to *all* atmospheric phenomena on Jupiter.

Now, look closely at the description of the Wisconsin glacier. Can you fill in the chart below? If you need help, ask your instructor.

Earlier Form of Glacier	**Later Form of Glacier**

1. What it did:

    a) _____

    _____

    b) _____

    _____

2. What it was like:

    a) _____

    _____

    b) _____

    _____

1. What it did:

    a) _____

    _____

    b) _____

    _____

2. What it was like:

    a) _____

    _____

    b) _____

    _____

What Caused the Change

1. _____

STEP FOUR: **Add to the pattern of the *topos***

Add the following to your Temporal Comparison: Science chart, under "Procedure."
>   2. Compare aspects before and after a natural change unique to the subject
>   a. May include description of changes that occur in a regular cycle
>   b. May include explanation of why the change occurs

Notice that points *a* and *b* are optional; the comparison of Jupiter includes *a* but not *b*, while the excerpt on the Wisconsin glacier contains *b* but not *a*.

Day Two: Writing a Temporal Comparison in Science, Part II

 Focus: Writing temporal comparisons of natural changes

Today, you'll write a brief temporal comparison that compares the Washington volcano Mount St. Helens (including nearby Spirit Lake) to itself before and after it erupted on May 18, 1980.

STEP ONE: **Read**

Read the following excerpts carefully.

> At the time Lewis and Clark saw it . . . [in 1806], Mount St. Helens stood 9,677 feet high . . . When Lewis viewed it, he described its shape as "a regular cone . . . completely covered in snow." In later years it was called the "Fuji of America" because of its strong similarity in shape to Japan's Mount Fuji.
>
> —Elin Woodger and Brandon Toropov, *Encyclopedia of the Lewis and Clark Expedition* (New York: Facts on File, 2004), p. 245.

> Within ten minutes of the eruption, an immense plume of pumice and ash leaped 13.6 miles into the atmosphere and continued roaring upward for nine hours. The volume of ash fall could have buried a football field to a depth of 150 miles. Mount St. Helens' height dropped from 9,677 feet to 8,363 feet, with a crater more than 2,000 feet deep.
>
> When the summit and north flank collapsed in a giant landslide, a huge lateral blast blew sideways, obliterating or knocking down trees. Rock and melting ice created mudflows in the stream valleys, uprooting 150 square miles of trees and tearing out bridges and houses. The devastation left a landscape bleak and gray.
>
> . . . Spirit Lake, once a crystal-clear alpine gem, is regaining its blue clarity. The lateral blast was moving fast when it snapped off thousands of trees. The slower landslide sludge hit the lake and swooshed back uphill to wash the trees back into the basin. Many of those trees still float in the lake; others have sunk and caught on the bottom, perhaps to become a future petrified forest.
>
> —Marilyn McFarlane and Christine Cunningham, *Quick Escapes: Pacific Northwest* (Guilford, Conn.: Insiders Guide, 2007), pp. 28, 30.

. . . Mount St. Helens was 9,677 feet tall. It was a beautiful snow-capped mountain, full of forests and wildlife. Birds soared in the clear air around the peak, while deer and elk nibbled on green grass and plants on the mountain's flanks. Squirrels ran from tree to tree and insects buzzed in the cold, clear air. Occasionally, bears could be seen catching fish in a rushing stream. During springtime, wildflowers such as lupine and fire-weed covered the slopes of Mount St. Helens. The area attracted hikers and campers because of its natural beauty and abundant wildlife.

—Carmen Bredeson, *Fiery Volcano: The Eruption of Mount St. Helens*
(Berkeley Heights, NJ: Enslow Publishers, 2012), p. 36.

The Mount St. Helens explosion was the greatest volcanic eruption in the coterminous United States (forty eight states) in historic times. This huge release of volcanic energy removed the top of the mountain, reducing its elevation 1,313 feet, to 8,364 feet. Approximately one cubic mile of material was displaced from the mountain, about 15 percent of which was new magma. The crater formed was about 1500 feet deep, broken on the north side to form a great "amphitheater" one by two miles across. From the blast alone, some 230 square miles were devastated in a fan-shaped area reaching to the Green River about 15 miles north.

—Thomas F Saarinen and James L. Sell, *Warning and Response to the Mount St. Helen's Eruption* (Albany, N.Y.: State University of New York Press, 1985), p. 13.

. . . Spirit Lake, the gem of St. Helens, and so picture perfect it had seemed like a caricature of a mountain scene, [was] altered totally. When the mountain blew apart, the world's largest recorded avalanche thundered through Spirit Lake. The water flew out of the basin in a wave that splashed 800 feet up the adjacent valley wall . . .

When the water came back down, it brought everything that was loose with it—dirt, trees, rocks, animal carcasses—and deposited it all back in the lake, the bottom of which by that time had risen 300 feet. Superheated gases carrying fragmented volcanic rock poured out of the volcano and flew into the lake on the afternoon of the eruption, raising the water temperature to nearly 100 degrees. All of the fish, their food chains, and habitats were gone . . . The water in the new Spirit Lake was 22 times as alkaline as it had been, and . . . contained high concentrations of manganese, iron, phosphate, sulfate, and chloride, which drastically altered the lake's chemistry.

—Rob Carson, *Mount St. Helens: The Eruption and Recovery of a Volcano* (Seattle, Wash.: Sasquatch Books, 1990), p. 109.

STEP TWO: **Chart**

Divide your own paper into three columns. At the top of the left-hand column, write "Before." In the middle column, write "After." At the top of the right-hand column, write "Cause."

Go back through the paragraphs from Step One and write descriptive information about Mount St. Helens and Spirit Lake before the eruption in the left column. In the center column, write information about the mountain and lake *after* the eruption. In the right-hand column, write information about the cause of the change (the eruption).

The beginning of your chart might look like this:

Before	After	Cause
9,677 feet high	Summit and north flank collapsed	Giant landslide

Aim to have at least five notes in the Before column, eight to nine notes in the After column, and five notes in the Cause column.

STEP THREE: **Write**

Using the information in your chart, write a subject-by-subject comparison of Mount St. Helens and Spirit Lake before and after the eruption.

Include a brief explanation of the cause of the change (that would be the eruption itself). This explanation does not need to be a descriptive sequence or a chronological narrative; it should simply tell the reader that the eruption occurred and should include a few helpful descriptive details. The explanation can either come in the middle of the composition or at the end.

The composition should have at least three paragraphs and should be at least 125 words in length (it can be longer).

When your work is finished, show it to your instructor.

Day Three: Sentence Transformations in Science Writing

Focus: Practicing skills in sentence transformation

Most of your sentence transformations have been done using examples from history or literature. Today, you'll work on transforming sentences from science essays.

STEP ONE: **Review**

Read carefully through the nine types of transformation on your Sentence Variety chart. Then, review the following instructions for transformation carefully.

To transform descriptive adjectives into nouns, look for adjectives that come right before the nouns they modify. Or, look for prepositional phrases beginning with "of" and see if they can be turned into descriptive adjectives.

To transform active verbs into passive, look for sentences with action verbs and direct objects.

Look for sentences with indirect objects to transform into objects of a preposition.

To transform a participle into an infinitive, look for an -ing word following an action verb.

To transform a main verb into an infinitive, pick a strong verb and see whether you are able to add one of the following verbs to it:

VERBS THAT ARE OFTEN FOLLOWED BY INFINITIVES

agree	aim	appear	arrange	ask	attempt
beg	begin	care	choose	consent	continue
dare	decide	deserve	dislike	expect	fail
forget	get	hesitate	hope	hurry	intend
leap	like	love	ought	plan	prefer
prepare	proceed	promise	refuse	remember	start
strive	try	use	wait	want	wish

To intensify an adjective, look for descriptive adjectives that either come before a noun or follow a linking verb.

To change a word into a phrase, metaphor, or kenning, look for strong and interesting nouns.

To change a positive statement to a negative statement, look for a strong statement. Then use your thesaurus to find antonyms for the nouns and verbs in the statement.

STEP TWO: **Transform**

In each of the following sentences, identify the element that can be transformed. (There may be more than one transformation possible.) Then, rewrite the sentence on your own paper, using the guidelines on your Sentence Variety Chart.

All of the sentences below are original, taken directly from the listed sources.

From J. Arthur Thomson, *The Outline of Science, Vol. 1: A Plain Story Simply Told* (New York: G. P. Putnam's Sons, 1922).

Blue, green, yellow, red, and white combine to give a glorious display of colour.

Play, we repeat, gives us a glimpse of the possibilities of the mammal mind.

The elephant at the Belle Vue Gardens in Manchester used to collect pennies from benevolent visitors.

When a visitor gave the elephant a halfpenny it used to throw it back with disgust.

From P. W. Atkins, *The Periodic Kingdom: A Journey into the Land of the Chemical Elements* (New York: Basic Books, 1995).

Magnesium was culled from its compounds by Davy in 1808, calcium in 1808 (also by Davy), and strontium in 1808 (Davy again).

By investigating the properties of X rays emitted by atoms, Moseley was able to count the positive charges of a nucleus.

Stars do not burn smoothly from their inception to their death.

The internal structure of atoms was determined by a succession of experiments in the late nineteenth and early twentieth centuries.

From Rachel Carson, *Silent Spring* (Boston: Houghton Mifflin, 1962).

Under primitive agricultural conditions the farmer had few insect problems.

When the public protests, confronted with some obvious evidence of damaging results of pesticide applications, it is fed little tranquilizing pills of half-truth.

There is a cheaper and better way to remove crabgrass than to attempt year after year to kill it out with chemicals.

As many examples show, the poison is carried in by rains and runoff from surrounding land.

Day Four: Copia Exercise
Negative and Positive Modifiers

 Focus: Understanding negative and positive modifiers

STEP ONE: Understand the purpose of negative and positive modifiers

Back in Week 22, you learned the technique of *varying by equivalence*. You learned that a positive statement can be rewritten as a negative, or vice versa.

Positive Statements	Negative Statements
They have a plentiful lack of wit.	They are not witty.
His attentions were over.	His attentions did not continue.
The prospect was exceedingly agreeable.	The prospect was not at all unpleasant.

Varying by equivalence can also be done for individual words in a sentence—particularly adjectives and adverbs. Look how Erasmus changed the positive adverb *greatly* as he varied his sentences.

Your letter pleased me greatly.
Your letter pleased me in no small measure.
Your letter pleased me in no small scale.

In the last two sentences, Erasmus transforms a single adverb into a phrase expressing the same meaning—but expressed negatively.

Usually, a positive adverb or adjective is the first one to come to your mind when you're writing. A negative restatement usually highlights some important comparison or contrast. The following three sentences are from Bill Bryson's bestseller *A Short History of Nearly Everything:*

> He was a bright but not outstanding student.
> Meteorites are not abundant and meteoritic samples not especially easy to get hold of.
> Putting things in order is not the easiest of tasks.

Why didn't Bryson just write the following?

> He was a bright, mediocre student.
> Meteorites are scarce, and meteoritic samples hard to get hold of.
> Putting things in order is a hard task.

Because, in each case, he was drawing a contrast between the negatively-phrased modifier and something else. In the first sentence, Bryson plays against the assumption that a bright student is *always* an outstanding student, by highlighting the reader's assumption that bright and outstanding are always parallel.

The second sentence comes right after a paragraph in which a scientist has been trying to figure out where to find very ancient rocks, which he wants to use in an effort to find the exact age of the Earth. The problem, says Bryson, is that "very ancient rocks" are extremely hard to get to. What did the scientist do?

> The assumption he made—rather a large one, but correct, as it turned out—was that many meteorites are essentially leftover building materials from the early days of the solar system, and thus have managed to preserve a more or less pristine interior chemistry. Measure the age of these wandering rocks and you would have the age also (near enough) of the earth.[52]

Much easier than digging miles down into the earth for layers of ancient rock, right? Well . . .

> As always, however, nothing was quite as straightforward as such a breezy description makes it sound. Meteorites are not abundant and meteoritic samples not especially easy to get hold of.[53]

The reader is expecting the scientist's solution to solve a problem—the lack of abundant, easily accessible ancient rocks. Bryson chooses the negative phrases "not abundant" and "not

---

52. Bill Bryson, *A Short History of Nearly Everything: Special Illustrated* Edition (Broadway, 2010), p. 156.
53. Ibid.

especially easy to get hold of" in order to highlight the difficulties that still exist. In comparison with ancient rocks, meteorites are *still* hard to get your hands on.

How about the third sentence? It is the introduction to a paragraph about biological classification which explains how a certain scholar took *forty years* to figure out a classification system:

> Putting things in order is not the easiest of tasks. In the early 1960s, Colin Groves of the Australian National University began a systematic survey of the 250-plus known species of primate. Oftentimes it turned out that the same species had been described more than once—sometimes several times—without any of the discoverers realizing that they were dealing with an animal that was already known to science. It took Groves four decades to untangle everything, and that was with a comparatively small group of easily distinguished, generally noncontroversial creatures. Goodness knows what the results would be if anyone attempted a similar exercise with the planet's estimated 20,000 types of lichens, 50,000 species of mollusk, or 400,000-plus beetles.[54]

Given how huge the task is, "not the easiest of tasks" is an ironic understatement, meant to contrast with the enormity of the job.

As you can see, choosing to use a negative or a positive modifier has to do with the feel or tone that you want to convey to the reader. The opposing meanings can be very subtle, and you may not always be able to express exactly why an author chooses one method over another. For now, just try to be aware of the differences that a change in modifiers might produce.

One more thing to keep in mind: Rephrasing a modifier might require a whole phrase, like this:

> He had a <u>secret</u> desire to be a superhero.
> He had a desire, <u>not known to anyone,</u> to be a superhero.

Or, a modifer can be changed with a single word.

> He had a <u>secret</u> desire to be a superhero.
> He had an <u>unrevealed</u> desire to be a superhero

STEP TWO: **Practice changing positive modifiers into negatives and vice versa**

Fill in the chart below, changing positives into negatives and vice versa. You don't have to get too creative (although you can if you want)—this is just to get you comfortable with the

---

54. Bryson, *A Short History*, p. 363.

idea. Remember that if you insert a phrase in place of a single word, you may also need to add punctuation.

If you have trouble finding a way to rephrase the sentence, follow these three steps:

1) Look up the adverb or adjective in the thesaurus.
2) Find the *antonyms* to the adverb or adjective.
3) Use an antonym (to transform a negative to a positive), or else put a negation in front of an antonym (to transform a positive to a negative).

Positive:	Negative:
_____	He was, not surprisingly, in a hurry.
The gift was generous.	_____
_____	She ran away, in a non-leisurely fashion.
Her speech was eloquent.	_____
The thunder was terrifying.	_____
_____	The dog ate without moderation.

STEP THREE: **Add to the Sentence Variety chart**

Add the following principle and illustration to the Sentence Variety chart. Note that the first example is of an adjective, while the second is an adverb.

positive modifier ⟷ negative modifier

He was cheerful this morning.
He was not unhappy this morning.

She drove without haste.
She drove slowly.

STEP FOUR: **Practice sentence variety**

The sentences below are adapted from Bill Bryson's bestselling nature book *A Walk in the Woods: Rediscovering America on the Appalachian Trail* (New York: Broadway Books, 1998). On your own paper, rewrite each underlined modifier so that positives become negatives and negatives become positives—just as Bill Bryson first wrote them. If you change a phrase to a word or vice versa, you may have to insert additional punctuation and/or conjunctions (and, but, or, nor, for, yet).

When you are finished, ask your instructor to show you Bryson's original sentences. How close were you?

A sign announced that this was <u>an exceptional</u> footpath, the <u>not unknown</u> Appalachian Trail.
Black bears, <u>not frequently</u>, attack.
All bears are agile, <u>in no way stupid</u>, and <u>not inconsiderably</u> strong, and they are always hungry.
With a grizzly, you should make for a <u>less than short</u> tree, since grizzlies <u>abhor</u> climbing.
With black bears, however, playing dead is <u>less than productive</u>, since they will <u>not cease</u> chewing on you until you are considerably past caring.
The bears were <u>unmistakably</u> startled, but <u>calmed</u> by the flash.
If I did happen upon a bear, I would be quite <u>without resources</u>.

WEEK 29: PREPARING TO WRITE ABOUT A LONGER WORK OF FICTION

Over the next two weeks, you'll work on applying the skills you've learned in story analysis to a longer work of fiction.

You'll be reading a classic retelling of the Robin Hood legend, by the well-known late nineteenth century writer Mary Macleod. It was originally published in 1906 in a longer collection called *A Book of Ballad Stories*. The retelling is a little more than 13,000 words long; it could be classified as a "novella" (shorter than a full-length novel but longer than a short story).

You will notice one strange contradiction in the novella. The very first line tells you that Robin Hood lived "in the days of Richard I" (Richard Lionheart ruled England 1189–1199). But later on, the king of England is called "Edward"—probably Edward I, who ruled 1272–1307 (although it could also refer to Edward II, 1307–1327, or Edward III, 1327–1377).

Why the difference? Apparently, in her introduction, Mary Macleod is referring to the sixteenth-century tradition that Robin Hood lived during the days of the Crusades; this was first suggested by the Renaissance historian John Mair in 1521. But her retelling is based on older versions of the Robin Hood folk tales. These earliest tales place Robin Hood during the reign of a "King Edward."

In all likelihood, the stories do come from 1272 or later, rather than from the time of Richard Lionheart.

Instead of dividing this week's work into days, I'll give you a simpler assignment: First, read *The Legend of Robin Hood* all the way through without stopping—just read for fun. Then, read back through it a second time, making a few notes as you go.

Follow the steps below. You and your instructor can divide your reading and note-taking up into as many different days as necessary.

STEP ONE: Read

Get comfortable and read *The Legend of Robin Hood* from beginning to end. **(It is found in Appendix I, on pages 437-460.)** You can do this reading over two days or more if necessary.

Enjoy the stories.

Don't forget to eat a cookie.

STEP TWO: **Take Notes**

Now, go back and reread *The Legend of Robin Hood* from the beginning, one more time. As you read, write down the following information for each chapter.

1) What is the title of the chapter?
2) Who is the main character?
3) What is the most important thing that happens to the main character in the chapter?
4) Who are the other important characters?
5) What is one important thing that happens to each of them?

To help you, here are my answers for the first chapter:

1) **Chapter One, Robin Hood and the Knight**
2) **Robin Hood**
3) **He gives money, clothes, and help to a poor knight**
4) **Little John, Sir Richard Lee**
5) **Little John goes with Sir Richard Lee; Sir Richard Lee becomes prosperous again**

Your answers might be slightly different—which is fine. Just be able to explain *why* you chose the answers you did. For example, even though so much of the chapter is about the knight Richard Lee, I chose Robin Hood as the main character because the chapter begins *and* ends with him.

When you're finished with your chapter notes, show them to your instructor.

Week 30: Writing About a Longer Work of Fiction

Day One: Think

 Focus: Understanding how individual sections of episodic fiction work

Last week, you took notes in order to remember the main events of *The Legend of Robin Hood*. Today, you'll use those notes and the story itself to write brief answers to a series of questions. These answers will help you construct your own composition later in the week.

STEP ONE: ~~Review~~

Read quickly back through your notes now, to remind yourself of the characters and events in the story.

Then, read the following definitions from Level One of this course carefully.

protagonist: the character who wants to get, become, or accomplish something
antagonist: the character, force, or circumstance that opposes the protagonist

hero/heroine: a central character with admirable qualities
villain: an antagonist with evil motives

conflict: the clash between protagonist and antagonist
story climax: the point of greatest tension or conflict
pivot point: the moment at which the main character changes goals, wants, or direction

STEP TWO: **Understand the form of episodic fiction**

The Legend of Robin Hood is a work of **episodic fiction.** Read the definition out loud now:

> **episodic fiction: a series of self-contained stories, connected
>   by common characters and/or an overall plot**

In episodic fiction, each chapter or story has its own protagonist and antagonist and its own conflict. These characters and conflicts work together to produce the larger story.

You are probably most familiar with episodic fiction from television. Most television series use the techniques of episodic fiction. Each TV show, or "episode," can be watched on its own—but each one also adds to the overall story that the TV series is telling as a whole. In some episodic TV, such as the series *Lost*, the overall story (the one told by *all* the episodes together) is so important that individual episodes may not make very much sense unless you've watched all the episodes before; the episodes are more like chapters in a regular novel. In other series, particularly comedies, the overall structure is much weaker. The characters and their stories do develop over time, but you can perfectly well watch an episode from the middle of the second or third or fourth season and understand it without difficulty. Comedy series, such as *I Love Lucy* or *Seinfeld*, are more likely to have stronger episodes and a weaker overall structure.

The classic children's novels *Five Children and It, Homer Price, The Moffats* and *Pippi Longstocking* all use an episodic structure. So does James Herriot's bestselling *All Creatures Great and Small*.

Add the definition of episodic fiction to your Literary Terms chart now.

STEP THREE: **Identify the literary elements of each episode**

Tomorrow, you and your instructor will discuss the overall structure and interpretation of the entire *Legend of Robin Hood*. Today, you'll prepare by identifying the protagonist, antagonist, and conflict in individual chapters.

When you identified the main character in each chapter (last week), you were naming the protagonist (with two exceptions . . . see the hints below). Now, ask yourself the following series of questions:

1) What does the protagonist want to do, become, or get?
2) What force or person is blocking the protagonist's goal? (This is the antagonist)
3) At what event, or in what way, or in what scene do the protagonist and the antagonist clearly clash with each other?
4) How is the clash resolved? (Or is it left unresolved?)

To help you out, I've done the first chapter below.

1) Robin Hood wants to help Sir Richard Lee and then be paid back.
2) Nothing keeps him from helping, but Richard Lee gets involved with the tournament, and that keeps him from getting back to Robin Hood.

3) They don't clash, but Robin Hood is still waiting at the end of the chapter.
4) Unresolved.

Using your own paper, follow my model for the remaining chapters. Don't worry too much about getting the "right" answer. The purpose of this exercise is to get you thinking more critically about the structure of the individual stories; there may be more than one "correct" way to analyze each one.

If you need help, ask your instructor. A few additional hints are below.

When you're finished, show your work to your instructor.

HINTS

Chapter Two, "Little John and the Sheriff of Nottingham": Although the chapter ends with the sheriff sleeping in the greenwood, the *real* conflict isn't between the sheriff and Little John. Who is much more active than the sheriff in opposing the protagonist?

Chapter Three, "How Robin Hood was Paid His Loan": This is really a continuation/resolution of the first chapter, with some of the same answers.

Chapter Four, "The Golden Arrow": Remember that Robin Hood is the protagonist, so the clash and resolution will involve Robin Hood, not supporting characters.

Chapter Five, "How the Sheriff Took Sir Richard Prisoner": In this chapter, something strange happens. The main character of the chapter is *not* the same as the protagonist. Remember, the protagonist has a want or goal that makes the action of the chapter unfold. Which character would that be? (Also, this chapter has the most obvious clash between protagonist and antagonist of *any* chapter!)

Chapter Six, "How the King Came to Sherwood Forest": The *antagonist* is the same as in Chapter Five.

Chapter Seven, "How Robin Hood Went Back to the Greenwood": In this chapter, a *circumstance* is the antagonist—not a person.

Chapter Eight, "Robin Hood and the Butcher": You will find the answers to questions 2–4 much simpler to find if you look for a want or goal that is not explicitly stated in the chapter—just implied.

Chapter Nine, "The Jolly Tanner": This chapter has the same antagonist as Chapters Five and Six.

Chapter Ten, "How Robin Hood Drew His Bow for the Last Time": As in Chapter Five, the main character is not the protagonist—he does not set the events of the chapter in motion. Who does that? Also, notice that there are *two* resolutions to this final chapter.

Day Two: Discuss

 Focus: Understanding the overall structure of episodic fiction

Today, your instructor will carry on a conversation with you. As you talk about *The Legend of Robin Hood,* you will write observations on the lines below. You'll use these to work on your brief essay later in the week.

STEP ONE: **Identify the overall plot structure**

First story-within-a-story: _____

_____

_____

Second story-within-a-story: _____

_____

_____

Robin Hood's goal: _____

_____

_____

Who opposes him? _____

_____

_____

What force opposes him? _____

_____

_____

The clash between protagonist and antagonist: _____

_____

_____

Resolution: _____

_____

_____

What sort of resolution is this? _____

_____

_____

STEP TWO: Discuss identity and concealment

1. _____

_____

2. _____

_____

3. _____

_____

4. _____

_____

5. _____

_____

6. _____

_____

7. _____

_____

The most successful transformation is:_____

_____

_____

_____

Days Three and Four: Write

Over the next two days, you will use your notes from last week and this week to construct an original critical essay of at least 375 words.

You will complete the following five steps. You and your instructor can decide how many steps to finish per day.

Step One: Write a brief narrative summary
Step Two: Write about the overall structure of *The Legend of Robin Hood*
Step Three: Write about identity and concealment
Step Four: Write an introduction and conclusion
Step Five: Proofread

You may show your work to your instructor at any point, but you do not *have* to turn in your essay until you have finished Step Five.

In at least one of the following steps, quote directly from *The Legend of Robin Hood.*

STEP ONE: Write a brief narrative summary

Begin your work by writing a brief narrative summary of *The Legend of Robin Hood.*

Summarizing a work of episodic fiction can be challenging. Follow these instructions:

1. Start off by explaining that *The Legend of Robin Hood* is episodic fiction. You don't have to use the phrase "episodic fiction," but if you do, be sure to define it for the reader.

2. Summarize briefly the events that happen in at least three of the stories. These can be one-sentence summaries, or a little longer—that's up to you. You will probably find your reading notes from last week very useful!

3. Describe briefly the importance of two or three important secondary characters.

You may do all of this in one paragraph, or you may spread it out over two or more. This part of the composition should be at least 120–125 words in length.

STEP TWO: **Write about the overall structure of** *The Legend of Robin Hood*

Using your notes from Day Two, write at least two paragraphs about the overall plot structure of *The Legend of Robin Hood*. In the first paragraph, explain what Robin Hood wants, what opposes him, what the primary clash of the story is, and how it is resolved. In the second paragraph, explain whether or not Robin Hood was successful, and why you came to that conclusion.

This part of your composition should also be at *least* 120–125 words. Remember, your entire composition will need to be at least 375 words.

STEP THREE: **Write about identity and concealment**

Now, write at least one paragraph about the ways in which the characters conceal their identities or disguise themselves. Begin with a sentence explaining that disguises are something that many characters use. Then, give at least two good examples.

Keep an eye on your word length. By now, your paper should be very close to 350 words or longer.

STEP FOUR: **Write an introduction and conclusion**

Write a brief opening paragraph (it can be a single long sentence or more) that identifies the book by its title and tells the reader who the author is. Your introduction should also say, very briefly, what Robin Hood sets out to do in the book, and whether or not he succeeds.

(Sometimes writers get stuck because they start writing with the introduction. In most cases, a good introduction is one of the last things you add to the essay!)

Then, write a concluding paragraph that gives your personal opinion about *The Legend of Robin Hood*. What parts did you enjoy, and why? What parts did you dislike? Why? What did you wish the author had done differently? What did the author do well?

STEP FIVE: **Proofread**

When you have finished Step Four, put your essay away for a few hours or overnight before proofreading.

Then, follow these proofreading steps.

1) Check to make sure that all five required elements are present.

2) Make sure that your finished essay is at least 375 words long.

3) Make sure that you have quoted from *The Legend of Robin Hood* at least once. Since your copy of the story is not an independent publication, you do not need to footnote your quote.

4) Read your paper out loud, listening for awkward or unclear sections and repeated words. Rewrite awkward or unclear sentences so that they flow more naturally.

5) Listen for information that is repeated more than once. Eliminate repetition of ideas.

6) Read through the paper one more time, looking for sentence fragments, run-on sentences, and repeated words. Correct fragments and run-on sentences. Listen for unnecessary repetition.

7) Check your spelling by looking, individually, at each word that might be a problem.

When you are finished proofreading, give your essay to your instructor.

WEEK 31: COMBINING THE *TOPOI* IN HISTORY

In your study of *topoi* so far, you've learned how to construct six different basic types of essay—chronological narratives, descriptions, biographical sketches, sequences, comparisons and contrasts, and explanations by definition. You've studied what elements belong to each one, and how they differ for history compositions and science compositions.

Now it's time to take your knowledge one step further.

Learning about the *topoi* is an important starting place, but when good, mature writers put together their own essays, they rarely follow any one of the *topoi* exactly. Instead, they combine, adding and subtracting elements to produce a piece of writing that flows smoothly forward.

Compare learning to write and learning to draw. When you start learning how to draw, you might start out working on basic shapes, and then go on to perspective drawings. Then you might practice drawing landscapes; then, still life scenes; after that, drawings of animals; after that, people.

These are all valuable skills. And once you become an artist, you'll probably spend some time using those skills just as you practiced them. If you do a portrait, you'll use everything you learned when you practiced drawing people. You'll probably draw some landscapes, and perhaps a few still life scenes.

But you might also strike out on your own and draw a landscape that has a person or two in it, plus an animal in the distance—or perhaps just a half-glimpsed animal. Or you might combine elements of still life and portraits together.

Over the next three weeks, you'll prepare for your final project by examining how elements from different *topoi* can be combined together into a single effective essay. In both history and science, you'll examine a classic piece of writing, identify the techniques and forms that the writer uses, and then practice writing your own composition.

Day One: Analyze the Model

 Focus: Understanding how writers combine elements

STEP ONE: **Review the** *topoi*

Before you begin today's work, read carefully through the following *topoi* in your Composition Reference Notebook. Don't just skim through them; pay attention to each element!

Chronological Narrative of a Past Event
Description of a Place
Description of a Person
Biographical Sketch
Sequence: History
Explanation by Comparison/Contrast
Explanation by Definition: Historical Object, Event, Place, or People Group
Temporal Comparison: History

To help keep your attention on the material, I recommend that you read the *topoi* out loud.

STEP TWO: **Read**

Read carefully through the following excerpt from "Julius Caesar Crossing the Rubicon," by the nineteenth-century historian and writer Jacob Abbott.

— — —

Julius Caesar Crossing the Rubicon

by Jacob Abbott

There was a little stream in ancient times, in the north of Italy, which flowed eastward into the Adriatic Sea, called the Rubicon. This stream has been immortalized by the transactions which we are now about to describe.

The Rubicon was a very important boundary, and yet it was in itself so small and insignificant that it is now impossible to determine which of two or three little brooks here running into the sea is entitled to its name and renown. In history the Rubicon is a grand, permanent, and conspicuous stream, gazed upon with continued interest by all mankind for nearly twenty centuries; in nature it is an uncertain rivulet, for a long time doubtful and undetermined, and finally lost.

The Rubicon originally derived its importance from the fact that it was the boundary between all that part of the north of Italy which is formed by the valley of the Po, one of the richest and most magnificent countries of the world, and the more southern Roman territories. This country of the Po constituted what was in those days called the hither Gaul, and was a Roman province. It belonged now to Caesar's jurisdiction, as the commander in Gaul.

All south of the Rubicon was territory reserved for the immediate jurisdiction of the city. The Romans, in order to protect themselves from any danger which might threaten their own liberties from the immense armies which they raised for the conquest of foreign nations, had imposed on every side very strict limitations and restrictions in respect to the approach of these armies to the capital. The Rubicon was the limit on this northern side. Generals commanding in Gaul were never to pass it. To cross the Rubicon with an army on the way to Rome was rebellion and treason. Hence the Rubicon became, as it were, the visible sign and symbol of civil restriction to military power.

As Caesar found the time of his service in Gaul drawing toward a conclusion, he turned his thoughts more and more toward Rome, endeavoring to strengthen his interest there by every means in his power, and to circumvent and thwart the designs of Pompey. He had agents and partisans in Rome who acted for him and in his name. He sent immense sums of money to these men, to be employed in such ways as would most tend to secure the favor of the people. He ordered the Forum to be rebuilt with great magnificence. He arranged great celebrations, in which the people were entertained with an endless succession of games, spectacles, and public feasts. When his daughter Julia, Pompey's wife, died, he celebrated her funeral with indescribable splendor. He distributed corn in immense quantities among the people, and he sent a great many captives home, to be trained as gladiators to fight in the theatres for their amusement. In many cases, too, where he found men of talents and influence among the populace, who had become involved in debt by their dissipations and extravagance, he paid their debts, and thus secured their influence on his side. Men were astounded at the magnitude of these expenditures, and, while the multitude rejoiced thoughtlessly in the pleasures thus provided for them, the more reflecting and considerate trembled at the greatness of the power which was so rapidly rising to overshadow the land.

It increased their anxiety to observe that Pompey was gaining the same kind of influence and ascendency, too. He had not the advantage which Caesar enjoyed in the prodigious wealth obtained from the rich countries over which Caesar ruled, but he possessed, instead of it, the advantage of being all the time at Rome, and of securing, by his character and action there, a very wide personal popularity and influence. Pompey was, in fact, the idol of the people . . . [and] considered himself as standing far above Caesar in fame and power . . .

In the meantime, the period was drawing near in which Caesar's command in the provinces was to expire; and, anticipating the struggle with Pompey which was about to ensue, he conducted several of his legions through the passes of the Alps and advanced gradually, as he had a right to do, across the country of the Po toward the Rubicon, revolving in his capacious mind, as he came, the various plans by which he might hope to gain the ascendency over the power of his mighty rival and make himself supreme.

He concluded that it would be his wisest policy not to attempt to intimidate Pompey by great and open preparations for war, which might tend to arouse him to vigorous measures of resistance, but rather to cover and conceal his designs, and thus throw his enemy off his guard. He advanced, therefore, toward the Rubicon with a small force. He established his headquarters at Ravenna, a city not far from the river, and employed himself in objects of local interest there in order to avert as much as possible the minds of the people from imagining that he was contemplating any great design. Pompey sent to him to demand the return of a certain legion which he had lent him from his own army at a time when they were friends. Caesar complied with this demand without any hesitation, and sent the legion home. He sent with this legion, also, some other troops which were properly his own, thus evincing a degree of indifference in respect to the amount of the force retained under his command which seemed wholly inconsistent with the idea that he contemplated any resistance to the authority of the government at Rome.

In the meantime, the struggle at Rome between the partisans of Caesar and Pompey grew more and more violent and alarming. Caesar, through his friends in the city, demanded to be elected consul. The other side insisted that he must first, if that was his wish, resign the command of his army, come to Rome, and present himself as a candidate in the character of a private citizen. This the constitution of the state very properly required. In answer to this requisition, Caesar rejoined that, if Pompey would lay down his military commands, he would do so too; if not, it was unjust to require it of him . . .

To a large part of the people of the city these demands of Caesar appeared reasonable. They were clamorous to have them allowed. The partisans of Pompey, with the stern and inflexible Cato at their head, deemed them wholly inadmissible and contended with the most determined violence against them. The whole city was filled with the excitement of this struggle, into which all the active and turbulent spirits of the capital plunged with the most furious zeal, while the more considerate and thoughtful of the population . . . trembled at the impending danger.

Pompey himself had no fear. He urged the Senate to resist to the utmost all of Caesar's claims, saying if Caesar should be so presumptuous as to attempt to march to Rome he could raise troops enough by stamping with his foot to put him down.

It would require a volume to contain a full account of the disputes and tumults, the manoeuvres and debates, the votes and decrees, which marked the successive stages of this quarrel . . . A thousand plans were formed, and clamorously insisted upon by their respective advocates, for averting the danger. This only added to the confusion, and the city became at length pervaded with a universal terror.

While this was the state of things at Rome, Caesar was quietly established at Ravenna, thirty or forty miles from the frontier. He was erecting a building for a fencing school there, and his mind seemed to be occupied very busily with the plans and models of the edifice which the architects had formed. Of course, in his intended march to Rome, his reliance was not to be so much on the force which he should take with him, as on the cooperation and support which he expected to find there. It was his policy, therefore, to move as quietly and privately as possible, and with as little display of violence, and to avoid everything which might indicate his intended march to any spies which might be around him, or to any other persons who might be disposed to report what they observed, at Rome. Accordingly, on the very eve of his departure, he busied himself with his fencing school, and assumed with his officers and soldiers a careless and unconcerned air, which prevented any one from suspecting his design.

In the course of the day, he privately sent forward some cohorts to the southward, with orders for them to encamp on the banks of the Rubicon. When night came, he sat down to supper as usual and conversed with his friends in his ordinary manner, and went with them afterward to a public entertainment. As soon as it was dark and the streets were still, he set off secretly from the city, accompanied by a very few attendants. Instead of making use of his ordinary equipage, the parading of which would have attracted attention to his movements, he had some mules taken from a neighboring bakehouse and harnessed into his chaise. There were torch-bearers provided to light the way. The cavalcade drove on during the night, finding, however, the hasty preparations which had been made inadequate for the occasion. The torches went out, the guides lost their way, and the future conqueror of the world wandered about bewildered and lost, until, just after break of day, the party met with a peasant who undertook to guide them. Under his direction they made their way to the main road again, and advanced then without further difficulty to the banks of the river, where they found that portion of the army which had been sent forward encamped and awaiting their arrival.

Caesar stood for some time upon the banks of the stream, musing upon the greatness of the undertaking in which simply passing across it would involve him. His officers stood by his side. "We can retreat *now*," said he, "but once across that river, we must go on."

He paused for some time, conscious of the vast importance of the decision, though he thought only, doubtless, of its consequences to himself. Taking the step which was now before him would necessarily end either in his realizing the loftiest aspirations of his ambition, or in his utter and irreparable ruin.

There were vast public interests, too, at stake, of which, however, he probably thought but little. It proved, in the end, that the history of the whole Roman world, for several centuries, was depending upon the manner in which the question now in Caesar's mind should turn.

There was a little bridge across the Rubicon at the point where Caesar was surveying it. While he was standing there, the story is, a peasant or shepherd came from the neighboring fields with a shepherd's pipe—a simple musical instrument made of a reed and used much by the rustic musicians of those days. The soldiers and some of the officers gathered around him to hear him play. Among the rest came some of Caesar's trumpeters, with their trumpets in their hands. The shepherd took one of these martial instruments from the hands of its possessor, laying aside his own, and began to sound a charge—which is a signal for a rapid advance—and to march at the same time over the bridge. "An omen! a prodigy!" said Caesar. "Let us march where we are called by such a divine intimation. The die is cast."

So saying, he pressed forward over the bridge, while the officers, breaking up the encampment, put the columns in motion to follow him.

STEP THREE: **Understand how *topoi* can be combined**

During this step, your instructor will carry on a dialogue with you. Keep your *topoi* chart next to the essay as you work.

Day Two: Prepare to Write

Focus: Reading sources for an
essay in history

Now that you've seen how an accomplished author combines *topoi* and uses elements from different forms, you'll start preparing to do the same in a historical essay of your own.

Your essay will be about Joan of Arc.

STEP ONE: **Read**

Today, you only have one step to perform. Before you start thinking about which *topoi* you will use, read through the following sources carefully, without stopping to take notes.

"The Story of Joan of Arc, the Maid Who Saved France." In William Patten, ed., *The Junior Classics, Vol. 7: Stories of Courage and Heroism* (New York: P. F. Collier & Son, 1912). [Page numbers are in parentheses]

— — —

(113) Over five hundred years ago, the children of Domremy, a little village on the border of France, used to dance and sing beneath a beautiful beech tree. They called it "The Fairy Tree." Among these children was one named Jeanne, the daughter of an honest farmer, Jacques d'Arc. Jeanne sang more than she danced, and though she carried garlands like the other boys and girls, and hung them on the boughs of the Fairies' Tree, she liked better to take the flowers into the parish church and lay them on the altars of St. Margaret and St. Catherine.

She was brought up by her parents (as she told (114) the judges at her trial) to be industrious, to sew and spin. She did not fear to match herself at spinning and sewing, she said, against any woman in Rouen. When very young, she sometimes went to the fields to watch the cattle. As she grew older, she worked in the house; she did not any longer watch sheep and cattle. But the times were dangerous, and when there was an alarm of soldiers or robbers in the neighborhood, she sometimes helped to drive the flock into a fortified island or peninsula, for which her father was responsible, in the river near her home. She learned her creed, she said, from her mother. Twenty years after her death, her neighbors, who remembered her, described her as she was when a child. Jean Morin said that she was a good industrious girl, but that she would often be praying in church when her father and mother did not know it. Jean Waterin, when he was a boy, had seen Joan in the fields, "and when they were all playing together, she would go apart and pray to God, as he thought, and he and the others used to laugh at her. When she heard the church bell ring, she would kneel down in the fields." All those who had seen Joan told the same tale: she was always kind, simple, industrious, pious and yet merry and fond of playing with the others.

In Joan's childhood France was under a mad king, Charles VI, and was torn to pieces by two factions, the party of Burgundy and the party of Armagnac. The English took advantage of these disputes, and overran the land. The two parties of Burgundy and Armagnac divided (115) town from town and village from village . . . Domremy was for the Armagnacs—that is, against the English and for the Dauphin, the son of the mad Charles VI. But at Maxey, a village near Domremy, the people were all for Burgundy and the English . . .

When Joan was between twelve and thirteen (the year 1424), so she swore, *a Voice came to her from God for her guidance*, but when first it came, she was in great fear. And it came, that Voice, about noonday, in the summer season, she being in her father's garden. Joan had not fasted the day before that, but was fasting when the Voice came. The Voices at first only told her to be a good girl, and go to church. The Voice later told her of the great sorrow there was in

France, and that one day she must go into France and help the country. She had visions with the Voices; visions first of St. Michael, and then of St. Catherine and St. Margaret. "I saw them with my bodily eyes, as I see you," she said to her judges," and when they departed from me I wept, and well I wished that they had taken me with them."

What are we to think about these visions and these Voices which were with Joan to her death?

(116) In 1428 only a very few small towns in the east still held out for the Dauphin, and these were surrounded on every side by enemies. Meanwhile the Voices came more frequently, urging Joan to go into France and help her country. She asked how she, a girl, who could not ride or use sword and lance, could be of any help? At the same time she was encouraged by one of the vague old prophecies which were common in France. A legend ran that France was to be saved by a Maiden from the Oak Wood, and there was an Oak Wood (*le bois chenu*) near Domremy. Some such prophecy had an influence on Joan, and probably helped people to believe in her. The Voices often commanded her to go to Vaucouleurs, a neighboring town which was loyal, and there meet Robert de Baudricourt, who was captain of the French garrison. Now, Robert de Baudricourt was a gallant soldier, but a plain practical man, very careful of his own interest, and cunning enough to hold his own among his many enemies . . .

Joan had a cousin who was married to one Durand Lassois, at Burey en Vaux, a village near Vaucouleurs. This cousin invited Joan to visit her for a week. At the end of that time she spoke to her cousin's husband. There was an old saying, as we saw, that France would be rescued by a Maid, and she, as she told Lassois, was that Maid. Lassois listened, and, whatever he may have thought of her chances, he led her to Robert de Baudricourt.

Joan came, in her simple red dress, and walked straight up to the captain. She told him that the Dauphin must keep quiet, and risk no battle, for, (117) before the middle of Lent next year (the year 1429), God would send him help. She added that the kingdom belonged, not to the Dauphin, but to her Master, who willed that the Dauphin should be crowned, and she herself would lead him to Reims, to be anointed with the holy oil.

"And who is your Master?" said Robert.

"The King of Heaven!"

Robert, very naturally, thought that Joan was crazed, and shrugged his shoulders. He bluntly told Lassois to box her ears and take her back to her father. So she had to go home; but here new troubles awaited her. The enemy came down on Domremy and burned it; Joan and her family fled to Neufchateau, where they stayed for a few days. When Joan looked from her father's garden to the church, she saw nothing but a heap of smoking ruins. These things only made her feel more deeply the sorrows of her country. The time was drawing near when she had prophesied that the Dauphin was to receive help from heaven—namely, in the Lent of 1429. On that year the season was held more than commonly sacred, for Good Friday and the Annunciation fell on the same day. So, early in January, 1429, Joan turned her back on Domremy, which she was never to see again. Her cousin Lassois came and asked leave for Joan to visit him again; so she said good-by to her father and mother, and to her friends.

She went to her cousin's house at Burey, and there she stayed for six weeks, hearing bad news of the siege of Orleans by the English . . .

(118) On February 12, the story goes, she went to Robert de Baudricourt. "You delay too long," she said. "On this very day, at Orleans, the gentle Dauphin has lost a battle."

Now the people of Vaucouleurs brought clothes for Joan to wear on her journey to the Dauphin. They were such clothes as men wear—doublet, hose, surcoat, boots, and spurs—and Robert de Baudricourt gave Joan a sword. Her reason was that she would have to be living alone among men-at-arms for a ten days' journey and she thought it was more modest to wear armor like the rest. Also, her favorite saint, St. Margaret, had done this once when in danger. Besides, in all the romances of chivalry, we find fair maidens fighting in arms like men, or travelling dressed as pages.

(119) On February 23, 1429, the gate of the little castle of Vaucouleurs, "the Gate of France," which is still standing, was thrown open. Seven travellers rode out, among them two squires, Jean de Nouillompont and Bertrand de Poulengy, with their attendants, and Joan the Maid.

"Go, and let what will come of it come!" said Robert de Baudricourt. He did not expect much to come of it. It was a long journey—they were eleven days on the road—and a dangerous. But Joan laughed at danger. "God will clear my path to the king, for to this end I was born." . . . On March 6, Joan arrived in Chinon where for two or three days the king's advisers would not let him see her. At last they yielded, and she went straight up to him, and when he denied that he was the king, she told him that she knew well who he was.

(120) "There is the king," said Charles, pointing to a richly dressed noble. "No, fair sire. You are he!"

"The Loss of France." From Susan Wise Bauer, *The History of the Renaissance World: From the Rediscovery of Aristotle to the Conquest of Constantinople* (New York: W. W. Norton, 2013)

Jeanne remained at Chinon with the king until April, planning the assault on the besiegers of Orleans. On April 27, she sent the Duke of Bedford a message (which he ignored) ordering him to surrender all of his properties and leave France. Then she began to travel towards Orleans at the head of the Dauphin's army. Two days later, she crossed the Loire.

Her energy and conviction had managed to transmit itself to the knights and captains who had been stalled behind the Dauphin's withdrawn generalship; and in three quick assaults on the French-English camps, the royalist army forced the besiegers to break camp and retreat by the end of the first week of May. It was the initial victory in a string of triumphs. Like a football team that has suddenly regained its confidence, the Dauphin's army followed the "Maid of Orleans" into battle after battle—and fought brilliantly. The English and Burgundian forces fell back and back. The English-held Tournelles surrendered on May 8; Jargeau in June; Troyes and Reims in July; St. Denis in August. With Reims finally back in his hands, the Dauphin mounted an elaborate coronation ceremony in the ancient cathedral, following the tradition established by the Frankish king Clovis centuries before.

Coronated and anointed, Charles now seemed to lose his will to tap into Jeanne d'Arc's electrical presence. The final step in establishing his lordship over France would be the routing of the English from Paris; but Charles was not enthusiastic about the attack, and Jeanne herself had underestimated the English strength in Paris. She had thought that the people would come over to the side of the rightfully crowned king of France, but there were too many Burgundians and English in the city. After a few initial assaults in late August, she led a major attack against Paris's walls on September 8, 1429. But, sensing division in their leadership, the French army faltered. Jeanne herself was badly injured, taking a serious arrow wound to the thigh. The royalist army finally retreated. Something had shifted; Jeanne's injury had turned the angel of the Lord into a vulnerable woman.[55]

The mysterious momentum of the French army had faded. By early September, Charles VII had decided to retreat across the Loire for the winter. By spring of 1430, he was still sitting, apathetically, at the northern city of Sully.

Hoping to recapture the old momentum, Jeanne d'Arc left him and went, with two thousand loyal soldiers, to the city of Compiegne. Compiegne had remained loyal to Charles VII, defying the English; she hoped to use the city as a base for a surprise attack on English troops nearby. Instead, she marched out

---

55. Clayton J. Drees, *The Late Medieval Age of Crisis and Renewal, 1300–1500: A Biographical Dictionary* (Greenwood Press, 2001), p. 252.

from its gates and was almost at once driven backwards by the Duke of Burgundy's men. "During that time," one of the soldiers who was present later wrote, "the captain [of Compiegne], seeing the great multitude of Burgundians and Englishmen ready to get on the bridge . . . raised the drawbridge of the city and closed the gate. So the Maid was shut outside, and only a few of her men were with her."[56]

Later accounts, including Holinshed's, suggest that the governor of Compiegne was in the pay of the English, and that Jeanne had been set up. However it happened, she was forced to surrender, and was taken captive to the Duke of Burgundy's camp at Marigny. To the English and Burgundians, she was the power that had resurrected Charles VII's army from the dead; she had to be not just removed from the war, but discredited. So she was treated not as prisoner of war, but as a heretic, accused of "many crimes, sorceries, idolatry, intercourse with demons, and other matters relative to faith and against faith."[57]

Charles VII made no effort to ransom her. No contemporary writer makes any mention of his thoughts on the subject; there is nothing but silence. Perhaps he was playing out one of those deep long-term strategies which occasionally surfaced during his reign; or perhaps his coronation had been the only goal all along; or, possibly, he was suffering from a spell of the pathological apathy that occasionally seized him. There is no way to know for sure. But after long and miserable imprisonment, Jeanne was finally put on trial for heresy at Rouen, in Normandy (safely English territory) on February 21, 1431.

. . . [S]he was condemned as an unrepentant heretic and sentenced to death by burning. The French court had been prepared (and perhaps hoping) for this eventuality all along: the punishment was carried out with immediate efficiency. On May 30, 1431, she was led out to the square of Rouen, where eight hundred armed men had assembled to supervise the execution. It was a hasty execution; the priest assigned to hear her last confession at the stake later wrote that the captain of the troops tried to hurry him through the confession so that he could dismiss his men for dinner.

— — —

56. Donald Spoto, *Joan: The Mysterious Life of the Heretic Who Became a Saint* (HarperCollins, 2007), p. 111.
57. Spoto, p. 118; Holinshed, p. 170.

The following pages are taken from R. S. Gower, *Joan of Arc* (New York: Charles Scribner's Sons, 1893).

The following excerpt is from page 6:

speak volumes.   From her childhood she showed an intense and ever-increasing devotion to things holy; her delight in prayer became almost a passion.   She never wearied of visiting the churches in and about her native village, and she passed many an hour in a kind of rapt trance before the crucifixes and saintly images in these churches. Every morning saw her at her accustomed place at the early celebration of her Lord's Sacrifice; and if in the afternoon the evening bells sounded across the fields, she would kneel devoutly, and commune in her heart with her divine Master and adored saints.   She loved above all things these evening bells, and, when it seemed to her the ringer grew negligent, would bribe him with some little gift — the worked wool from one of her sheep or some other trifle — to remind him

THE CALL.   7

in the future to be more instant in his office. That this little trait in Joan is true, we have the testimony of the bell-ringer himself to attest.

This devotion to her religious duties had not the effect of making Joan less of a companion to her fellow-villagers.   She could not have been so much beloved by them as she was had she held herself aloof from them : on the contrary, Joan enjoyed to play with the lads and village lasses ; and we hear of her swiftness of foot in the race, of her gracefulness in the village dance, either by the stream or around an old oak-tree in the forest, which was said to be the favourite haunt of the fairies.

Often in the midst of these sports Joan would break away from her companions, and enter some church or chapel, where she placed garlands of flowers around statues of her beloved saints.

Thus passed away the early years of the maiden's gentle life, among her native fields, with nothing especially to distinguish her from her companions beyond her goodness and piety.   A great change, however, was near at hand.   The

The following excerpt is from page 11:

been less propitious. A soldier named Bertrand de Poulangy, who was one of the garrison of Vaucouleurs, was an eye-witness of the meeting. He accompanied Joan of Arc later on to Chinon, and left a record of the almost brutal manner with which Baudricourt received the Maid. From this soldier's narrative we possess one of the rare glimpses which have come down to us of the appearance of the heroine : not indeed a description of what would be of such intense interest as to make known to us the appearance and features of her face ; but he describes her dress, which was that then worn by the better-to-do agricultural class of Lorraine peasant women, made of

12   *JOAN OF ARC.*

rough red serge, the cap such as is still worn by the peasantry of her native place.

It is much to be regretted that no portrait of Joan of Arc exists either in sculpture or painting. A life-size bronze statue which portrayed the Maid kneeling on one side of a crucifix, with Charles VII. opposite, forming part of a group near the old bridge of Orleans, was destroyed by the Huguenots ; and all the portraits of Joan painted in oils are spurious. None are earlier than the sixteenth century, and all are mere imaginary daubs. In most of these Joan figures in a hat and feathers, of the style worn in the Court of Francis I. From various contemporary notices, it appears that her hair was dark in colour, as in Bastien Lepage's celebrated picture, which supplies as good an idea of what Joan may have been as any pictured representation of her form and face. Would that the frescoes which Montaigne describes as being painted on the front of the house upon the site of which Joan was born could have come down to us. They might have given some conception of her appearance. Montaigne saw those frescoes on his way to Italy, and says that all the front of the house was painted with representations of her deeds, but even in his day they were much injured.

The excerpt below is from page 159:

> Beaupère now began questioning Joan of Arc regarding 'her voices,' and one can imagine how eagerly this portion of the prisoner's examination must have been listened to by all present.
>
> 'When did you first hear the voices?' asked Beaupère.
>
> 'I was thirteen,' answered Joan, 'when I first heard a voice coming from God to help me to live well.   That first time I was much

---

160   *JOAN OF ARC.*

alarmed.   The voice came to me about mid-day; it was in the summer, and I was in my father's garden.'

'Had you been fasting?' asked Beaupère.

J.—'Yes, I had been fasting.'

B.—'Had you fasted on the day before?'

J.—'No, I had not.'

B.—'From what direction did the voices come?'

J.—'I heard the voice coming from my right —from towards the church.'

B.—'Was the voice accompanied with a bright light?'

J.—'Seldom did I hear it without seeing a bright light.   The light came from the same side as did the voice, and it was generally very brilliant.   When I came into France I often heard the voices very loud.'

B.—'How could you see the light when you say it was at the side?'

To this question Joan gave no direct answer, but she said that when she was in a wood she would hear the voices coming towards her.

'What,' next asked Beaupère, 'what did you think this voice which manifested itself to you sounded like?'

J.—'It seemed to me a very noble voice, and I think it was sent to me by God.   When I heard it for the third time I recognised it as being the voice of an angel.'

B.—'Could you understand it?'

J.—'It was always quite clear, and I could easily understand it.'

The following pages are taken from Francis C. Lowell, *Joan of Arc* (Boston: Houghton, Mifflin and Co., 1897).

The following excerpt is from page 53:

On Wednesday morning a message came from Charles, and they rode on to Chinon. The town is built February upon a meadow beside the river Vienne; behind 23, 1429. it rises a high perpendicular ledge on which the castle stood. At once a fortress and a palace, it had thick walls, huge towers, and deep moats, which protected great buildings but just constructed, containing lofty rooms lighted by

54   JOAN OF ARC.

large mullioned windows. Joan reached the town about noon, and dined at an inn; after dinner she rode around the western end of the cliff, through a gloomy ravine, made darker by the high walls of the castle, up to its eastern entrance, where the drawbridge crossed a moat hewn in the solid rock. She was led past the modern buildings, across another drawbridge, into the strongest part of the hold, and there lodged in a great tower called of Coudray.[1]

The excerpt to the right is from pages 55 & 56:

Five hundred years ago, however contemptible personally a king might be, his personality was important to his kingdom. Seldom has a king lived who deserved greater contempt than did Charles VII. Weak in body and mind, idle, lazy, luxurious, and cowardly, he was naturally the puppet of his worst courtiers, and the despair of those who hoped for reform.[2] "How many times have poor human creatures come to you to bewail the grievous extortion practiced upon them! Alas, well might they cry, 'Why sleepest thou, O Lord!' But they could arouse neither you nor those about you." So wrote an excellent official who helped to make illustrious the later years of the reign.[3]

The child of a crazy father and a licentious mother, Charles, as has been said already, was at times frivolous and splendor-loving, at times gloomy and solitary. "Never a king lost his kingdom so gayly," was a saying fathered upon La Hire, a fierce Gascon soldier, and the acknowledged wit of France.[4] Most of the money that the king could raise was spent in luxurious living or given to favorites. He had pledged Chinon itself to La Trémoille, until the favorite became dissatisfied with the

56   JOAN OF ARC.

security, as being of too little value and too likely to be taken by the English.[1] Charles's extravagance often left him wretchedly poor, and so the story went about that a cobbler, who had mended one of his boots and could not get payment, tore out the work and left the king to walk about in holes.

The following excerpt is also from page 56:

On reaching Chinon, Joan at once asked to see the Dauphin, but this his advisers would not allow. Some of them went to her and inquired her errand. At first she refused to speak to any one except Charles; but when she was told that he would not see her unless she first told her errand, she said to them plainly that she had two commands laid upon her by the King of Heaven, one, to raise the siege of Orleans, the other, to lead Charles to Rheims that he might be crowned and consecrated there. Meantime, Metz and Poulengy were talking everywhere about her goodness, and the wonderful safety they had enjoyed during the long journey which they had taken together.[3]

Joan's visitors were not disinclined to believe her inspired, but it seemed possible that her inspiration might come from hell rather than from heaven. For Charles to receive a witch into his presence would endanger his person, and, besides, would greatly discredit his majesty.[4]

CHINON.   57

Certain clerks and priests, accordingly, men expert in discerning good spirits from bad, were appointed to examine Joan. They could find no harm in her, but yielded to her simple faith, and told Charles that, as she professed to bring him a message from God, at least he ought to hear her. He yielded reluctantly, and fixed a time for the audience, some two or three days after her arrival.[1]

It was evening, and the great hall of the palace, lighted by dozens of torches, was filled with curious courtiers and with the royal guard. Louis of Bourbon, count of Vendôme, led Joan into the room, dressed in black and gray, — the man's dress she had worn upon her journey. She had been praying, and beside the glare of the torches, she saw the light which usually came with her voices. As she entered, Charles drew aside, thinking to puzzle her and try her miraculous powers, but by the counsel of her voices, as she afterwards said, she knew him, and made to him a dutiful obeisance. "Gentle Dauphin," she began, "I have come to you on a message from God, to bring help to you and to your kingdom." She went on to declare more particularly that she was bidden to raise the siege of Orleans and to conduct him to Rheims.[2]

The following illustration is found in Gower's biography of Joan of Arc:

STREET IN CHINON.

Days Three and Four: Take Notes for a History Composition

Focus: Taking notes

Over the next two days, you'll take notes on the sources about Joan of Arc. You'll then spend the first half of next week writing your essay.

There are three steps to this assignment. You and your instructor can decide how much work you should do on each day.

STEP ONE: **Choose tentative *topoi* and elements**

To take notes effectively, you'll need to make a tentative decision about the the *topoi* that you'll include in your essay.

Look back through the following *topoi* in your Composition Reference Notebook. Keeping in mind the sources that you read in Day Two, choose at least three *topoi* that you might be able to use in an essay about Joan of Arc. Four is even better.

Remember that you don't have to include *every* element in the chosen *topoi*; you can just incorporate one or two aspects into your final paper.

Chronological Narrative of a Past Event
Description of a Place
Description of a Person
Biographical Sketch
Sequence: History
Explanation by Comparison/Contrast
Explanation by Definition: Historical Object, Event, Place, or People Group
Temporal Comparison: History

Once you've made your choice, show your selections to your instructor. Ask for help if you need it.

STEP TWO: **Prepare to take notes**

At the top of a sheet of notebook paper, or at the beginning of a new word processing document, enter the name of the first *topos* that you intend to use. Then, write a brief phrase or sentence describing the person, historical period, place, or other phenomenon that the *topos* will cover. You might also find it useful to jot down the aspects you might want to include.

For example, if the first *topos* you decided to include was "Chronological Narrative of a Past Event," you might then write, "Joan of Arc's life, from Hearing Voices to Leading the

French Army" or "The French War with the English, from Joan's Arrival in Chinon to her Capture by the English." If you chose "Description of a Person," you could then write "The Dauphin Charles—What Others Think, Character Qualities, Behaviors, Notoriety."

The heading on your paper should help you keep in mind, as you go through your sources and take notes, exactly what kinds of information you're looking for. Otherwise, you may end up taking too many notes that you don't need (and won't use.)

Do the same for the rest of your selected *topoi*, using a different page for each heading.

STEP THREE: **Take notes**

Spend the rest of your time taking notes on the sources about Joan of Arc.

Remember to pick and choose only those facts and details that will support the *topoi* you've chosen. You do not need to write down *every* fact and detail—that would give you far too much information! Having too much information can be paralyzing when you sit down to write.

Aim to have at least five or six to eight notes about each *topos*, but do not take more than fifteen notes for any single *topos*.

As before, you can choose which note-taking method suits you best:

1) Go through the sources one time each, placing each relevant bit of information from each source on the appropriate page of notes as you go. OR

2) Pick the first *topos* and go through all four sources, looking for answers. Do the same for the second *topos*, and then the third, and so on.

NOTE: The excerpt from *The History of the Renaissance World* is from the manuscript—at the time of this writing, the book had not yet been typeset, so there are no page numbers for you to reference. When there are no page numbers for a source, use this notation:

(Bauer, n.p.)

which simply means: This piece of information came from Bauer, no page number.

I have provided you with what might be the first four or five notes on a sample *topos*, below. Follow this model.

If you need help, ask your instructor. When you are finished, show your work to your instructor.

Description of a Person
The Dauphin Charles—What Others Think,
Character Qualities, Behaviors, Notoriety

Had fits of "pathological apathy" (Bauer, n.p.)
Sometimes played out "deep long-term strategies" as a king (Bauer, n.p.)
"Weak in body and mind, idle, lazy, luxurious and cowardly (Lowell, p. 55)
The "puppet" of his courtiers (Lowell, p. 55)

Week 32: Combining the *Topoi* In History And Science

This week, you'll draft and finalize your composition combining *topoi* in history—and you'll also make a start at understanding how science writers combine *topoi*.

Days One and Two: Write

 Focus: Combining *topoi*
into a history composition

Over the next two days, you'll write a composition of at least 300 words that uses elements from at least three different *topoi*. Longer is fine; 300 is a bare minimum.

Your assignment has six steps.

Step One: Draft the main *topos*
Step Two: Add other *topoi*
Step Three: Provide an introduction and conclusion
Step Four: Construct the Works Cited page
Step Five: Title
Step Six: Proofread

Read through the instructions for all six steps before you begin to write.

Together, you and your instructor should decide how much time to spend on each step.

STEP ONE: Draft the main *topos*

In the model you examined at the beginning of Week 31, Jacob Abbott used the Chronological Narrative of a Past Event as the "skeleton" for his essay—the primary organizational form. He then inserted shorter forms and selected elements of other *topoi* into it.

Before you start to write, decide which of the *topoi* you've taken notes on will serve as your "skeleton." Choose one that has plenty of notes to go with it. (The Chronological Narrative of a Past Event and the Biographical Sketch will probably be the simplest *topoi* to use, but the Description of a Person might be a possibility as well.)

Using your notes and referring to your reference chart, write a draft of the main *topos*.

Be sure to look back at your chart, reminding yourself of the elements that should belong in the *topos*.

Aim for at least 150 words; try to get closer to 200 words if possible. Be sure to cite at least *two* sources and to include at least one direct quote.

When you cite your sources, you do not need to cite the names of the chapters (given in quotation marks for your reference), just the book titles.

STEP TWO: **Add other *topoi***

Look back over your notes and decide which *topoi* or elements you will add to your composition. If necessary, glance back at the essay by Jacob Abbott that began Week 31. Notice how he borrows aspects from Description of a Person, Comparison/Contrast, and Definition in order to flesh out his Chronological Narrative of a Past Event.

Decide where the *topoi* or elements will be located in your composition. Draft the *topoi* or elements and insert them into your essay. You must add elements from at least two different *topoi*. You may need to rearrange paragraphing or slightly rewrite some of your existing sentences so that the new elements fit into your composition smoothly. (If your original composition was a Description of a Person, it's perfectly fine to use elements from another Description of a Person as one of your additional *topoi*—so if you described Joan, you could add descriptions of Charles or vice versa.)

You should aim to have a total of at least 250 words by the end of this step; longer is better!

STEP THREE: **Provide an introduction and conclusion**

Choose an introduction and a conclusion from your Introductions and Conclusions chart. You may pick any introduction and conclusion—but make sure that they don't repeat the same information.

To write an introduction by history that uses a brief scene or an introduction by anecdote that uses an invented scene, you may need to reread the sources from Week 31. You may also find the additional excerpts below helpful (although you may need to look up some of the terms used).

Each introduction and conclusion should be at least two sentences long and should be placed in separate paragraphs, not incorporated into the existing paragraphs of the composition.

Remember that your final word count must be over 300.

Diane Stanley, *Joan of Arc* (New York: HarperCollins, 2002).

> (page xli) . . . [B]y 1453, the English were gone and the war was over
> . . . With Rouen back in French hands, Charles finally had access to the
> transcript of Joan's trial. Though he had not tried to save her, the king now
> set about clearing her name. A royal commission concluded that the trial
> had been fraudulent and driven by political aims . . .
>
> Finally, on July 7, 1456, more than six years after Charles began to look
> into the matter, and (page xlii) twenty-five years after Joan's death, a second
> verdict was announced. "The trial and sentence being tainted with fraud,"
> the conviction of heresy was considered "null, invalid, worthless, without
> effect and annihilated," and Joan was "washed clean . . . absolutely."
>
> The document was read at the cemetery of Saint-Ouen, where Joan
> had recanted out of fear. The next day, it was read again in the Old Mar-
> ket, where she gave up her life. There, the king erected a stone cross in her
> memory.
>
> In 1920, almost five hundred years after her death, Joan of Arc was
> made a saint by the Catholic Church.

Jules Michelet, *Joan of Arc* (Ann Arbor, Mich.: University of Michigan Press, 1967).

> We have a touching testimony about Joan's piety, that of her child-
> hood friend, her bosom friend, Haumette, younger than she by three or four
> years. "How often," Haumette says, "I went to her father's house . . . She
> was a very good girl, simple and sweet. She loved to go to church and to holy
> places. She would spin and do household chores like other girls . . . She went
> to confession frequently. She blushed when she was told that she was too
> devout, that she went to church too often." A peasant, who was also called a
> witness, adds that she nursed the sick and gave alms to the poor. "I know it
> for certain," he said; "I was a child then, and she took care of me." (p. 8)
>
> Joan of Arc was rehabilitated by papal decree, in 1456, after a long
> inquiry promoted by the king. On January 27, 1894, the slow process
> of canonization was formally begun. On January 6, 1904, Pope Pius X
> declared Joan entitled to the designation *Venerable*. On December 13, 1908,
> the decree of *beatification* was published; in 1920 . . . Pope Benedict XV
> declared Joan of Arc a saint. (p. 132)

STEP FOUR: **Construct the Works Cited page**

At the top of a separate sheet of paper, center the words "Works Cited." In proper form, list the sources you used to write your essay.

STEP FIVE: **Title**

Give your composition a title that describes the primary *topos* you decided to use.

For example, if I wrote a chronological narrative of past events that covered the events of Joan of Arc's call by the voices, up to her arrival at Chinon, I might title it:

The Beginning of Joan of Arc's Mission

or

Joan of Arc: From Call to Acceptance by the King

or

How Joan of Arc Went to War

Notice that the first title simply names the period of Joan's life that the composition covers. The second uses Joan's name as the title, inserts a colon, and then describes the period of her life that will be discussed by putting it into a subtitle. The third describes the overall result— what happened at the end of the chronological narrative.

Your instructor has other sample titles for you to look at, should you be completely unable to come up with an idea.

STEP SIX: **Proofread**

Before you hand your composition to your instructor, go through the following proofreading steps very carefully.

1) Check to make sure that you have used elements from at least three different *topoi*, plus an introduction and a conclusion.

2) Make sure that your finished essay is at least 300 words long. Longer is better!

3) Make sure that you have quoted from at least one source and cited at least two sources.

4) Read your paper out loud, listening for awkward or unclear sections and repeated words. Rewrite awkward or unclear sentences so that they flow more naturally.

5) Listen for information that is repeated more than once. Eliminate repetition of ideas.

6) Read through the paper one more time, looking for sentence fragments, run-on sentences, and repeated words. Correct fragments and run-on sentences. Listen for unnecessary repetition.

7) Check your spelling by looking, individually, at each word that might be a problem.

When your paper is ready, give it to your instructor.

Day Three: Analyze the Model

> Focus: Understanding how writers
> combine elements

STEP ONE: **Review the *topoi***

Before you begin today's work, read carefully through the following *topoi* in your Composition Reference Notebook. Don't just skim through them; pay attention to each element!

Chronological Narrative of a Scientific Discovery
Scientific Description
Sequence: Natural Process
Explanation by Comparison/Contrast
Explanation by Definition: Natural Object or Phenomenon
Temporal Comparison: Science

To help keep your attention on the material, I recommend that you read the *topoi* out loud.

STEP TWO: **Read**

Read carefully through the following essay, "Dr. William Harvey," by A. Dickson Wright. It was first published in *New Scientist* magazine, June 6, 1957.

You may not be familiar with a "blue pencil," referred to in the conclusion of the essay. In the days before computers, a blue pencil was traditionally used by copy editors to mark mistakes and corrections on written pages, because blue would not show up when it was photocopied. Blue pencils are no longer used, but to "blue pencil" something still means "to correct it."

— — —

Dr. William Harvey

by A. Dickson Wright

The outstanding figure in the history of British medicine is undoubtedly Dr. William Harvey, whose name is a household word to every doctor through-out the world and who yet seems to be little known to the public at large. Medi-cine might almost be divided into the pre- and post-Harveian epochs. What was it, then, that he did to transform medicine? Quite briefly, he was the first to quit the school of wild conjecture which had dominated medical thought for

1500 years and in its place to establish the experimental method. This method involved three things: first, a line of thought leading to a crucial experiment; second, the performance of the experiment; and third, the deduction therefrom.

This method led him to discover the circulation of the blood, a thing which had mystified the medical world till his time. The arteries were supposed to contain gases or foul vapours, and the heart, which is partitioned into two cavities, was supposed to supply the blood to the body at fever heat. The blood was also supposed to pass from one side of the heart to the other, and when it was pointed out that there were no apertures, the retort was that the openings were too small for the human eye to see . . . There are no openings normally between the two sides of the heart, yet up to Harvey's time this was thought to be so.

Harvey demonstrated that at each beat of the heart a spray of blood left the two sides of the heart, one directed towards the lungs and the other to the body generally. As soon as the blood left the heart, the heart muscle slackened and the heart valves closed to prevent the return of the blood, so that it had to pursue its way through the lungs and the body. Having completed the passage the blood returned to the heart by the veins, but to the opposite side of the heart from that which it originated, and then the figure-of-eight circulation was repeated again. It was a wonderful and simple method, the blood being aerated on one side of the heart and the aerated blood sent to the body from the other. The amount discharged from each side had to be equal, or there would be piling up of blood on one side or the other.

William Harvey first started to speak in public of this discovery in the year that Shakespeare died (1616) and he waited for twelve years till he published his book entitled *Exercitatio Anatomica de Motu cordis et Sanguinis in Animalibus* (Anatomical exercise on the Motion of the Heart and Blood in Animals). The year of publication was 1628, the place Frankfurt and Latin the language, and in this remark-able book of 72 pages he announced his dis-covery, backing it with beautifully conceived experiments which he made on various animals—the deer of King Charles's forests,  rabbits, frogs, toads, snakes, snails, and even the translucent shrimp.

The publication of this book provoked a storm in the world of medicine such had never been seen before. Abuse was spewed over Harvey in every lan-guage of the world: he came to be regarded as a quack, and his private practice faded away. Nevertheless he maintained a dignified silence and persevered with his research. He was willing to demonstrate his experiments to any who wished to see . . .

Twenty years were to pass before Harvey made his first written answer to the critic (Riolan, anatomist of Paris) and this was couched in the kindest and most courteous terms. As the years went by agreement grew and grew, and when he died of a stroke at Roehampton . . . the old man of nearly eighty years was the beloved and respected leader of medicine in [England]. Every doctor of eminence joined his funeral procession . . .

The life that ended on 3 June 1657 . . . had begun on 1 April 1578, in Folkestone. Harvey's parents were well-to-do citizens of that town, and Harvey enjoyed the best education obtainable. He went to King's School Canterbury, at the age of ten . . . then to Cambridge at the age of fifteen. After four years there studying the arts, he went to Padua, near Venice, to study medicine . . .

Returning to Cambridge with his Padua degree . . . Harvey received his Cambridge degree in medicine at the age of 24. With this wonderful education behind him, he married the daughter of Queen Elizabeth's doctor. Nothing was lacking to make a successful career, and this followed with great speed—physician to St. Bartholomew's Hospital, to James I, and to Charles I.

Harvey's closing years were saddened by the Civil War, which broke out when he was 64. In spite of his age, as physician to King Charles he followed him to the wars. He was at the battle of Edgehill, which was a victory for Charles, and looked after the young princes who were to become Charles II and James II. While he was away at the wars the mob looted his house in London, and some of his writings were lost for ever . . .

The great importance of Harvey's discovery was that it revolutionised the concept of how life was maintained in the human body through the constant irrigation of the tissues by a vast network of blood vessels, varying from the main artery with a calibre of two thumbs down to the finest blood vessels (capillaries), the diameter of which is one-tenth of a human hair. The aggregate length of these vessels is immense, estimated at thousands of miles, and yet they are filled with only twelve pints of blood. The heart provides the power, beating without cessation, and in a life of seventy years makes 3,500 million beats. The blood circulates at a remarkable speed, completing the circuit of the whole body in twelve seconds, or passing through the 100 miles of blood vessels in the brain in two seconds.

The construction of such a system would provide a nightmare for an engineer.

Harvey thus opened up a wonderful prospect; the anatomists found that the anatomy they had taught had to be corrected to fit in with the new concept. The physician at last began to think with logic and reason, and the treatment of every disease was benefited by the new discovery. The harmful ritualistic practice of bleeding was exposed as useless. The surgeon benefited by preventing loss of blood at operations.

In recent years the surgery of the heart and circulation has developed at an amazing speed, though in the field of research there are thousands of questions still to be answered. Many other circulations besides that of the blood have been discovered in the 100,000 miles of tubes which our bodies are estimated to contain. One might say that the body consists of tubes and life consists of circulations.

Yet if Harvey returned to the world today, 350 years after his discovery, and became acquainted with all our advances, and if in one of his hands was placed the little book of 72 pages which he published in 1628, and in the other a blue pencil, he could read the book through without once using the pencil.

Of what other scientific book could this be said?

STEP THREE: **Understand how *topoi* can be combined**

During this step, your instructor will carry on a dialogue with you. Keep your *topoi* chart next to the essay as you work.

Day Four: Prepare to Write

 Focus: Reading sources for an essay in science

Now that you've seen how an accomplished author combines *topoi* and uses elements from different forms in a science essay, you'll start preparing to do the same in a composition of your own.

STEP ONE: **Read**

Today, you only have one step to perform. Before you start thinking about which *topoi* you will use or what your exact topic will be, read through the following sources carefully, without stopping to take notes.

Elizabeth Miles, *Louis Pasteur* (Chicago: Heinemann-Raintree, 2009), p. 4.

– – –

In 1822, Louis Pasteur was born into a world that was very different from ours. Terrible illnesses such as typhoid fever and cholera spread fast, killing millions of people. When Louis was 10 years old, cholera arrived in France, the country where he lived. Thousands of townspeople died after suffering from symptoms such as fever and vomiting.

Few medicines existed, and no one understood why people caught diseases from each other. The importance of hygiene in controlling the spread of germs was not known. People did not wash their hands or keep their homes clean. Even hospitals were dangerous places to go because the rooms were dirty.

— — —

Lisa Zamosky, Thomas B. Ciccone, and Ronald Edwards, *Louis Pasteur* (Mankato, Minn.: Compass Point Books, 2009), p. 7.

— — —

Sheep and cattle were dying all over France. It was the 1870s, and farmers had no idea why their livestock were dropping dead. France's farm economy was in trouble.

French scientist Louis Pasteur believed harmful microorganisms were the cause. But no one believed his so-called germ theory. Even doctors didn't think germs could cause infection or disease. They didn't wash their hands or clean their instruments before operating on patients.

Pasteur didn't let the skeptics stop him. He continued to study and experiment. In 1877, German scientist Heinrich Hermann Robert Koch discovered the bacterium that was killing sheep and cattle. The disease was called anthrax. Pasteur went to work to find a way to protect them from this deadly disease. By 1881, he developed a vaccine, but he had to convince the people of France it would work.

In 1882, Pasteur finally had the chance to try out his vaccine. He injected it into 25 healthy sheep; another 25 healthy sheep were not vaccinated. Then Pasteur gave all 50 sheep a deadly dose of anthrax. The 25 vaccinated sheep survived, and the rest died within three days. Pasteur had proved that his vaccine worked.

— — —

Kendall Haven, *100 Greatest Science Discoveries of All Time* (Westport, Conn.: Greenwood Publishing, 2007), p. 77.

— — —

Yogurt and other dairy products soured and curdled in just a few days. Meat rotted after a short time. Cow's and goat's milk had always been drunk as fresh milk. The consumer had to be near the animal since milk soured and spoiled in a day or two.

Then Louis Pasteur discovered that microscopic organisms floated everywhere in the air, unseen. It was these microorganisms that turned food into deadly, disease-ridden garbage. It was the same microscopic organisms that entered human flesh during operations and through cuts to cause infection and disease. Pasteur discovered the world of microbiology and developed the theory that germs cause disease. . . .

Many scientists believed that microorganisms had no parent organism. Instead, they spontaneously generated from the decaying molecules of organic matter to spoil milk and rot meat. Felix Pouchet, the leading spokesman for this group, and had just published a paper claiming to prove this thesis.

Pasteur thought Pouchet's theory was rubbish. Pasteur's earlier discovery that microscopic live organisms (bacteria called yeasts) were always present during, and seemed to cause, the fermentation of beer and wine, made Pasteur suspect that microorganisms lived in the air and simply fell by chance onto food and all living matter, rapidly multiplying only when they found a decaying substance to use as nutrient.

— — —

Robert P. Gaynes, *Germ Theory: Medical Pioneers in Infectious Diseases* (Washington, D.C.: ASM Press, 2011), pp. 152, 169.

— — —

(152) Pasteur was familiar with and intensely interested in the process of making wine. He knew, for example, that wine was slightly acidic. He also knew that the anti-microbial effects of heat on microorganisms were more successful in an acidic environment. He experimented to find a temperature that would kill the unwanted microorganisms (bacteria) and still leave the process and the taste of wine unaffected. He further discovered [in 1858] that the heat would not affect the wine making process if applied after all the oxygen originally present in the bottle had become exhausted. We know this process as pasteurization. Pasteurization was successfully applied to wine, beer, cider, vinegar, and, of course, milk . . .

(169) In the last few years of his life, Pasteur was weak and ill . . . He died on 28 September 1895. He was given the rare honor for a scientist of a state funeral. Thousands lined the streets of Paris to pay their respects. His remains were placed in a crypt in the Institute that bears his name [the Pasteur Institute, opened in 1888].

— — —

Stephen Feinstein, *Louis Pasteur: The Father of Microbiology* (Berkeley Heights, N.J.: Enslow Publishers, 2008), pp. 105–107.

— — —

(105) Finally, in 1884, Pasteur produced a [rabies] vaccine. [He and his partner, Dr. Roux] experimented by transferring the rabies from infected animals to healthy ones. They placed spinal cord tissue from the sick (106) animals in direct contact with the brains of the healthy animals. Pasteur and Roux then vaccinated an animal that already had rabies to see if the vaccine protected the infected animal. They repeated the experiment many times . . . Now they needed to vaccinate a person to see if their method would protect humans who had been bit by a rabid animal.

In July 1885, nine-year-old Joseph Meister was brought to Pasteur's laboratory in Paris. Joseph had been attacked by a rabid dog, and his parents were afraid he would die. Pasteur vaccinated the (107) boy and he survived. Meister was the first person to be successfully vaccinated against rabies.

News of Pasteur's successful development of a rabies vaccine spread quickly . . . More and more people came to Pasteur for help, and he realized that his small laboratory was no longer big enough. He needed a full-scale clinic . . . [O]n November 14, 1888, the Pasteur Institute opened in Paris, with Pasteur as its director.

— — —

Albert Keim and Louis Lumet, *Louis Pasteur*, trans. Frederic Taber Cooper (New York: Frederick A. Stokes, 1914).

NOTE: Be sure to stop and look up any words that you do not understand! This source uses the old-fashioned word for rabies, *hydrophobia*.

---

160   PASTEUR

the walls of the garden, in testimony of his valour and devotion.

The studies pursued by Pasteur and his pupils were at this epoch extended to every malady of microbic origin, but more particularly to hydrophobia, that terror of the country districts, and which the illustrious scientist was determined to vanquish by the combined power of genius and persistence. He was interrupted for a few weeks by the obligation of representing France at the celebration of the tri-centenary of the University of Edinburgh, in company with Messrs. Caro, Gréard, de Lesseps, Guizot and Eugène Guillaume. In London the French delegates found a private parlor car awaiting them, thanks to Mr. Younger, a Scotch brewer, who wished in this manner to thank Pasteur for his studies in relation to beer. It was a recognition of the fine generosity of the French savant, who had enriched commerce and manufactures to the extent of millions, while refusing to retain anything for himself. And that is one of the brightest sides of the glory of France.

CHAPTER VIII

HYDROPHOBIA

MAD dogs were formerly the terror of the country-side. The mysterious character of the malady, its frightful consequences to those whom it attacked, classed it among those scourges of the fields against which no certain remedy was known. In ancient times Pliny the Elder advised those who had been bitten to eat the liver of the dog who had done the harm, while Gallian prescribed as a remedy the eyes of crabs! During the middle ages, which were haunted by mad dogs, the remedies used were omelettes made of ground oyster shells and cauterisation of the wound with red-hot irons; but most frequently they stifled the unhappy sufferers between two mattresses. In the eighteenth century a Lieutenant of Police

161

162   PASTEUR

named Lenoir founded a prize of twelve hundred pounds, to be awarded by the Royal Society of Medicine to the author of the best paper on the methods of curing hydrophobia. It was won by a certain Dr. Roux, a physician at Dijon, and, among the methods of saving those who had been bitten, he recommended cauterisation with hot irons, and more especially with antimony tri-chloride ("butter of antimony").

In the eighteenth century the problem of hydrophobia, although it had been studied more scientifically, had made but little progress, until Pasteur caused a sensation by discovering its solution. He began his researches in 1880 with the collaboration of Doctors Chamberland, Roux and Thuillier. We cannot follow them through all the details of the long succession of exceedingly delicate experiments that often had to be commenced all over again in order to obtain assured results; but a very simple summary will make it clear that Pasteur's genius was as fruitful as ever, and that his illness had

HYDROPHOBIA   163

in no wise impaired his qualities as an experimenter.

On the 10th of December, 1880, Pasteur, being informed by Dr. Lannelongue that he had under treatment, at Trousseau a five-year-old child who had been bitten by a mad dog, went to obtain a specimen of his saliva. In the saliva he discovered a microbe, which was not that of hydrophobia, and which, when injected into rabbits, caused their death within two days of a different disease. Nevertheless, the saliva contained the microbes of hydrophobia, but they lost all their virulence within twenty-four hours. Since rabies chiefly affects the nerve centres, Pasteur inoculated rabbits and dogs with the cranial marrow of rabid dogs. The subjects inoculated developed hydrophobia after a greater or less lapse of time, and the experiments became difficult to follow and to control. In order to hasten the period of inoculation, Pasteur conceived the idea of injecting the matter containing the germs directly into the dogs' skulls; but the idea of trepanning, neces-

164   PASTEUR

sitated by the injection, was repugnant to him.

"He could witness, without much distress, a simple operation such as subcutaneous inoculation," writes M. Roux, "although even then, if the animal cried a little, Pasteur would be overcome with pity and make his escape, lavishing on the victim words of consolation and encouragement, which would have seemed comical if they had not been so touching. The thought that a dog's skull would have to be perforated was most unpleasant to him. He was keenly anxious to have the experiment tried, yet he shrank from seeing it undertaken. I did it one day when he was absent. The following day, when I reported to him that the intracranial inoculation offered no difficulties, he fell to pitying the dog:

" 'Poor beast! Its brain is no doubt ruptured; it must be paralysed.'

"Without reply, I descended to the basement to get the animal, and brought it back with me to the laboratory. Pasteur was not fond of dogs, but when he saw this one, full of spirits

HYDROPHOBIA   165

and curiously exploring the premises, he exhibited the keenest satisfaction and began to lavish terms of endearment upon it. He felt an infinite gratitude towards this particular dog for having stood the trepanning so well, and thus having put an end to all his scruples in regard to future trepanning." [1]

The experiment succeeded, and the period of inoculation was reduced to twenty days, and it was demonstrated that the principal seat of the malady was in the nervous centres. To the first results, which were of a theoretic character, Pasteur became ambitious to add others of a practical nature. Was it possible to render dogs immune to hydrophobia after they had been bitten, as he had rendered cattle and sheep immune to anthrax? And could this immunity be extended to man?

The problem was quite complex, for he did not know the microbe of hydrophobia, which had barely been detected by Dr. Roux, in the

* L'Oeuvre Médicale de Pasteur, by Dr. Roux. Agenda du Chimiste, 1896.

---

166   PASTEUR

form of points almost imperceptible under the most powerful microscopes. It was here that the inventive genius of Pasteur displayed itself. Since he could not cultivate these microbes in appropriate liquids and attenuate them according to the method that he had used in the case of anthrax and chicken cholera, he conceived the idea of cultivating them from rabbit to rabbit, and in this way he obtained a fixed maximum of virulence which reduced the period of inoculation to seven days. But how was the virus to be transformed into vaccine? Pasteur observed that the infected marrows, when brought into contact with dry air, lost their virulence in proportion to the length of time they were exposed, becoming almost harmless after fifteen days.

The attenuated virus having been found by a process which, although hardly scientific, was certain, the next facts to ascertain were: First, whether inoculation with this vaccine virus would render dogs resistant to hydrophobia; and, secondly, whether inoculation would pre-

HYDROPHOBIA   167

vent the disease from appearing and developing in animals that had been bitten.

The experiments were long and full of difficulties. The laboratory in the Rue d'Ulm no longer sufficed to contain all the subjects. The State placed at Pasteur's disposal more extensive quarters at Villeneuve-l'Etang, near Saint-Cloud. Finally his experiments achieved this double result: Hydrophobia could be communicated to animals by inoculation; and, on the other hand, inoculation with attenuated virus rendered dogs resistant to hydrophobia, and prevented the disease from appearing in those that had been bitten.

Pasteur was sure of the efficacy of his discovery, but he hesitated to apply his method to human beings.

"I have not yet dared to make any attempt upon man," he wrote to the Emperor of Brazil, "in spite of my confidence as to the result, and in spite of the numerous opportunities that have been offered me since my last lecture at the Academy of Sciences. I am too much

---

168   PASTEUR

afraid of a failure, which may compromise my future plans. I want first to collect a multitude of successful cases of the treatment of animals. In this respect matters are going well. I already have numerous examples of dogs rendered immune after having been bitten. I take two dogs, and I cause them to be bitten by another dog that is mad. I vaccinate one of them, and I leave the other without treatment; the latter dies of hydrophobia; the one that was vaccinated is immune.

"But, no matter to what extent I should multiply these examples of the prophylaxis of hydrophobia in dogs, it seems to me that my hand would inevitably tremble when the time came to apply the treatment to a human being.

"Here is where the high and powerful initiative of the Sovereign of a State might intervene most profitably for the greatest good of humanity. If I were king or emperor, or even President of the Republic, this is the way in which I should exercise my right to pardon prisoners condemned to death. I should offer

HYDROPHOBIA   169

the condemned man, through his lawyer, on the eve of his client's execution, the choice between imminent death and an experiment consisting of preventive inoculation of hydrophobia for the purpose of rendering his constitution immune to that disease. Aside from the risks of these experiments, the life of the condemned man would be spared. In case the experiments should succeed—and, in point of fact, I am sure they would—in order to protect society, which had previously condemned the criminal, he could be kept in custody for the rest of his life.

"Every condemned man would accept. For the only thing which a condemned man fears is death.

"This brings me to the question of cholera, which Your Majesty also had the goodness to discuss with me. Neither Doctors Strauss and Roux nor Dr. Koch have succeeded in infecting animals with cholera. Hence there is a great uncertainty regarding the bacillus which Dr. Koch believes to be the cause of cholera.

We ought to be allowed to try to give cholera to criminals condemned to death by making them swallow cultures of these bacilli. As soon as the malady should make its appearance the remedies regarded as most efficacious could immediately be administered.

"I attach so much importance to these measures that, if Your Majesty should share my views, I would gladly set out for Rio Janeiro, despite my age and state of health, in order to devote myself to this sort of study of the prophylaxis of hydrophobia, or the contagion of cholera, and the remedies to be applied to it." (Letter cited by M. Vallery-Radot, in *La Vie de Pasteur*.)

His conscience became so troubled by this weight of responsibility that the famous scientist even thought of inoculating himself, when at last his experiments, repeatedly tried upon animals, gave such unmistakable results that he decided to apply his methods to human beings.

The first inoculation was given to a boy nine

years old, an Alsatian, named Joseph Meister, who had been seriously bitten by a mad dog on the 6th of July, 1885. He had fourteen wounds, and was in a lamentable state. The treatment began with the injection of the least virulent vaccine obtained from infected marrow fourteen days old. The child stood it admirably, but Pasteur became anxious, distressed to the point of sleeplessness, when it became necessary to pass on to the virulent vaccines. How would the young patient respond to them? He stood them all without any apparent trouble, and two months from the time that he was first attacked not a sign of hydrophobia had developed. Nor did young Meister subsequently ever show any symptom of it.

Then came another lad, who had played the part of hero, a young shepherd by the name of J. B. Jupille, who successfully underwent the second treatment for hydrophobia. This boy, fifteen years of age, had fought with a mad dog on the lands of Villers-Farlay, in the Jura, in order to save his comrades, five other young

shepherds. He had been badly bitten in the struggle, and his case was more serious than that of Meister, because a whole week had passed between the day on which he had received his wounds and that on which he could be inoculated. Like the first patient, he received the hypodermic from Dr. Grancher, with the assistance of Vulpian, on Tuesday, October 29th, 1885; and, after a series of injections of vaccines, he was immune to hydrophobia.

It was at the meeting of the Academy of Sciences, held October 26th, 1885, that Pasteur made his communication on the subject of hydrophobia, preventive vaccination and vaccination after bites, as applied to men. Dr. Vulpian responded and paid homage to the genius of Pasteur:

"The Academy will not be surprised if, as a member of the section of medicine and surgery, I ask the floor in order to express the sentiments of admiration inspired in me by the communication of M. Pasteur. These will be

shared, I am convinced, by the medical profession as a whole.

"Hydrophobia, that terrible disease against which all therapeutic efforts have hitherto failed, has at last found its remedy. M. Pasteur, who has had no precursor but himself along this route, has been led through a series of researches, uninterruptedly pursued for years, to create a method of treatment by the aid of which it is possible to prevent, beyond all question, the development of hydrophobia in a man recently bitten by a mad dog. I say, beyond all question, because, after what I have seen in M. Pasteur's laboratory, I cannot myself doubt the permanent success of this treatment, whenever it is applied in its full extent within a few days after the bite has been received.

"It becomes at once necessary to take steps towards the organisation of a public system of treatment for hydrophobia, according to the Pasteur method. Every individual bitten by a mad dog ought to be able to benefit by this great discovery, which puts the seal of glory upon our illustrious colleague, and is destined to redound greatly to the honour of our country."

It was Pasteur's destiny never to triumph through any of his discoveries until after he had overcome desperate resistance. The value of his method was questioned by a large part of the profession, he was ridiculed, and the comic papers published caricatures upon his work.

Pasteur's enemies, who had not even yet disarmed in the presence of his genius, renewed their attacks in connection with a failure which occurred in December, 1885, the death of a young girl, Louise Lepelletier, who had been inoculated thirty-seven days after she was bitten. Nevertheless, all resistance and all perfidy disappeared beneath the immense flood of enthusiasm which had been aroused by Pasteur's discoveries. A public system of vaccination against hydrophobia was installed, and people flocked there from all parts of France and from every other country. Within one year

and two months, from October, 1885, to December, 1886, 2,682 persons who had been bitten were treated there, and out of this number only 31 succumbed. The efficacy of the method had been demonstrated.

Pasteur took an interest in the children whom he treated, and lavished caresses and presents on them. He wrote to them, after the course of treatment was over, trying to keep watch of their subsequent lives, and urging upon them the advantages of honesty and industry. The great man, surrounded with the halo of glory, and over-burdened with his labours and his thoughts, found himself paternally drawn towards these little ones—and they were his best source of repose.

The following article appeared in *The American Food Journal*, Vol. 12, No. 1 (January, 1917).

P a s t e u r i z a t i o n

By Dr. Adolph Gehrmann
of the Columbus Laboratories of Chicago

The organic source of food materials gives nature opportunity to destroy them by drying, disintegration and decomposition. Of these, decomposition is most active. Louis Pasteur proved conclusively that bacteria were the cause of decomposition. His researches were first conducted to bring science to bear on the great question of spontaneous generation. He was strongly opposed by other scientists who believed that life could start from dead substance. This theory was completely exploded by Pasteur's interesting experiments. He found that by boiling broth or other putrescible liquids they could be preserved if protected from dirty air, and that it was not the air itself but the floating particles in it that carried bacteria which induced the decomposition. When the air was clean, as it was high up in the Alps after a snow storm, or when it had been heated and all the suspended particles burnt, it could be passed over broth without causing decay. In the course of these experiments it was found by Pasteur that a single boiling would in some cases suffice to preserve broth, but that in other cases two or three boilings were necessary to preserve it. The cause of this variation was found in the fact that some bacteria developed a more resistant stage of life in that they formed spores. These spores resist all destructive action much better than the growing bacteria. We now call the spore a resting state and the growing bacteria a vegetative state.

These resting and vegetative states are analogous to seeds and growing plants. One preserves life over the winter and during drought, while the other is the growing active plant. When mixed bacteria are present in broth, milk, wort, must or on meat or vegetables, some of the bacteria are very likely to be in this spore state and their destruction by heat is much more difficult.

Some very active decomposition bacilli, such as the potato bacillus, have spores that will still live and grow even after having been boiled for several hours, but as soon as they sprout and are in the vegetative state, a few minutes boiling will kill the growing bacteria. All of these demonstrations lead to what we call fractional sterilization, or a killing of decomposition bacteria by several short period heatings far enough apart to allow the spores to sprout into vegetative cells that can be easily killed.

The problem of preserving milk becomes complicated when we know the intricate composition of this valuable food. It contains everything necessary to support life and is very easily decomposed or digested. If its delicate constituents are changed by boiling, it is not as easily digested by the child and nutrition is unbalanced. The practical application to milk must therefore bring about a killing of bacteria as far as possible, and yet not damage the milk or change its taste to any extent. The degree and the length of time of heating must be very carefully regulated to that temperature which kills bacteria and not above that which changes the albumens of the milk. This temperature range is between 55° and 60° C. or 130° to 140° F. If the temperature goes much above this for any length of time, some of the albumens or the ferments of the milk may be changed. Practically, these principles are the guides in applying pasteurization. Two methods are used, one called the holding method in which the heating is held at the named temperature for a few minutes —15, 20, 30—with or without agitation, according to the device used, and the other is called the flash method in which the heat is raised momentarily to a higher temperature and is

Photograph from McIntosh Stereopticon Co.
FLASH METHOD PASTEURIZER.

Another side of fractional sterilization is that some materials or mixtures can be preserved by this method which would be injured by too long boiling and their properties changed. This is true of gelatins, albumens and sugars. In order to avoid damaging the material to be preserved, and at the same time accomplish preservation, fractional sterilization is practiced. Another advantage is its use in preserving for a short time. The vegetative bacteria begin their destructive activities at once when they get into suitable food material while spores are resting and do not cause any change until they sprout. This sprouting of spores requires some time, from several hours to several days, according to whether or not the temperature is suitable. If milk, for instance, that contains all kinds of bacteria, is heated a few minutes and the growing bacteria killed, the spores can be prevented from sprouting by cold, and the milk thus preserved for several days.

The method of killing part of the bacteria for short preservation has come to be called pasteurization from the name of its discoverer.

Pasteurization is more used as a means of preserving milk and beer than any other materials. All of the studies of the bacteriology of milk show that the really dangerous bacteria in it are in a vegetative state, or do not form spores. A short heating will therefore kill the undesirable bacteria and, if carefully conducted, will not damage the milk.

as quickly reduced. This latter method is not always uniform in action because some particles of milk might burn when hot pipes or plates are used over which the milk is allowed to run. We have also pasteurization in the bottle and in bulk. In the former the milk is protected in a closed bottle, but cannot be easily agitated to get the heat evenly distributed. In the bulk method there is the disadvantage that dust and bacteria from the air at once fall into the milk and its protection from contamination is very difficult.

The principles of milk pasteurization have not changed to any extent for half a century, but the number of devices discovered for applying it is constantly increasing. In 1893, at the World's Fair, a division of the dairy exhibit was assigned to pasteurizing machinery. Now, an entire exposition could be made of the machinery and allied activities connected with pasteurization, extending from the single bottle in the nursery to the supply amounting to thousands of bottles for some large city. As a health protecting system, pasteurization of milk alone is of inestimable value. As has been intimated, practically all of the dangerous bacteria of milk are without spores and can be killed by pasteurization. From the cow's udder there are the pus bacteria and streptococci and tubercle bacilli, and these are destroyed, and those from dirt, as typhoid, cholera and dysentery bacteria, are also killed. Truly, a wonderfully protecting method when conscientiously applied.

WEEK 33: COMBINING THE *TOPOI* IN SCIENCE

Days One and Two: Take Notes for a Science Composition

Focus: Taking notes

Over the next two days, you'll take notes for a science composition, just as you did for your Joan of Arc essay. You'll then spend the second half of the week writing your essay.

There are three steps to this assignment. You and your instructor can decide how much work you should do on each day.

STEP ONE: **Choose tentative *topoi* and elements**

To take notes effectively, you'll need to make a tentative decision about the *topoi* that you'll include in your essay.

Look back through the following *topoi* in your Composition Reference Notebook. Keeping in mind the sources that you read last week, choose at least three *topoi* that you might be able to use in an essay about Pasteur and/or Pasteur's accomplishments. Four is even better.

Remember that you don't have to include *every* element in the chosen *topoi*; you can just incorporate one or two aspects into your final paper.

Chronological Narrative of a Scientific Discovery
Scientific Description
Biographical Sketch
Sequence: Natural Process
Explanation by Comparison/Contrast
Explanation by Definition: Natural Object or Phenomenon
Temporal Comparison: Science

Once you've made your choice, show your selections to your instructor. Ask for help if you need it.

STEP TWO: **Prepare to take notes**

As you did for your last writing assignment, write the name of each *topos* that you've selected at the top of a new page (whether notebook paper or word processing document). Then, write a brief phrase or sentence describing exactly what that *topos* will cover. For example, if the first *topos* you decided to include was "Chronological Narrative of a Scientific Discovery," you might then write "The Rabies Vaccine."

The heading on your paper should help you keep in mind, as you go through your sources and take notes, exactly what kinds of information you're looking for. Otherwise, you may end up taking too many notes that you don't need (and won't use).

STEP THREE: **Take notes**

Spend the rest of your time taking notes on the sources.

Remember to pick and choose only those facts and details that will support the *topoi* you've chosen. You do not need to write down *every* fact and detail—that would give you far too much information! Having too much information can be paralyzing when you sit down to write.

Aim to have at least five or six to eight notes about each *topos*, but do not take more than fifteen notes for any single *topos*. (Some comparisons and sequences might have only three to four pieces of information in them.)

As before, you can choose which note-taking method suits you best:

1) Go through the sources one time each, placing each relevant bit of information from each source on the appropriate page of notes as you go. OR

2) Pick the first *topos* and go through all four sources, looking for answers. Do the same for the second *topos*, and then the third, and so on.

I have provided you with what might be the first four or five notes on a sample *topos*, below. Follow this model.

If you need help, ask your instructor. When you are finished, show your work to your instructor.

Chronological Narrative of a Scientific Discovery:

The Rabies Vaccine

Before Pasteur, "no one understood why people caught diseases" or "the spread of germs" (Miles, p. 4)

"Even doctors didn't think germs could cause infection or disease" (Zamosky et al., p. 7)

Pasteur produced vaccine in 1884 (Feinstein, p. 105)

Tested by placing "spinal cord tissue from the sick animals in direct contact with the brains of the healthy animals" (Feinstein, pp. 105–106)

Then, vaccinated Joseph Meister in 1885 after he was attacked by rabid dog (Feinstein, p. 106)

Days Three and Four: Write

 Focus: Combining *topoi*
into a science composition

Over the next two days, you'll write a composition of at least 300 words that uses elements from at least three different *topoi*. Longer is fine; 300 is a bare minimum.

Like last week's Joan of Arc essay, your assignment has six steps.

Step One: Draft the main *topos*
Step Two: Add other *topoi*
Step Three: Provide an introduction and conclusion
Step Four: Construct the Works Cited page
Step Five: Title
Step Six: Proofread

Review through the instructions for all six steps before you begin to write.

Together, you and your instructor should decide how much time to spend on each step.

STEP ONE: **Draft the main *topos***

In the essay about William Harvey that you examined last week, the author used the Chronological Narrative of a Scientific Discovery as the "skeleton" for his essay—the primary organizational form. He then inserted a compact biographical sketch as well as selected elements of other *topoi* into it.

Before you start to write, decide which of the *topoi* you've taken notes on will serve as your "skeleton." Choose one that has plenty of notes to go with it. (The Chronological Narrative of a Scientific Discovery and the Biographical Sketch will probably be the simplest *topoi* to use.)

Using your notes and referring to your reference chart, write a draft of the main *topos*.

Be sure to look back at your chart, reminding yourself of the elements that should belong in the *topos*.

Aim for at least 150 words; try to get closer to 200 words if possible. Be sure to cite at least *two* sources and to include at least one direct quote.

STEP TWO: **Add other *topoi***

Look back over your notes and decide which *topoi* or elements you will add to your composition. If necessary, glance back at A. Dickson Wright's essay in Week 32. Notice how he borrows aspects from a Sequence: Natural Process as well as Scientific Description, Explanation by Definition, and Temporal Comparison to flesh out his combination of chronological narrative and biographical sketch.

Decide where the *topoi* or elements will be located in your composition. Draft the *topoi* or elements and insert them into your essay. You must add elements from at least two different *topoi*. You may need to rearrange paragraphing or slightly rewrite some of your existing sentences so that the new elements fit into your composition smoothly.

You should aim to have a total of at least 250 words by the end of this step; longer is better!

STEP THREE: **Provide an introduction and conclusion**

Choose an introduction and a conclusion from your Introductions and Conclusions chart. You may pick any introduction and conclusion—but make sure that they don't repeat the same information.

To write an introduction by history that uses a brief scene or an introduction by anecdote that uses an invented scene, you may need to reread the sources from Week 32. You may also ask your instructor to show you the sample introductions and conclusions provided for the Joan of Arc essay; this may help you to come up with introductions and conclusions for this composition.

Each introduction and conclusion should be at least two sentences long and should be placed in separate paragraphs, not incorporated into the existing paragraphs of the composition.

Remember that your final word count must be over 300.

STEP FOUR: **Construct the Works Cited page**

At the top of a separate sheet of paper, center the words "Works Cited." In proper form, list the sources you used to write your essay.

STEP FIVE: **Title**

Give your composition a title that describes the primary *topos* you decided to use.

For example, if I wrote a chronological narrative of scientific discovery that dealt with Louis Pasteur's discovery of an anthrax vaccine, I might title it:

Louis Pasteur and the Anthrax Vaccine

or

How Louis Pasteur Discovered a Vaccine for Anthrax

or

Louis Pasteur: Discoverer of the Anthrax Vaccine

Notice that the first title simply couples the scientist and the result of his discovery together. The second describes a process—the steps that Pasteur went through to get to that result. The third uses Pasteur's name as the title, inserts a colon, and then describes his role in discovering the vaccine in the subtitle.

Your instructor has other sample titles for you to look at, should you be completely unable to come up with an idea.

STEP SIX: **Proofread**

Before you hand your composition to your instructor, go through the following proofreading steps very carefully.

1) Check to make sure that you have used elements from at least three different *topoi*, plus an introduction and a conclusion.

2) Make sure that your finished essay is at least 300 words long. Longer is better!

3) Make sure that you have quoted from at least one source and cited at least two sources.

4) Read your paper out loud, listening for awkward or unclear sections and repeated words. Rewrite awkward or unclear sentences so that they flow more naturally.

5) Listen for information that is repeated more than once. Eliminate repetition of ideas.

6) Read through the paper one more time, looking for sentence fragments, run-on sentences, and repeated words. Correct fragments and run-on sentences. Listen for unnecessary repetition.

7) Check your spelling by looking, individually, at each word that might be a problem.

When your paper is ready, give it to your instructor.

WEEKS 34 THROUGH 36: FINAL PROJECT

At the end of Level 1 of this course, you carried out an independent project that drew on all the skills you had practiced over the year. Now that you're at the end of Level 2, you'll do the same.

Over the course of this year, you've added new *topoi* to your arsenal of writing tools. You've also practiced more advanced note-taking and research skills. You've learned to brainstorm for your subject, and you've begun to see how different *topoi* can fit together to create a more interesting and complex composition.

Instead of two weeks (like last year), you'll have three weeks to work on this project. Instead of beginning with your *topoi* list, like you did last year, you'll start with brainstorming. And instead of a minimum of two *topoi* in your paper, you'll need to use at least three.

I won't be dividing up your weeks into days. Instead, I'll give you a number of steps, with a suggestion of how many hours you should spend on each step. These are only suggested times. Writers work, read, and think at *very* different speeds!

You can also choose to spend more time on the project and stretch it out over additional weeks. You can take additional time to illustrate your final composition with drawings, graphs, charts, maps and diagrams—or not.

But however you decide to approach this final composition, it must:

1. Include at least three of the *topoi* in your reference chart.
2. Be at least 1,250 words in length (that's five to seven typed, double-spaced pages).
3. Make use of at least four sources.
4. Include footnotes and a Works Cited page.

Over the next three (or so) weeks, you'll carry out twelve steps. Don't be intimidated by the number; dividing the big task of writing your paper into a number of smaller steps makes it simpler, not harder, to do.

Here's an overview of your plan:

Step One: Create brainstorming maps	1–2 hours
Step Two: Resource collection	3 hours . . . or possibly more
Step Three: Pre-reading, Part I	2–3 hours
Step Four: Choose tentative *topoi* and elements	1 hour
Step Five: Pre-reading, Part II	3–4 hours

Step Six: Take notes	3–4 hours
Step Seven: Draft the main *topos*	3–4 hours
Step Eight: Add other *topoi*	2–3 hours
Step Nine: Provide an introduction and conclusion	60–90 minutes
Step Ten: Title	20 minutes
Step Eleven: Construct the Works Cited page	30 minutes
Step Twelve: Proofread	2 hours

STEP ONE: **Create brainstorming maps (1–2 hours)**

Turn back to Week 8, and read carefully through the instructions for Day One (brainstorming in history) and Day Two (brainstorming in science). Following the instructions, create two brainstorming maps for history and two for science.

Go through this process even if you think you already know what you want to write about. Every brainstorming map that you create forces your brain to make new connections; you may find a new perspective on a subject you think you already understand, or discover a topic that's even more interesting than the one you've already picked. And, if you discover during Step Two that resources for your original idea are few and far between, you'll already have a couple of alternative topics lined up.

STEP TWO: **Resource collection (3 hours . . . or possibly more)**

This will be your most time-consuming task, because it requires you to visit the library and collect your resources.

Before you can settle on the *topoi* you'll include in your composition, you need to have some idea of what information is out there and available to you.

Your goal is to end up with six sources that tell you something helpful about your general subject area. But you should start out by reading a couple of encyclopedia articles on your subject.

In Level One of this course, I told you not to use Wikipedia. Here's what I said:

> *You may not use Wikipedia. Wikipedia is not professionally edited or fact-checked. Anyone can post anything on Wikipedia. Usually, other users will identify and remove mistakes—but if you happen to use Wikipedia five minutes after someone has posted bad information (which people sometimes do just for fun), you won't realize that you're writing down false facts.*

That's still true. But I'm going to relax my anti-Wikipedia stance for this step, and allow you to start off by consulting Wikipedia entries that relate to your subject.

Why? Because this is only the first pre-reading stage. Your goal right now is just to figure out what terms and phrases you should search for in your first library visit. Don't plan on using *anything* you find on Wikipedia in your composition. But if Wikipedia can point you towards phrases and words that will help you search for resources that have been professionally edited and fact-checked, you'll get a jump on your research.

Once you're armed with keywords and phrases to search for (remember, you haven't settled on the form of your composition yet—so you don't know whether a chronological narrative, an explanation by definition, a biographical sketch, or some other *topos* will best suit your subject), prepare for a library visit by making an initial list of titles to look for, using your local library's online catalog. If you need a refresher, reread the instructions for Week 8, Days Three to Four.

If you're unable to find more than one or two books, you should choose another subject area definition and try using its keywords for your search. And if *none* of your subject area definitions are giving you good keywords for searching, you might consider choosing another brainstorming map.

You should finish making up your preliminary list of titles before you visit the library. Once you're there, ask the reference librarian for help finding the books, if necessary. Glance on either side of the titles to see whether nearby books might also have something interesting to say about your subject area.

Pull at least 10–12 books off the shelf and take them to a place where you can examine them more closely. Using the index, make sure that at least one of the keywords in your subject area appears in the book.

Try to bring home at least six books that relate to your subject.

STEP THREE: **Pre-reading, Part I (2–3 hours)**

In the last two writing assignments, you began your research by just reading—not taking notes, or looking for facts, but just reading.

Read the chapters or sections of each book that relate to your topic. Don't take notes yet—you don't know what information you'll need. But be sure to use bookmarks (torn slips of notebook paper are fine) or Post-It Notes to mark pages where you find interesting information.

STEP FOUR: **Choose tentative *topoi* and elements (1 hour)**

Now that you've read through your resources, you should have some idea of what *topoi* might fit your subject material. Do the books about your topic contain plenty of chronological events? How about biographical details and personal descriptions? Descriptive sequences of natural cycles?

Just as you did in your last two assignments, settle on *topoi* that you might want to use to organize your paper. Since your paper will need to include at least three *topoi*, choose at least four. Five would be safer. Inevitably, when you start taking notes, you discover that you had less information than you thought in at least one area!

Before you go on to the next step, read through the *topoi* you've chosen carefully. Reading out loud always helps you to concentrate.

STEP FIVE: **Pre-reading, Part II (3–4 hours)**

Now return to your bookmarked/Post-It marked pages and reread them carefully.

You're still not taking notes. Remember: in the last two assignments, you read your sources first, before even *thinking* about note taking. The more familiar you are with your material, the simpler the note-taking process will be.

As you read, keep your chosen *topoi* in mind. If you realize that one of your *topoi* won't work, cross it off your list. If you find material that would support another *topos*, add it.

STEP SIX: **Take notes (3–4 hours)**

Just as you did in the last two assignments, write the name of each *topos* at the top of a sheet of notebook paper (or word processing document). Add an explanatory phrase that describes the content the *topos* will cover. (If you need to review, look back at Week 31, Days Three and Four, Step Two).

Then, take your notes.

Remember to pick and choose only those facts and details that will support the *topoi* you've chosen. You do not need to write down *every* fact and detail—that would give you far too much information! Having too much information can be paralyzing when you sit down to write.

Aim to have at least eight or nine notes about each *topos*, but do not take more than twenty notes for any single *topos*.

Choose which note-taking method suits you best:

1) Go through the sources one time each, placing each relevant bit of information from each source on the appropriate page of notes as you go. OR

2) Pick the first *topos* and go through all four sources, looking for answers. Do the same for the second *topos*, and then the third, and so on.

STEP SEVEN: **Draft the main *topos* (3–4 hours)**

Which one of your pages contains the most notes? That's the *topos* that should probably be the "skeleton," the primary organizational form, of your composition.

Decide which *topos* will be at the center of your composition. Using your notes and referring to your reference chart, write a draft of the main *topos*.

Be sure to look back at your chart, reminding yourself of the elements that should belong in the *topos*.

STEP EIGHT: **Add other *topoi* (2–3 hours)**

Look back over your notes and decide which *topoi* or elements you will add to your composition.

Decide where the *topoi* or elements will be located in your composition. Draft the *topoi* or elements and insert them into your essay. You must add elements from at least two different *topoi*. You may need to rearrange paragraphing or slightly rewrite some of your existing sentences so that the new elements fit into your composition smoothly.

STEP NINE: **Provide an introduction and conclusion (60–90 minutes)**

Choose an introduction and a conclusion from your Introductions and Conclusions chart. You may pick any introduction and conclusion—but make sure that they don't repeat the same information.

Each introduction and conclusion should be at least two sentences long and should be placed in separate paragraphs, not incorporated into the existing paragraphs of the composition.

STEP TEN: **Title (20 minutes)**

Choose a title for your paper. This should be more descriptive than simply the name of the person, object, or phenomenon you're writing about. Remember that you can use the following format:

Name [of person, object, phenomenon]: Why it's important

OR

Name [of person, object, phenomenon]: What happened to it

STEP ELEVEN: **Construct the Works Cited page (30 minutes)**

At the top of a separate sheet of paper, center the words "Works Cited." In proper form, list the sources you used to write your essay.

STEP TWELVE: **Proofread (2 hours)**

Before you hand your composition to your instructor, go through the following proofreading steps very carefully.

1) Check to make sure that you have used elements from at least three different *topoi*, plus an introduction and a conclusion.

2) Make sure that your finished essay is at least 1,250 words long.

3) Make sure that you have cited at least four sources.

4) Read your paper out loud, listening for awkward or unclear sections and repeated words. Rewrite awkward or unclear sentences so that they flow more naturally.

5) Listen for information that is repeated more than once. Eliminate repetition of ideas.

6) Read through the paper one more time, looking for sentence fragments, run-on sentences, and repeated words. Correct fragments and run-on sentences. Listen for unnecessary repetition.

7) Check your spelling by looking, individually, at each word that might be a problem.

8) Check the formatting of your footnotes and your Works Cited page.

9) Read your title out loud. Does it give the reader a good sense of what your composition will cover?

When your paper is ready, give it to your instructor.

Certificate of Completion

This certifies that

_____

*Has successfully completed Level Two
of Writing with Skill
and is now able to research and write
chronological narratives, descriptions,
biographical sketches, sequences, definitions,
and comparisons with proper documentation
and mechanics.*

_____   _____
DATE   SUSAN WISE BAUER

APPENDIX I

Literature

The Open Window

by Saki

"My aunt will be down presently, Mr. Nuttel," said a very self-possessed young lady of fifteen; "in the meantime you must try and put up with me."

Framton Nuttel endeavoured to say the correct something which should duly flatter the niece of the moment without unduly discounting the aunt that was to come. Privately he doubted more than ever whether these formal visits on a succession of total strangers would do much towards helping the nerve cure which he was supposed to be undergoing.

"I know how it will be," his sister had said when he was preparing to migrate to this rural retreat; "you will bury yourself down there and not speak to a living soul, and your nerves will be worse than ever from moping. I shall just give you letters of introduction to all the people I know there. Some of them, as far as I can remember, were quite nice."

Framton wondered whether Mrs. Sappleton, the lady to whom he was presenting one of the letters of introduction, came into the nice division.

"Do you know many of the people round here?" asked the niece, when she judged that they had had sufficient silent communion.

"Hardly a soul," said Framton. "My sister was staying here, at the rectory, you know, some four years ago, and she gave me letters of introduction to some of the people here."

He made the last statement in a tone of distinct regret.

"Then you know practically nothing about my aunt?" pursued the self-possessed young lady.

"Only her name and address," admitted the caller. He was wondering whether Mrs. Sappleton was in the married or widowed state. An undefinable something about the room seemed to suggest masculine habitation.

"Her great tragedy happened just three years ago," said the child; "that would be since your sister's time."

"Her tragedy?" asked Framton; somehow in this restful country spot tragedies seemed out of place.

425

"You may wonder why we keep that window wide open on an October afternoon," said the niece, indicating a large French window that opened on to a lawn.

"It is quite warm for the time of the year," said Framton; "but has that window got anything to do with the tragedy?"

"Out through that window, three years ago to a day, her husband and her two young brothers went off for their day's shooting. They never came back. In crossing the moor to their favourite snipe-shooting ground they were all three engulfed in a treacherous piece of bog. It had been that dreadful wet summer, you know, and places that were safe in other years gave way suddenly without warning. Their bodies were never recovered. That was the dreadful part of it." Here the child's voice lost its self-possessed note and became falteringly human. "Poor aunt always thinks that they will come back someday, they and the little brown spaniel that was lost with them, and walk in at that window just as they used to do. That is why the window is kept open every evening till it is quite dusk. Poor dear aunt, she has often told me how they went out, her husband with his white waterproof coat over his arm, and Ronnie, her youngest brother, singing 'Bertie, why do you bound?' as he always did to tease her, because she said it got on her nerves. Do you know, sometimes on still, quiet evenings like this, I almost get a creepy feeling that they will all walk in through that window—"

She broke off with a little shudder. It was a relief to Framton when the aunt bustled into the room with a whirl of apologies for being late in making her appearance.

"I hope Vera has been amusing you?" she said.

"She has been very interesting," said Framton.

"I hope you don't mind the open window," said Mrs. Sappleton briskly; "my husband and brothers will be home directly from shooting, and they always come in this way. They've been out for snipe in the marshes today, so they'll make a fine mess over my poor carpets. So like you menfolk, isn't it?"

She rattled on cheerfully about the shooting and the scarcity of birds, and the prospects for duck in the winter. To Framton it was all purely horrible. He made a desperate but only partially successful effort to turn the talk on to a less ghastly topic, he was conscious that his hostess was giving him only a fragment of her attention, and her eyes were constantly straying past him to the open window and the lawn beyond. It was certainly an unfortunate coincidence that he should have paid his visit on this tragic anniversary.

"The doctors agree in ordering me complete rest, an absence of mental excitement, and avoidance of anything in the nature of violent physical exercise," announced Framton, who laboured under the tolerably widespread delusion that total strangers and chance acquaintances are hungry for the least detail of one's ailments and infirmities, their cause and cure. "On the matter of diet they are not so much in agreement," he continued.

"No?" said Mrs. Sappleton, in a voice which only replaced a yawn at the last moment. Then she suddenly brightened into alert attention - but not to what Framton was saying.

"Here they are at last!" she cried. "Just in time for tea, and don't they look as if they were muddy up to the eyes!"

Framton shivered slightly and turned towards the niece with a look intended to convey sympathetic comprehension. The child was staring out through the open window with a dazed horror in her eyes. In a chill shock of nameless fear Framton swung round in his seat and looked in the same direction.

In the deepening twilight three figures were walking across the lawn towards the window; they all carried guns under their arms, and one of them was additionally burdened with a white coat hung over his shoulders. A tired brown spaniel kept close at their heels. Noiselessly they neared the house, and then a hoarse young voice chanted out of the dusk: "I said, Bertie, why do you bound?"

Framton grabbed wildly at his stick and hat; the hall door, the gravel drive, and the front gate were dimly noted stages in his headlong retreat. A cyclist coming along the road had to run into the hedge to avoid imminent collision.

"Here we are, my dear," said the bearer of the white mackintosh, coming in through the window, "fairly muddy, but most of it's dry. Who was that who bolted out as we came up?"

"A most extraordinary man, a Mr. Nuttel," said Mrs. Sappleton; "could only talk about his illnesses, and dashed off without a word of goodbye or apology when you arrived. One would think he had seen a ghost."

"I expect it was the spaniel," said the niece calmly; "he told me he had a horror of dogs. He was once hunted into a cemetery somewhere on the banks of the Ganges by a pack of pariah dogs, and had to spend the night in a newly dug grave with the creatures snarling and grinning and foaming just above him. Enough to make anyone lose their nerve."

Romance at short notice was her speciality.

The Monkey's Paw

by W. W. Jacobs

Part I

Without, the night was cold and wet, but in the small parlour of Laburnum villa the blinds were drawn and the fire burned brightly. Father and son were at chess; the former, who possessed ideas about the game involving radical chances, putting his king into such sharp and unnecessary perils that it even provoked comment from the white-haired old lady knitting placidly by the fire.

"Hark at the wind," said Mr. White, who, having seen a fatal mistake after it was too late, was amiably desirous of preventing his son from seeing it.

"I'm listening," said the latter, grimly surveying the board as he streched out his hand. "Check."

"I should hardly think that he's come tonight," said his father, with his hand poised over the board.

"Mate," replied the son.

"That's the worst of living so far out," bawled Mr. White with sudden and unlooked-for violence. "Of all the beastly, slushy, out of the way places to live in, this is the worst. Path's a bog, and the road's a torrent. I don't know what people are thinking about. I suppose because only two houses in the road are let, they think it doesn't matter."

"Never mind, dear," said his wife soothingly; "perhaps you'll win the next one."

Mr. White looked up sharply, just in time to intercept a knowing glance between mother and son. The words died away on his lips, and he hid a guilty grin in his thin grey beard.

"There he is," said Herbert White as the gate banged to loudly and heavy footsteps came toward the door.

The old man rose with hospitable haste and opening the door, was heard condoling with the new arrival. The new arrival also condoled with himself, so that Mrs. White said, "Tut, tut!" and coughed gently as her husband entered the room followed by a tall, burly man, beady of eye and rubicund of visage.

"Sergeant-Major Morris, " he said, introducing him.

The Sergeant-Major took hands and taking the proffered seat by the fire, watched contentedly as his host got out whiskey and tumblers and stood a small copper kettle on the fire.

At the third glass his eyes got brighter, and he began to talk, the little family circle regarding with eager interest this visitor from distant parts, as he squared his broad shoulders in the chair and spoke of wild scenes and doughty deeds; of wars and plagues and strange peoples.

"Twenty-one years of it," said Mr. White, nodding at his wife and son. "When he went away he was a slip of a youth in the warehouse. Now look at him."

"He don't look to have taken much harm," said Mrs. White politely.

"I'd like to go to India myself," said the old man, just to look around a bit, you know."

"Better where you are," said the Sergeant-Major, shaking his head. He put down the empty glass and, sighing softly, shook it again.

"I should like to see those old temples and fakirs and jugglers," said the old man. "what was that that you started telling me the other day about a monkey's paw or something, Morris?"

"Nothing." said the soldier hastily. "Leastways, nothing worth hearing."

"Monkey's paw?" said Mrs. White curiously.

"Well, it's just a bit of what you might call magic, perhaps." said the Sargeant-Major off-handedly.

His three listeners leaned forward eagerly. The visitor absent-mindedly put his empty glass to his lips and then set it down again. His host filled it for him again.

"To look at," said the Sergeant-Major, fumbling in his pocket, "it's just an ordinary little paw, dried to a mummy."

He took something out of his pocket and proffered it. Mrs. White drew back with a grimace, but her son, taking it, examined it curiously.

"And what is there special about it?" inquired Mr. White as he took it from his son, and having examined it, placed it upon the table.

"It had a spell put on it by an old Fakir," said the Sergeant-Major, "a very holy man. He wanted to show that fate ruled people's lives, and that those who interfered with it did so to their sorrow. He put a spell on it so that three separate men could each have three wishes from it."

His manners were so impressive that his hearers were conscious that their light laughter had jarred somewhat.

"Well, why don't you have three, sir?" said Herbert White cleverly.

The soldier regarded him the way that middle age is wont to regard presumptuous youth. "I have," he said quietly, and his blotchy face whitened.

"And did you really have the three wishes granted?" asked Mrs. White.

"I did," said the sergeant-major, and his glass tapped against his strong teeth.

"And has anybody else wished?" persisted the old lady.

"The first man had his three wishes. Yes," was the reply, "I don't know what the first two were, but the third was for death. That's how I got the paw."

His tones were so grave that a hush fell upon the group.

"If you've had your three wishes it's no good to you now, then, Morris," said the old man at last. "What do you keep it for?"

The soldier shook his head. "Fancy I suppose," he said slowly. "I did have some idea of selling it, but I don't think I will. It has caused me enough mischief already. Besides, people won't buy. They think it's a fairy tale, some of them; and those who do think anything of it want to try it first and pay me afterward."

"If you could have another three wishes," said the old man, eyeing him keenly, "would you have them?"

"I don't know," said the other. "I don't know."

He took the paw, and dangling it between his forefinger and thumb, suddenly threw it upon the fire. White, with a slight cry, stooped down and snatched it off.

"Better let it burn," said the soldier solemnly.

"If you don't want it, Morris," said the other, "give it to me."

"I won't," said his friend doggedly. "I threw it on the fire. If you keep it, don't blame me for what happens. Pitch it on the fire like a sensible man."

The other shook his head and examined his possession closely. "How do you do it?" he inquired.

"Hold it up in your right hand, and wish aloud," said the sergeant-major, "But I warn you of the consequences."

"Sounds like the 'Arabian Nights'," said Mrs. White, as she rose and began to set the supper. "Don't you think you might wish for four pairs of hands for me?"

Her husband drew the talisman from his pocket, and all three burst into laughter as the Sergeant-Major, with a look of alarm on his face, caught him by the arm.

"If you must wish," he said gruffly, "wish for something sensible."

Mr. White dropped it back in his pocket, and placing chairs, motioned his friend to the table. In the business of supper the talisman was partly forgotten, and afterward the three sat listening in an enthralled fashion to a second installment of the soldier's adventures in India.

"If the tale about the monkey's paw is not more truthful than those he has been telling us," said Herbert, as the door closed behind their guest, just in time to catch the last train, "we shan't make much out of it."

"Did you give anything for it, father?" inquired Mrs. White, regarding her husband closely.

"A trifle," said he, colouring slightly, "He didn't want it, but I made him take it. And he pressed me again to throw it away."

"Likely," said Herbert, with pretended horror. "Why, we're going to be rich, and famous, and happy. Wish to be an emperor, father, to begin with; then you can't be henpecked."

He darted around the table, pursued by the maligned Mrs. White armed with an antimacassar.

Mr. White took the paw from his pocket and eyed it dubiously. "I don't know what to wish for, and that's a fact," he said slowly. It seems to me I've got all I want."

"If you only cleared the house, you'd be quite happy, wouldn't you!" said Herbert, with his hand on his shoulder. "Well, wish for two hundred pounds, then; that'll just do it."

His father, smiling shamefacedly at his own credulity, held up the talisman, as his son, with a solemn face, somewhat marred by a wink at his mother, sat down and struck a few impressive chords.

"I wish for two hundred pounds," said the old man distinctly.

A fine crash from the piano greeted his words, interrupted by a shuddering cry from the old man. His wife and son ran toward him.

"It moved," he cried, with a glance of disgust at the object as it lay on the floor. "As I wished, it twisted in my hand like a snake."

"Well, I don't see the money," said his son, as he picked it up and placed it on the table, "and I bet I never shall."

"It must have been your fancy, father," said his wife, regarding him anxiously.

He shook his head. "Never mind, though; there's no harm done, but it gave me a shock all the same."

They sat down by the fire again while the two men finished their pipes. Outside, the wind was higher than ever, and the old man started nervously at the sound of a door banging upstairs. A silence unusual and depressing settled on all three, which lasted until the old couple rose to retire for the rest of the night.

"I expect you'll find the cash tied up in a big bag in the middle of your bed," said Herbert, as he bade them goodnight, "and something horrible squatting on top of your wardrobe watching you as you pocket your ill-gotten gains."

He sat alone in the darkness, gazing at the dying fire, and seeing faces in it. The last was so horrible and so simian that he gazed at it in amazement. It got so vivid that, with a little uneasy laugh, he felt on the table for a glass containing a little water to throw over it. His hand grasped the monkey's paw, and with a little shiver he wiped his hand on his coat and went up to bed.

Part II

In the brightness of the wintry sun next morning as it streamed over the breakfast table he laughed at his fears. There was an air of prosaic wholesomeness about the room which it had lacked on the previous night, and the dirty, shriveled little paw was pitched on the side-board with a carelessness which betokened no great belief in its virtues.

"I suppose all old soldiers are the same," said Mrs White. "The idea of our listening to such nonsense! How could wishes be granted in these days? And if they could, how could two hundred pounds hurt you, father?"

"Might drop on his head from the sky," said the frivolous Herbert.

"Morris said the things happened so naturally," said his father, "that you might if you so wished attribute it to coincidence."

"Well don't break into the money before I come back," said Herbert as he rose from the table. "I'm afraid it'll turn you into a mean, avaricious man, and we shall have to disown you."

His mother laughed, and following him to the door, watched him down the road; and returning to the breakfast table, was very happy at the expense of her husband's credulity. All of which did not prevent her from scurrying to the door at the postman's knock, nor prevent her from referring somewhat shortly to retired Sergeant-Majors of bibulous habits when she found that the post brought a tailor's bill.

"Herbert will have some more of his funny remarks, I expect, when he comes home," she said as they sat at dinner.

"I dare say," said Mr. White, pouring himself out some beer; "but for all that, the thing moved in my hand; that I'll swear to."

"You thought it did," said the old lady soothingly.

"I say it did," replied the other. "There was no thought about it; I had just—What's the matter?"

His wife made no reply. She was watching the mysterious movements of a man outside, who, peering in an undecided fashion at the house, appeared to be trying to make up his mind to enter. In mental connection with the two hundred pounds, she noticed that the stranger was well dressed, and wore a silk hat of glossy newness. Three times he paused at the gate, and then walked on again. The fourth time he stood with his hand upon it, and then with sudden resolution flung it open and walked up the path. Mrs White at the same moment placed her hands behind her, and hurriedly unfastening the strings of her apron, put that useful article of apparel beneath the cushion of her chair.

She brought the stranger, who seemed ill at ease, into the room. He gazed at her furtively, and listened in a preoccupied fashion as the old lady apologized for the appearance of the room, and her husband's coat, a garment which he usually reserved for the garden. She then waited as patiently as her sex would permit for him to broach his business, but he was at first strangely silent.

"I—was asked to call," he said at last, and stooped and picked a piece of cotton from his trousers. "I come from 'Maw and Meggins.'"

The old lady started. "Is anything the matter?" she asked breathlessly. "Has anything happened to Herbert? What is it? What is it?"

Her husband interposed. "There there mother," he said hastily. "Sit down, and don't jump to conclusions. You've not brought bad news, I'm sure sir," and eyed the other wistfully.

"I'm sorry—" began the visitor.

"Is he hurt?" demanded the mother wildly.

The visitor bowed in assent. "Badly hurt," he said quietly, "but he is not in any pain."

"Oh thank God!" said the old woman, clasping her hands. "Thank God for that! Thank—"

She broke off as the sinister meaning of the assurance dawned on her and she saw the awful confirmation of her fears in the other's averted face. She caught her breath, and turning to her slower-witted husband, laid her trembling hand on his. There was a long silence.

"He was caught in the machinery," said the visitor at length in a low voice.

"Caught in the machinery," repeated Mr. White, in a dazed fashion, "yes."

He sat staring out the window, and taking his wife's hand between his own, pressed it as he had been wont to do in their old courting days nearly forty years before.

"He was the only one left to us," he said, turning gently to the visitor. "It is hard."

The other coughed, and rising, walked slowly to the window. "The firm wishes me to convey their sincere sympathy with you in your great loss," he said, without looking round. "I beg that you will understand I am only their servant and merely obeying orders."

There was no reply; the old woman's face was white, her eyes staring, and her breath inaudible; on the husband's face was a look such as his friend the sergeant might have carried into his first action.

"I was to say that Maw and Meggins disclaim all responsibility," continued the other. "They admit no liability at all, but in consideration of your son's services, they wish to present you with a certain sum as compensation."

Mr. White dropped his wife's hand, and rising to his feet, gazed with a look of horror at his visitor. His dry lips shaped the words, "How much?"

"Two hundred pounds," was the answer.

Unconscious of his wife's shriek, the old man smiled faintly, put out his hands like a sightless man, and dropped, a senseless heap, to the floor.

Part III

In the huge new cemetery, some two miles distant, the old people buried their dead, and came back to the house steeped in shadows and silence. It was all over so quickly that at first they could hardly realize it, and remained in a state of expectation as though of something else to happen—something else which was to lighten this load, too heavy for old hearts to bear.

But the days passed, and expectations gave way to resignation—the hopeless resignation of the old, sometimes mis-called apathy. Sometimes they hardly exchanged a word, for now they had nothing to talk about, and their days were long to weariness.

It was about a week after that the old man, waking suddenly in the night, stretched out his hand and found himself alone. The room was in darkness, and the sound of subdued weeping came from the window. He raised himself in bed and listened.

"Come back," he said tenderly. "You will be cold."

"It is colder for my son," said the old woman, and wept afresh.

The sounds of her sobs died away on his ears. The bed was warm, and his eyes heavy with sleep. He dozed fitfully, and then slept until a sudden wild cry from his wife awoke him with a start.

"THE PAW!" she cried wildly. "THE MONKEY'S PAW!"

He started up in alarm. "Where? Where is it? What's the matter?"

She came stumbling across the room toward him. "I want it," she said quietly. "You've not destroyed it?"

"It's in the parlour, on the bracket," he replied, marveling. "Why?"

She cried and laughed together, and bending over, kissed his cheek.

"I only just thought of it," she said hysterically. "Why didn't I think of it before? Why didn't you think of it?"

"Think of what?" he questioned.

"The other two wishes," she replied rapidly. "We've only had one."

"Was not that enough?" he demanded fiercely.

"No," she cried triumphantly; "We'll have one more. Go down and get it quickly, and wish our boy alive again."

The man sat in bed and flung the bedclothes from his quaking limbs. "Good God, you are mad!" he cried aghast. "Get it," she panted; "get it quickly, and wish—Oh my boy, my boy!"

Her husband struck a match and lit the candle. "Get back to bed," he said unsteadily. "You don't know what you are saying."

"We had the first wish granted," said the old woman, feverishly; "why not the second?"

"A coincidence," stammered the old man.

"Go get it and wish," cried his wife, quivering with excitement.

The old man turned and regarded her, and his voice shook. "He has been dead ten days, and besides he—I would not tell you else, but—I could only recognize him by his clothing. If he was too terrible for you to see then, how now?"

"Bring him back," cried the old woman, and dragged him towards the door. "Do you think I fear the child I have nursed?"

He went down in the darkness, and felt his way to the parlour, and then to the mantel-piece. The talisman was in its place, and a horrible fear that the unspoken wish might bring his mutilated son before him ere he could escape from the room seized upon him, and he caught his breath as he found that he had lost the direction of the door. His brow cold with sweat, he felt his way round the table, and groped along the wall until he found himself in the small passage with the unwholesome thing in his hand.

Even his wife's face seemed changed as he entered the room. It was white and expectant, and to his fears seemed to have an unnatural look upon it. He was afraid of her.

"WISH!" she cried in a strong voice.

"It is foolish and wicked," he faltered.

"WISH!" repeated his wife.

He raised his hand. "I wish my son alive again."

The talisman fell to the floor, and he regarded it fearfully. Then he sank trembling into a chair as the old woman, with burning eyes, walked to the window and raised the blind.

He sat until he was chilled with the cold, glancing occasionally at the figure of the old woman peering through the window. The candle-end, which had burned below the rim of the china candlestick, was throwing pulsating shadows on the ceiling and walls, until with a flicker larger than the rest, it expired. The old man, with an unspeakable sense of relief at the failure of the talisman, crept back back to his bed, and a minute afterward the old woman came silently and apathetically beside him.

Neither spoke, but lay silently listening to the ticking of the clock. A stair creaked, and a squeaky mouse scurried noisily through the wall. The darkness was oppressive, and after lying for some time screwing up his courage, he took the box of matches, and striking one, went downstairs for a candle.

At the foot of the stairs the match went out, and he paused to strike another; and at the same moment a knock came so quiet and stealthy as to be scarcely audible, sounded on the front door.

The matches fell from his hand and spilled in the passage. He stood motionless, his breath suspended until the knock was repeated. Then he turned and fled swiftly back to his room, and closed the door behind him. A third knock sounded through the house.

"WHAT'S THAT?" cried the old woman, starting up.

"A rat," said the old man in shaking tones—"a rat. It passed me on the stairs."

His wife sat up in bed listening. A loud knock resounded through the house.

"It's Herbert!"

She ran to the door, but her husband was before her, and catching her by the arm, held her tightly.

"What are you going to do?" he whispered hoarsely.

"It's my boy; it's Herbert!" she cried, struggling mechanically. "I forgot it was two miles away. What are you holding me for? Let go. I must open the door."

"For God's sake don't let it in," cried the old man, trembling.

"You're afraid of your own son," she cried struggling. "Let me go. I'm coming, Herbert; I'm coming."

There was another knock, and another. The old woman with a sudden wrench broke free and ran from the room. Her husband followed to the landing, and called after her appealingly as she hurried downstairs. He heard the chain rattle back and the bolt drawn slowly and stiffly from the socket. Then the old woman's voice, strained and panting.

"The bolt," she cried loudly. "Come down. I can't reach it."

But her husband was on his hands and knees groping wildly on the floor in search of the paw. If only he could find it before the thing outside got in. A perfect fusillade of knocks reverberated through the house, and he heard the scraping of a chair as his wife put it down in the passage against the door. He heard the creaking of the bolt as it came slowly back, and at the same moment he found the monkey's paw, and frantically breathed his third and last wish.

The knocking ceased suddenly, although the echoes of it were still in the house. He heard the chair drawn back, and the door opened. A cold wind rushed up the staircase, and a long loud wail of disappointment and misery from his wife gave him the courage to run down to her side, and then to the gate beyond. The streetlamp flickering opposite shone on a quiet and deserted road.

The Legend Of Robin Hood

retold by Mary MacLeod

Chapter One

Robin Hood and the Knight

In the days of Richard I there lived a famous outlaw who was known by the name of Robin Hood. He was born at Locksley in the county of Nottingham, and was of noble origin, for he is often spoken of as "Earl of Huntingdon." Robin was very wild and daring, and having placed his life in danger by some reckless act, or possibly through some political offence, he fled for refuge to the greenwood. His chief haunts were Sherwood Forest in Nottinghamshire, and Barnsdale in Yorkshire. Round him soon flocked a band of trusty followers. An old chronicler states that Robin Hood "entertained an hundred tall men and good archers." They robbed none but the rich, and killed no man except in self-defence. Robin "suffered no woman to be oppressed or otherwise molested; poor men's goods he spared, abundantly relieving them" with spoils got from abbeys or the houses of rich people.

Robin Hood's exploits were widely known, and although the poorer classes were all on his side, those in authority were naturally incensed against him. Many attempts were made to seize him, and large rewards were offered for his capture. He was often in danger of his life, and had many narrow escapes, but so daring was his courage, and so quick and clever his wit and resource that he always contrived to get clear away.

An old tradition says that the father of Robin was a forester, a renowned archer. On one occasion he shot for a wager against the three gallant yeomen of the north country—Adam Bell, Clym-of-the-Clough, and William of Cloudesly, and the forester beat all three of them.

The mother of Robin Hood was a niece of the famous Guy, Earl of Warwick, who slew the blue boar; her brother was Gamwel of Great Gamwel Hall, a squire of famous degree, and the owner of one of the finest houses in Nottinghamshire.

When the other outlaws flocked to Robin Hood they begged him to tell them what sort of life they were to lead, and where they were to go, what they were to take and what to leave, what sort of people they were to rob, and whom they were to beat and to bind—in short, how they were to act in every circumstance.

"Have no fear, we shall do very well," answered Robin. "But look you do no harm to any husbandman that tilleth with his plough, nor to any good yeoman that walketh in the greenwood, nor to any knight or squire who is a good fellow. And harm no folk in whose company is any woman.

"But fat rascals, and all who have got rich by pilfering, canting, and cheating, those you may beat and bind, and hold captive for ransom. And chiefly the Sheriff of Nottingham—look you, bear him well in mind."

And his followers promised to pay heed to his words, and carry them out carefully.

Chief among the band of outlaws known as "Robin Hood's merry men" was "Little John," so called because his name was John Little, and he was seven feet high. Robin Hood was about twenty years old when he first came to know Little John, and they got acquainted in this way. Robin was walking one day in the forest when coming near a brook he chanced to spy a stranger, a strong lusty lad like himself. The two met in the middle of a long narrow bridge, and neither would give way. They quarrelled as to which should be the master, and finally agreed to fight with stout staves on the bridge, and whichever fell into the water, the other was to be declared to have won. The encounter was a stiff one, but finally the stranger knocked down Robin Hood, and tumbled him into the brook. Robin bore no malice, but owned at once the other had got the best of it, and seeing what a stout nimble fellow he was, persuaded him to join his band of archers, and go and live with them in the greenwood.

Next to Little John the chief man was Will Scarlet, who in reality was Robin's own cousin or nephew, young Gamwel of Gamwel Hall. Having slain his father's steward either by accident or in some brawl, young Will fled to his kinsman, Robin Hood, in Sherwood Forest, where, as in the case of Little John, he first made his acquaintance by fighting with him. As young Will on this occasion happened to be dressed very smartly in silken doublet and scarlet stockings Robin Hood dubbed him "Will Scarlet," by which name he was always afterwards known.

Besides these two famous outlaws there were many others of lesser note who from time to time joined the band. Among them may be mentioned "Gilbert of the white hand" who was almost as good an archer as Robin himself; Allen-a-Dale, whose bride Robin Hood helped him to secure; Much, the son of a miller; George-a-Green; Friar Tuck; Will Stutely, who was taken prisoner by the Sheriff of Nottingham and nearly hanged, but was rescued from the gallows by the gallant yeomen; Arthur-a-Bland, the sturdy tanner of Nottingham, who beat Robin when they fought with staves; the jolly tinker of Banbury who went out to arrest Robin, but ended by joining his band, and the chief ranger of Sherwood Forest, who did the same.

Lastly, there was the bonny maid of noble degree, who was known in the north country as Maid Marian. She had loved Robin Hood when they were young together, in the days when he was still the Earl of Huntingdon, but spiteful fortune forced them to part. Robin had to fly for refuge to the greenwood, and Maid Marian, unable to live without him, dressed herself like a page, with quiver and bow, sword and buckler, and went in search of him. Long and wearily she ranged the forest, and when the lovers met they did not know each other, for Robin, too, had been obliged to disguise himself. They fought as foes, and so sore was the fray that both were wounded, but Robin so much admired the valour of the stranger lad that he bade him stay his hand, and asked him to join his company. When Marian knew the voice of her lover she quickly made herself known to him, and great was the rejoicing. A stately banquet was quickly prepared, which was served in a shady bower, and they feasted merrily, while all the tall and comely yeomen drank to the health of Robin Hood's bride. So for many years they dwelt together with great content in the greenwood.

It happened one day as Robin Hood stood under a tree in Barnsdale that Little John went up to him, and said:

"Master, if you would dine soon, would it not be well?"

"I do not care to dine," answered Robin, "until I have some bold baron or stranger guest to eat with us, or else some rich rascal who will pay for the feast, or else some knight or squire who dwells in these parts."

"It is already far on in the day; now heaven send us a guest soon, so that we may get to dinner," said Little John.

"Take thy good bow in thy hand," said Robin, "and let Will Scarlet and Much go with thee, and walk up to the Sayles and so to Watling Street. There wait for some strange guest whom it may very well chance you will meet. Be it earl or baron, or abbot or knight, bring him here to lodge; his dinner shall be ready for him."

So these three good yeomen, Little John, Will Scarlet, and Much went off to the great high-road which is known as Watling Street, and there they looked east and they looked west, but not a man could they see. But as they looked in Barnsdale, by a little private path there came a knight riding, whom they soon met. Very dreary and woebegone seemed this traveller; one foot was in the stirrup, the other dangled outside; his hood hung down over his eyes; his attire was poor and shabby; no sorrier man than he ever rode on a summer's day.

Little John bent low in courtesy before him.

"Welcome, sir knight! Welcome to the greenwood! I am right glad to see you. My master hath awaited you fasting these three hours."

"Who is your master?" asked the knight.

"Robin Hood, sir," answered Little John.

"He is a brave yeoman; I have heard much good of him," said the knight. "I will go in company with you, my comrades. My purpose was to have dined to-day at Blyth or Doncaster."

So the knight went with the yeomen, but his face was still sad and careworn, and tears often fell from his eyes. Little John and Will Scarlet brought him to the door of the lodge in Barnsdale, where the outlaws were staying at that time, and as soon as Robin saw him he lifted his hood courteously, and bent low in token of respect.

"Welcome, sir knight, welcome. I am right glad to see you. I have awaited you fasting, sir, for the last three hours."

"God save thee, good Robin, and all thy fair company," returned the knight pleasantly.

Robin brought clear water from the well for the guest to wash himself from the dust of travel, and then they sat down to dinner. The meal was spread under the trees in the greenwood, and rarely had the stranger seen a repast so amply furnished. Bread and wine they had in plenty, and dainty portions of deer, swans and pheasants, plump and tender, and all kinds of water-fowl from the river, and every sort of woodland bird that was good for eating.

Robin heaped his guest's plate with choice morsels, and bade him fall to merrily.

"Eat well, sir knight, eat well," he urged him.

"Thanks, thanks," said the knight. "I have not had such a dinner as this for three weeks. If I come again into this country, Robin, I will make as good a dinner for you as you have made for me."

"Thanks for my dinner, good knight, when I have it," returned the outlaw. "I was never so greedy as to crave for dinner. But before you go, would it not be seemly for you to pay for what you have eaten? It was never the custom for a yeoman to pay for a knight."

"I have nothing in my coffers that I can proffer, for shame," said the knight.

"Go, Little John, and look," said Robin. "Now swear to me that you are telling the truth," he added to his guest.

"I swear to you, by heaven, I have no more than ten shillings," said the knight.

"If you have no more than that I will not take one penny," said Robin. "And if you have need of any more I will lend it you. Go now, Little John, and tell me the truth. If there be no more than ten shillings, not one penny of that will I touch."

Little John spread out his mantle on the ground ready to hold any treasure he might find, but when he looked in the knight's coffer he saw nothing but one piece of money of the value of half a pound. He left it lying where it was, and went to tell his master.

"What tidings, John?" asked Robin.

"Sir, the knight is true enough."

"Fill a cup with the best wine, and hand it first to the knight," said Robin. "Sir, I much wonder that your clothing is so thin. Tell me one thing, I pray. I trow you must have been made a knight by force, or else you have squandered your means by reckless or riotous living? Perhaps you have been foolish and thriftless, or else have lost all your money in brawling and strife? Or possibly you have been a usurer or a drunkard, or wasted your life in wickedness and wrong-doing?"

"I am none of those things, by heaven that made me," declared the knight. "For a hundred years my ancestors have been knights. It has often befallen, Robin, that a man may be disgraced, but God who waits in heaven above can amend his state. Within two or three years, my neighbours knew it well, I could spend with ease four hundred pounds of good money. Now I have no goods left but my wife and my children. God has ordained this until He see fit to better my condition."

"In what manner did you lose your riches?" asked Robin.

"By my great folly and kindness," was the answer. "I had a son, who should have been my heir. At twenty years old he could joust right well in the field. Unhappily the luckless boy slew a knight of Lancashire, and to pay the heavy penalty exacted from him to save his rights I was forced to sell all my goods. Besides this, Robin, my lands are pledged until a certain day to a rich abbot living close by here at St. Mary's Abbey."

"What is the sum?" asked Robin.

"Sir, four hundred pounds, which the abbot lent me."

"Now, if you lose your land what will become of you?" asked Robin.

"I will depart in haste over the salt sea to Palestine. Farewell, friend, there is no better way." Tears filled the knight's eyes, and he made a movement to go. "Farewell, friends, farewell! I have no more that I can pay you."

But Robin stopped him as he would have gone.

"Where are your friends?" he asked.

"Sir, there are none who will know me now. When I was rich enough at home they were glad to come and flatter me, but now they all run from me. They take no more heed of me than if they had never seen me."

The knight's sorrowful story so touched the hearts of Little John and Will Scarlet that they wept for pity.

"Come, fill of the best wine," cried Robin. "Come, sir, courage! Never be downcast! Have you any friends from whom you can borrow?"

"None," replied the knight.

"Come forth, Little John, and go to my treasury," said Robin. "Bring me four hundred pounds, and look that you count it out carefully."

Then forth went Little John, and with him went Will Scarlet, and he counted out four hundred pounds. But Much, the miller's son, did not look very well pleased to see all this money going into the hands of a stranger.

"Is this wisely done?" he muttered.

"What grieves you?" said Little John. "It is alms to help a noble knight who has fallen into poverty. Master," he went on to Robin Hood, "his clothing is full thin; you must give the knight a suit of raiment to wrap himself in. For you have scarlet and green cloth, master, and plenty of rich apparel. I dare well say there is no merchant in England who has a finer store."

"Give him three yards of cloth of every colour," said Robin Hood, "and see that it be well meted out."

Little John took no other measure than his bow, and every handful he measured he leapt over three feet.

"What devilkin's draper do you think you are?" asked little Much in half-angry astonishment.

Will Scarlet stood still and laughed.

"John may well give him good measure," he said. "It cost *him* but light."

Little John paid no heed to their scoffing, but quietly went on with his task.

"Master," he said to Robin Hood, when he had put aside a bountiful store for their guest, "you must give the knight a horse to carry home all these goods."

"Give him a grey courser, and put a new saddle on it," said Robin.

"And a good palfrey as befits his rank," added little Much.

"And a pair of boots, for he is a noble knight," said Will Scarlet.

"And what will you give him, Little John?" asked Robin.

"Sir, a pair of shining gilt spurs to pray for all this company. God bring him safely out of all his trouble."

The poor knight scarcely knew how to thank them for all their goodness.

"When shall the day be for me to pay back the money you have lent me?" he said. "What is your will?"

"This day twelve-month under this greenwood tree," said Robin. "It were a great shame," he added, "for a knight to ride alone without squire, yeomen, or page to walk by his side. I will lend you my man, Little John, to be your lad. He may stand you in yeoman stead if ever you are in need."

As the knight went on his way he thought how well matters had happened for him, and when he looked on Barnsdale he blessed Robin Hood. And when he thought of Will Scarlet, Much, and Little John he blessed them for the best company he had ever been in.

"To-morrow I must go to York town to St. Mary's Abbey," he said to Little John, "and to the abbot of that place I have to pay four hundred pounds. If I am not there by to-morrow night my lands will be lost for ever."

The next day he strode out of the abbot's hall, all his care gone; he flung off his worn raiment, put on his good clothing, and left the other lying where it fell. He went forth singing merrily, back to his own home at Wierysdale, and his lady met him at the gate.

"Welcome, my lord," said his wife. "Sir, are all your possessions lost?"

"Be merry, dame," said the knight, "and pray for Robin Hood that his soul may always dwell in bliss. He helped me out of my distress; had it not been for his kindness we should have been beggars. The abbot and I are in accord; he is served with his money; the good yeoman lent it me as I came by the way."

★

The good knight, whose name was Sir Richard Lee, dwelt in prosperity at home till he had four hundred pounds all ready to pay back Robin Hood. He provided himself with a hundred bows made with the best string, and a hundred sheaves of good arrows with brightly burnished heads. Every arrow was an ell long, well dressed with peacock's feathers, and they were all inlaid with silver so that it was a goodly sight to see. The knight provided himself also with a hundred men, well armed, and clothed in white and red, and in the same fashion he attired himself. He bore a lance in his hand, and a man led the horse which carried his change of apparel. And thus he rode with a light heart to Barnsdale.

As he drew near a bridge he was forced to tarry awhile, for there was a great wrestling, and all the best yeomen of the West Country had flocked to it. A good game had been arranged, and valuable prizes were offered. A white bull had been put up, and a great courser, with saddle and bridle all burnished with gold, a pair of gloves, a red gold ring, and a pipe of wine in prime condition. The man who bore himself the best would carry off the prize.

Now there was a certain worthy yeoman there who ought by rights to have been awarded the prize, but because he was a stranger the other wrestlers were jealous, and all set on him unfairly. As he was far from home and had no friends there, he would certainly have been slain if it had not been for the knight who, from the place where he stood, saw what was going on. He took pity on the yeoman, and swore no harm should be done to him, for the love he bore to Robin Hood. He pressed forward into the place, and his hundred archers followed him, with bows bent and sharp arrows to attack the crowd. They shouldered every one aside, and made room for Sir Richard Lee to make known what he had to say.

Then the knight took the yeoman by the hand, and declared he had fairly won the prize. He bought the wine from him for five marks, and bade that it should be broached at once, and that every one who wished should have a draught. Thus good humour and jollity were restored, and the rest of the sports went on merrily.

The knight tarried till the games were done, and in the meanwhile it came to be three hours after noon. And all this time Robin had waited fasting for the coming of the knight to whom twelve months before he had lent the four hundred pounds.

Chapter Two

Little John and the Sheriff of Nottingham

It will be remembered that when the poor knight left Robin Hood in the forest Little John went with him to act as his yeoman. He stayed for some time in Sir Richard's service, and a light and pleasant post he found it, for he was free to do pretty much as he liked.

It happened one fine day that the young men of Nottingham were eager to go shooting, so Little John fetched his bow, and said he would meet them in a trial of skill. While the match was going on, the Sheriff of Nottingham chanced to pass, and he stood for a while near the marks to watch the sport.

Three times Little John shot, and each time he cleft the wand.

"By my faith, this man is the best archer that ever I saw," cried the sheriff. "Tell me now, my fine lad, what is your name? In what county were you born, and where do you dwell?"

"I was born at Holderness," said Little John, "and when I am at home men call me Reynold Greenleaf."

"Tell me, Reynold Greenleaf, will you come and live with me? I will give you twenty marks a year as wages."

"I have a master already, a noble knight," answered Little John. "It would be better if you would get leave of him."

The sheriff was so pleased with the prowess of Little John that he wanted to get him into his own service, so he went to the knight, and it was agreed the sheriff should have him for twelve months. Little John was therefore given at once a strong horse, well equipped, and now behold him the sheriff's man.

But Little John had not forgotten Robin Hood's words of warning about the sheriff; he knew him to be a false and greedy man, and a ruthless enemy to the outlaws, and Little John was always thinking how he could pay him out for his treachery.

"By my loyalty and truth," said Little John to himself, "I will be the worst servant to him that ever he had."

Little John soon found that his new place was little to his liking. The other servants were not well pleased to see the newcomer; they were jealous of the favour shown to him at first by his master, and treated him with rudeness and contempt. The sheriff himself was very mean; he wished to secure Little John for his service, for he knew such a comely lad and fine archer would do him credit, but once he was sure of him he paid no heed to seeing that he was properly lodged and fed.

It happened one day the sheriff went out hunting, and Little John was left at home forgotten. No meal was served to him, and he was left fasting till noon. As he was by this time very hungry he went to the steward, and asked civilly for something to eat.

"Good sir steward, I pray thee give me to dine," he said. "It is too long for Greenleaf to be so long fasting, therefore I pray thee, steward, give me my dinner."

"I've had no orders," said the steward rudely. "Thou shalt have nothing to eat or to drink till my lord comes back to town."

"Rather than that I'll crack thy head," said Little John.

The steward started forward to the buttery, and shut fast the door, but Little John gave him such a rap on his back it almost broke in two—as long as he lived he would be the worse for the blow. Then Little John put his foot to the door, and burst it open, and Little John went in and helped himself plentifully to both ale and wine.

"Since you will not dine, I will give you to drink," he said to the steward; "though you live for a hundred years you shall remember Little John."

He ate and drank for as long as he chose, and the steward dared say nothing, for he was still smarting from the blow. But the sheriff had in his employ a cook, a bold, sturdy man, and he was no coward either.

"A fine sort of fellow you are to dwell in a house and ask for dinner thus," he cried, and he dealt Little John three good blows.

"I vow I am very well pleased with those strokes of yours," said Little John, "and before I leave this place you shall be tested better."

He drew his good sword, and the cook seized another, and they went for each other then and there. Neither had any thought of giving in, but both meant to resist stoutly. There they fought sorely for a whole hour, and neither could in any way harm the other.

"Thou art truly one of the very best swordsmen that ever I saw," said Little John. "Couldst thou shoot as well with a bow thou shouldst go with me to the greenwood. Thou wouldst have from Robin Hood twenty marks a year as wages, and a change of clothing twice a year."

"Put up thy sword, and we will be comrades," said the cook.

He fetched at once for Little John a right good meal—dainty venison, good bread, and excellent wine—and they both ate and drank heartily. When they had well feasted they plighted their troth together that they would be with Robin that self-same night. Then they ran as fast as they could to the sheriff's treasury, and though the locks were of good steel they broke them every one. They carried off all the silver plate—vessels, dishes, gold pieces, cups, and spoons, nothing was forgotten.

They took also the money—three hundred and three pounds—and then they went off straight to Robin Hood in the forest.

"God save thee, my dear master," cried Little John.

"Welcome art thou, and also that fair yeoman whom thou bringest with thee," said Robin Hood. "What tidings from Nottingham, Little John?"

"The proud sheriff greeteth thee well, and sendeth you here by me his cook and his silver vessels and three hundred and three pounds," said Little John.

"I dare take my oath it was never by his good will these goods come to me," laughed Robin.

Thus they all made merry in the greenwood, and said the sheriff had been rightly paid for the greed and tyranny with which he performed the duties of his office, for by bribery and oppression he had got his ill-earned wealth.

Presently Little John bethought him of a shrewd device by which they could still further get the better of him. He ran into the forest here and there, and when he had gone about five miles it fell out as he wished; he came across the sheriff himself hunting with hound and horn. Little John was mindful of his manners, and went and knelt on his knee before him, and saluted him courteously.

"Why, Reynold Greenleaf, where hast thou been now?" cried the sheriff.

"I have been in the forest," said Little John, "and there I have seen a wondrous sight, one of the finest I ever yet saw. Yonder I saw a right gallant hart; his colour is green. Seven score of deer in a herd altogether are with him. His antlers are so sharp, master, I durst not shoot, for dread lest they should slay me."

"By heaven, I would fain see that sight," said the sheriff.

"Turn thy steps thither, then, at once, dear master," said Little John. "Come with me; I will show you where he lies."

The sheriff rode off, and Little John ran beside him, for he was full smart of foot. Through the forest they went, and by-and-by they came to Robin Hood in the midst of his band of yeomen.

"Lo, there is the master hart," said Little John. The sheriff stood still in dismay, and he was a sorry man.

"Woe worth thee, Reynold Greenleaf, thou hast betrayed me."

"Ye are to blame, master, I swear," said Little John. "When I was at home with you I was misserved of my dinner."

Then the outlaws made their guest sit down to supper with them, which he did with no good will, for he would fain have departed to his home at Nottingham. He was served on his own silver dishes, and when he saw his beautiful cups and vessels the sheriff for sorrow could not eat.

"Cheer up, sheriff," urged Robin Hood. "For the sake of Little John thy life is granted thee. What, man, eat and be merry! Here is fine fat venison served in a goodly vessel."

By the time they had well supped, the day was done. Robin then bade his men strip the sheriff of his fine clothes, his hose and his shoes, his kirtle, and the large handsome coat all trimmed with fur—and to give him in their place a green mantle to wrap himself in. He further bade his sturdy lads all to lie round the sheriff in a circle under the greenwood tree, so that he might see them, and know there was no chance of escape.

It was a sorry night the sheriff passed, cold and shivering, in his shirt and breeches, on the hard ground; small wonder that his bones ached, and that he sighed piteously for his soft warm bed at home.

"Come, come, sheriff, cheer up!" said Robin; "for this is our order, you know, under the greenwood tree."

"This is a harder order than any anchorite or friar!" groaned the sheriff. "For all the gold in merry England I would not dwell here long."

"Thou wilt dwell here with me for the next twelve months," said Robin. "I shall teach thee, proud sheriff, to be an outlaw."

"Before I lie here another night, Robin, smite off my head rather, and I'll forgive it thee," said the sheriff. "Let me go, for pity's sake!" he begged, "and I will be the best friend that ever thou hadst."

"Before I let thee go, thou shalt swear me here an oath," said the outlaw. "Swear on my sword that thou wilt never seek to do me harm by water or by land. And if thou find any of my men, by night or by day, thou shalt swear on thy oath to help them all thou canst."

There was no other way to get back his freedom, so the sheriff was compelled to take the oath demanded by Robin. Then he was allowed to depart, and he went back to Nottingham a sad and sorry man, feeling that he had had more than enough of the greenwood to last him a very long time.

Chapter Three

How Robin Hood was Paid His Loan

Twelve months had come and gone since Robin Hood lent four hundred pounds to the poor knight to redeem his land, and now the day had arrived when he had promised to pay back the money.

The sheriff had returned to Nottingham, and Robin Hood and his merry men were left in the greenwood.

"Let us go to dinner," said Little John.

"Nay, not yet," said Robin. "Now I fear our friend the knight is likely to prove false, for he comes not to pay back the money, according to his word."

"Have no doubt, master," said Little John, "for the sun has not yet gone to rest."

"Take thy bow," said Robin, "and let Much and Will Scarlet go with you, and walk up into the Sayles, and to Watling Street, and wait there for some stranger guest, for you may well chance upon one there. Whether he be messenger or mountebank, rich man or poor man, he shall share dinner with me."

Forth then started Little John, half-angry and half-troubled, and under his green mantle he girded on a good sword.

The three yeomen went up to the Sayles; they looked east and they looked west, and not a man could they see.

But all the time Robin kept thinking of the knight who had promised to return that day with the borrowed money.

"I marvel much he does not come," he said. "I fear he does not mean to keep faith."

"Have no doubt, master," said Little John. "You have no need, I say."

Sir Richard Lee, meanwhile, who had tarried to see the wrestling, came while it was still daylight to fulfil his promise. He went straight to Barnsdale, and there he found Robin Hood and his band under the greenwood tree. Directly the knight saw Robin, he dismounted from his palfrey, and saluted him courteously on one knee.

"God save thee, good Robin Hood, and all this company."

"Welcome, welcome, noble knight," said Robin. "I pray thee tell me what need driveth thee to the greenwood? I am right glad to see thee. Why hast thou been so long in coming?"

"The abbot and the high justice have been trying to get hold of my land," said the knight.

"Hast thou thy land again?"

"Yea, and for that I thank God and thee. But take not offence that I have come so late in the day. On my journey hither I passed by some wrestling, and there I helped a poor yeoman who was being wrongly put behind by the others."

"Nay, by my faith, for that I thank thee," said Robin. "The man that helpeth a good yeoman, his friend will I be."

"Have here the four hundred pounds you lent me," said the knight, "and here is also twenty marks for your courtesy."

"Nay, keep it and use it well yourself," said Robin, "and thou art right welcome under my trysting-tree. But what are all those bows for, and those finely feathered arrows?"

"They are a poor present to thee," said the knight.

Then Robin Hood bade Little John go to his treasury and fetch four hundred pounds, and he insisted on the knight's accepting this money as a gift.

"Buy thyself a good horse and harness, and gild thy spurs anew," he said laughingly. "And if thou lack enough to spend come to Robin Hood, and by my truth thou shalt never lack while I have any goods of my own. Keep the four hundred pounds I lent thee, and I counsel thee never leave thyself so bare another time."

So good Robin Hood relieved the gentle knight of all his care, and they feasted and made merry under the greenwood tree.

Chapter Four

The Golden Arrow

The knight took his leave and went on his way, and Robin Hood and his merry men lived on for many a day in Barnsdale.

Now the Sheriff of Nottingham proclaimed a grand sport to be held—that all the best archers of the north country should come one day and shoot at the butts, and that a prize should be given to the best archer.

The butts were to be set in a glade in the forest and he who shot the best of all should receive an arrow, the like of which had never been seen in England, for the shaft was to be of silver, and the head and feathers of red gold.

Now all this was a device of the sheriff's to try to enthrall the outlaws, for he imagined that when such matches took place Robin Hood's men without any doubt would be the bowmen there.

Tidings of this came to Robin Hood in the forest, and he said: "Come, make ready, my lads, we will go and see that sport. Ye shall go with me, and I will test the sheriff's faith, and see if he be true."

With that a brave young man, called David of Doncaster, stepped forward.

"Master," he said, "be ruled by me, and do not stir from the greenwood. To tell the truth I am well informed yonder match is a wile. The sheriff has devised it to entrap us."

"That sounds like a coward," said Robin; "thy words do not please me. Come what will of it, I'll try my skill at yonder brave archery."

Then up spoke brave Little John.

"Let us go thither, but come, listen to me, and I will tell you how we can manage it without being known. We will leave behind us our mantles of Lincoln green, and we will all dress differently so that they will never notice us. One shall wear white, another red, a third one yellow, another blue. Thus in disguise we will go to the sport, whatever may come of it."

When they had their bows in order and their arrows well feathered there gathered round Robin seven score of stalwart young men.

When they came to Nottingham they saw the butts set out fair and long, and many were the bold archers who came to shoot. The outlaws mixed with the rest to prevent all suspicion, for they thought it more discreet not to keep together.

"Only six of you shall shoot with me," said Robin to his men. "The rest must stand on guard with bows bent so that I be not betrayed."

The sheriff looked all round, but amidst eight hundred men he could not see what he suspected.

The outlaws shot in turn, and they all did so well that the people said that if Robin Hood had been there, and all his men to boot, none of them could have surpassed these men.

"Ay," quoth the sheriff ruefully, rubbing his head. "I thought he would have been here; I certainly thought he would, but though he is bold he doesn't dare to appear."

His speech vexed Robin Hood to the heart. "Very soon," he thought angrily, "thou shalt well see that Robin Hood *was* here."

Some cried blue jacket, another cried brown, and a third cried brave yellow, but a fourth man said: "Yonder man in red hath no match in the place."

Now that was Robin Hood himself, for he was clothed in red. Three times he shot, and each time he split the wand. To him, therefore, was delivered the golden arrow as being the most worthy. He took the gift courteously, and would have departed back to the greenwood; but the Sheriff of Nottingham had by this time marked him, and had no mind to let him go so easily. The alarm was raised; they cried out on Robin Hood, and great horns were blown to summon help to capture him.

"Treachery! treason!" cried Robin. "Full evil art thou to know! And woe to thee, proud sheriff, thus to entertain thy guest! It was otherwise thou promised me yonder in the forest. But had I thee in the greenwood again, under my trysting-tree, thou shouldst leave me a better pledge than thy loyalty and truth."

Then on all sides bows were bent, and arrows flew like hail; kirtles were rent, and many a stout knave pricked in the side. The outlaws shot so strong that no one could drive them back, and the sheriff's men fled in haste.

Robin saw the ambush was broken, and would fain have been back in the greenwood, but many an arrow still rained on his company. Little John was hurt full sorely, with an arrow in his knee, and could neither ride nor walk.

"Master," he cried, "if ever thou loved me, and for the meed of my service that I have served thee, let never that proud sheriff find me alive! But take thy sword and smite off my head, and give me deep and deadly wounds, so that no life be left in me."

"I would not that, John—I would not thou wert slain for all the gold in merry England!" cried Robin.

"God forbid that thou shouldst part our company, Little John," said Much.

He took Little John up on his back, and carried him a good mile, and more. Often he laid him down on the ground, and turned to shoot those who came after, and then he took him up and carried him on again. So the outlaws fought their way, step by step, back to the forest.

A little within the wood there was a fair castle, with a double moat, and surrounded by stout walls. Here dwelt that noble knight, Sir Richard Lee, to whom Robin Hood had lent the four hundred pounds to redeem his land.

He saw the little company of outlaws fighting their way along, so he hastened to call them to come and take shelter in his castle.

"Welcome art thou, Robin Hood! Welcome!" he cried, as he led them in. "Much I thank thee for thy comfort and courtesy and great kindness to me in the forest. There is no man in the world I love so much as thee. For all the proud Sheriff of Nottingham, here thou shalt be safe!—Shut the gates, and draw the bridge, and let no man come in!" he shouted to his retainers. "Arm you well; make ready; guard the walls! One thing, Robin, I promise thee: here shalt thou stay for twelve days as my guest, to sup, and eat, and dine."

Swiftly and readily tables were laid and cloths spread, and Robin Hood and his merry men sat down to a good meal.

Chapter Five

How the Sheriff Took Sir Richard Prisoner

The Sheriff of Nottingham was wroth when he heard that Robin Hood and his band of outlaws had taken refuge in the knight's castle. All the country was up in rout, and they came and besieged the castle. From his post outside the walls the sheriff loudly proclaimed that the knight was a traitor, and was shielding the king's enemy against the laws and right.

"I am ready to answer for the deeds I have done here by all the lands I possess, as I am a true knight," was Sir Richard's answer. "Go on your way, sirs, and leave me alone in peace until ye know our king's will, what he will say to you."

The sheriff, having had his answer, curt and to the point, rode forth at once to London to carry the tale to the king.

He told him of the knight, and of Robin Hood, and of the band of bold archers which the latter kept up.

"The knight boasts of what he has done to aid these outlaws," said the sheriff. "He would be lord, and set you at nought through all the north country."

"I will be at Nottingham within the fortnight," said the king, "and I will seize Robin Hood, and also that knight. Go home, sheriff, and do as I bid thee. Get ready enough good archers from all the country round about."

So the sheriff took his leave, and went home to Nottingham to do as the king commanded.

Robin meanwhile had left the castle, and had gone back to the greenwood, and Little John, as soon as he was whole from the arrow-shot in his knee, went and joined him there. It caused great vexation to the sheriff to know that Robin Hood once more walked free in the forest, and that he had failed of his prey; but all the more he was resolved to be revenged on Sir Richard Lee. Night and day he kept watch for that noble knight; at last, one morning when Sir Richard went out hawking by the riverside, the sheriff's men-at-arms seized him, and he was led bound hand and foot to Nottingham.

When Sir Richard's wife heard that her husband had been taken prisoner, she lost no time in seeking help. Mounting a good palfrey, she rode off at once to the greenwood, and there she found Robin Hood and all his men.

"God save thee, Robin Hood, and all thy company! For the love of heaven, grant me a boon! Let not my wedded lord be shamefully slain. He is taken fast bound to Nottingham, all for the love of thee!"

"What man hath taken him?" asked Robin.

"The proud sheriff," said the lady. "He has not yet passed on his way three miles."

Up then started Robin as if he were mad.

"Arm, lads! Arm and make ready! By heaven, he that fails me now shall never more be man of mine!"

Speedily good bows were bent, seven score and more, and away went the outlaws, full speed over hedge and ditch, in chase of the sheriff's men, When they came to Nottingham, there in the street they overtook the sheriff.

"Stay, thou proud sheriff—stay and speak with me!" said Robin. "I would fain hear from thee some tidings of our king. By heaven, these seven years have I never gone so fast on foot, and I swear it bodeth no good for thee."

He bent his bow, and sent an arrow with all the might he could; it hit the sheriff so that he fell to the ground, and lay there stunned, and before he could rise to his feet Robin drew his sword and smote off his head.

"Lie thou there, proud sheriff, traitor and evildoer!" said Robin. "No man might ever trust to thee whilst thou wert still alive!"

Now the two sides fought hand to hand. Robin Hood's men drew their shining swords, and laid on so heavily that they drove down the sheriff's men one after another.

Robin Hood ran to Sir Richard Lee, and cut his bonds in two, and, thrusting a bow into his hand, bid him stand by him.

"Leave thy horse behind thee, and learn to run on foot," he counselled him. "Thou shalt go with me to the greenwood through mire and moss and fen. Thou shalt go with me to the forest, and dwell with me there, until I have got our pardon from Edward, our king."

Chapter Six

How the King Came to Sherwood Forest

Tidings of the sheriff's death were sent to King Edward in London, and he came to Nottingham with a great array of knights to lay hold of Sir Richard Lee and Robin Hood, if that were possible. He asked information from men of all the country round, and when he had heard their tale and understood the case he seized all the lands belonging to Sir Richard Lee. He went all through Lancashire, searching far and wide, till he came to Plumpton Park, and everywhere he missed many of his deer. There he had always been wont to see herds in large numbers, but now he could scarcely find one deer that bore any good horn.

The king was furiously wroth at this.

"By heaven I would that I had Robin Hood here before me to see him with my own eyes," he exclaimed. "And he that shall smite off the knight's head and bring it here to me shall have all the lands belonging to Sir Richard Lee. I will give them him with my charter, and seal it with my hand for him to have and to hold, for evermore."

Then up spoke a good old knight who was very faithful and loyal.

"Ay, my liege lord the king, but I will say one word to you," he said. "There is no man in this country who will have the knight's lands as long as Robin can go or ride and carry bow in hand. If any one try to possess them he will assuredly lose his head. Give them to no man, my lord, to whom you wish any good."

The king dwelt for many months in Nottingham, but no man came to claim the knight's lands, nor could he ever hear of Robin Hood in what part of the country he might be. But always Robin went freely here and there, roving wherever he chose over hill and valley, slaying the king's deer, and disposing of it at his will.

Then a head forester, who was in close attendance on the king, spoke up, and said:

"If you would see good Robin you must do as I tell you. Take five of the best knights that are in your train, and go down to yonder abbey, and get you monks' habits. I will be your guide to show you the way, and before you get back to Nottingham I dare wager my head that you will meet with Robin if he be still alive. Before you come to Nottingham you shall see him with your own eyes."

The king hastened to follow the forester's counsel; he and his five monks went to the abbey, and speedily disguised themselves in the garb of monks, and then blithely returned home through the greenwood. Their habits were grey; the king was a head taller than all the rest, and he wore a broad hat, just as if he were an abbot, and behind him followed his baggage-horse, and well-laden sumpters, and in this fashion they rode back to the town.

They had gone about a mile through the forest under the linden trees when they met with Robin Hood standing in the path with many of his bold archers.

"Sir abbot, by your leave, ye must bide awhile with us," said Robin, seizing the king's horse. "We are yeomen of this forest, we live by the king's deer, and we have no other means. But you have both churches and rents, and full great plenty of gold; give us some of your store for charity's sake."

"I brought no more than forty pounds with me to the greenwood," said the pretended abbot. "I have been staying at Nottingham for a fortnight with the king, and I have spent a great deal on many of the fine lords there. I have only forty pounds left, but if I had a hundred I would give it thee."

Robin took the forty pounds, and divided it into two parts; half he gave to his men, and bade them be merry with it, and the other half he returned to the king.

"Sir, have this for your spending," he said courteously. "We shall meet another day."

"Thanks," said the king. "But Edward our king greeteth you well; he sends thee here his seal, and bids thee come to Nottingham to dine and sup there."

He took out the broad seal, and let him see it, and Robin at the sight of it, knowing what was right and courteous, knelt in reverence.

"I love no man in all the world so well as I do my king," he said. "Welcome is my lord's seal, and welcome art thou, monk, because of thy tidings. Sir abbot, for love of my king thou shalt dine with me to-day under my trysting-tree."

Forth he led the king with all gentle courtesy, and many a deer was slain and hastily dressed for the feast. Then Robin took a great horn and blew a loud blast and seven score of stalwart young men came ready in a row, and knelt on their knee before Robin in sign of salutation.

"Here is a brave sight," said the king to himself. "In good faith his men are more at his bidding than mine are at mine."

Dinner was speedily prepared, and they went to it at once, and both Robin and Little John served the king with all their might. Good viands were quickly set before him—fat venison, fish out of the river, good white bread, good red wine, and fine brown ale. The king swore he had never feasted better in his life.

Then Robin took a can of ale, and bade every man drink a health to the king. The king himself drank to the king, and so the toast went round, and two barrels of strong old ale were spent in pledging that health.

"Make good cheer, abbot," said Robin, "and for these same tidings thou hast brought thou art doubly welcome. Now before thou go hence thou shalt see what life we lead here in the greenwood, so that thou mayest inform the king when ye meet together."

The meal was scarcely over when up started all the outlaws in haste, and bows were smartly bent. For a moment the king was sorely aghast, for he thought he would certainly be hurt. But no man intended ill to him. Two rods were set up, and to them all the yeomen flocked to try their skill at archery. The king said the marks were too far away by fifty paces, but he had never seen shooting such as this. On each side of the rods was a rose garland, and all the yeomen had to shoot within this circle. Whoever failed of the rose garland had as penalty to lose his shooting gear, and to hand it to his master, however fine it might be, and in addition to this he had to stand a good buffet on the head. All that came in Robin's way he smote them with right good will.

When his own turn came Robin shot twice, and each time cleft the wand, so also did the good yeoman Gilbert. Little John and Will Scarlet did not come off so well, and when they failed to hit within the garland they each got a good buffet from Robin.

But at his last shot, in spite of the way in which his friends had fared, Robin, too, failed of the garland by three fingers or more.

"Master, your tackle is lost," said Gilbert. "Stand forth and take your pay."

"If it be so there is no help for it," said Robin. "Sir abbot, I deliver thee mine arrow; I pray thee, sir, serve thou me."

"It falleth not within my order, by thy leave, Robin, to smite any good yeoman, for fear lest I grieve him," said the king.

"Smite on boldly; I give thee full leave," said Robin.

The king at these words at once folded back his sleeves, and gave Robin such a buffet that it nearly knocked him to the ground.

"By heaven, thou art a stalwart friar," cried Robin. "There is pith in thine arm; I trow thou canst shoot well."

Then King Edward and Robin Hood looked each other full in the face, and Robin Hood gazed wistfully at the king. So also did Sir Richard Lee, and then he knelt down before him on his knee. And all the wild outlaws, when they saw Sir Richard Lee and Robin Hood kneeling before the king, also knelt down.

"My lord the King of England, now I know you well," said Robin. "Mercy, of thy goodness and thy grace, for my men and me! Yes, before heaven, I crave mercy, my lord the king, for me and for my men."

"Yes, I grant thee thy petition," said the king, "if thou wilt leave the greenwood, thou and all thy company, and come home with me, sir, to my court, and dwell with me there."

"I will swear a solemn vow that so it shall be," said Robin. "I will come to your court to see your service and bring with me seven score and three of my men. But unless I like well your service, I shall soon come back to the forest, and shoot again at the dun deer, as I am wont to do."

Chapter Seven

How Robin Hood Went Back to the Greenwood

"Hast thou any good cloth that thou wilt sell to me now?" said the king.

"Yes, three and thirty yards," said Robin.

"Then I pray thee, Robin, sell me some of it for me and my company."

"Yes, I will," said Robin. "I should be a fool if I did not, for I trow another day you will clothe me against Christmas."

So the king speedily cast off his coat, and donned a garment of green, and so did all his knights. When they were all clad in Lincoln green and had thrown aside their monks' grey habits, "Now we will go to Nottingham," said the king.

They bent their bows, and away they went, shooting in the same band, as if they were all outlaws. The king and Robin Hood rode together, and they shot "pluck-buffet" as they went by the way—that is to say, whoever missed the mark at which he aimed was to receive a buffet from the other; many a buffet the king won from Robin Hood, and good Robin spared nothing of his pay.

"Faith," said the king, "thy game is not easy to learn; I should not get a shot at thee though I tried all this year."

When they drew near Nottingham, all the people stood to behold them. They saw nothing but mantles of green covering all the field; then every man began saying to another: "I dread our king is slain; if Robin Hood comes to the town, he will never leave one of us alive." They all hastened to make their escape, both men and lads, yeomen and peasants; the ploughman left the plough in the fields, the smith left his shop, and old wives who could scarcely walk hobbled along on their staves.

The king laughed loud and long to see the townsfolk scurry off in this fashion, and he commanded them to come back. He soon let them understand that he had been in the forest, and that from that day for evermore he had pardoned Robin Hood. When they found out the tall outlaw in the Lincoln green was really the king, they were overjoyed; they danced and sang, and made great feasting and revelry for gladness at his safe return.

Then King Edward called Sir Richard Lee, and there he gave him his lands again, and bade him be a good man. Sir Richard thanked the king, and paid homage to him as the true and loyal knight he had always been.

So Robin Hood went back to London with the king, and dwelt at court. But before many months had gone he found all his money had melted away, and that he had nothing left. He had spent over a hundred pounds and now had not enough to pay the fees of his followers. For everywhere he went he had always been laying down money both for knights and squires, in order to win renown. When he could no longer afford to pay their fee, all the new retainers left him, and by the end of the year he had none but two still with him, and those were his own faithful old comrades, Little John and Will Scarlet.

It happened one day some young men of the court went out to shoot, and as Robin Hood stood with a sad heart to watch them, a sudden great longing for his old life in the greenwood came over him.

"Alas!" he sighed, "my wealth has gone! Once on a time I too was a famous archer, sure of eye and strong of hand; I was accounted the best archer in merry England. Oh, to be back once more in the heart of the greenwood, where the merry does are skipping, and the wind blows through the leaves of the linden, and little birds sit singing on every bough! If I stay longer with the king, I shall die of sorrow!"

So Robin Hood went and begged a boon of the king.

"My lord the King of England, grant me what I ask! I built a little chapel in Barnsdale, which is full seemly to see, and I would fain be there once again. For seven nights past I have neither slept nor closed my eyes, nor for all these seven days have I eaten or drunk. I have a sore longing after Barnsdale; I cannot stay away. Barefoot and doing penance will I go thither."

"If it be so, there is nothing better to be done," said the king. "Seven nights—no longer—I give thee leave to dwell away from me."

Thanking the king, Robin Hood saluted him and took his leave full courteously, and away he went to the greenwood.

It was a fair morning when he came to the forest. The sun shone, the soft green turf was strewn with flowers that twinkled like stars, and all the air rang with the song of birds. The cloud of care and sorrow rolled away from Robin's spirit, and his heart danced as light as a leaf on the tree.

"It is long since I was here last," he said, as he looked around him. "I think I should like to shoot once more at the deer."

He fitted an arrow to his bow, and away it sped to its mark, and down dropped a fine fat hart. Then Robin blew his horn. And as the blast rang out, shrill and sweet and piercing, all the outlaws of the forest knew that Robin Hood had come again. Through the woodland they gathered together, and fast they came trooping, till in a little space of time seven score stalwart lads stood ready in order before Robin. They took off their caps, and fell on their knee in salutation.

"Welcome, our master! Welcome, welcome back to the greenwood!" they shouted.

Chapter Eight

Robin Hood and the Butcher

It happened one day when Robin Hood was in the forest that he saw a jolly butcher with a fine mare, who was going to market to sell his meat.

"Good morrow, good fellow, what food have you there?" said Robin. "Tell me what is your trade, and where you live, for I like the look of you."

"No matter where I live," answered the man. "I am a butcher, and I am going to Nottingham to sell my flesh."

"What's the price of your flesh?" said Robin. "And tell me, too, the price of your mare, however dear she may be, for I would fain be a butcher."

"Oh, I'll soon tell you the price of my flesh," replied the butcher. "For that, with my bonny mare, and they are not at all dear, you must give me four marks."

Robin Hood agreed at once to the bargain.

"I will give you four marks. Here is the money; come, count it, and hand me over the goods at once, for I want to be a butcher."

So the man took the money, and Robin took the mare and the cart of meat, and went on to Nottingham to begin his new trade. He had a plan in his mind, and in order to carry it out he went to the sheriff's house, which was an inn, and took up his lodging there.

When the butchers opened their shops Robin boldly opened his, but he did not in the least know how to sell, for he had never done anything of the kind before. In spite of this, however, or rather because of it, while all the other butchers could sell no meat Robin had plenty of customers, and money came in quickly. The reason of this was that Robin gave more meat for one penny than others could do for three. Robin therefore sold off his meat very fast, but none of the butchers near could thrive.

This made them notice the stranger who was taking away all their custom, and they began to wonder who he was, and where he came from. "This must be surely some prodigal, who has sold his father's land, and is squandering away his money," they said to each other. They went up to Robin to get acquainted with him. "Come, brother, we are all of one trade," said one of them; "will you go dine with us?"

"By all means," answered Robin, "I will go with you as fast as I can, my brave comrades." So off they hastened to the sheriff's house, where dinner was served at once, and Robin was chosen to sit at the head of the table and say grace.

"Come, fill us more wine; let us be merry while we are here," he cried. "I'll pay the reckoning for the wine and good cheer however dear it may be. Come, brothers, be merry. I'll pay the score, I vow, before I go, if it costs me five pounds or more."

"This is a mad blade," said the butchers, but they laughed and made haste to eat and drink well at Robin's expense.

Now the sheriff, who was of a very shrewd and grasping nature, had not failed to remark this handsome young butcher lad who was so very lavish of his money, and who sold his meat in the market so much cheaper than any one else. If there were good bargains to be made he determined to make his own profit out of them. "He is some prodigal," he said to himself, "who has sold land, and now means to spend all the money he has got for it." If Robin were able to sell his meat so cheap it occurred to the sheriff that probably he possessed a great deal of cattle, and would most likely be ready to part with them for a very low price. "Hark'ee, good fellow, have you any horned beasts you can sell me?" he asked in a lordly way.

"Yes, that I have, good master sheriff, two or three hundred," answered Robin. "And I have a hundred acres of good free land, if it would please you to see it. I'll hand it over to you as securely as ever my father did to me."

The sheriff, quite pleased to think of the fine bargain he was likely to make, saddled his palfrey, and taking three hundred pounds in gold in his portmanteau, went off with Robin Hood to see his horned beasts. Away they rode till they came to the forest of Sherwood, and then the sheriff began to look about him in some alarm.

"God preserve us this day from a man they call Robin Hood," he said earnestly.

When they had gone a little further Robin Hood chanced to spy a hundred head of good fat deer, who came tripping quite close.

"How like you my horned beasts, good master sheriff? They are fat and fair to see, are they not?"

"I tell you, good fellow, I would I were gone, for I like not your company," said the sheriff, now very ill at ease.

Robin set his horn to his mouth, and blew three blasts, and immediately Little John and all his company came flocking up.

"What is your will, master?" asked Little John.

"I have brought hither the Sheriff of Nottingham to dine with thee to-day."

"He is welcome," said Little John; "I hope he will pay honestly. I know he has gold enough, if it is properly reckoned, to serve us with wine for a whole day."

Robin took off his mantle and laid it on the ground and from the sheriff's portmanteau he counted out three hundred pounds in gold. Then he led him through the forest, set him on his dapple-grey palfrey, and sent him back to his own home.

Chapter Nine

The Jolly Tanner

About this time there was living in Nottingham a jolly tanner whose name was Arthur-a-Bland. Never a squire in Nottingham could beat Arthur, or bid him stand if he chose to go on. With a long pike-staff on his shoulder he could clear his way so well he made every one fly before him.

One summer's morning Arthur-a-Bland went forth into Sherwood Forest to see the deer, and there he met Robin Hood. As soon as Robin saw him he thought he would have some sport, so he called to him to stand.

"Why, who art thou, fellow, who rangest here so boldly?" he said. "In sooth, to be brief, thou lookst like a thief who comes to steal the king's venison. I am a keeper in the forest; the king puts me in trust to look after the deer. Therefore I must bid thee stand."

"If you be a keeper in this forest, and have so great authority," answered the tanner, "yet you must have plenty of helpers in store before you can make me stop."

"I have no helpers in store, nor do I need any. But I have good weapons which I know will do the deed."

"I don't care a straw for your sword or your bow, nor all your arrows to boot," said Arthur-a-Bland. "If you get a knock on your pate, your weapons will be no good."

"Speak civilly, good fellow," said Robin, "or else I will correct thee for thy rudeness, and make thee more mannerly."

"Marry, see how you'll look with a knock on your head!" quoth the tanner. "Are you such a goodly man? I care not a rush for your looking so big. Look out for yourself, if you can."

Then Robin Hood unbuckled his belt, and laid down his bow, and took up a staff of oak, very stiff and strong.

"I yield to your weapons, since you will not yield to mine," said Robin. "I, too, have a staff, not half a foot longer than yours. But let me measure before we begin, for I would not have mine to be longer than yours, for that would be counted foul play."

"The length of your staff is nothing to me," said the tanner. "Mine is of good stout oak; it is eight feet and a half long, and it will knock down a calf—and I hope it will knock down you."

At these rude and mocking words, Robin could not longer forbear, but gave the tanner such a crack on the head that the blood began to flow. Arthur quickly recovered, and gave Robin in return such a knock that in a few minutes blood ran trickling down the side of his face. As soon as he felt himself so badly hurt, Robin raged like a wild boar, while Arthur-a-Bland laid on so fast it was almost as if he were cleaving wood. Round about they went, like wild boars at bay, striving to maim each other in leg or arm or any place. Knock for knock they dealt lustily, so that the wood rang at every blow, and this they kept up for two hours or more.

But at last Robin was forced to own that he had met his match, and he called to the sturdy stranger to stay.

"Hold thy hand, hold thy hand, and let our quarrel drop!" he cried. "For we may thrash our bones all to smash here, and get no good out of it. Hold thy hand, and hereafter thou shalt be free in the merry forest of Sherwood."

"Thank you for nothing!" retorted Arthur. "I have bought my own freedom. I may thank my good staff for this, and not you."

"What tradesman are you, good fellow, and where do you dwell?"

"I am a tanner, and in Nottingham I have worked for many years. If you will come there, I vow and protest I will tan your hide for nothing."

"Heaven have mercy, good fellow, since you are so kind and obliging," said Robin. "If you will tan my hide for nothing, I'll do as much for you. But come, if you will forsake your tanner's trade, to live here with me in the greenwood, my name is Robin Hood, and I swear faithfully to give you good gold and wages."

"If you are Robin Hood, as I think very well you are, then here's my hand," said the tanner. "My name is Arthur-a-Bland. We two will never part. But tell me, where is Little John? I would fain hear of him, for we are allied, through our mother's family, and he is my dear kinsman."

Then Robin blew a loud, shrill blast on his bugle, and instantly Little John came quickly tripping over the hill.

"Oh, what is the matter? Master, I pray you tell me!" cried Little John. "Why do you stand there with your staff in your hand? I fear all is not well."

"Yes, man, I do stand here, and this tanner beside me has made me stand," said Robin. "He is a fine fellow, and master of his trade, for he has soundly tanned my hide."

"He is to be commended if he can do such a feat," said Little John. "If he is so sturdy, we will have a bout together, and he shall tan my hide too."

"Hold your hand," said Robin; "for, as I understand he is a good yeoman of your own blood; his name is Arthur-a-Bland."

Then Little John flung away his staff as far as he could, and running up to Arthur-a-Bland, threw his arms around his neck. Both were ready and eager to be friends, and made no attempt to hide their delight at the meeting, but wept for joy. Then Robin Hood took a hand of each, and they danced all round the oak-tree, singing:

"For three merry men, and three merry men,
And three merry men we be!

And ever hereafter, as long as we live,
We three will be as one;
The wood it shall ring, and the old wife sing,
Of Robin Hood, Arthur, and John."

Chapter Ten

How Robin Hood Drew His Bow for the Last Time

But there came a day at last when Robin Hood had to bid farewell to the greenwood where he and his merry men had spent so many happy years. Word was sent to the king that the outlaws waxed more and more insolent to his nobles and all those in authority, and that unless their pride was quelled the land would be overrun.

A council of state was therefore called, to consider what was best to be done. Having consulted a whole summer's day, at length it was agreed that some one should be sent to seize Robin Hood and bring him before the king.

A trusty and most worthy knight, called Sir William, was chosen for this task.

"Go you hence to that insolent outlaw, Robin Hood," said the king, "and bid him surrender himself without more ado, or he and all his crew shall suffer. Take a hundred valiant bowmen, all chosen men of might, skilled in their art, and clad in glittering armour."

"My sovereign liege, it shall be done," said the knight. "I'll venture my blood against Robin Hood, and bring him alive or dead."

A hundred men were straightway chosen, as proper men as were ever seen, and on midsummer day they marched forth to conquer the bold outlaw.

With long yew-bows and shining spears they marched in pomp and pride, and they never halted nor delayed till they came to the forest.

"Tarry here, and make ready your bows, that in case of need you may follow me," said the knight to his archers. "And look you observe my call. I will go first, in person, with the letters of our good king, duly signed and sealed, and if Robin Hood will surrender we need not draw a string."

The knight wandered about the forest, till at length he came to the tent of Robin Hood. He greeted the outlaw, and showed him the king's letter, whereupon Robin sprang to his feet and stood on guard.

"They would have me surrender, then, and lie at their mercy?" quoth Robin. "Tell them from me that shall never be while I have seven score of good men."

Sir William, who was a bold and hardy knight, made an attempt to seize Robin then and there, but Robin was too quick to be caught, and bade him forbear such tricks. Then he set his horn to his mouth, and blew a blast or two; the knight did the same.

Instantly from all sides archers came running, some for Robin Hood, some for the knight.

Sir William drew up his men with care, and placed them in battle array. Robin Hood was no whit behind with his yeomen. The fray was stern and bloody. The archers on both sides bent their bows, and arrows flew in clouds. In the very first flight the gallant knight, Sir William, was slain; but nevertheless the fight went on with fury, and lasted from morning until almost noon. They fought till both parties were spent, and only ceased when neither side had strength to go on. Those of the king's archers that still remained went back to London with right good will, and Robin Hood's men retreated to the depths of the greenwood.

But Robin Hood's last fight was fought, and of all the arrows that ever he shot, there was but one yet to fly. As he left the field of battle he was taken ill, and he felt his strength fail, and the fever rise in his veins.

His life was ebbing fast away, and now he was too weak to go on.

Then he remembered his little bugle-horn, which still hung at his side, and setting it to his mouth, he blew once, twice, and again—a low, weak blast.

Away in the greenwood, as he sat under a tree, Little John heard the well-known call, but so faint and feeble was the sound it struck like ice to his heart.

"I fear my master is near dead, he blows so wearily!"

Never after hart or hind ran Little John as he ran that day to answer his master's dying call. He raced like the wind till he came to where Robin was, and fell on his knee before him.

"Give me my bent bow in my hand," said Robin Hood, "and I will let fly a broad arrow, and where this arrow is taken up, there shall you dig my grave.

"Lay me a green sod under my head,
And another at my feet;
And lay my bent bow at my side,
Which was my music sweet;
And make my grave of gravel and green,
Which is most right and meet."

So Robin Hood drew his bow for the last time, and there where the arrow fell, under a clump of the greenwood trees, they dug the grave as he had said, and buried him.

Appendix II

Poetry

The Armful
by Robert Frost

For every parcel I stoop down to seize   1
I lose some other off my arms and knees,   2
And the whole pile is slipping, bottles, buns—   3
Extremes too hard to comprehend at once,   4
Yet nothing I should care to leave behind.   5
With all I have to hold with, hand and mind   6
And heart, if need be, I will do my best   7
To keep their building balanced at my breast.   8
I crouch down to prevent them as they fall;   9
Then sit down in the middle of them all.   10
I had to drop the armful in the road   11
And try to stack them in a better load.   12

The Road Not Taken
by Robert Frost

Two roads diverged in a yellow wood,   1
And sorry I could not travel both
And be one traveler, long I stood
And looked down one as far as I could
To where it bent in the undergrowth;

Then took the other, as just as fair,   6
And having perhaps the better claim
Because it was grassy and wanted wear,
Though as for that the passing there
Had worn them really about the same,

And both that morning equally lay   11
In leaves no step had trodden black.
Oh, I marked the first for another day!
Yet knowing how way leads on to way
I doubted if I should ever come back.

I shall be telling this with a sigh   16
Somewhere ages and ages hence:
Two roads diverged in a wood, and I,
I took the one less traveled by,
And that has made all the difference.

The Highwayman
by Alfred Noyes

PART ONE

I
The wind was a torrent of darkness among the gusty trees,   1
The moon was a ghostly galleon tossed upon cloudy seas,
The road was a ribbon of moonlight over the purple moor,
And the highwayman came riding—
    Riding—riding—
The highwayman came riding, up to the old inn-door.

II
He'd a French cocked-hat on his forehead, a bunch of lace at his chin,   7
A coat of the claret velvet, and breeches of brown doe-skin;
They fitted with never a wrinkle: his boots were up to the thigh!
And he rode with a jewelled twinkle,
    His pistol butts a-twinkle,
His rapier hilt a-twinkle, under the jewelled sky.

III
Over the cobbles he clattered and clashed in the dark inn-yard,   13
And he tapped with his whip on the shutters, but all was locked and barred;
He whistled a tune to the window, and who should be waiting there
But the landlord's black-eyed daughter,
    Bess, the landlord's daughter,
Plaiting a dark red love-knot into her long black hair.

IV
And deep in the dark old inn-yard a stable-wicket creaked   19
Where Tim the ostler listened; his face was white and peaked;
His eyes were hollows of madness, his hair like mouldy hay,
But he loved the landlord's daughter,
    The landlord's red-lipped daughter,
Dumb as a dog he listened, and he heard the robber say—

V
"One kiss, my bonny sweetheart, I'm after a prize to-night,   25
But I shall be back with the yellow gold before the morning light;
Yet, if they press me sharply, and harry me through the day,
Then look for me by moonlight,

Watch for me by moonlight,
I'll come to thee by moonlight, though hell should bar the way."

VI

He rose upright in the stirrups; he scarce could reach her hand,   31
But she loosened her hair i' the casement! His face burnt like a brand
As the black cascade of perfume came tumbling over his breast;
And he kissed its waves in the moonlight,
     (Oh, sweet, black waves in the moonlight!)
Then he tugged at his rein in the moonlight, and galloped away to the West.

PART TWO

I

He did not come in the dawning; he did not come at noon;   37
And out o' the tawny sunset, before the rise o' the moon,
When the road was a gypsy's ribbon, looping the purple moor,
A red-coat troop came marching—
     Marching—marching—
King George's men came marching, up to the old inn-door.

II

They said no word to the landlord, they drank his ale instead,   43
But they gagged his daughter and bound her to the foot of her narrow bed;
Two of them knelt at her casement, with muskets at their side!
There was death at every window;
     And hell at one dark window;
For Bess could see, through her casement, the road that *he* would ride.

III

They had tied her up to attention, with many a sniggering jest;   49
They had bound a musket beside her, with the barrel beneath her breast!
"Now, keep good watch!" and they kissed her.
     She heard the dead man say—
Look for me by moonlight;
     Watch for me by moonlight;
I'll come to thee by moonlight, though hell should bar the way!

IV

She twisted her hands behind her; but all the knots held good!   56
She writhed her hands till her fingers were wet with sweat or blood!
They stretched and strained in the darkness, and the hours crawled by like years,

Till, now, on the stroke of midnight,
    Cold, on the stroke of midnight,
The tip of one finger touched it! The trigger at least was hers!

V

The tip of one finger touched it; she strove no more for the rest!   62
Up, she stood up to attention, with the barrel beneath her breast,
She would not risk their hearing; she would not strive again;
For the road lay bare in the moonlight;
    Blank and bare in the moonlight;
And the blood of her veins in the moonlight throbbed to her love's refrain .

VI

Tlot-tlot; tlot-tlot! Had they heard it? The horse-hoofs ringing clear;   68
Tlot-tlot, tlot-tlot, in the distance? Were they deaf that they did not hear?
Down the ribbon of moonlight, over the brow of the hill,
The highwayman came riding,
    Riding, riding!
The red-coats looked to their priming! She stood up, straight and still!

VII

Tlot-tlot, in the frosty silence! *Tlot-tlot,* in the echoing night!   74
Nearer he came and nearer! Her face was like a light!
Her eyes grew wide for a moment; she drew one last deep breath,
Then her finger moved in the moonlight,
    Her musket shattered the moonlight,
Shattered her breast in the moonlight and warned him—with her death.

VIII

He turned; he spurred to the West; he did not know who stood   80
Bowed, with her head o'er the musket, drenched with her own red blood!
Not till the dawn he heard it, his face grew grey to hear
How Bess, the landlord's daughter,
    The landlord's black-eyed daughter,
Had watched for her love in the moonlight, and died in the darkness there.

IX

Back, he spurred like a madman, shrieking a curse to the sky,   86
With the white road smoking behind him and his rapier brandished high!
Blood-red were his spurs i' the golden noon; wine-red was his velvet coat,
When they shot him down on the highway,
    Down like a dog on the highway,

And he lay in his blood on the highway, with the bunch of lace at his throat.

X

And still of a winter's night, they say, when the wind is in the trees,   92
When the moon is a ghostly galleon tossed upon cloudy seas,
When the road is a ribbon of moonlight over the purple moor,
A highwayman comes riding—
    Riding—riding—
A highwayman comes riding, up to the old inn-door.

XI

Over the cobbles he clatters and clangs in the dark inn-yard;   98
He taps with his whip on the shutters, but all is locked and barred;
He whistles a tune to the window, and who should be waiting there
But the landlord's black-eyed daughter,
    Bess, the landlord's daughter,
Plaiting a dark red love-knot into her long black hair.

Appendix III

Works Cited

Abbott, Jacob. "Julius Caesar Crossing the Rubicon." In William Patten, ed., *The Junior Classics, Vol. 7: Stories of Courage and Heroism*. New York: P. F. Collier & Son, 1912.

Alcott, Louisa May. *Little Women*. New York: Signet Classics, 2012.

"Alfred Noyes, Poet, Dies at 77; Noted for 'The Highwayman.'" *New York Times*, June 29, 1958, pp. 1, 68.

Anderson, Audrey. "The Venus Flytrap's Circle of Life." In Susan Wise Bauer, *Writing With Skill, Level Two Student Workbook*. Charles City, Va.: Peace Hill Press, 2013.

Atkins, P. W. *The Periodic Kingdom: A Journey into the Land of the Chemical Elements*. New York: Basic Books, 1995.

Backman, Dana, and Michael A. Seeds. *Universe: Solar System, Stars, and Galaxies*. Boston: Cengage Learning, 2011.

Bartlett, Patricia. *Reptiles & Amphibians for Dummies*. New York: Wiley, 2003.

Bauer, Susan Wise. *The History of the Renaissance World: From the Rediscovery of Aristotle to the Conquest of Constantinople*. New York: W. W. Norton, 2013.

————. *Writing With Skill, Level One Student Workbook*. Charles City: Peace Hill Press, 2012.

Behme, Bob. "Pan for gold this summer—here's how and where." *Popular Mechanics*, Vol. 142, no. 1 (July 1974), pp. 82-85.

Bell, H. G. *Life of Mary Queen of Scots*. Vol. II. Edinburgh: William Brown, 1890.

Bennett, Matthew, et al. *Fighting Techniques of the Medieval World, AD 500—AD 1500: Equipment, Combat Skills, and Tactics*. Amber Books/St. Martin's Press, 2005/2006.

Berkin, Carol, et al. *Making America: A History of the United States, Vol. 1: To 1877*. Brief 5th ed. Boston: Wadsworth, 2011.

Bess, Nancy Moore. *Bamboo in Japan*. New York: Kodansha America, Inc., 2001.

Bidner, Jenni. *Is My Cat a Tiger? How Your Pet Compares to its Wild Cousins*. New York: Lark Books, 2006.

Brause, Rita S. "School Days—Then and Now." *Anthropology & Education Quarterly,* Vol. 18, no. 1 (Mar. 1987), pp. 53-55.

Breay, Claire. *Magna Carta: Manuscripts and Myths.* London: British Library, 2002.

Bredeson, Carmen. *Fiery Volcano: The Eruption of Mount St. Helens.* Berkeley Heights, NJ: Enslow Publishers, 2012.

Brenner, Joël Glenn. *The Emperors of Chocolate.* New York: Crown Business, 2000.

Bryson, Bill. *A Short History of Nearly Everything.* New York: Random House, 2004.

———. *A Short History of Nearly Everything: Special Illustrated Edition.* New York: Broadway Books, 2010.

———. *A Walk in the Woods: Rediscovering America on the Appalachian Trail.* New York: Broadway Books, 1998.

Buchanan, Rita, and Roger Holmes, eds. *Taylor's Master Guide to Gardening.* New York: Houghton Mifflin Co., 1994.

Burroughs, Edgar Rice. *Tarzan of the Apes.* New York: A.L. Burt Company Publishers, 1914.

Burton, Maurice, ed. *The International Wildlife Encyclopedia.* Vol. 1. New York: Marshall Cavendish Corp., 1989.

Calhoun, D. D. *The Book of Brave Adventures.* New York: The Macmillan Co., 1915.

Calvino, Italo. *If on a winter's night a traveler.* New York: Harcourt, 1981.

Cameron, Vicki. *Don't Tell Anyone, But—: UFO Experiences in Canada.* Burnstown, Ont., Canada: General Store Pub. House, 1995.

Campbell, Ballard C., ed. *Disasters, Accidents and Crises in American History.* New York: Infobase Publishing, 2008.

Carroll, Lewis. "The Lobster Quadrille." In *Alice's Adventures in Wonderland.* New York: The Macmillan Company, 1920.

Carson, Rachel. *Silent Spring.* Boston: Houghton Mifflin, 1962.

Carson, Rob. *Mount St. Helens: The Eruption and Recovery of a Volcano.* Seattle, Wash.: Sasquatch Books, 1990.

Catton, Bruce. *A Stillness at Appomattox.* New York: Anchor Books, 1990.

Chamberlain, Harold W. "Queer Things about Frogs." *St. Nicholas,* Vol. 20, no. I (Nov. 1892-Apr. 1893), pp. 837-838.

Clarkson, Peter. *Volcanoes.* Stillwater, Minn.: Voyageur Press, Inc., 2000.

Comins, Neil F., and William J. Kaufmann. *Discovering the Universe.* New York: W. H. Freeman, 1996.

Compton-Hall, Richard. *The First Submarines: The Beginnings of Underwater Warfare.* Penzance, Cornwall: Periscope Publishing, 2003.

Connah, Graham. *Three Thousand Years in Africa: Man and His Environment in the Lake Chad Region of Nigeria.* Cambridge: Cambridge University Press, 1981.

Cornell, David. *Bannockburn: The Triumph of Robert the Bruce.* New Haven: Yale University Press, 2009.

Cosman, M.P., and L. G. Jones. *Handbook to Life in the Medieval World.* New York: Facts on File, 2008.

Conant, Roger, Robert C. Stebbins, and Joseph T. Collins. *Peterson First Guide: Reptiles and Amphibians.* New York: Houghton Mifflin Company, 1992.

Cremin, Dennis H., and Elan Penn. *Chicago: A Pictorial Celebration.* New York: Sterling Publishing Co., Inc., 2006.

Cromwell, Sharon. *Dred Scott v. Sandford: A Slave's Case for Freedom and Citizenship.* Mankato, Minn.: Compass Point Books, 2009.

Cross, Richard. "Duns Scotus: *Ordinatio.*" In John Shand, ed., *Central Works of Philosophy, Volume 1: Ancient and Medieval.* Montreal: McGill-Queens, 2005.

Crouch, Tom D. *The Bishop's Boys: A Life of Wilbur and Orville Wright.* New York: W.W. Norton, 1989.

Cullina, William. *Native Ferns, Moss, and Grasses: From Emerald Carpet to Amber Wave.* Boston: Houghton Mifflin, 2008.

Daintith, John, and William Gould. *Astronomy.* New York: Facts on File, 2006.

Davison, Edward. "The Poetry of Alfred Noyes." *The English Journal,* Vol. XV, no. 4 (Apr. 1926), pp. 247-255.

Dawson, James. *Australian Aborigines.* Melbourne: Walker May & Co., 1881.

Decker, Robert, and Barbara Decker. *Volcanoes.* 4th ed. San Francisco: W. H. Freeman & Co., 2006.

Diamond, Jared. *Collapse: How Societies Choose to Fail or Succeed.* New York: Penguin, 2005.

Dickens, Charles. *Oliver Twist.* New York: Vintage, 2012.

Dineen, Jacqueline. *Natural Disasters: Volcanoes.* Mankato, Minn.: The Creative Company, 2005.

Dixon-Engel, Tara, and Mike Jackson. *The Wright Brothers: First in Flight.* New York: Sterling Publishing, 2007.

Elkins-Tanton, Linda T. *Jupiter and Saturn.* New York: Chelsea House, 2006.

Ellyard, David, and Wil Tirion. *The Southern Sky Guide.* Cambridge: Cambridge University Press, 1993.

Estes, Eleanor. *The Middle Moffat.* New York: Harcourt, 2001.

Feinstein, Stephen. *Louis Pasteur: The Father of Microbiology.* Berkeley Heights, N.J.: Enslow Publishers, 2008.

Franklin, Benjamin. *The Autobiography of Benjamin Franklin.* New York: Dover Publications, 1996.

Friedman, Norman. *U.S. Submarines Since 1945: An Illustrated Design History.* Annapolis, Md.: U.S. Naval Institute, 1994.

Gaynes, Robert P. *Germ Theory: Medical Pioneers in Infectious Diseases.* Washington, D.C.: ASM Press, 2011.

Gehrmann, Adolph. "Pasteurization." *The American Food Journal,* Vol. 12, no. 1 (Jan. 1917) pp. 96.

Glancey, Jonathan. *Eyewitness Companions: Architecture.* New York: DK Publishing, 2006.

"The Gold Country." *Life* (Feb. 2, 1948), pp. 44.

Goldberg, Gale Beth. *Bamboo Style.* Layton, Utah: Gibbs Smith, Publisher, 2002.

Gollon, Matilda, ed. *The Big Idea Science Book.* New York: DK Publishing, 2010.

Gower, R.S. *Joan of Arc.* New York: Charles Scribner's Sons, 1893.

Grant, Tom. *The Platypus: A Unique Mammal.* Sydney, Australia: University of New South Wales Press, 1995.

Greenberg, Ethan. *Dred Scott and the Dangers of a Political Court.* Lanham, Md.: Lexington Books, 2009.

Gunderson, Cory Gideon. *The Dred Scott Decision.* Edina, Minn.: ABDO Publishing Company, 2004.

Guo, Rongxing. *Territorial Disputes and Resource Management: A Global Handbook.* New York: Nova Science Publishers, 2007.

Hahn, Emily. *Mary, Queen of Scots.* New York: Random House, 1953.

Haven, Kendall. *100 Greatest Science Discoveries of All Time.* Westport, Conn.: Greenwood Publishing, 2007.

Hawthorne, Nathaniel. *Young Goodman Brown and Other Tales.* Oxford: Oxford University Press, 2009.

Heaney, Seamus. *Beowulf: A New Verse Translation.* New York: W. W. Norton, 2001.

Hemming, John. *The Conquest of the Incas.* New York: Harcourt, Inc., 1970.

Hill, Marquita K. *Understanding Environmental Pollution.* 3rd ed. Cambridge: Cambridge University Press, 2010.

Hossell, Karen Price. *The Emancipation Proclamation.* Chicago: Heinemann Library, 2006.

Johnson, Rebecca L. *A Journey Into a Wetland.* Minneapolis: Carolrhoda Books, 2004.

Kaiser, James. *Grand Canyon: The Complete Guide*. 4th ed. Santa Monica, Calif.: Destination Press, 2011.

Kalman, Bobbie. *Peru: The People and Culture*. New York: Crabtree Publishing Company, 2003.

Keim, Albert, and Louis Lumet. *Louis Pasteur*. Trans. Frederic Taber Cooper. New York: Frederick A. Stokes, 1914.

Keller, Helen. *The Story of My Life*. New York: Doubleday, Page & Company, 1903.

Kirk, Stephen. *First in Flight: The Wright Brothers in North Carolina*. Winston-Salem, NC: John F. Blair, 2003.

Kops, Deborah. *Machu Picchu*. Minneapolis: Twenty-First Century Books, 2009.

Koupelis, Theo. *In Quest of The Universe*. 6th ed. Sudbury, Mass.: Jones & Bartlett Learning, 2010.

Krueger, Karl. "By Post to Peace." *The Rotarian* (Jan. 1928), pp. 38-39.

Lacroix, Paul, and Robert Naunton. *Manners, Custom and Dress during the Middle Ages and during the Renaissance Period*. Whiteface, MT: Kessinger Publishing, 2010.

Laity, Julie J. *Deserts and Desert Environments*. Oxford: Wiley-Blackwell, 2008.

Lamb, Charles. "A Few Words on Christmas." In Charles Lamb et al., *The Works of Charles Lamb: Vol. IV, Essays and Sketches*. New York: E. O. Dutton & Co., 1903.

Lang, Kenneth R., and Charles A. Whitney. *Wanderers in Space: Exploration and Discovery in the Solar System*. Cambridge: Cambridge University Press, 1991.

Lewis, Daphne, and Carol A. Miles. *Farming Bamboo*. Washington, D.C.: Smithsonian Institute/Daphne B. Lewis and Carol Miles, 2007.

Lowell, Francis C. *Joan of Arc*. Boston: Houghton, Mifflin, and Co., 1897.

Mackenzie, Donald. *The Flooding of the Sahara*. London: Sampson Low, 1877.

Macleod, Mary. *A Book of Ballad Stories*. New York: F.A. Stokes Company, 1906.

Majumdar, A.K. Basu. *Rabindranath Tagore: The Poet of India*. New Delhi: Indus Publishing Company, 1993.

Markham, Clements Robert. *The Incas of Peru*. New York: E. P. Dutton and Co., 1910.

Marshall Cavendish Corporation. *Encyclopedia of the Aquatic World*. New York: Marshall Cavendish, 2004.

McColl, R. W. *Encyclopedia of World Geography*. Vol. 1. New York: Facts on File, 2005.

McFarlane, Marilyn and Christine Cunningham. *Quick Escapes: Pacific Northwest*. Guilford, Conn.: Insiders Guide, 2007.

McGhee, Karen, and George McKay. *The Encyclopedia of Animals: A Complete Visual Guide.* Washington, D.C.: National Geographic, 2007.

McPherson, Stephanie Sammartino, and Joseph Sammartino Gardner. *Wilbur & Orville Wright: Taking Flight.* Minneapolis: Lerner Publishing Group, 2004.

Mead, Charles Williams. *The Musical Instruments of the Inca.* Washington, D.C.: The American Museum of Natural History, 1903.

Michelet, Jules. *Joan of Arc.* Ann Arbor, Mich.: University of Michigan Press, 1967.

Miles, Elizabeth. *Louis Pasteur.* Chicago: Heinemann-Raintree, 2009.

Miller, Donald L. *City of the Century: The Epic of Chicago and the Making of America.* New York: Simon & Schuster, 1996.

Milne, A.A. *The Complete Tales and Poems of Winnie-the-Pooh.* New York: Dutton Children's Books, 2001.

Mitchel, John. *Jail Journal: or, Five Years in British Prisons.* New York: Office of the "Citizen," 1854.

Mittelbach, Margaret, and Michael Crewdson. *Carnivorous Nights: On the Trail of the Tasmanian Tiger.* New York: Random House, 2005.

Mollenhoff, David V. *Madison: A History of the Formative Years.* Madison: The University of Wisconsin Press, 2003.

Müller-Schwarze, Dietland. *The Beaver: Natural History of a Wetlands Engineer.* Ithaca, NY: Comstock, 2003.

Myers, Jack, and John Rice. *The Puzzle of the Platypus: And Other Explorations of Science in Action.* Honesdale, Penn.: Boyds Mills Press, 2008.

Naden, Corinne J., and Rose Blue. *Dred Scott: Person or Property?* Tarrytown, NY: Benchmark Books, 2005.

Niazi, Nozar, and Rama Gautam. *How to Study Literature: Stylistic and Pragmatic Approaches.* New Delhi, India: PHI, Ltd., 2010.

Nihoul, Jacques C. J. et al., eds. *Dying and Dead Seas: Climatic Versus Anthropic Causes.* Boston: Kluwer Academic Publishers, 2003.

Olsen, Penny. *Upside Down World: Early European Impressions of Australia's Curious Animals.* Canberra, A.C.T.: National Library of Australia, 2010.

Parker, R. O. *Introduction to Food Science.* Albany, N.Y.: Delmar, 2003.

Parker, Steve. *Protozoans, Algae & Other Protists.* Mankato, Minn.: Compass Point Books, 2009.

Parramore, Lynn. *Reading the Sphinx.* New York: Palgrave Macmillan, 2008.

Patten, William, ed. *The Junior Classics, Vol. 7: Stories of Courage and Heroism.* New York: P. F. Collier & Son, 1912.

Pielou, E.C. *A Naturalist's Guide to the Arctic.* Chicago: The University of Chicago Press, 1994.

Pinch, Geraldine. *Egyptian Mythology: A Guide to the Gods, Goddesses, and Traditions of Ancient Egypt.* Oxford: Oxford University Press, 2002.

Pliny the Younger. *The Letters of the Younger Pliny.* Trans. and ed. Betty Radice. New York: Penguin Books, 1963.

———. "Pliny to Tacitus," trans. Cynthia Damon. In Ronald Mellor, ed., *The Historians of Ancient Rome: An Anthology of the Major Writings,* second ed. New York: Routledge, 2004.

Plumbe, George Edwards. *Chicago: The Great Industrial and Commercial Center of the Mississippi Valley.* Chicago: The Civic-Industrial Committee of the Chicago Association of Commerce, 1912.

Preston, Richard. *Panic in Level Four: Cannibals, Killer Viruses and Other Journeys to the Edge of Science.* New York: Random House, 2008.

Ray, Mohit K., ed. *Atlantic Companion to Literature in English.* New Delhi, India: Atlantic Publishers, 2007.

Richards, John F. *The Mughal Empire.* Cambridge: Cambridge University Press, 1995.

Rhys, Grace. *About Many Things.* London: Methuen, 1920.

Rohrbough, Malcolm J. *Days of Gold: The California Gold Rush and the American Nation.* Berkeley, Calif.: University of California Press, 1997.

Rowling, J. K. *Harry Potter and the Chamber of Secrets.* New York: Scholastic, 2000.

Rue, Leonard Lee. *Beavers.* Stillwater, Minn.: Voyageur Press, 2002.

Saarinen, Thomas F., and James L. Sell. *Warning and Response to the Mount St. Helen's Eruption.* Albany, N.Y.: State University of New York Press, 1985.

Shipman, James T., Jerry D. Wilson, and Aaron Todd. *An Introduction to Physical Science.* 12th ed. Boston: Houghton Mifflin, 2009.

Simmons, Arthur Thomas, and Ernest Stenhouse. *A Class Book of Physical Geography.* London: Macmillan & Co., 1912.

Skog, Jason. *The Dred Scott Decision.* Mankato, Minn.: Compass Point Books, 2006.

Stade, George, and Karen Karbiener, eds. *Encyclopedia of British Writers, 1800 to Present.* Volume 2. New York: Facts on File, 2009.

Stanley, Diane. *Joan of Arc.* New York: HarperCollins, 2002.

Swift, Jonathan. *Gulliver's Travels.* New York: Dover, 1996.

Thomas, Isabel. *Lion vs. Tiger.* Chicago: Heinemann Library, 2007.

Thomson, J. Arthur. *The Outline of Science, Vol. 1: A Plain Story Simply Told.* New York: G. P. Putnam's Sons, 1922.

Tierra, Michael. *Treating Cancer with Herbs: An Integrative Approach.* Twin Lakes, Minn.: Lotus Press, 2003.

Twain, Mark. *The Autobiography of Mark Twain.* New York: Harper Perennial, 2000.

Underwood, Gary. *Spirit of the Incas.* Clayton South: Blake Education, 2006.

Van Gelder, Robert. "An Interview with Mr. Alfred Noyes, Who Finds Great Danger in the Literature of This Age." *New York Times*, April 12, 1942, BR2.

Van Horn, Carl E., and Herbert A. Schaffner, eds. *Work in America: An Encyclopedia of History, Policy and Society.* Santa Barbara, Calif.: ABC-CLIO, Inc., 2003.

Varner, Eric R. *Mutilation and Transformation: Damnatio Memoriae and Roman Imperial Portraiture.* Leiden: Brill, 2004.

Wallin, Craig. *Golden Harvest: How to Grow the Four Most Profitable Specialty Crops.* Anacortes, Wash.: HeadStart Publishing, 2012.

Wells, H.G. *The Time Machine: An Invention.* Kettering: Manor House, 1895.

Weir, Jane. *Max Planck: Revolutionary Physicist.* Mankato, Minn.: Capstone Press, 2009.

Whitaker, John O. and William John Hamilton. *Mammals of the Eastern United States.* Ithaca, N.Y.: Comstock, 1998.

White, Stewart Edward. *The Forty-niners: A Chronicle of the California Trail and El Dorado.* New Haven: Yale University Press, 1920.

Widmaier, Eric P. *Why Geese Don't Get Obese (And We Do).* New York: W. H. Freeman, 1999.

Winterson, Jeanette. *Lighthousekeeping.* Boston: Houghton Mifflin Harcourt, 2006.

Woodger, Elin, and Brandon Toropov. *Encyclopedia of the Lewis and Clark Expedition.* New York: Facts on File, 2004.

Woolfson, M. M. *Materials, Matter & Particles: A Brief History.* London: Imperial College Press, 2010.

Wright, A. Dickson. "Dr. William Harvey." *New Scientist* (Jun. 1957), pp. 11-13.

Wright, Orville, and Fred C. Kelly. *How We Invented the Airplane: An Illustrated History.* New York, David McKay, 1953.

Young, David C. *A Brief History of the Olympic Games.* Oxford: Blackwell Publishing, 2004.

Zamosky, Lisa, Thomas B. Ciccone, and Ronald Edwards. *Louis Pasteur.* Mankato, Minn.: Compass Point Books, 2009.

Zimmer, Carl. "Fatal Attraction." *National Geographic,* Vol. 217, no. 3 (March 2010), pp. 80-82.

Appendix IV

Permissions

ABC-CLIO, LLC:*100 Greatest Science Discoveries of All Time*, Kendall Haven. Copyright © (2007) by Libraries Unlimited. Reproduced with permission of ABC-CLIO, LLC.

Capstone Global Library, LLC: Excerpted from the work entitled: *The Emancipation Proclamation* © 2006 by Heinemann Library, an imprint by Capstone Global Library, LLC Chicago, Illinois. All rights reserved.

Cengage Learning: From Parker. Introduction to Food Science, 1E. © 2003 Delmar Learning, a part of Cengage Learning, Inc. Reproduced by permission. www.cengage.com/permissions

Capstone: Excerpted from the work entitled: *The Dred Scott Decision* © 2006 by Compass Point Books, an imprint by Capstone. All rights reserved.

Capstone: Excerpted from the work entitled: *Dred Scott v. Sandford: A Slave's Case for Freedom and Citizenship* © 2009 by Compass Point Books, an imprint by Capstone. All rights reserved.

Compass Point Books: *Hatshepsut: Egypt's First Female Pharaoh*, Pamela Dell. Copyright © 2009 by Compass Point Books. All rights reserved.

The Creative Company: *Natural Disasters: Volcanoes*, Jacqueline Dineen. Copyright © 2004 by The Creative Company. All rights reserved.

DK Publishing: *The Big Idea Science Book*, Matilda Gollon, ed. Copyright © 2010 by DK Publishing. All rights reserved.

Headstart Publishing: *Golden Harvest: How to Grow the Four Most Profitable Speciality Crops*, Craig Wallin. Anacortes, Wash.: HeadStart Publishing, 2012.

Houghton Mifflin Harcourt Publishing Company: from *Lighthousekeeping*, Jeanette Winterson. Copyright © 2004 by Jeanette Winterson. Reprinted by permission of Houghton Mifflin Harcourt Publishing Company. All rights reserved.

Houghton Mifflin Harcourt Publishing Company: Excerpt from *Native Ferns, Moss and Grasses* by William Cullina. Copyright © 2008 by New England Wild Flower Society. Reprinted by permission of Houghton Mifflin Harcourt Publishing Company. All rights reserved.